T0334423

Economic Systems of Foraging, Agricultural, and Industrial Societies

Drawing upon the disciplines of economics, anthropology, and history, and employing a new and unified analytic approach, Frederic L. Pryor reformulates in this book the entire field of comparative economic systems. He examines large samples of foraging (hunting, gathering, and fishing), agricultural, and industrial economies to explore four key questions: What are the distinct economic systems found in each group? Why do certain societies or nations have one economic system rather than another? What impact do economic systems have on the performance of the economy? How do these economic systems develop and change? The results provide a context that allows us to move beyond the chaos of case studies and ideological assertions to gain an overview of the development of economic systems over the millennia. It also raises a series of new analytic and empirical issues that have not hitherto been systematically explored.

Frederic L. Pryor, a Senior Research Scholar at Swarthmore College, is one of the world's leading specialists in the comparative study of economic systems. His career has spanned both the academic and the consulting worlds. In addition to teaching at Swarthmore, Professor Pryor has been affiliated with the University of California, Stanford, the University of Michigan, Indiana University, and several universities in France and Switzerland. His academic work includes the authorship of twelve books, including *Economic Evolution and Structure: The Impact of Complexity on the U.S. Economic System* (1996), *Who's Not Working and Why: Employment, Cognitive Skills, Wages, and the Changing U.S. Labor Market* (1999, coauthored with David L. Schaffer), and *The Future of U.S. Capitalism* (2002), all published by Cambridge University Press. He has also written more than one hundred articles in professional journals, primarily on the comparative study of different economic systems. As an economic consultant and researcher, Professor Pryor has worked at a variety of positions for the World Bank, several departments of the U.S. government, the Danish government, the Commonwealth of Pennsylvania, the Soros International Economic Advisory Group in Ukraine, the Hoover Institution, the Brookings Institution, and the Wissenschaftszentrum Berlin. He also serves on the boards of several nonprofit institutions.

Other Books by the Author

The Communist Foreign Trade System. 1963.

Public Expenditures in Communist and Capitalist Nations. 1968.

Property and Industrial Organization in Communist and Capitalist Nations. 1973.

The Origins of the Economy: A Comparative Study of Distribution in Primitive and Peasant Economies. 1977.

A Guidebook to the Comparative Study of Economic Systems. 1985.

Revolutionary Grenada: A Study in Political Economy. 1986.

The Political Economy of Poverty, Equity, and Growth: Malaŵi and Madagascar. 1990.

The Red and the Green: The Rise and Fall of Collectivized Agriculture in Marxist Regimes. 1992.

Economic Evolution and Structure: The Impact of Complexity on the U.S. Economic System. 1996.

Who's Not Working and Why?: Employment, Cognitive Skills, Wages, and the Changing U.S. Labor Market (with David L. Schaffer). 1999.

The Future of U.S. Capitalism. 2002.

Economic Systems of Foraging, Agricultural, and Industrial Societies

FREDERIC L. PRYOR

Swarthmore College

CAMBRIDGE
UNIVERSITY PRESS

CAMBRIDGE
UNIVERSITY PRESS

University Printing House, Cambridge CB2 8BS, United Kingdom

One Liberty Plaza, 20th Floor, New York, NY 10006, USA

477 Williamstown Road, Port Melbourne, VIC 3207, Australia

314-321, 3rd Floor, Plot 3, Splendor Forum, Jasola District Centre, New Delhi - 110025, India

103 Penang Road, #05-06/07, Visioncrest Commercial, Singapore 238467

Cambridge University Press is part of the University of Cambridge.

It furthers the University's mission by disseminating knowledge in the pursuit of
education, learning and research at the highest international levels of excellence.

www.cambridge.org
Information on this title: www.cambridge.org/9780521613477

© Frederic L. Pryor 2005

First published 2005

A catalogue record for this publication is available from the British Library

Library of Congress Cataloging in Publication data
Pryor, Frederic L.
Economic systems of foraging, agricultural, and industrial societies / Frederic L. Pryor.
p. cm.
Includes bibliographical references and index.
ISBN 0-521-84904-7 (hardback) – ISBN 0-521-61347-7 (pbk.)
1. Comparative economics. I. Title.
HB90.P789 2005
330.9 – dc22   2004019666

ISBN 978-0-521-61347-7 Paperback

To Kathleen and her family

Contents

Tables and Charts

Tables

Charts

Appendices

The appendices can only be found online at either <http://us.cambridge.org/titles/0521849047.htm> or the author's home page <www.swarthmore.edu/ SocSci/Economics/fpryor1>. The texts of the appendices are in PDF format; the Statistical Appendices, in EXCEL format.

The reference A2: 20 means page 20 of the appendices for Chapter 2; the reference SA2: 1 means page 1 of Statistical Appendix 2.

Appendices Tables

Appendix Chart

Statistical Appendices Tables

Preface

I have long been discontented with the field of comparative economic systems and this book is the result of my efforts to show what I think this discipline should be about.

In the twentieth century, comparative economists focused too narrowly on industrialized economies and paid little attention to preindustrial societies. Because these latter societies have been rapidly disappearing, we are losing an important part of our potential subject matter. Comparative economists also have few overarching approaches to deal usefully with a wide variety of market and nonmarket economies in a coherent fashion. Although case studies of an enormous number of market and nonmarket economies are available, the literature is so rich and varied that it is difficult to gain perspective. What is necessary, of course, is to look at a large number of societies with different types of economic systems with the same analytic tools. In dealing with preindustrial economic systems, this also requires a considerable familiarity not just with economics but with history and anthropology as well.

For several decades, I have been writing in my mind a book that would analyze foraging (hunting, gathering, fishing), agricultural (herding, planting), and industrial/service economic systems with a unified analytic approach that would take advantage of the rich factual information on these economies now at hand – the kind of book that nineteenth-century social scientists tried to write without adequate factual materials and case studies. But, when I finally had time to sit down and put my thoughts on paper, I was appalled at the inapplicability of many of my ideas and the enormity of the task. Various foundations also did not think the project feasible and refused to fund me. I started this research to prove that these doubts – expressed by others as well as myself – were misguided and to validate my vision of how comparative economics should be carried out. Although my new approach now seems feasible and the book is finished, I send it to press with considerable trepidation, for many important questions remain unanswered.

Completion of the research would not have been possible without the assistance of other scholars, many of whom may disagree with the approach or the conclusions or both, but who were willing to put aside their reservations.

For supplying data or information on particular societies or countries, I would like to thank George S. Argyropoulos, John Baldwin, Fredrik Barth, Thea Bosten-Eurlings, Pamela Crossley, Thomas Cusack, Ethel Dunn, Robert Fernea, Clifford Geertz, Hildred Geertz, Jane Goodale, Gregory Grossman, Christopher Hallpike, Paul Harrison, George Hewitt, Murray Klee, Arvelod E. Kuprava, Edward Lazear, H. Arlo Nimmo, Emiko Ohnuki-Tierney, Walter Park, Stu Pettingrew, Steven Piker, Leandro Prados de la Escosura, Dennis Quinn, John Ridley, and A. Maria Toyoda. I am especially grateful to Erik Buyst, Robert Carneiro, Angus Maddison, Leandro Prados de la Escosura, and Jaap Sleifer for allowing me access to unpublished research materials and data.

For reading drafts of all or most of this book, I would like to express my appreciation to Robert Carneiro and James Stodder. For commenting on different chapters, I would like to thank Robert Duplessis, Stephen Golub, Bruce Grant, Vladimir Kontorovich, James Kurth, Bruce A. Maxwell, Stephen A. O'Connell, Virginia Adams O'Connell, Dean Peabody, Steven Piker, Daniel A. Pryor, Zora Pryor, Scott Redenius, Bernard Saffran, F. M. Scherer, David Smith, Michael Speirs, and Larry Westphal, as well as members of the Tri-College Brown Bag Lunch, who offered many useful suggestions on various chapters.

The cluster analyses could never have been carried out without the patient help of Bruce Maxwell. I used his computer program and plied him with countless questions and pleas for help. I would also like to thank Shana Carleyolsen, Tom Dee, Gudmund Iversen, Philip Jefferson, Bruce Maxwell, Martin Rio, and Casey Smith for their extremely helpful statistical and computer advice, as well as the overburdened inter-library loan staff of Swarthmore College. Finally, Victoria Wilson-Schwartz, Leslie English, and Nancy Hulan provided invaluable editorial advice.

My greatest debt is to Zora, who patiently put up with missed vacations, unfulfilled household chores, and long hours in my office so that I could finish this book.

PART ONE

ORIENTATION

ONE

Introduction

An *economic system* comprises the totality of institutions and organizations that specify property relations within a given society and that channel and influence the distribution of goods and services. This dry definition covers an amazing diversity of economies at all levels of development: the altruistic foragers of the Kalahari Desert in southern Africa; the highly competitive fishing societies on the Canadian Pacific coast; the egalitarian Lepcha farmers of Sikkim; the intricately structured caste agriculturalists in Uttar Pradesh, India; the industrialized market economies of West Europe; and the former centrally planned economies of East Europe.

How can we make sense of this exuberant profusion, which represents a tribute to humanity's ingenuity at organizing itself? In this book, I look at economic systems in a comparative fashion and ask four key questions about them: Is the number of these systems infinite or do particular institutions and organizations consistently cluster together in a few distinct patterns? If such patterns exist, are they a function of the environment, the social or political structure, or the level of economic development; or are they relatively independent entities? What impact do economic systems have on the performance of the economy? How do they originate, develop, and change?

Although traditional economic theories may help us to approach these questions in a systematic fashion, such theories do not provide many answers. More specifically, we have few believable deductive analyses about which particular institutions and organizations cluster together, not just for industrial/service economies but also for those with other *foci of production*, namely foraging (hunting, gathering, or fishing) and agriculture (plant production and herding). This theoretical confusion was clearly illustrated in a bizarre debate in the 1950s and 1960s about the possibility of

3

convergence of both centrally planned and market economies toward some "social optimum" in between.[1]

Although the lack of a credible deductive theory of economic systems is certainly not fatal to analysis, it means that we run the double risk of including too few or too many factors in defining such systems. It also means we must approach the four questions posed previously in a more inductive fashion. Only in this way can we develop the stylized facts that would give us a deeper understanding of institutional structures and also bridge the gap between abstract considerations and the concrete reality of economic systems. In brief, this is not a book of airy, high-level generalizations about economic systems, nor is it an attempt to construct a generalized "theory of economic systems," nor is it a methodological treatise telling others to do what I am too lazy to carry out myself. Rather, I present what I have learned by studying a large number of preindustrial and industrial economies and by looking for groups of complementary economic institutions which, in turn, define different types of economic systems. The results of such an exercise provide a factual basis for theorizing and a systematic formulation of testable hypotheses, thus permitting us to move away from the ideological approaches that have dominated most comparisons of economic systems.

One major conclusion of this study is that for any focus of production, we can isolate a small number of coherent types of economic systems. This is important because, as in biology, the genus (the type of economic system) provides perspective on the individual species (the economy that exemplifies it), so that the accidental or unique elements can be separated from those the economy has in common with other members of the same genus. Conversely, through careful study of a given species, we may be able to isolate mechanisms that operate in other species of the same genus. More specifically, determination of the economic systems provides an analytical framework within which a variety of economic activities can be placed in context for further analysis. In the case of preindustrial societies, for instance, this means that certain economic activities can now be understood as integral parts of the economic system, whereas other activities (often receiving considerable attention) can be viewed as unique aspects of the particular society.

I also show that traditional classifications, such as feudalism or capitalism, are not very helpful and that we need to reexamine the various types of

---

[1] Nobel laureate Jan Tinbergen was a particular strong advocate of convergence, whereas other economists of lesser professional stature (including myself) argued against it (the debate is reviewed in Pryor, 1973b: 356–71). Subsequent events in East Europe suggest that Tinbergen was dead wrong. The question of institutional coherence is inescapable and we cannot simply pick and choose particular institutions that appeal to us and combine them in an economic system. I discuss this issue in greater detail in Chapter 8.

economic systems from a different perspective. Such an intellectual framework must be flexible enough to embrace the full spectrum of economic and social phenomena but firm enough to retain its unifying elements even as it changes in response to new information.

Isolating different types of economic systems is a relatively straightforward statistical exercise. Once accomplished, I can also demonstrate that they are relatively independent of social, political, and environmental influences but highly dependent on the level of economic development. Serious difficulties arise in exploring the other two major questions that guide this study. To assess the impact of the type of economic system on economic performance and to gain an understanding of systemic change, we can make some detailed empirical investigations for industrial/service economic systems. For agricultural economies, such an exploration also is possible, although in much less detail; and for foraging economies, the lack of suitable data prevents such assessment. In studying the transformation of different types of economic systems, we are also limited by the availability of information to certain broad issues: namely, the factors underlying the transition from foraging to agriculture and from agriculture to industry. For the same reasons, my explorations of the origins of types of economic systems are also limited.

Aside from the four questions underlying this analysis, delineation of a particular economic system allows us to view the institutions structuring economic activities as a whole and, in turn, to relate these patterns to a variety of particular questions we may be investigating. Thus, delineation of the economic systems allows us to step beyond reference to specific economic customs or behaviors to see more general networks of complementary institutions.

The broad focus of this book will, I hope, provide those interested in the various social sciences with a broad synthesis of economic systems, so that they can begin to see connections that they have hitherto overlooked in the chaos of unrelated facts and case studies of various economies. I have also tried to write this book so it would be comprehensible to those at various levels of expertise, placing technical materials in footnotes and appendices. The latter can be found either at <http://us.cambridge.org/titles/0521849047. htm> or at <www.swarthmore.edu/SocSci/Economics/fpryor1>.

A. Some Basic Concepts

Because this study looks at the preindustrial world from quite a different perspective than that of most economists, anthropologists, and historians, it employs a set of concepts and a vocabulary whose meaning is somewhat different in the various social science disciplines. To avoid confusion, it is important to define four crucial and abstract concepts used throughout this study.

1. The Economy

The *economy* consists of all activities aimed at the production of goods and services, their distribution, and their consumption. It reflects the specific ways in which the members of the society make their living and survive, what technologies are employed, and the specific behaviors associated with various economic activities. Consider certain aspects of a simple nomadic foraging economy. Its members spend part of their day hunting, gathering, or (for certain groups) fishing. All humans, as well as certain species of apes, employ tools for foraging; and both humans and some nonhuman primates, such as chimpanzees, make these tools as well.[2] Within all primate species, some foraged products are also distributed. Most of the differences between the economic activities of human and nonhuman primates, however, appear to be quantitative, not qualitative,[3] and all animals (both social and nonsocial) have an economy. Nevertheless, the division of labor is more extensive among humans than among their nonhuman primate cousins; and the distribution and property relationships among humans are more articulated and structured by rules (e.g., norms of sharing of the meat of large game) that are more extensive and are enforced by consensus, rather than by force.[4] As will shortly become evident, only human societies have deliberate institutions, and it is these institutions that define the type of economic system.

2. Economic Institutions

Economic institutions are, according to Douglass C. North (1998: 79), "the humanly devised constraints that structure human interaction. They are made up of formal constraints (e.g., rules, laws, constitutions), informal

---

[2] Comparing the complexity of these tools, William C. McGrew (1992: 131–42) found little difference between those of the Tasmanian aborigines and those of the chimpanzees of Tanzania.

[3] This generalization is based on a long comparative survey (Pryor, 2003b) of the economies of various species of nonhuman primates.

[4] Boehm (2004) offers the interesting argument that the defining of individually killed large game as communal property to be shared is a distinctively human trait not found in nonhuman primates.

constraints (e.g., norms of behavior, conventions, self-imposed codes of conduct), and their enforcement characteristics. Together they define the incentive structure of societies and specifically economies." They also facilitate the organization and conduct of transactions between members of the society and, crucial to their effectiveness, employ various enforcement mechanisms, which can be based on habits, rules of morality, customs, rights, or coercion. Institutions influence beliefs and behaviors of individuals and groups and, thus, the preferences and priorities expressed through both public and private decisions (Engerman and Sokoloff, 2003).[5]

I would add to this definition of economic institutions that these constraints must be *deliberately* set; and, in turn, two criteria must be met to determine the "deliberateness" of such constraints:

(a) The behavior of members of the society must be individualistic. Such behavior includes strategizing, forming friendships, expressing oneself artistically, inventing, or displaying a distinct personality. In this respect, the differences between human and nonhuman primates also appear quantitative, not qualitative.

(b) The institutions of one group must differ significantly from those of other groups of the same species in similar ecological circumstances. Nonhuman primates do not meet this second aspect of deliberateness: primatologists have found few behavioral differences among the economic behavior (and the rules inferred from it) of different groups (bands) of the same species, at least for those economic activities occupying a significant amount of time.[6]

In brief, despite considerable differences in the economies of different bands of the same species, nonhuman primates have no real economic institutions according to this criterion. By way of contrast, as I show in Chapters 2 and 3, different groups of human nomadic foragers have had not only very different economies but also a profusion of different property and distribution institutions channeling their economic activities. From an economic

---

[5] Another useful discussion of institutions is by Baslé (2002).

[6] See Pryor (2003b). For example, although baboon troops may differ considerably in the amount of their hunting and meat eating, in no troop do these figure as salient elements of their time budget or diet. The exchange of grooming services, on the other hand, is a much more important group activity among baboons, and patterns of exchange vary little from troop to troop. Although the patterns of grooming differ significantly *between* species of nonhuman primates, up to now primatologists have found few differences *within* a given species.

point of view, it is the existence of institutions that distinguishes humans from other animals.[7]

Of course, it is often difficult to determine exactly what these institutions are if they are not embodied in constitutions, laws, books of "correct conduct," or survey results. In preliterate societies, however, anthropologists can ask members of the society about these institutions (and then try to resolve conflicting opinions) or can infer them from the behavior of members of that society. For instance, does a person who takes a tool from the house of its original owner incur punishment when the removal is discovered? As I argue in later chapters, rules of property are found in human societies at all levels of development; we must discard the notion that at a very early stage of human society, our ancestors made no distinction between mine and thine (i.e., the notion of *primitive communism*).

3. Economic Organizations

Let us continue with the distinctions made by Douglass C. North (1998: 81): "If institutions are the rules of the game, organizations and their entrepreneurs are the players. *Organizations* are made up of groups of individuals bound together by some common purpose to achieve certain objectives. Organizations include political bodies (e.g., political parties, the Senate, a city council, regulatory bodies), economic bodies (e.g., firms, trade unions, family farms, cooperatives), social bodies (e.g., churches, clubs, athletic associations), and educational bodies (e.g., schools, universities, vocational centers)." Although these examples focus on industrial/service rather than preindustrial economies, North's basic idea can be applied to all human economies.

---

[7] Others have argued, incorrectly I believe, that the economies of human and nonhuman primates differ on three other grounds. (1) Some claim the existence of communal property is the key, but I have dealt with this issue elsewhere (Pryor, 2004). (2) Some claim that nonhuman primates have no general concept of property. But, in fact, many species of primates have a strong sense of territoriality (Pryor, 2003b), and some have a sense of personal property as well. For instance, in the Yerkes Laboratory (a large outdoor reserve), chimpanzees performed various tasks and earned tokens to be later exchanged for food; they soon began to hoard the tokens and became "hysterical" when other animals came near their cache (Dare, 1974). (3) Some note that nonhuman primates are relatively self-sufficient and rely very little on exchange. However, many human societies also manifest a high degree of economic self-sufficiency within the nuclear family (although not quite as high as among nonhuman primates). For instance, if we assign values to home-produced goods and services, we find that even in an advanced industrial nation, such as the United States in the latter half of the twentieth century, home-produced goods and services amounted to roughly 50 percent of total personal consumption (Eisner, 1989: Table 1).

Human nomadic foragers have many different types of economic organizations. The most important economic interactions occur within the family, where adult males and females spend a significant portion of their time in joint activities for production, consumption, and distribution.[8] But, other joint economic activities outside the family can also be specified: for instance, foraging parties, food sharing, competitive feasts, and so forth. So it seems we humans are qualitatively distinguished from our simian cousins and other animals by our (deliberate) economic institutions and organizations.[9]

4. The Economic System, the Mode of Production, and the New Institutional Economics

As previously defined, the economic system comprises the entire configuration of institutions. The economic system and the economy are concepts that direct our attention to the same phenomena but from very different perspectives and levels of abstraction.

In studying preindustrial societies, however, most anthropologists have focused primarily on the economy. For agricultural economies, they have investigated various production techniques – swidden, use of irrigation, and types of tools – and they may have dealt with a few key economic institutions, such as tenancy arrangements or the organization of work parties. For foraging societies, most anthropologists have also focused for the most part on the economy, as Binford (2001) did in his monumental synthesis. But, for a complete description of any given preindustrial society, of course, we must investigate both the economy and the economic system.

My focus on economic systems, specified in terms of the overall pattern of economic institutions and organizations defining property relations and the distribution of goods and services, is relatively standard in the West, at least among those working within the mainstream tradition of Anglo-American economics. Implicit in the term "economic system" is the notion that certain institutions are complementary to others and, as a result, are usually found together. Some refer to this phenomenon as reflecting the "logic of institutions," a concept which, unfortunately, is seldom spelled out or

---

[8] One possible exception to my generalization about the importance of joint economic activities within the family is the Ik of Uganda (Turnbull, 1972), but this was a semi-starving society, whose long-term survival was in doubt.

[9] Certain types of insects, such as ants, do have complex economies with a division of labor and systems of exchange, so in this respect they have more "advanced" economic organizations than our primate cousins. But their economic organization seems to function on the basis of instinct, so that they also do not meet the criterion of deliberateness.

investigated carefully. By contrast, the cluster analysis employed throughout this book focuses on these complementarities. Moreover, in the latter part of this book, I carefully examine how the logic of institutions influences systemic change, a new issue for comparative economists.

Relatively few economists have analyzed the economic systems of tribal and peasant economic systems in terms of their constituent institutions and organizations. Anthropologists who study these economies are more likely than economists to write from a Marxist perspective and to focus on the *mode of production*, a broader concept than the economic system. Some clarification of these contrasting approaches to preindustrial economies is in order.

A mode of production consists of both *forces of production* and *relations of production*. The former term includes the level of technology, the environment and natural resources, and the physical and human capital available to the economy; the latter term roughly corresponds to my concept of economic system.

Of course, discussing the forces of development in a methodical fashion requires measurement; and, at this point, problems arise. Different aspects of the forces of production require quite different measures. For a measure of economic development in preindustrial economies, I use an ingenious index of "cultural complexity" devised by Robert Carneiro (1970). This measure covers a wide variety of tangible and intangible aspects of the society's culture, including a large number that directly reflect technology and the division of labor.[10]

Because the connotations of both "cultural" and "complexity" differ greatly from one field of social science to another, I relabel Carneiro's scale as the "level of economic development" because it reflects what economists mean by that concept. As a measure of economic development in industrial/service economies, I use the per capita gross domestic product (GDP), calculated for each country in 1990 dollar prices. For characterizing other aspects

---

[10] Carneiro (1970) looked at particular traits reflecting functions common to all societies and selected those aspects of material culture that allow a simple coding yielding an unambiguous scale to rank societies according to their level of development. More specifically, he developed a Guttman scale with several hundred cumulative indicators that cover various aspects of the division of labor, level of technology, architecture, social organization, political organization, law and judicial processes, warfare, religion, ceramics and art, transportation, and special knowledge and practices. In his measure, he focused on only those indicators that could be used in a Guttman scale and did not include other kinds of complexity, such as that embodied in kinship or religious beliefs, which did not allow such scaling. Because his various indicators have little overlap with those I employ in defining the economic system, my use of his scale does not involve any circular reasoning. The estimation technique for those societies not coded by Carneiro is described in Appendix 2-2.

of the forces of production, such as the physical environment, I use a number of indicators, including evapo-transpiration (a measure of the moisture available for plant growth), effective temperature (a measure capturing the average temperature and the length of the growing season), soil quality, topography, and so forth. For measures of physical capital, I use an approximation of the capital intensity of production; and, as a measure of human capital, an approximation of literacy or of education in the population.

The concept of mode of production has many inadequacies, which I have discussed elsewhere (Pryor, 1982a). For the purposes of this book, I find that separating the forces and relations of production and considering the former as external to the economic system, rather than as intrinsic to it, has three major advantages. Most important, my approach permits us to test propositions about the correlation (or lack thereof) between economic system and levels of economic development; in other words, to see if the former evolves in a unilineal fashion or whether different types of economic systems can exist at the same level of economic development. Furthermore, the dispute over whether the relations or forces of production have causal priority ceases to be an ideological catfight and becomes an empirical question instead. Finally, for preindustrial societies, the separation of these two aspects of the mode of production allows us to move away from lavishing almost exclusive attention to the forces of production, which is customary in this literature, to giving more attention to the relations of production.

My particular treatment of types of economic systems is related to that of the "new institutional economics," which also focuses on economic institutions and organizations. But, although the new institutional economics has a microeconomic focus and deals with institutions and organizations primarily as phenomena in isolation from each other, I deal with these phenomena from a more macro-viewpoint and consider how specific institutions and organizations within an economy are interrelated. Nevertheless, of the four key questions asked by comparative economists outlined previously, the new institutional economics deals with all but one: what particular configurations of the institutions and organizations within an economy occur together and what might underlie such complementarities.

B. Classification of Economic Systems

1. Common Approaches for Classifying Economic Systems

The various property relations and methods of distribution of goods and services occurring together and defining an economic system do not appear randomly in human societies. If they did, there would be an infinite number of types of economic systems. Rather, they are somehow related to each other in some type of pattern. Because these overall patterns are relatively few in number, as I will show, we can use them to devise a schema for sorting societies into groups. In turn, this permits a more methodical and comprehensive analysis of these economic systems, of how they function and how they change, than is possible with scattered case studies. But how do we determine meaningful categories for defining an economic system? Of the several methods usually employed, each has serious faults.

Some analysts merely take a few characteristics of an economy and use them to classify the type of economic system.[11] For modern industrial/service economies, such characteristics may be the "spirit" of the system: for instance, the U.S. entrepreneurial model, the French statist model, the Swedish socialist model, or the Japanese concensus model. Such a holistic approach papers over the problem of specifying the exact institutional differences between economies. Or, these selected characteristics might be the share of government ownership in the means of production, the relative importance of government expenditures or regulation, the dominant ideology, the most important economic values (individualistic, social, communitarian), the most usual structure of enterprises, and so forth. This approach, however, is usually an ad hoc procedure, because little attempt is made to link the selected criteria with the full range of other economic institutions and organizations that structure the society in question. Such an approach can be justified, however, when the analyst cannot get adequate data on the society's full range of economic institutions (the discussion in Chapter 8, for example).

Some scholars have posited various "ideal types," which is a more "theoretical" approach. That is, they focus on certain aspects of the economic institutions and organizations that their theory tells them are important, set up the corresponding categories of economic systems, and then place the various economies in the appropriate conceptual boxes. Such an approach has been widely employed from the middle of the nineteenth century up to the end of the twentieth century.[12] In some cases, the characteristic is relatively general: for instance, the primary method of distributing goods

---

[11] The various essays on modern industrial/service economies in Coates (2002: volume I) provide examples of this practice. For preindustrial societies, Netting (1977) has a brief but useful survey of this approach.

[12] A nineteenth-century example is found in the work of Bruno Hildebrand, who classified economic systems according to their reliance on barter, money, or credit in their transfer of goods and services. Bert F. Hoselitz (1960) notes the ambiguity of this type of analysis: do these categories

and services (e.g., market, centrally planned, traditional) or the type of market (e.g., free competition, regulated competition, dominance of monopolies). This method of classification helps to organize discussion and where the distinctions between economic systems appear obvious – for instance, those between industrial/service economies that are market driven and those that are centrally planned – it allows performance comparisons to be made with a minimum of fuss. Indeed, on many occasions, I have used such an approach myself. But, seldom are the roles of other economic institutions or the justifications for the classification schema made very clear. Moreover, as Richard Grassby sourly notes (1999: 2), ideal types are "fictive generalizations about the predominant characteristics of a particular society, projected from selected historical facts and intended to serve as a basis for universal analysis." As in the previously described procedure, usually only two or three features are singled out as crucial, so we cannot be sure that the most important institutions and organizations in that economy are taken into account. As a result, we also have no assurance that the categories are very meaningful in helping us answer the central questions that I raise at the beginning of this chapter.

Yet, others have based their classification on the implications of some particular theory of how the economy functions. The best-known application of such an approach toward preindustrial societies is probably that of Marx and Engels. But, their theory is a highly abstract model of systemic change, fleshed out with the bits of ethnographic knowledge at their disposal (often drawn from the American lawyer/anthropologist Lewis Henry Morgan). It was not based on a formal analysis of foraging and agricultural societies, and many Marxist anthropologists have acknowledged the difficulties in applying such concepts as class struggle or exploitation to societies in which the requisite property institutions for defining classes are either absent or incipient. I have not found these theoretical approaches to have yielded propositions that are at once intriguing and empirically verifiable.

Finally, a set of miscellaneous approaches deserves passing reference. Some scholars have simply classified economic systems according to the schema in common parlance, using terms such as "feudalism," "agrarian capitalism," and so forth. Then, they somehow squeeze the data into the

---

represent phases of a temporal sequence (*economic stages*), *ideal types* of economic system, or the most important *economic principles* underlying the functioning of an economy.

A twentieth-century example of an ideal type schema is provided by Brian Hayden (1995), who divided preindustrial economic systems into those where important economic activities are carried out in independent households and those where such activities are carried out by more broadly based corporate groups within the community.

schema, however tight the fit. Such a "commonsense" solution may make the results of any further analysis easily understandable by others, but it does little to address the disadvantages of the classification schema itself. Other scholars have argued that the concept of economic system is superfluous, but they offer conflicting reasons to buttress their case.[13] I do not believe their arguments seem tenable or worth the space to refute.

2. My Approach for Classifying Economic Systems

Given the huge volume of case-study materials, the lack of any general schema for distinguishing economic systems, and the resulting intellectual chaos, one should approach the classification problem with a certain humility. If we have no satisfactory theory of how the clustering of economic institutions and organizations occur, we can tackle the problem inductively.

More specifically, I start with variables representing a series of institutions and organizations and define each as a dimension of the economic system, an approach that allows multidimensional statistical techniques to be employed. I focus on institutions and organizations that might have an important impact on the economy (at least as suggested by case studies of particular societies) and that are related to the system of property or distribution. Given these various dimensions, I then look for a cluster of economies with similar configurations of institutions and organizations.

More technically, I calculate the distances in this multidimensional space defined by the selected institutions and organizations between each society and every other society and employ a pattern-recognition technique called cluster analysis to determine which societies are closest to each other – that is, which institutions and organizations cluster together. The clusters of economies that appear most similar define, in turn, the different types of economic systems.

Chart 1-1 presents a simplified example in two-dimensional space. To be very concrete, let us assume that all economic systems have only different degrees of two institutions: slavery (A) and land rental (B). For each society, we can designate this configuration by an x on the graph. At first glance, the economies fall into three clusters (Q, R, and S), whose boundaries I have

---

[13] Some claim that most economies are so different that comparisons are misleading and each must be considered in isolation, a view associated in anthropology with Franz Boaz and his followers. Others take the opposite position and argue that each economy can be analyzed using standard economic tools as if they were market economies, a purely formalistic view found in the writings of some economists particularly enamored with neoclassical economics.

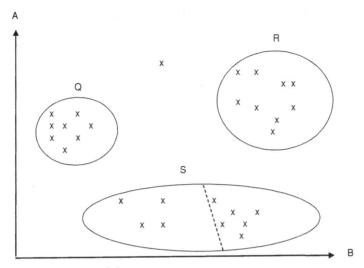

Chart 1-1. Designation of clusters.
Note: The axes A and B, respectively, represent the two possible institutions in this simplified example, slavery and land rental. The position of each society (x) is determined by the degree to which these two institutions play a part in its economy. Q, R, and S represent the derived clusters.

sketched. These clusters are bunched somewhat differently, with cluster Q the most tightly packed and cluster S, the most loosely. One economy, in the upper middle portion of the graph, does not fall clearly into any of the three clusters; different estimations of the clusters might put it in either Q or R. Fortunately, as I show in later chapters, such situations are relatively rare.

The chart illustrates another problem, however, that is quite common in this procedure. Might it be better to consider cluster S as really two clusters, with the dashed line marking the boundaries of each? We face a tradeoff. On the one hand, according to the principle of Occam's razor, entities (types of economic systems, in this case) should not be multiplied unnecessarily, and we should have as few clusters as possible.[14] On the other hand, increasing the number of clusters reduces the error in defining each cluster. Obviously, if we have twenty-nine societies (each with an x on the

---

[14] In modern information theory, this means that we should keep theoretical complexity to a minimum, where complexity is defined mathematically as the number of bits used to represent the model generating the clusters. A model with ten parameters, each with two possible values (1 or 0), would be of equal complexity to a model with one parameter with 1,024 potential values.

graph), we will have no error in our description if we define twenty-nine clusters. If, however, eight x's cluster near each other and another nine x's are also close to each other but not to the first group, and a third group of eleven x's also forms a distinct cluster, we lose relatively little information about the grouping of economic systems by reducing the twenty-nine clusters to three.

At this juncture, it is useful to draw upon the principle of the *minimum description length* (MDL), defined by Jorma Rissanen (1989: 79 ff.), who worked from a "stochastic information-theoretic" approach. This technique combines the positive value of additional information gained by increasing the number of clusters with the negative value of the resulting greater theoretical complexity (both determined using information theory), thereby arriving at a description length used for determining the optimal number of clusters. More specifically, the first step is to calculate the description length associated with each of various numbers of clusters for the data under examination. The optimal number of clusters (the MDL) is simply where the gain in information is exactly counterbalanced by the increase in complexity.[15] A computer program (written by Bruce Maxwell and described in Maxwell, Pryor, and Smith, 2002) allows an easy calculation of the MDL over a range of numbers of clusters. Once the optimal number of clusters (the number of economic systems) is selected, the program prints out the list of economies in each, as well as certain properties of each cluster, so that we can gain a quantitative idea of how often particular institutions occur together.

The optimal number of clusters, I must emphasize, may not be very helpful if the isolated clusters are very broad (in terms of Chart 1-1, if the lines defining the clusters encompass a very large area). A useful statistic to investigate this matter compares the variance of the distance of every point (a nation or society) with every other point in the sample and the summed variance for each cluster of the distance of every point within the cluster with every other point in the same cluster. Such a calculation tells us how much of the differences among the various economies is and is not explained by the calculated clusters. Thus, if the MDL calculations determine that three clusters are optimal and if, within each of these clusters, all countries have the same institutional configuration, the reduction-in-variance is 100 percent. By way of

---

[15] In cases where the MDL was roughly equal for two adjacent numbers of clusters, I selected the number of clusters yielding the most interesting results. In these cases, the various societies in all but one of the clusters were generally the same, but one particular cluster was split in two (in Chart 1-1, this would most likely occur with cluster S).

contrast, if the points to be clustered are randomly scattered over the multi-dimensional space, the calculated reduction-in-variance may be only 10 percent and distinctive economic systems cannot be meaningfully determined – a situation that, fortunately, I did not encounter. Appendix 1–2 contains some further technical notes on the cluster analysis.

This is, of course, an inductive rather than deductive way of defining economic systems. Although such an approach appears "objective," it cannot be used heedlessly. The analyst must base the calculations on unbiased information and select thoughtfully the dimensions by which the clusters are to be defined (in Chart 1-1, slavery and land rental). The number of relevant institutions and organizations is, of course, related to the complexity of the economy: for foraging, agricultural, and industrial/service economic systems I selected, respectively, ten, twenty-two, and forty.[16] From the basis of the case materials at hand, I chose aspects of property relations and the distribution of goods and services that I had some reason to believe might have an impact on the functioning of the economy. My choice was confined, however, to those aspects for which I could collect sufficient comparable information for most of the societies in the sample. For the preindustrial societies, I drew upon data from more than 700 ethnographic sources (plus a number of letters to various ethnographers); for the industrial/service economies, I could, fortunately, draw upon statistics published by international organizations and studies by other economists.

Although such an approach focuses on the characteristics of economic systems at a single point in time, a fuller understanding of these systems requires us also to determine how they change over time. That is, we must ascertain both their static and dynamic elements. For this reason, I look at the role of economic systems in the transition from foraging to agriculture and from agriculture to industry. For advanced industrial market economies, I also look briefly at their systemic changes over the twentieth century.

The economic systems derived from the cluster analysis may look like ideal types, yet they differ in three respects. They are empirically derived, and not deduced from a particular theory about economic systems that may (or may not) be correct. Moreover, the starting point for the analysis takes

---

[16] I might add that only a small number of the institutions I chose proved helpful in distinguishing economic systems. For instance, for the agricultural societies, neither the inheritance arrangements nor the extent to which food was redistributed through a central organization (the government, the church, or a "big man") was a defining element of the economic system. That is, they varied more among societies with a given type of economic system than between types of economic systems.

into account many different dimensions, rather than one or two that capture the fancy of the investigator. Finally, many societies with a given economic system lacked *some* of the characteristics defining the system, even though its patterns of institutions and organizations matched the system type in the most important respects.[17]

In the final analysis, the "correctness" of my procedure can be determined only by asking whether my results make sense, provide new insights into the functioning of these economies, and help to answer important questions. I believe they do, but on this matter readers must make up their own mind.

C. Problems of Analysis

1. Basic Expositional Strategy

In this study, I divide my analysis of economic systems into three distinct sections that focus, respectively, on foraging, agriculture, and industrial/service economies.[18] Each of these types of economies has a distinctive focus of production and, as a result, the key dimensions of their economic systems are also very different. The three sections of the book are separate units and can be read independently of the others.

In the first chapter of each section, I isolate the various types of economic systems on the basis of a cross-sectional (or synchronic) study – that is, one that looks at various societies at a pinpointed year to derive the economic systems through a cluster analysis. Of course, this type of analysis overlooks certain vital aspects of historical change and the mutation of the economic system as the level of economic development rises or falls. Furthermore,

---

[17] I weight each of the dimensions equally, so that the cluster analysis yields a single pattern. If, for theoretical reasons, certain dimensions are considered more important than others, then a different pattern might emerge. Because the empirical analysis in the following chapters shows that usually only a handful of dimensions serve to distinguish one economic system from another, such a weighting procedure does not seem necessary.

[18] This way of differentiating economies is, of course, not original and can be traced back at least as far as the early nineteenth century, when Lewis Henry Morgan characterized the three types as savagery, barbarism, and civilization (or city-based). Such labels, however, may sound harsh to the tender ears of contemporary readers and I use more bland and neutral terms.

To name the economies in this order – foraging, agricultural, and industrial/service – implies nothing about their relative standards of living or productivity. As I point out in Chapter 3, many foraging peoples ate better and worked far fewer hours than those living in agricultural societies.

such developments can be imperceptible or sudden; they can affect only a single important institution or organization, or the entire system; and their impact on the performance of the economy can be limited or large.

The second chapter in each section, therefore, deals with how the various types of economic systems change. Although the paucity of appropriate historical data for preindustrial societies prevents many types of time-series analyses, we can still gain some perspective on the certain causal elements involved in systemic changes from one focus of production to another. For the industrial/service economies, more exact temporal comparisons can be made.

2. Problems of Causation

Which factors determine why a particular society has one type of economic system rather than another at a certain point in time? Many anthropologists and economists accept Karl Polanyi's argument that preindustrial economies are embedded in a social, cultural, and political matrix and that the origin of the economic system is, therefore, not an "economic" question. I take this argument seriously and spend considerable effort examining the association between the types of economic systems and different social, cultural, and political variables that are most appropriate to this argument. Of course, a cross-section analysis can tell you whether the economic system is related to these noneconomic factors, but we cannot know in which direction the arrow of causation points. In most cases, as it turns out, the correlations between economic system and the various social and political factors are statistically insignificant, which suggests that the economic system is not caused by these noneconomic factors and, instead, is an independent entity that should be studied by itself. It is, thus, legitimate to focus most of our attention on economic considerations alone.

The relationship between the types of economic systems and the physical environments in which they are located presents somewhat different problems. Cultural ecologists such as Netting (1975) have devoted enormous effort to demonstrating the relationship between different environmental variables and the functioning of the economy. In some cases, the linkage between the environment and certain features of the economic system are also readily apparent. For instance, foraging societies located closer to the North or South Pole rely less on gathering and are also more likely to practice food storage than those living closer to the Equator, where growing seasons are longer; such storage, in turn, presumes a certain type of private property.

Nevertheless, my analysis will show that environmental factors appear to play only a minor causal role in determining the economic system, an example where the distinction between the economic system and the economy is crucial.

The greatest difficulty in causation arises from the interrelations between the economic system and the level of economic system. One common view was expressed by the economist Yegor Gaidar, who was in charge of economic reforms when he was First Deputy Chairman of the Council of Ministers of the Russian Federation. Apropos of the fall of communism, he thundered: "Henceforth books on comparative economic systems will be found on the shelves dealing with economic development."[19] He was assuming, as do many, that the functional requirements for an economic system to be effective at any given level of economic development are so restrictive that only one economic system is optimal at that level.

This book is based on the opposite assumption: namely, that at a given level of economic development, several different economic systems can function effectively, although their performance in particular areas might be different. (In anthropology, this might be called a belief in "multilayered evolution.") Nevertheless, it is vital to take into account explicitly the relation between types of economic systems and the level of economic development. Therefore, in examining all causal relationships between the type of economic system and particular variables (either performance indicators or various environmental, social, cultural, political, or environmental factors), I employ regression techniques that allow us to distinguish the separate influences of the variables under consideration and the level of economic development.

A final serious problem in determining causal relationships arises because particular causal factors may operate differently in a particular economy over time and at a single point in time over many different economies. For instance, in highly industrialized economies, the ratio of public expenditures to the per capita GDP has risen considerably over the last century in all countries; but, at a single point in time, this ratio is not significantly related to the per capita GDP. For industrial/service economic systems, we can address this problem quite directly because a certain amount of similar quantitative information is available for both time-series and cross-section analyses. For preindustrial economic systems, however, we have no such information, so

---

[19] This is quoted by Rosser and Rosser (2004: 575) from Gaidar's address to a meeting of the International Economic Association in Moscow in August 1992.

the results of any cross-section analysis must be interpreted with caution when considering historical developments.

3. Data Problems

For industrial/service economies, I could obtain a useful sample by focusing on the OECD countries, supplemented in several instances by a sample of developing economies. In most cases, I could collect suitable data by drawing either upon standard statistical sources or the estimations of other economists.

For preindustrial economies, I have drawn on the Standard Cross-Cultural Sample (SCCS), compiled by George Peter Murdock and Douglas R. White (1969). This consists of 186 societies spread over the globe (they originally had planned to select one society from each of the two hundred "culture areas" of the world, but found that this research design could not be completely implemented). They pinpointed each society to a particular time and community, usually when some reliable observer (traveler, missionary, trader, colonial agent, or anthropologist) first visited the society and wrote about it in sufficient detail to impart important ethnographic information. I chose just over half of the SCCS societies for close examination. More specifically, I included all of those societies for which the predominant focus of production was foraging or agriculture (i.e., relatively "pure cases") and omitted those where both foraging and agriculture were significant sources of food – the "mixed cases." About three quarters of the foraging societies in my sample were in North and South America; although the agricultural societies in my sample had a wider geographical distribution, certain regions of the world were also not well represented.

Does my use of the SCCS lead to biased results? According to J. Patrick Gray (1996), the SCCS is not "a representative sample that would gladden the heart of a sampling theorist." Nevertheless, it is possible to isolate its particular biases (discussed in detail in Appendix 1-1) and compensate for them in the analysis. Even more important, for the purpose of isolating economic systems, it is not so vital to have a totally random sample as to have a sample that exhibits the wide variety of ways in which particular institutions and organizations can be combined and rearranged. Further, in most cases, the types of economic systems I isolate were not confined to one geographical area but found in widely scattered places on the globe. Thus, cultural diffusion (i.e., the borrowing of traits by one society from another) does not appear to be a serious objection to the validity of my analysis.

For the preindustrial societies, I also focus on one individual community and speak of this community as "the society," making it in some way "representative" of a larger grouping of neighboring communities. Such a shortcut was unavoidable because, in most cases, reliable information for the society as a whole was not available. Nevertheless, important inferences about the wider society can be made by examining the impact of external influences on the economy of the community under examination. For instance, we can tell much about the Incan empire as a whole from the extractions transferred to the capital by individual villages. In the analysis, I try to compensate in a qualitative fashion for the community-centered nature of the available data.

I coded most of the data for the preindustrial societies myself, a procedure with two advantages: it ensured consistency of coding and it gave me a detailed familiarity with each society in the sample.[20] Of course, such a procedure also has a serious disadvantages: namely, that no tests for accuracy or bias in the coding could be performed by comparing the results of two or more independent coders. I tried, nevertheless, to take certain precautions to minimize any coding biases. For instance, I tried to compare my codes with those of others who had coded the same or similar variables.

4. Problems of Methodological Bias

Those carrying out any type of cross-cultural comparison must develop analytic categories of their own. They cannot rely on the ways in which members of the various societies understood their own institutions because this would make comparisons impossible with any large sample. Such a procedure, of course, raises the hackles of those who believe that each society is so unique that useful comparisons cannot be made with others.[21]

---

[20] It also spared me the extremely time-consuming job of training undergraduates to code the data (I had no access to graduate anthropology students) and then getting them to persist for several years at a job that took me a year of full-time work to carry out myself. The greatest problems any coder faces arise for societies described only in scattered ethnographic sources or in ethnographies that focused primarily on noneconomic matters, and different coders would find it difficult to handle these problems in the same way.

[21] More technically, I use an "etic" rather than an "emic" approach. Unlike "modern anthropologists," I believe that no society is *sui generis* and that comparisons employing consistent categories of analysis allow us to gain perspective not just on individual societies but also on a series of broader anthropological issues. Many of these anthropologists also argue that the etic approach introduces ethnocentrism and should be totally replaced by a more "holistic" analysis based on how these preindustrial peoples understand themselves and their society. Such arguments are frivolous because the particular choice of an etic or emic approach should depend on the analytical issue under examination.

Other inconsequential objections might be raised, particularly by those wedded to traditional analytic methods, which do not warrant a detailed response.[22]

Because this study is an exercise in positive rather than normative economics, it is not my purpose to assess morally the economic arrangements within any society. Thus, bias does not enter the analysis in this way. Obviously, in caste-organized villages, such as those found in India up to the end of World War II, many peasants had to pay handsomely for economic services that, for religious reasons, they were not allowed to perform themselves. But, I treat these matters solely as facts, not as a pulpit for moral outrage. In such cases, the truly important value judgments are made not by economists but by those inside the society who believe the economic system to be unfair and work to change it.[23]

Other problems of bias arise from the selection of the societies to examine. It is, of course, impossible to investigate all of the preindustrial economies in world history, especially since most have not been very adequately described. Moreover, if we wish to study the economic systems of many preindustrial societies, particularly outside of Europe, we are forced to rely on descriptions by Westerners only in the last half millennium. This raises the problem of contamination of my sample. More specifically, since the beginning of the age of Western exploration in the fifteenth century, almost all non-Western preindustrial societies have been influenced, at least to some degree, by direct or indirect contact with the West and by modern technologies and institutions, such as money.

To minimize the effect of these outside influences, I have usually chosen societies for which the data come from years close to that of first contact with

---

[22] At various stages of this research, professional anthropologists have criticized my methodology by accusing me of having "evolutionist, materialist, and functional" conceptions of preindustrial societies. Because I explicitly test for relationships between the types of economic systems and the development index, I do not assume evolutionism but rather test it as an hypothesis. Similarly, because I also test for relationships between a variety of social, cultural, and political variables, it is hard for me to see how such alleged materialist or functional biases have influenced my results.

[23] I should add that the economic teachings of major religions such as Islam, Buddhism, or Christianity are often so ambiguous that they are not very helpful in assessing economic systems from a moral standpoint (Pryor, 1985c, 1990a, 1991, and 1993). Although it would have been extremely useful to bring the practice (in contrast to the teachings) of religion into the analysis, particularly in looking at the social and cultural correlates of the economic system, I could not derive meaningful codes of such practices to carry this out. In certain cases, for instance, why Middle Eastern countries did not industrialize (discussed briefly in Chapter 6), the role of religion appears very important; by contrast, recent evidence (Rodrik, *et al.*, 2003) suggests that the role of Protestantism in industrialization in Christian countries has been overdrawn.

the West, but such a solution is not perfect.[24] A different way of addressing the problem is to ask how much these preindustrial societies have changed over the millennia until the pinpointed date. Archaeological evidence suggests that for some, such as the !Kung San (Ju/'hansi) of the Kalahari Desert, appear to have changed relatively little over the past three or four centuries, and their rock drawings from many centuries ago portray activities quite similar to those pursued in 1950, the pinpointed date.[25] Other societies in my sample made technological advances over the millennia, but there is no evidence that their economic systems changed significantly. Most of the agricultural societies discussed in this book, however, were pinpointed within the last century and a half, so that problems of Western influence are more serious. In particularly, certain long-lasting institutions, such as slavery, were forcibly eliminated by more powerful Western nations, and certain new institutions, such as wage labor, were introduced. I try to handle these problems in a qualitative way in the discussion.

Several other methodological pitfalls also deserve note. Certain economic systems might have existed in the far distant past, only to become extinct during the last half-millennium. This could have come about, for instance, because such systems provided a quick transition from foraging to agriculture and then disappeared, whereas other foraging societies survived to be described by Westerners only because they were much slower to make the transition and became frozen in time. Therefore, it is difficult to determine whether my delineation of economic systems is exhaustive and covers all that ever existed.

Finally, some of the non-Western preindustrial peoples in my sample that were found in the last century or so lived in isolated or extreme environments, such as the Yahgan of Tierra del Fuego. Their habitats might not have been typical for most of our distant ancestors. Problems of representativeness of my sample arising from such circumstances are not as serious as they might appear because, as noted previously, environmental factors have relatively little impact on the economic system.

---

[24] It also raises the question of whether any of the societies in my sample are "pure." For instance, although many foraging societies had little direct contact with the West, some had considerable contact over many centuries with more advanced agricultural societies. Conversely, although many agricultural societies had trade contacts with the West, the impacts of these contacts on the economic system were, in some cases, minimal.

[25] Archaeological evidence provides us with some useful information about economies in the past – for instance, about the relation between climatic shifts and changes in subsistence production. But, such information often reveals little about the ancient economic systems or the component economic institutions.

Despite these and other problems, little suggests that the endogenous forces influencing the economic system in the societies in my sample were more different in the distant past than in more recent years. Readers, however, must judge the relevance of my results for other societies and situations for themselves.

D. Plan of Attack

Chapters 2 and 3 focus on foraging economic systems; Chapters 4 and 5, on agricultural systems; and Chapters 6 through 8 on city-based industrial/service societies. In the even-numbered chapters, I outline the exact criteria for property ownership and distribution used to define various economic systems, present the results, and analyze the impact of different environmental, social, and political variables on the various systems. In the odd-numbered chapters, the analysis is usually more qualitative by default because we have relatively few case studies of the transition of foraging societies to agriculture and, although studies on the transition from agriculture to industry (the "industrial revolution") abound, they do not allow for easy quantification.

I survey more than two hundred different economies in this study. In the text, however, I usually summarize these data in terms of averages for each type of economic system. I describe and present all of the underlying data used in the empirical analysis – coded both by myself and by others – in the appendices to avoid smothering readers with details.

The use of the cluster analysis allows us to define economic systems in terms of complementary institutions. The theoretical problem that remains to be solved is whether these institutional complementarities are the result of economic forces (sometimes characterized as the "logic of institutions") or of particular political or social factors.

We have a vast territory to cover and some of the terrain is quite rugged. Nevertheless, the aerial view that I provide in the following chapters allows the contours of the land to be clearly seen without forcing the reader to face the rigors of a land expedition. So buckle your seatbelts, put your tray tables and seats in an upright position, and prepare for takeoff.

PART TWO

FORAGING SOCIETIES

TWO

Economic Systems of Foragers

In past millennia, foraging (hunting, gathering, or fishing) proved a highly successful method of adaptation, allowing humans to spread and survive over most land areas on the planet. In the analysis of preindustrial societies, it is tempting to group together all foraging societies because they operated in quite different ways from those based primarily on agriculture. But, as I show herein, more insights can be gained by looking at their different types of economic systems.

Given the fact that very few "pure" foraging societies now exist, it is necessary to rely on how these societies functioned at some pinpointed date many years ago. As a result, this is an exercise in historical analysis, utilizing the vast store of ethnographies written over the past centuries to arrive at new insights. Because all of the societies in my sample have greatly changed since the pinpointed date, I use the past tense in discussing them. The sample, reviewed in detail, includes forty-four different foraging societies from Africa, Asia, Australia, and the Americas.

The major conclusions can be readily stated: Foraging societies reveal six quite distinct economic systems, whose different organizing principles are readily interpretable. Such economic systems are, in most cases, unrelated to those ecological, social, and political variables that have received the bulk of attention by anthropologists. In brief, these economic systems are independent entities worthy of study by themselves.

The first section discusses the sample and the institutional variables selected for defining an economic system. The next section presents the results of the cluster analysis and the different institutional components of the six types of economic systems. In the remaining discussion, I look briefly at the impact of the type of economic system on performance; examine much more extensively the relation of economic systems to important environmental, social, political, and other economic variables of interest; and then consider certain paths along which these foraging economic systems might have evolved.

A. The Data Base

1. The Sample

As noted in Chapter 1, I draw the societies used for my sample (Table 2-1) from the 186 preindustrial societies throughout the world that are included in the SCCS of George P. Murdock and Douglas R. White (1969). Of these societies in the SCCS, forty-four can be considered to be foraging, which I define as directly obtaining 75 percent or more of their food from hunting, gathering, or fishing (variables 2-7, 2-8, and 2-9 in Appendix 2-2). The pinpointed dates for slightly less than two thirds of these societies were during or earlier than the nineteenth century. Although the foraging societies in my sample were not necessarily "pristine" at their pinpointed date, my reading of the relevant ethnographies suggests that they maintained their aboriginal characteristics to a sufficient degree that the results have validity for foraging societies with less contact with the West.

The sample is geographically skewed because about half of the foraging societies were in North America and another quarter in South America.[1] For the purpose of isolating economic systems, however, it is not as vital to have a totally geographically random sample as to have a sample with sufficient *variety* that different combinations and permutations of particular institutions and organizations can be explored. My sample allows such an approach because the type of cluster analysis I employ can separate out small clusters of societies if their particular configurations of institutions and organizations were greatly different from the others in the sample. It is also important to note that in most cases, the types of economic systems I isolate by the cluster analysis were not confined to one geographical area; rather, they were found scattered over the globe. Thus, cultural diffusion (when one society borrowed certain aspects of its economic system from unrelated neighbors, or when a single culture spread over a wide area so that neighboring societies were very similar) does not muddle the results.

---

[1] Of the 1,260 societies in the "Revised Ethnographic Atlas" (Divale and Gray, 2001), about three quarters were in North America. The SCCS and the EA samples differ only slightly in the relative importance of food from the three types of foraging activities.

Table 2-1. *Foraging societies used in the sample*

SCCS Number	Society	Location	Date	SCCS Number	Society	Location	Date
2	!Kung	Namibia	1950	131	Haida	Canada	1875
9	Hadza	Tanzania	1930	132	Bellacoola	Canada	1880
13	Mbuti	Congo (Zaire)	1950	133	Twana	USA	1860
77	Semang	Malaysia	1925	134	Yurok	USA	1850
79	Andamanese	Andaman Isles	1860	135	Pomo (Eastern)	USA	1850
80	Vedda	Sri Lanka	1860	136	Yokuts (Lake)	USA	1850
86	Badjau	Philippines	1963	137	Paiute (North)	USA	1870
90	Tiwi	Australia	1929	138	Klamath	USA	1860
91	Aranda	Australia	1896	139	Kutenai	USA	1890
96	Manus	Admiralty Isles	1929	140	Gros Ventre	USA	1880
118	Ainu	Japan	1880	147	Comanche	USA	1870
119	Gilyak	Sakhalin Island	1890	148	Chiricahua	USA	1870
120	Yukaghir	Russia	1850	162	Warrau	Venezuela	1935
122	Ingalik	Alaska	1885	173	Sirionó	Bolivia	1942
123	Aleut	Alaska	1800	174	Nambicuara	Brazil	1940
124	Copper Esk.	Canada	1915	178	Botocudo	Brazil	1884
125	Montagnais	Canada	1910	179	Shavante	Brazil	1958
126	Micmac	Canada	1650	180	Aweikoma	Brazil	1932
127	Saulteaux	Canada	1930	182	Lengua	Paraguay	1889
128	Slavey	Canada	1940	183	Abipon	Argentina	1750
129	Kaska	Canada	1900	185	Tehuelche	Argentina	1870
130	Eyak	Alaska	1890	186	Yahgan	Chile	1865

Note: SCCS = Standard Cross-Cultural Sample. The sample is described in various essays in Barry and Schlegel (1980), and my numbering of societies follows that of the SCCS.

Such a geographic spread of particular economic systems also means that the close contact between agricultural and foraging societies, a phenomenon more frequently found in Africa than in the Americas, did not influence the designation of types of economic system *per se*, even though it may have influenced particular aspects of the economies of societies in the two areas. In selecting the dimensions by which the economic system is to be defined, I have also tried to avoid including characteristics found in only one particular geographical region (e.g., the potlatch), preferring rather to test later for their presence in types of economic systems already defined.

2. Institutional Characteristics to Define Types of Economic Systems: Distribution

By distribution institutions I mean those that structure exchanges and transfers – that is, two-way and one-way movements of goods and services within a society. Economists (e.g., Pryor, 1977c; Stodder, 1995a, 1995b) have formulated a number of propositions about distribution in foraging societies, mostly relating the type and importance of particular institutions to the level of economic development of the society, its major foraging activities and associated risks, and the size and complexity of its community.

Whereas it would be important to focus on all types of distribution, I have chosen four distinct types of institutions that allow estimates to be made for all societies in the sample.[2] Two of the four distribution institutions concern particular aspects of sharing, a protean concept that covers both one-way transfers and two-way exchanges. More specifically, sharing can represent (a) an outright gift; (b) scrounging or tolerated theft; (c) some type of delayed reciprocity; or (d) an intended reciprocal exchange that actually turns out to be a gift because the receiver cannot – or will not – return the favor.[3] It is also possible that the actors in the transaction do not keep proper mental books and believe that the gift was reciprocated when it was not, a situation documented for the Takamiut Eskimo (Pryor and Graburn, 1980). The other two distributional dimensions concern the presence of trade/barter and the

---

[2] A principal component analysis of these four institutional variables reveals that about 41 percent of the variation between them can be explained by a single latent variable (factor), whereas the next two factors explain a very much lower share of the variation. For this reason, I judge these institutions to be "distinct."

[3] I include "demand-reciprocity" as sharing because this type of transaction really represents a forced gift. Some analysts also designate a simultaneous exchange of goods or services as "sharing," but I classify these transactions as market/barter exchange, even though strong elements of reciprocity may be involved.

presence of taxation/tribute. More specifically, the distribution dimensions I use in the analysis are as follows:[4]

(a) *Wealth inequality, an indirect sharing variable* (1-4). This approaches the phenomenon of sharing indirectly by looking at results. More specifically, I use a rough estimate of the degree of income or wealth inequality. It can be argued that if sharing is frequent, then wealth should be relatively evenly distributed, both because wealth would be equalized in the process and because people would be less inclined to accumulate wealth since others might claim part of it. Wealth and income are not the same and it is also possible for extensive sharing to have occurred – even with a highly unequal distribution of wealth – if the distribution of income was highly unequal and the sharing was not of sufficient magnitude to eliminate wealth differences. Because more information is available on wealth than on income, I could only code the wealth inequalities. It should be added, however, that this inequality variable is strongly correlated with social inequality (1-17), which, of course, confirms the common observation that in many of these foraging societies, social status was judged by relative wealth usually reflecting a higher income, a topic to be discussed in greater detail.

(b) *Direct food sharing* (1-5). This compound variable focuses on direct food sharing and has two parts. The first reflects the degree to which foraged food was divided on the spot where obtained. For instance, in some societies, parts of a killed animal were distributed among those in the hunting group to which the person bringing the animal down belonged; in other cases, the entire kill was kept by the successful hunter. The second part of the measure indicates in-camp sharing, which could be estimated only from qualitative descriptions of particular activities associated with eating (e.g., the Copper Eskimo brought plates of their food to other igloos). Obviously, such sharing was high when the society featured either demand-sharing (where a person could demand a gift from another, a phenomenon discussed by Woodburn, 1998) or its cousin, demand-reciprocity (where one person gave another a gift and then demanded something specific in return).[5] The magnitudes

---

[4] The number of the variable, explained in more detail in Appendices 2-1 and 2-2, is placed in parentheses. The first number refers to the appendix (e.g., 2-11 is the eleventh variable discussed in Appendix 2-2 and it is also the 11th column in Table SA-2). The actual data used in this chapter are presented in spreadsheets in Statistical Appendix Tables SA-1 and SA-2.

[5] Although I would have liked to include demand-sharing as a separate variable, the early ethnographic literature is unreliable because the outside observers were usually visiting the society

involved of other types of sharing, for instance, that occurred through scrounging or tolerated theft, are more difficult to quantify and could not be included in the estimate.[6]

(c) *The relative importance of trade/barter* (1-6). By trade/barter, I mean two-way transactions, either within the society or with another society, in which the exchange rate appeared to have varied. This means that I exclude reciprocal change where the price is fixed. Although all of the societies in my sample traded with other tribes, only slightly more than a third featured significant internal trade or barter.[7]

(d) *The presence of taxation or tribute* (1-7). In the foraging societies under examination, this meant that the political leader received a portion of the foraged foodstuffs from others (a type of centric transfer). These leaders, in turn, would either keep such food for their own consumption; redistribute it, in whole or in part, to other members of the community at a later date; or use it for communal activities such as feasts or receiving visitors.[8] Of the forty-four societies in the sample, only six had this type of distribution. It can be argued that such a taxation method was most likely to occur in a foraging society where the community had a relatively fixed residence; otherwise, disgruntled families might split away and try to join other local groups where they could keep a larger share of their foraged foods. Such a prediction (using 1-14 as the explanatory variable) is validated at a statistically significant level, but the correlation coefficient is low.

---

from time to time and talking with informants, rather than living there and observing economic life in action. Therefore, we cannot be certain if demand-sharing existed in some of these societies, and my attempts to code this variable (1-25) reveals a noticeable bias in that the data are most uncertain for those societies where the presence or absence of demand-sharing was not explicitly mentioned in the ethnographies.

[6] Although this coding is the best that can be made, it clearly represents only an educated guess. It should also be added that the relative differences between societies on this indicator did not seem very great: for the forty-four societies, the coefficient of variation (the standard deviation divided by the mean) was only 33 percent, in contrast to 88 percent for wealth differences.

[7] Such data suggest that "external trade" preceded "internal trade." In an earlier study (Pryor 1977c), I obtained a different result. The discrepancy between the two studies arises for two reasons. First, only about a quarter of the sixty societies in the earlier study lived primarily on the results of foraging (the remainder relied primarily on crop production or animal husbandry), so the sample of foraging societies was small. Second, of the eleven societies that appeared in both samples, new information led me to change my mind about the codings of several.

[8] I exclude from taxation/tribute the type of distribution practiced, for instance, by the Lengua Indians of Paraguay. They would bring game to the chief, who then immediately divided it equally among all members of the community. I classified this type of distribution as "sharing."

3. Institutional Traits to Define Types of Economic Systems: Property

I define "property" as the exclusive use of tangible or intangible assets by the "owner," a relationship that is socially enforced in some way. A number of social scientists have analyzed foraging economies from this approach (recently, for instance, Hann 1998; Bowles and Choi, 2003). Nevertheless, many of their propositions are difficult to test empirically, except those relating property institutions to the level of economic development, the mobility of the society, or some aspect of the environment requiring food storage.

I have chosen six distinct types of property institutions.[9] Five of them focus on ownership of income-producing assets – namely, land, food inventories, people (slaves), magical healing powers, and marriage rights.[10] The last institution focuses on the importance of transfers of property through inheritance, in contrast to the destruction of property upon death.

(a) *Possession of land* (1-8). This type of ownership is a composite variable covering both "territoriality" and private property in land. Territoriality refers to the exclusive use of a particular area by a specific group of people for a certain period of time in a manner that is recognized by others or that is enforced by group efforts (e.g., warfare). Of course, the "owners" of the land can give permission for others to enter or use the land, but they must first be asked and they can refuse the request. Private property covers the exclusive possession by individuals or families of particular pieces of land for a particular purpose. Territoriality and private ownership of land are not coterminous. For instance, the Kutenai of northern Montana and southern British Columbia were a territorial society that held their land in common and recognized no family or

---

[9] A principal component analysis of these six institutional variables reveals that about 32 percent of the variation between them can be explained by a single latent variable (factor), whereas the next factors explain considerably lower share of the variation. For this reason, I judge these institutions to be "distinct."

[10] Woodburn (1982) specifies other types of important property relations that I tried to take into account. These included the rights held by men over their female kin, who are then bestowed in marriage; or exclusive ownership of the means of production requiring considerable labor (boats, stockades, pit traps). I found the marriage rights (1-23) difficult to code and, as it turns out, such property rights did not seem related to any of the economic systems that I distinguish. The ownership of the means of production did not serve to distinguish the societies because in all cases where such labor-intensive capital goods could be found, they were usually the private property of the maker.

individual claims to exclusive use of a specified part. By way of contrast, the Copper Eskimo of northern Canada were a nonterritorial society, but they recognized the rights of individuals or families to particular areas for fishing for shorter or longer durations. The analysis of private property in land is further complicated by the fact that land can be private for one purpose but not for another. For instance, among the Slavey in the Canadian Northwest Territory, the land was divided up among families for the private trapping of small animals, who generally lived only in a small area. Nevertheless, moose or caribou, which roamed randomly over large areas, could be hunted anywhere by anyone.[11]

In my sample, all but seven societies exhibited at least some type of territoriality behavior. For some societies, defense of territory was very difficult – for instance, where the home range was very large or marshy or mountainous. Still others lived in quite rich areas and the population densities were not apparently high enough to trigger competition over food resources and, as a consequence, territoriality.[12] Of the seven nonterritorial societies in the sample, three recognized private claims on land or trees, but in only one society were these private claims economically important. Of the thirty-seven territorial societies, roughly three quarters also recognized certain private claims on land or trees, but in only 40 percent of these did such private claims have economic importance; these included cases of private ownership of fishing sites along rivers or trapping areas (the origins of these types of property rights have been the subject of fierce debate among anthropologists). The most notable exception to the common belief that private property in land can be found only at high levels of economic development was the Yahgan, a society with a low level of development living in Tierra del Fuego. Small groups of individuals related by blood hunted and fished along a certain shore area and, within this area, each nuclear family had its own exclusive section.

(b) *Private food stocks* (1-9). Although food stocks were handy for survival, they were not completely necessary if the society was located where food could be gathered over the entire year – for instance, in hot and humid climates or when animals or fish could be caught in all months. If the

---

[11] An interesting parallel in the animal world occurs among sunbirds; according to Gill (1995: 330), they have territories and do not tolerate others of their species near choice flowers. Nevertheless, they will peacefully sit side by side in a bush to catch passing insects. The literature on the ecological economics of territorial defense is extensive.

[12] These included the Hazda of Tanzania (primarily gatherers) and the Twana of northwest Washington State (primarily fishers).

society was nomadic, however, such stocking of food may not have been feasible because it would have involved some complex logistical efforts, especially when stocks had to be carried on a person's back because of lack of other means of transport such as boats or horses.

Some anthropologists, such as Binford (1980) and Woodburn (1982), have placed great stress on the importance of food storage for determining many other aspects of the economy and society. As I show herein, it played some – but not a major – role in defining the economic system. In passing, it should also be noted that a number of accepted propositions about the presence of food storage were not validated by the data in this study.[13]

I did not code the ownership of other movable goods. All of the societies in the sample recognized the private possession of personal items (e.g., clothing, pots, and tents) and means of production (e.g., canoes, sleds, bows and arrows, bolos, horses, and hunting dogs). Obviously, the possession of means of production had an influence on the availability of food to the possessor. The private possession of personal items was sometimes limited, however, by demand-sharing, although even this type of exchange recognized that one person had the original right to the object.

(c) *Slavery* (1-10). This represents ownership of other human beings. Certain problems in coding, however, arise with some societies, such as the Abipone of the Argentinean pampas, who captured slaves but treated them as family members so that they would not steal a horse and run away. Such cases I define as "half-slavery." I also count as slaveholding those societies that practiced slavery previous to the pinpointed date of my sample but were forced to give up this practice upon contact with the West.

(d) *Economically important intangibles* (1-11). Most foraging societies had important intangibles – for instance, songs, dances, stories, powers of prediction, hunting prowess, or healing lore. In some of these societies, such intangibles were held by many people; whereas in others, they were held by only a few who, in some cases, used these exclusive rights for

---

[13] For instance, Testart (1982) argues that food storage is related to the complexity of the society, a sedentary way of life, and socio-economic inequalities. Dividing my sample into two groups, those with and without food storage (1-9) and using T tests, I found no significant difference in societies with and without food storage with regard either to the development index (2-6) or to fixity of residence (1-18). On the other hand, as pointed out herein, food storage was related to socio-economic inequalities. As Goland (1991) points out, certain environmental variables that I have not taken into account may have played a critical causal role.

economic gain; for instance, when a medicine man (or shaman or priest) was rewarded for his healing services with gifts or when the possessor of a chant was given gifts for teaching it to a younger member of the tribe. The coding of this phenomenon focuses on how such intangibles were used and whether their owners were able to obtain considerable economic return from them. Because many ethnographers have paid little attention to the matter of payment except in the case of healing powers and the economic benefits derived therefrom, I focus exclusively on the ownership of healing powers.

(e) *One-way wealth transfers at marriage* (1-12). In some societies, a considerable amount of tangible wealth passed at marriage in one direction, either from the groom's family to the bride's family or the reverse. We can, therefore, consider ownership of marriage rights of a daughter or a son as an important source of intangible wealth. Other types of marital arrangement, such as bride service, sister exchange, or simple gifts, did not involve significant amounts of wealth; and in some societies, a woman retained ownership of her dowry so that no wealth transfer to the groom's family was involved. As shown herein, in most cases the father of the bride held such intangible rights.

(f) *Inheritance arrangements for goods and other wealth* (1-13). In some foraging societies, a considerable share of personal property was buried with its owner or burned or destroyed in other ways. Whatever the local justification for not transmitting this property to potential heirs (e.g., that the possessions are permeated with the spirit of the late owner, which would be defiled if the object were owned by others), the practice implies that intergenerational accumulation of goods was not an important activity and, therefore, we might expect that property rights were less rigidly enforced than in societies with greater stress on accumulation. In determining inheritance customs, I could not take into account giving away assets as gifts before death, but this practice did not seem very important in most of the societies in my sample.

B. The Types of Economic Systems

For a given environment and relative importance of gathering, hunting, and fishing, the daily economic life of foragers in different societies was often quite similar. It seems likely, therefore, that the various types of economic systems would be distinguished by different orientations of these daily activities. That is, some societies would have a strong communal (and sharing) orientation; in others, a political element would seem crucial; whereas still others would have a more economic orientation in which accumulation of particular types of assets would provide a vital focus of their activities.

1. The Estimations

Using the technique described in Chapter 1, I found that the optimal number of clusters (types of economic systems) could be either five or six. After examining the results from each calculation, it seemed to me that the results from the six clusters provided more insights for the rest of the analysis.[14]

The results of these calculations, shown in Table 2-2, can be quickly summarized. They show six very distinct types of economic systems; further, both the economic systems and many of their components were strongly related to the level of economic development. Before examining the types of economic systems and the institutions that distinguish them from each other, it is necessary to examine the impact of the level of economic development.

2. The Role of Economic Development

The average levels of economic development of the six types of economic systems fall into three groups along the development scale. The classic and transition foragers have a significantly lower level of economic development than the others in the sample (at a 0.05 level of statistical significance), the politically oriented and the physical-capital–oriented economic systems have a significantly higher level. Although such results suggest that foraging economic systems pass through several stages in the course of their economic development, I provide some contrary evidence.

As the previously cited studies have argued from theoretical grounds, many of the institutional indicators are strongly related to the level of economic development. One way of examining this relationship is to determine

---

[14] These results represent a revision of an earlier version of this chapter (Pryor, 2003c). In the recalculations of the MDL, I carried out fifty rather than fifteen estimations. The number of times the program indicated the optimality of five or six was about the same. For both cases, the grouping of societies was roughly similar except for the "economically oriented societies" that split into two groups, one emphasizing human capital, the other emphasizing physical capital. These distinctions are discussed herein. In this discussion, I also use more powerful and appropriate statistical tests than in the earlier version.

The clustering procedure for six clusters accounts for 52 percent of the differences among these societies (i.e., the variance of the multidimensional distance of every society with every other society). In most of these ten runs of the cluster program, the six clusters consisted of roughly the same societies (more exactly, the various societies fell in the same clusters 90 percent of the time). If a society fell into one cluster less than 70 percent of the time, I eliminated it from all calculations except for the development elasticity.

Table 2-2. *Defining characteristics of foraging economic systems*

Variable Number	Description	Range	Devel. Elast.	Average Scores						Total Sample
				Classic	TRN	HWO	IWO	PO	PCO	
	Number of societies in sample			6	10	6	6	5	7	40
2-6	Average level of development (Carneiro scale)	0–600		12.0^-	17.4^-	28.8	32.8	44.0^+	44.7^+	28.7
Distribution institutions										
1-4	Wealth inequality (1 = equal)	0–3	+0.40	1.00^-	1.25^-	2.67^+	2.58^+	$1.90^{-?}$	2.71	1.96
1-5	Food sharing (0 = low)	0–4	$-0.15^?$	2.33	3.14^+	2.57	1.69^+	2.09	1.99	2.38
1-6	Market/barter (1 = little)	1–5	+0.28	1.67^-	3.05	3.08	3.75	4.00	3.29	3.11
1-7	Tax/tribute (0 = none)	0–1	+0.11	0.00^-	0.00^-	0.17	0.00^-	1.00^+	0.00^-	0.15
Property institutions										
1-8	Land possession (none = 0)	0–4	+0.15	1.50	2.30^+	1.33	1.25	1.60	$2.64^{+?}$	1.85
1-9	Food storage (none = 1)	1–3	+0.34	1.00^-	1.30	2.25	1.58	2.10	2.29	1.71
1-10	Slave holding (none = 1)	1–3	+0.10	1.17	1.00^-	2.42^+	1.25	1.00^-	1.43	1.35
1-11	Intang. wealth (1 = many hold)	1–3	+0.23	1.08^-	2.30	$2.92^{+?}$	$2.92^{+?}$	2.80	1.93^-	2.30
1-12	Marriage wealth transfers (1 = none)	1–3	+0.13	1.08	1.10	1.33	2.83^+	1.40	1.14	1.44
1-13	Inheritance (1 = no inherit.)	1–3	+0.22	1.42^-	1.80	1.83	2.00	2.10	2.71^+	1.98

Note: TRN = transitional system; HWO = human-wealth–oriented; IWO = intangible-wealth–oriented; PO = politically oriented; PCO = physical-wealth–oriented. The development elasticity (devel. elast.) indicates the percentage change in the indicator under examination to a 1 percent change in the level of economic development. For all the values in the table, boldface indicates statistical significance; if there is no question mark in the superscript, the level of significance is 0.05; otherwise, it is 0.10. The significance tests for the average scores are made when the development level is held constant (a procedure explained in the text) and, in the superscript, the sign indicates the direction of significance.

The labels for the economic systems are explained in the text. The individual codings, as well as their sources, are described in greater detail in Appendix 2-1. The variable number refers to the number of the variable in the Appendix and also in Statistical Appendix Tables SA-1 and SA-2, which gives the values for the different societies and indicators.

whether the indicator is related to the Carneiro scale I use to measure economic development when we leave aside considerations of the type of economic system. More specifically, I calculate the percentage change in the indicator of the institution that occurs when the level of economic development increases 1 percent (the "development elasticity") using an ordinary least-squares regression. If it is statistically significant, it means that relationship with the level of economic development is important to take into account.[15] For instance, if the level of economic development increased 1 percent, my indicator of the inequality of wealth would increase 0.40 percent. Six of the institutional indicators are significantly (at the 0.05 level) related to the level of economic development, while a seventh reveals the same relationship but at a lower level of statistical significance. Such results offer considerable support to the results of theoretical models linking different types of distribution and property institutions to the level of economic development. By way of contrast, three of the indicators (i.e., land possession, slave holding, and transfers of wealth at marriage) were not related to the level of economic development in any meaningful way.

Table 2-2 also shows the average value of the societies with a given type of economic system for the ten institutional variables. To be able to interpret such averages, however, it is necessary to separate out the impact of the level of economic development so that we are just looking at the relationship between the economic system and the institutional variable under examination. This can be easily accomplished with a simple regression calculation.[16]

Once the impact of the development level is taken into account, distinguishing the orientation of the six types of economic systems becomes easier. In the columns labeled "average scores" in Table 2-2, I made boldface all the statistically significant relationships between institutional variables

---

[15] For anthropologists more accustomed to thinking of these matters in terms of a Guttman scale, a significant coefficient means that if the societies were lined up according to their relative level of economic development (cultural complexity) on the horizontal axis and if the value of the variable were plotted on the vertical axis, that particular indicator would scale; that is, if it were included in the development scale, it would fit quite well. The ability to scale decreases as the significance level falls.

[16] More specifically, to determine whether the type of economic system can be explained by a particular institutional indicator, I calculated regressions of the following type:

$$EcSys = a + b\ DevLev + cI,$$

where EcSys is a dummy variable that is equal to 1 if the society has the specified economic system and equal to 0 if it doesn't; DevLev is the level of economic development (variable 2-6); I is the indicator under examination; and a, b, and c are the calculated regression coefficients. For ten indicators and six economic systems, this required calculating sixty regressions. Because the variable to be explained is equal to either 1 or 0, I used a probit-regression technique.

and the economic system, noting in the superscript the direction of the relationship; the question marks indicate that the significance levels are 0.10 rather than 0.05 (i.e., the results are less reliable). For instance, the classic foragers have a significantly lower degree of market/barter exchange than other societies in the sample, whereas they do not significantly differ with regard to direct food sharing. This determination of the level of significance is important. Although the societies associated with each economic system are more similar to each other than to those in other clusters, the societies within each cluster exhibit a certain variation and, thus, such a calculation tells us if a particular institutional characteristic especially distinguishes that economic system from all of the others.

It also becomes clear, when closely examining the significance differences for particular institutions for each type of economic system, that the major differences lie in the orientation of the system. I label the types of economic systems by these orientations and, in the following discussion, look briefly at the defining characteristics of each of the six systems.

3. Societies with the Lowest Average Levels of Economic Development

The two types of economic systems in this group both had a strong communal orientation, particularly with regard to institutions of distribution.

a. Classic Foragers

I designate those societies in this cluster with the very lowest average level of economic development as "classic foragers" because they exhibited most of the stereotypical characteristics that some analysts have mistakenly assumed to epitomize all foraging societies. They comprised six societies (15 percent of the total sample) and were found only in Africa and South America. This group included such societies as the Sirionó in eastern Bolivia and the !Kung San (Ju/'hansi) in Namibia. Except for direct food sharing, the average values of their indicators of distribution institutions were noticeably lower than those of other economic systems.

Looking only at those institutions that were significantly different than those in other societies (when factoring out the impact of their level of economic development), some clear patterns also emerge. Regarding distribution, they had lower amounts of market or barter activity and also lower amounts of tax or tribute of foraged food that they had to give to their leaders. Although they did not have significantly more direct food sharing, their significantly lower inequality in wealth suggests that they did not have great differences in their individual consumption levels.

Regarding property, knowledge of healing techniques and magic was widespread and not monopolized by a few for economic gain. This group of societies had no inheritance, which means that all consumer and producer goods of the deceased (e.g., clothes, pottery, and spears) were destroyed at death. And they had no long-term food storage, which meant that their nourishment depended solely on what they were able to gather within a short period. They did not, as some might expect, score significantly lower in land possession.

b. Transition Foragers

The transition foragers included ten societies, or 25 percent of the sample. They included the Semang of Malasia, the Aranda of Australia, the Montagnais of Canada, and the Yahgan at the southern tip of South America.

Generally speaking, the transition foragers had somewhat higher values on almost all institutional indicators than the classic foragers. Nevertheless, for three out of the four distribution institutions, they also appeared more "communal" than the other societies – namely, low wealth inequality, higher food sharing, and low taxation/tribute. Only with regard to market or barter activities did they seem roughly similar to the other societies.

Regarding their property institutions, they were significantly different in having no slaves and in having considerable possession of land, primarily in the form of small-group ownership of relatively exclusive foraging grounds. Such results cast considerable doubt on the oft-repeated Marxist proposition that ownership in preindustrial societies emerged only at relatively high stages of economic development.

4. Societies with a Middle Level of Average Economic Development

The two economic systems in this group had less of a communal orientation in distribution and a more distinct orientation toward particular forms of wealth than the previous two cases.

a. Human-Wealth–Oriented Societies

The human-wealth–oriented foragers comprised six societies or 15 percent of the sample, all in the Americas. They ranged from the Tehuelche in Argentina to the Eyak in Alaska, with the Comanche in the southwestern

United States in between. The societies with this economic system had a particular type of economic orientation that emphasized wealth embodied in human beings.

Regarding distribution, the societies with this economic system had greater inequalities of wealth, which suggests less sharing in general; such wealth, however, was not significantly more likely to be passed on after death. Their property institutions were distinct in having significantly more slavery than other societies in the sample, even though they were primarily nomadic. Moreover, these societies appeared also to have had a greater concentration of intangible wealth that served as a source of income, such as healing magic.

b. Intangible-Wealth–Oriented Societies

The intangible-wealth–oriented foragers included six societies or 15 percent of the sample and ranged over the world, from the Badjau in the Philippines, to the Abipon in Argentina, to the Gros Ventre in the northwestern United States.

Of the various societies in the sample, those with this type of economic system appeared to have the least communal forms of distribution of goods and services. More specifically, they revealed a low degree of sharing with regard to food and other commodities as well; this, in turn, reflected a high inequality of wealth. The property institutions of intangible-wealth–oriented foragers were unique because of the importance of the transfers of wealth at marriage, manifested in bridewealth. That is, a man's ownership of the marriage rights of his daughters served as a significant source of wealth to him. Moreover, like the human-wealth–oriented societies, they appeared to have also had a greater concentration of another source of intangible wealth serving as a source of income: namely, as healing magic.

5. Societies with High Levels of Average Economic Development

a. Politically Oriented Societies

The politically oriented foragers comprised five societies or 12.5 percent of the sample. They appeared worldwide and ranged from the Ainu in Japan, to the Warrau in Venezuela, to the Lake Yokut of California.

The most distinctive distribution trait of politically oriented societies was the importance of taxes or tributes in the form of foraged foodstuffs given (paid) to the political leaders. These leaders, however, did not necessarily keep such payments (which would represent one-way centric transfers) but, for the most part, they redistributed them or used them for community ceremonial or diplomatic purposes. Their low inequalities of wealth suggest that the leaders did not use such payments for personal wealth accumulation. Their property institutions appeared relatively similar to other societies, except for their absence of slavery.

b. Physical-Wealth–Oriented Societies

The physical-wealth–oriented foragers included seven societies or 17.5 percent of the sample. All were found on the northern rim of the Pacific and ranged from the Gilyak of the Sakhalin Islands of Russia, to the Aleut of Alaska, to the Bellacoola of the western part of Canada.

The physical-wealth–oriented foragers were little different from most of the societies in the sample with regard to distribution institutions. Their property institutions were distinct in that they had a significantly higher amount of inheritance, a feature tied to the fact that all of these societies used relatively capital-intensive means of production such as boats or elaborate hunting weapons. They also had less concentrated holdings of intangible wealth, which could be used to obtain income. Finally, their economic system appeared to feature significantly more private possession of land.

6. A Brief Summary

Defining types of economic systems in terms of property and distribution institutions leads to a clustering that makes intuitive sense. The classic and transition foragers had the lowest average levels on the development index and were characterized by more communal elements in their distribution institutions. At a somewhat higher level of economic development, the human-wealth– and intangible-wealth–oriented foragers had less communal elements in their distribution and particularly distinct forms of wealth related to possession of slaves, healing magic, and marriage rights. At the highest levels of economic development, the politically oriented foragers featured important transfers of food to political leaders, and inheritance of wealth played an important role in the economic systems of the physical-wealth–oriented foragers.

The six types of foraging economic systems that I have defined were not necessarily the only such economic systems that ever existed. Some foraging societies, which had made a rapid transition to agriculture, might have had certain institutional characteristics not shared by the societies in my sample, which were more conservative and never made the transition.

C. The Impact of Particular Foraging Economic Systems on Economic Performance

We have few historical records for most preindustrial economic systems as to how their economies have performed over time. Indeed, we have relatively few studies of their economic accomplishments – for instance, their efficiency at a single point in time. And what information we do have for one society is generally not easily comparable with information from other societies. As a result, we cannot determine the impact of the economic system on economic performance using the standard type of approach, which I follow for exploring the impact of the economic systems of industrial/service economies later in this book.

A case-study approach of certain extreme situations might be more fruitful to determine the impact of the type of foraging economic system on economic performance. To what extent, for instance, did the economic system determine the way in which a foraging society responded to a famine? It seems unlikely that societies with classic, transition, or politically oriented economic systems would allow certain members of their society to starve while others had sufficient food. (Such was the case, as documented by Turnbull, 1972, for the Ik of Uganda.) In societies with human-wealth–, intangible-wealth–, and physical-wealth–oriented economic systems, by way of contrast, this behavior might have been possible. Similarly, the human-wealth–, physical-wealth–, and politically oriented foragers might have coped more adequately (and/or disintegrated less quickly) following contact with the West than societies with other types of economic systems. These are examples of the ways in which societal change can be analyzed with the typology developed in the previous section.

The various questions I raise can be answered only by detailed ethnographic studies of specific societies, using the concept of economic system as one of many analytic tools to transcend the particularities of a society. Distinguishing the various types of economic systems is only the first step in a much longer line of inquiry. I challenge anthropologists to reexamine their ethnographic data to determine whether the concept of economic system allows new insights into the economic performance of particular societies.

D. Determinants/Correlates of Economic Systems

1. Some Preliminaries

As noted previously, few foraging economies have a recorded history and, thus, we have few adequate and systematic records of how they came to have the economic system that they did at the time of contact with the West.[17] As a result of this contact, most of these foraging economic systems changed drastically in a few decades, so that we are left only with a snapshot at a single point in time and with little idea about how they would have evolved in isolation.

All is not lost, however. We can, for instance, look at various correlates of these economic systems and try to infer if they played a causal role in the formation of the economic system. Although the direction of the arrow of causality is sometimes unclear, no significant correlation would indicate that the factor under consideration probably played no causal role in the formation of the economic system.

This task is particularly important because it is a strongly held tenet of faith among almost all anthropologists that economies and economic systems were not relatively independent entities worthy of study but rather were embedded in a larger structure and were predominantly determined by the environmental, social, and political forces operating within that society upon which they focus their loving attention. Many economists, under the influence of Karl Polanyi, hold a similar view. Although it is not my deliberate intention to smash the idols of these groups, I do feel it necessary to explore the validity of this preciously held belief. Without wishing to spoil the suspense, let me add that in most cases, few significant correlations can be found, which means that although such variables might have influenced the economy, the various types of economic systems were *not* embedded in a meaningful way in a wider societal matrix, varied forces specified previously did *not* determine the economic system and, as a result, such economic systems are worthy of study as independent entities.

In the following discussion, I examine the role of a series of environmental, social structural, and political variables, as well as certain economic variables lying outside the economic system.[18]

---

[17] Some suggest that important clues to the origins of particular preindustrial economic systems can be gained by examining their myths of origin, but this advice is difficult to follow. For instance, the Genesis story gives few concrete clues about the evolution of the economic system of the ancient Hebrews (one attempt to explore these problems is by Pryor and Beach, 1995). Although archaeological evidence teaches us something about the earlier economy of some of these preindustrial societies, it tells us much less about the institutions and organizations that channeled their economic activities.

[18] In all cases, I calculated ordinary least-square regressions of the following type:

$$\text{Ind} = a + b\,\text{DevLev} + c\,\text{EcSys},$$

where Ind is the institutional indicator under examination, DevLev is the level of economic development; EcSys is a dummy variable that is equal to 1 if the society has the specified economic system and equal to 0 if it doesn't; and a, b, and c are the calculated regression coefficients. I used this regression form because it is unclear in which direction causality runs, and this regression form is more familiar than the probit form used previously.

2. Environmental Factors

Because foragers depend for their livelihood on the natural environment, it would seem likely that the physical environment would have an enormous impact on their economic systems, but Table 2-3 shows surprisingly few statistically significant correlations that would allow us to understand why the societies had their particular types of economic systems or how these systems evolved.

The classic foragers were distinguished only by the fact that they were found in areas with a relatively low famine threat. Living in Eden, no environmental necessity forced them to change their way of life. The transition foragers lived in environments not significantly different from any of the other societies in the sample. Such a correlation exercise gives no usable clues as to the evolution of these economic systems.

Of the next three economic systems on the development scale, the human-wealth–oriented foragers lived in significantly higher absolute latitudes and in areas with less available water (evapo-transpiration) for subsistence purposes; the intangible-wealth–oriented foragers were more likely to live in hotter climates; and the politically oriented foragers lived in areas with a higher agricultural potential. Although they did not utilize this potential, they did have a natural advantage for any future development of agriculture. Although these geographical factors were undoubtedly related to the way in which these societies made their living, any causal linkage with the economic system is not readily apparent.

For the physical-wealth–oriented foragers, however, the situation was quite different. They lived in areas with high absolute latitudes, low temperatures, low agricultural potential, and low amounts of water for subsistence purposes. Given such an environment, wresting a living required considerable effort. Conditions for gathering were harsher, which forced them more into fishing and the hunting of large animals, both of which required considerable capital investment. Under such circumstances, the economic waste of destroying a person's goods upon death was obvious and it is not surprising that inheritance was an important means of acquiring property in such societies.

The shares of food foraged through gathering, hunting, and fishing were tied, to a certain extent, to the geographical indicators. Of gathered foodstuffs, the lower share among human-wealth–oriented foragers and the higher share among politically oriented foragers were undoubtedly a function of the relative favorability of their respective environments for the growth of edible plants. The significantly lower amount of fishing among

Table 2-3. *Environmental and subsistence characteristics of foraging economic systems*

Variable Number	Description	Range	Devel. Elast.	Average Scores						Total Sample
				Classic	TRN	HWO	IWO	PO	PCO	
	Number of societies in sample			6	10	6	6	5	7	40
2-6	Average level of development (Carneiro scale)	0–600		12.0⁻	17.4⁻	28.8	32.8	44.0⁺	44.7⁺	28.7
Averages of geographical variables										
2-5	Absolute latitude	0–180°	+0.66	16.1	26.9	48.3⁺	26.1	34.8	55.6⁺	34.4
2-10	Effective temperature	C°	−0.17	18.2	17.2	12.6	17.8⁺?	13.7	11.1⁻	15.3
2-11	Evapo-transpiration	mm	−0.13	943	947	407⁻?	950	585	454⁻?	734
2-12	Famine threat (1 = low)	1–4	+0.24	1.60⁻?	2.48	2.39	2.04	2.85	2.93	2.39
2-13	Agricultural potential (4 = low)	4–23	−0.13?	18.2	16.3	13.3	16.0	18.0⁺	10.7⁻	15.3
1-20	Contact with West (1 = low)	1–2	+0.12?	1.25	1.35	1.75	1.33	1.60	1.71	1.49
Average percentage of subsistence										
2-7	Gathering	0–100%	−0.37	0.45	0.32	0.17⁻?	0.23	0.32⁺?	0.17	0.28
2-8	Hunting	0–100%	−0.09	0.45	0.35	0.47	0.32	0.32	0.31	0.37
2-9	Fishing	0–100%	+0.50	0.05⁻	0.30	0.37	0.38	0.32	0.51	0.33

Note: TRN = transitional system; HWO = human–wealth–oriented; IWO = intangible–wealth–oriented; PO = politically–oriented; PWO = physical–wealth–oriented. The development elasticity (devel. elas.) indicates the percentage change in the indicator under examination to a 1 percent change in the level of economic development. For all the values in the table, bold-face indicates statistical significance; if there is no question mark in the superscript, the level of significance is 0.05; otherwise, it is 0.10. The significance tests for the average scores are made when the development level is held constant (a procedure explained in the text) and, in the superscript, the sign indicates the direction of significance.

These labels for the economic systems are explained in the text. The individual codings, as well as their sources, are described in greater detail in Appendix 2-1. The sum of the average percentages of subsistence may not equal 100 percent because some of the societies rely on agricultural production (up to 25 percent) and on agricultural products as well. The values for each society are given in Statistical Appendix Tables SA-1 and SA-2.

49

the classic foragers appears due to the fact that few of these societies were located near sites where reliance on fishing would provide a secure source of food.

Thus, although these foraging economies were undoubtedly influenced by the environment, these meager statistical results for the different types of economic systems suggest that the relative reliance on different types of foraging for subsistence had little direct impact on the economic system. Combined with the conclusion that, except for the physical-wealth–oriented foragers (and possibly the classic foragers), geographical conditions appeared to have little direct causal influence on the economic systems, we are forced to search for causal influences on the economic system in other spheres.

3. Social Structural Variables

Table 2-4 reveals that two economic systems had a significant connection with certain important social structural variables. The intangible-wealth–oriented foragers featured transfers of wealth to the bride's family. As noted previously, this was directly related to the finding that the societies with this economic system were more likely to feature general transfers of wealth upon marriage. The politically oriented societies were more likely to feature large communal structures for living or large multifamily homes. Such living arrangements facilitated the transfer of foraged food to the political leader, who would then redistribute such foodstuffs. That is, the communities functioned in some ways more like a family, where the father redistributed food, than like a state with a formal tax and/or transfer system. For both of these two types of economic systems, it seems likely that the economic system and the social structural variable emerged together, rather than one causing the other.

The remaining four types of economic systems reveal little of interest: The transitional foragers and the physical-wealth–oriented foragers did not seem statistically different with respect to these social structural variables than other societies in the sample. The classical foragers were more likely to feature monogamy than other marriage forms. The human-wealth–oriented foragers were significantly more likely to have husbands and wives living in their own homes (or separate houses for each wife) and they were more likely to feature households with multiple wives. None of these relationships support any credible causal connection between social structural variables and these four economic systems.

Table 2-4. Social structural characteristics of foraging economic systems

Variable Number	Description	Range	Devel. Elast.	Average Scores						
				Classic	TRN	HWO	IWO	PO	PCO	Total Sample
Number of societies in sample				6	10	6	6	5	7	40
2-6	Average level of development (Carneiro scale)	0–600		**12.0**⁻	**17.4**⁻	28.8	32.8	**44.0**⁺	**44.7**⁺	28.7
Averages of social-structure variables										
2-18	Corporate descent groups (1 = none)	0–1	+0.08	0.17	0.30	0.33	0.17	0.40	0.57	0.33
2-19	Household form (1 = many in one house; 4 = small households)	1–4	−0.03	2.83	3.00	**3.33**⁺?	3.17	**2.40**⁻	2.86	2.95
2-20	Family form (1 = nuclear)	1–4	+0.04	2.50	1.70	**3.50**⁺	1.67	2.20	2.29	2.25
2-21	Marital form (1 = monogamous)	1–3	−0.03	**2.50**⁺?	2.10	2.33	2.00	2.20	2.00	2.18
2-22	Marital wealth direction (1 = to bride's family)	1–4	+0.09	3.17	3.10	3.33	**1.67**⁻	3.40	3.14	2.98
2-23	Postmarital residence (1 = matrilocal)	1–4	+0.21	2.00	3.00	3.33	2.83	2.60	3.00	2.85
2-24	Cousin marriages allowed (1 = all cousins; 6 = none)	1–6	−0.02	3.67	4.56	4.17	5.17	4.00	4.14	4.31
Averages of sex-role variables										
1-17	Social differentiation (1 = low)	1–3	+0.36	**1.00**⁻?	**1.00**⁻?	**2.00**⁺	1.83	1.60	2.14	1.55
2-14	Female power (1 = low)	1–7	+0.01	5.25	4.86	4.67	**6.33**⁺?	4.00	5.50	5.20
2-15	Male aggression (1 = low)	1–6	+0.12	4.40	2.75	5.00	3.33	4.33	4.33	3.86
2-16	Male dominance (1 = no)	1–3	+0.13	1.60	1.71	2.25	1.33	2.20	1.67	1.76
2-17	Female contribution to food supply (0 = none)	0–10	−0.25	0.35	0.34	0.25	0.37	0.26	0.26	0.31

Note: TRN = transitional system; HWO = human–wealth–oriented; IWO = intangible–wealth–oriented; PO = politically oriented; PCO = physical–wealth–oriented; PWO = physical-wealth–oriented. The development elasticity (devel. elas.) indicates the percentage change in the indicator under examination to a 1 percent change in the level of economic development. For all the values in the table, boldface indicates statistical significance; if there is no question mark in the superscript, the level of significance is 0.05; otherwise, it is 0.10. The significance tests for the average scores are made when the development level is held constant (a procedure explained in the text) and, in the superscript, the sign indicates the direction of significance.

These labels for economic system are explained in the text. The individual codings, as well as their sources, are described in greater detail in Appendix 2-1. The values for each society are given in Statistical Appendix Tables SA-1 and SA-2.

51

4. Social Inequality and Inequality between the Sexes

To reflect the degree of social differentiation or social inequality among free (nonslave) individuals, I coded the societies in my sample along a three-point scale: those where general egalitarianism prevailed; those in which individuals or families were socially ranked; and those in which there were at least two distinct classes that transmitted their status through inheritance. (Castes did not occur among foragers.) Social differentiation was highly and positively correlated with wealth inequalities.[19] Although both of these variables were also significantly correlated with the presence of slavery, the coefficient of determination was much lower. Another type of social inequality was between men and women. Using data on the female contribution to subsistence and on female power, male aggression, and male dominance, few significant differences appear among the different types of economic systems.

5. Political Variables

Most of the indicators of political variables shown in the upper panel of Table 2-5 do not show any significant relationship with the economic system. Although the classic foragers appeared to have less warfare with other societies, it does not seem as if the economic system played a causal role. More specifically, two aspects of the societies with the classic economic system seemed more responsible: namely, that they were nomadic and characterized by small communities.[20] Although, as we might expect, the politically oriented societies showed greater political centralization (a variable that takes into account various aspects of power), it seems likely that the taxation system was neither a cause nor an effect of such centralization but, rather, the two characteristics emerged together.

---

[19] The unadjusted coefficient of determination (R^2) is 0.56; for the next two correlations, the unadjusted coefficient of variation is roughly equal to 0.23 for both.

[20] The calculated regression is:

$$\text{ExC} = 2.324^* + 0.235^* \text{ SLC} - 0.302^* \text{ FR} - 0.679 \text{ ES} \qquad R^2 = 0.2702$$
$$\quad\;\;(0.408)\quad (0.104)\qquad\;\; (0.133)\qquad (0.378) \qquad \text{Size of sample} = 39$$

where:

ExC = frequency of external conflict (2-27)

SLC = size of local community (1-19)

FR = fixity of residence (the opposite of nomadism) (1-18)

ES = economic system (where classic foragers are coded as 1, and all other societies are coded as 0) (1-3)

Standard errors are in parentheses under the calculated coefficients.

Table 2-5. *Some economic and political characteristics of foraging economic systems*

Variable Number	Description	Range	Devel. Elast.	Average Scores						
				Classic	TRN	HWO	IWO	PO	PCO	Total Sample
Number of societies in sample				6	10	6	6	5	7	40
2-6	Average level of development (Carneiro scale)	0–600		**12.0**⁻	17.4⁻	28.8	32.8	**44.0**⁺	**44.7**⁺	28.7
Political variables										
1-16	Political centralization (0 = little)	0–4	**+0.34**	0.04	0.33	1.17	0.67	**2.40**⁺	0.86	0.81
2-25	Overall conflict (1 = low)	1–3	+0.18	2.00	2.11	2.67	2.33	2.25	2.33	2.29
2-26	Internal conflicts (1 = low)	1–3	+0.08	2.00	1.89	1.83	1.67	1.50	2.00	1.83
2-27	External conflicts (1 = low)	1–3	+0.20	**1.00**⁻?	1.80	2.50	2.33	2.00	1.83	1.94
Other economic variables										
1-18	Locational fixity (1 = nomadic)	1–5	**+0.50**	1.83	1.55	2.17	2.50	3.60	3.36	2.40
1-19	Size of local group (1 = <50)	1–6	**+0.31**	1.83	1.30	2.58	2.92	2.40	2.50	2.16
1-21	Gambling present (1 = little)	1–3	+0.13	1.17	**1.30**⁻?	**2.92**⁺	2.08	2.10	1.93	1.85
1-22	Potlatch presence (1 = none)	1–3	+0.09	1.00	1.00	1.50	1.17	1.00	**1.71**⁺	1.23

Note: TRN = transitional system; HWO = human-wealth–oriented; IWO = intangible-wealth–oriented; PO = politically oriented; PWO = physical-wealth–oriented. The development elasticity (devel. elas) indicates the percentage change in the indicator under examination to a 1 percent change in the level of economic development. For all the values in the table, boldface indicates statistical significance; if there is no question mark in the superscript, the level of significance is 0.05; otherwise, it is 0.10. The significance tests for the average scores are made when the development level is held constant (a procedure explained in the text) and, in the superscript, the sign indicates the direction of significance.

These labels for economic system are explained in the text. The individual codings, as well as their sources, are described in greater detail in Appendix 2-1. The values for each society are given in Statistical Appendix Tables SA-1 and SA-2.

6. Other Economic Variables

The bottom panel of Table 2-5 shows the results of correlation analysis between some miscellaneous economic variables and the economic system. It is noteworthy that the types of economic systems did not significantly differ either with regard to the degree of nomadism or the size of the local group. For my sample, the presence of the potlatch occurred only in societies in the northwest coast of North America and three of these societies number among the physical-wealth–oriented societies. The explanation of the presence of gambling among human-wealth–oriented societies and the lack thereof among transition foragers I must leave for others.

7. A Brief Conclusion

Negative conclusions are seldom very exciting and, in this section, the major result is that little evidence supports a causal relation between the various social and political variables and the types of economic systems, except in some special cases. This conclusion, however, has considerable importance because it strongly suggests that the types of economic systems were not primarily a function of these "broader" causal forces but rather were independent entities worthy of study by themselves. Of course, some can still claim that the economic systems of these foraging societies were embedded in a social and political matrix, but all this really means is that the people carrying out various economic activities within a given society had particular social and political relationships to each other. It might also represent a confusion between the economy, which was influenced by these forces, and the economic system. Such a claim does not mean that these social and political relationships determined the economic institutions that structured distribution and property relations.

It may seem surprising that the environment appeared to play only a small role in the emergence of most types of foraging economic systems. The exceptions were the physical-wealth–oriented societies, which were located in harsh areas where considerable capital goods – either boats or elaborate hunting gear – were necessary to survive. This, in turn, appeared to play an important role in the inheritance system and certain other economic institutions defining the economic system. The fact that the classic foragers were found in areas where famines were less frequent might also have played a causal role in their communal orientation.

E. Evolution of Foraging Economic Systems

The development elasticities presented herein and the significant correlation between the level of economic development and the various types of economic systems raise some interesting issues about the evolution of types of economic systems. These results suggest that in previous centuries (or millennia), the societies in the sample with higher levels of economic development had to have had at an earlier time the same types of economic systems as those in the sample with a lower level of economic development. But, if possible, such a stage-theory hypothesis needs to be empirically tested, which raises some problems because we have little evidence of the types of economic systems of these societies in the past that would provide direct evidence on this issue.[21] Fortunately, the hypothesis can be empirically investigated in an indirect fashion by exploring a sample of societies with somewhat less reliance on foraging for their subsistence, asking how these societies developed, and then using the results to work backward.

As noted previously, I define foraging societies as those relying 75 percent or more on foraging as the source of their food. For this analysis, I draw from the SCCS all of the thirteen "intermediate societies" – that is, those which relied 55 to 75 percent on foraging for their food. If the societies in this new sample passed through a definite series of economic systems over the course of their economic development, then they should have most resembled the politically oriented and the physical-wealth–oriented societies – that is, the societies in the foraging sample that had the highest level of development. In a supervised cluster analysis, we start with the economic systems (derived previously) of all of the foraging societies and then investigate which type of economic system each of the intermediate societies in the new sample most closely resembled.

The results, presented in Appendix 2-3, very clearly reject the stage-theory hypothesis. More specifically, four of the thirteen societies most closely resembled the transition foragers; four, the human-wealth–oriented foragers; four, the physical-wealth–oriented foragers; and the remaining society, the intangible-wealth–oriented foragers. Thus, the economic systems of these intermediate societies show no signs either of resembling only the systems of the economically most advanced foragers or of passing through stages

---

[21] Carneiro (1969) does show that his development scale, developed from cross-section evidence, can also be profitably used in analyzing the development of single societies through time; for instance, Anglo-Saxon England from 450 to 1087 C.E.

with particular types of economic systems before making the transition to agriculture.

The most reasonable interpretation of these results is that most of the various types of foraging economic systems provided distinct economic platforms from which the transition to agriculture was made. I present evidence supporting this conjecture in the next chapter, where the focus is on the transition to agriculture. And, using this interpretation of the results of the supervised cluster analysis to look backward at the origins of the various types of foraging economic systems, we can speculate that the special orientations of certain societies allowed them to achieve particular levels of economic development very quickly. Thus, it might not have been necessary for those societies with the highest level of economic development to have passed through all of the types of economic systems at lower levels of economic development. Unfortunately, neither the stage-theory approach nor my own counter-conjecture can be verified with the available empirical evidence.

F. A Brief Summary

As noted at the beginning of this chapter, in many respects the daily economic life of foragers was similar throughout the world, once we take into account the different physical environments in which they lived and the different ways in which they split their time among gathering, hunting, and fishing. Their societies featured a spectacular variety of different social and political institutions that, unfortunately, have blinded us to the different economic institutions and systems that also distinguish them. Moreover, these economic systems were, for the most part, quite independent of the social and political institutions, being neither a cause nor an effect of them.

Most generally, the various types of economic systems can be classified by the clusters of particular institutions that orient their economic life. At the lowest level of economic development, the classic and transition foragers featured the most "communal" distribution systems, with considerable emphasis on the sharing of food. They differed in that the classic foragers had less market/barter activities and the transition foragers featured more possession – either private or group – of land. At the relatively middle levels of economic development, both the human-wealth and the intangible-wealth foraging societies featured a relatively small group of people in possession of healing magic, which could be used for economic gain. The former were also more likely to have some form of slavery and the latter were more likely to use marriage rights as a source of wealth. At the highest levels of economic development, the politically oriented foragers had a system of taxation/tribute, while the physical-wealth–oriented foragers held considerable wealth in the form of capital equipment – a necessity in their environment – which they transferred to their heirs upon death.

The six economic systems define key economic parameters of these foraging societies. This is not, however, the end of the story because these system designations also provide a context to analyze a variety of other economic activities not discussed herein that may be structured by or related to the economic system. In brief, we have a more precise way of determining which activities are unique to the society, which are related to the system, and which are common to all foraging societies.

The empirical analysis also shows that many of the property and development institutions were strongly related to their level of economic development. Although the functional prerequisites for a society to survive economically at a particular level of economic development appeared to narrow the types of economic systems that could exist, several different types of economic systems were consistent with these requirements.

Because these types of economic systems structured the daily economic life of these foragers, their influence must undoubtedly have been reflected not just in objectively measured activities, such as their social interactions or their child-raising practices, but also in the way these people saw themselves – for instance, their values, their myths, and their own explanations of why they followed certain procedures in carrying out particular economic activities. In sum, the kind of analysis carried out herein provides a new perspective from which to understand these foraging societies in their entirety – and, thereby, our own history.

THREE

From Foraging to Farming

Hunting, gathering, and fishing economies can change from one type of foraging economic system to another, and it is as important to understand these dynamic aspects of the system as it is to know the static elements of the system at a single point in time. Unfortunately, the evidence for such systemic transformations of these economies is skimpy and, as a result, this type of systemic transformation has received relatively little attention in the ethnographic literature. Foraging systems can also change into agricultural systems. The evidence for this transition – the "neolithic revolution" – is more abundant and has engendered a vast literature, but I am uncomfortable with it.

When discussing the transition from foraging to farming, most archaeologists and anthropologists adopt a bottom-up approach and usually rest their argument on a small number of cases, generalizing from these results to all transitions in other places.[1] Such a procedure rests on the dubious assumption that the transition proceeded in a similar fashion all over the world. By way of contrast, economists have adopted a top-down approach. In previous years, they usually started from one or more of four general propositions about the causes of the transition (Weisdorf: 2003a): that it was a result of diminishing returns in foraging as the population increased; that it was a result of a general decrease in foraging productivity arising from a change in climate or an extinction of the plants and animals being foraged; that it was a result of a rise in the productivity of agriculture due to the invention or borrowing of more productive techniques in farming; or that it was a result of a shift in preferences for nonfood items that could be

---

[1] Gebauer and Price (1992) draw from the anthropology literature and list thirty-eight different hypothesized causes for the transition to agriculture. In this chapter, I deal only with the most plausible.

obtained only by exchanging agricultural goods. More recently, economists have constructed interesting and sophisticated mathematical models incorporating these various causal factors.[2] But this economic literature provides little evidence on the relative importance of the various causes embodied in their models because everything depends on the values of particular coefficients for which no data are provided. In some cases, moreover, one has the impression that these economists have spent little time familiarizing themselves with the primary ethnographic sources to see how these foraging economies in transition actually functioned. I find it necessary to approach the topic differently. In Chapter 2, I show that the transition to agriculture did not necessarily occur by foraging societies passing through a series of economic systems (stages) before making the transition and that several different foraging economic systems could have served as a platform for the transition. In this chapter, I follow the bottom-up approach adopted by archaeologists and anthropologists but differ from them by looking at a great many preindustrial societies all over the world in the past five centuries. More specifically, I rely on a study of foraging and agricultural societies described by Westerners from the sixteenth to the twentieth centuries that are contained in the SCCS, discussed in the previous chapter, and examine a series of environmental, social, and economic variables related to this transition from foraging to agriculture to determine their relative importance in the process.

Although I am generalizing from cross-section evidence from the relatively recent past to events that occurred over a long period of time in the far-distant past, there is little to suggest that the causal mechanisms underlying the transition many millennia ago were very much different from those in more recent years. Nevertheless, this means that my results present a plausible but not definitive argument. In studying the transition to agriculture, two serious and interrelated issues immediately arise:

Why was the appearance of agriculture so sudden? Humans (genus *Homo*) have been on earth in one form or another for several million years, and the anatomically modern man – the kind of person who wouldn't look out of place shopping at the local Wal-Mart – for about 100,000 years. Archaeologists tell us, however, that "agriculture" suddenly appeared only about 10,000 years ago and that, in the next 8,000 years, it became the primary source of food for the vast majority of human societies. In this chapter, I present evidence suggesting that agriculture, at least as a minor source of

---

[2] The most interesting include Olsson (2003); Olsson and Hibbs (forthcoming); and Weisdorf (2003b).

food, existed long before 10,000 years ago and, further, that the domestication of plants and animals did not represent a dramatic technological advance. This means that the real issue is not why it appeared so suddenly or how it was invented, but why it spread so fast.

Why would any society adopt agriculture? Various studies show that agriculturalists usually worked much longer for their food than foragers, especially in the early stages of the adoption of agriculture.[3] Rindos (1984: 94) also cites evidence that extensive natural stands of wild wheat in the Near East were quite as productive as many of the older varieties of domesticated wheat. Cohen (1977b) and Hayden (1993: 220) argue that those early societies relying primarily on agriculture were less well nourished than their foraging cousins and just as prone, or even more prone, to famine (more evidence on this follows). Some also claim that agriculturalists in villages often suffered from more diseases than nomadic foragers.

The first step in my analysis is to define "agriculture," a conceptual problem that is more complicated than it first appears. I then examine three of the most important conjectured causes for the spread of agriculture – environmental, social/political, and demographic – and show that, by themselves, none can satisfactorily explain the development and/or spread of agriculture in all societies. Finally, I argue that the origin/spread of agriculture was a process with quite different causes in different places so that a general theory of the transition to agriculture does not seem a useful tactic. A more promising approach is an examination of the costs, benefits, and risks of agriculture in specific situations, especially when it is combined with particular attention to the positive feedback process involving demographic growth and sedentarism.

A. Agriculture and Related Subsistence Activities

Determining whether a society practices "agriculture" raises problems. Agriculture involves both modifying the environment and manipulating the genetic material of plants or animals (i.e., domestication) to increase labor productivity in obtaining food. For plant production, agriculture also involves several distinct tasks: preparing the land and planting; certain nurturing activities such as fertilizing, irrigating, weeding, and warding off predators; and, finally, harvesting the crop and selecting seeds to store for

---

[3] Binford (1968) and Sahlins (1972) forcefully raised this issue and since then it has received considerable attention. Time budgets of subsistence activities for a number of preindustrial societies are presented by Hayden (1993: 139) and Kelly (1995: 20).

next year. For meat production, agriculture involves breeding, feeding, and protecting the animals. To decide where the line should be drawn between agriculture and related subsistence activities, some distinctions need to be made.

1. Proto-Plant-Production

Proto-plant-production[4] places a greater emphasis on managing the environment for plant production than on nurturing the crops or deliberately manipulating the genetic materials of the plants. As a result, it also requires only a few of the tasks noted previously. Several examples of proto-agriculture deserve brief mention.

FIRE-STICK AGRICULTURE. Certain tribes in Australia, North America, and elsewhere set fire to fields to encourage the growth of new plants by burning away the underbrush and the coarse tops of the old grass (O'Dea, 1992; Keeley, 1995; Mulvaney and Kamminga, 1999: 60–62). The ash from the burning also served as a fertilizer. In some cases, the purpose was merely to raise hunting productivity by attracting grazing animals to the young grass; in other cases, to supply seed and nut crops that would later be gathered for subsistence. Some societies (e.g., Shoshonians of the Great Basin in the United States) took this practice a step further by planting wild seeds in the burned field and later harvesting the crop (Keeley, 1995).

TENDING TUBERS. In northern Australia, the long yam was a dry-season staple. When harvesting it, certain groups would leave the top of the tuber attached to the tendril of the vine to ensure that it would grow again the following year (O'Dea, 1992).

WATERING FIELDS. Certain foraging societies, such as the Owens Valley Paiute of California, flooded fields containing wild root crops to encourage their growth (Keeley, 1995).

SOIL AERATION. Some Australian aboriginal tribes engaged in extensive turning of the soil to collect edible roots and tubers, a practice that encouraged their growth the next year (Mulvaney and Kamminga, 1999: 87).

---

[4] Proto-animal-husbandry has received much less attention, although certain practices among reindeer hunters who followed the herd, culled it, and employed other techniques to manage it (Bender, 1975: 2) might be so classified. When most authors speak of proto-agriculture, they really mean proto-plant-production.

SEMI-SOWING. In various parts of the world, some societies would broadcast wild seeds on fresh alluvial silts (Watson, 1995). The Menomini Indians of Wisconsin purposely allowed some of the wild rice they harvested to fall back into the water to ensure a crop the next year (Cohen, 1977a: 21). The Kumeyaay tribe on the California–Mexico border transplanted various plants and trees (Smith, 1995).

Quantitative analyses of the various practices of proto-agriculture are rare, with the exception of the work of Keeley (1995, 1999). From a regression analysis of the practice of burning fields among various groups of Shoshone and Paiute of the Great Basin in the United States, Keeley concludes (1995: 271): "The most important variables for explaining the intensification of plant exploitation, including cultivation of wild plants, are, in order of decreasing importance, ecological 'latitude,' precipitation, and population pressure. Population pressure plays only a minor, but still essential, role in intensifying plant exploitation. Social demand and social complexity are completely irrelevant." By "social demand," he refers to the need for a food surplus to support higher social classes, a high ceremonial intensity, or giveaway feasts.

Most early proto-agriculturalists seemed to understand well what they were doing. According to some anthropologists, we should no longer consider gatherers and hunters as a ragged and scruffy band of nomads. Kent V. Flannery (1968) declares that, instead, "they appear as a practiced and ingenious team of lay botanists who know how to wring the most out of a superficially bleak environment . . . We know of no human group on earth so primitive that they are ignorant of the connection between plants and the seeds from which they grow and this is particularly true of groups . . . [utilizing] seasonal plant resources." Cohen (1977a: 18–22) discussed other evidence along these lines.

Nevertheless, we will never know how the original connection between seeds and plant growth came about – a seminal insight in the true sense of the term. We can speculate (as have Rindos, 1984; and Tudge, 1998), however, that proto-plant-production was practiced for tens of thousands of years before the so-called "neolithic revolution" of 10,000 years ago and, most likely, began in the middle Paleolithic. Unfortunately, the sites of proto-plant-production have not left sufficient archaeological traces to support this conjecture. Nevertheless, it seems highly likely that extensive proto-plant-production preceded full-scale agriculture because it allowed the accumulation of knowledge about plant production.

To anticipate discussion later in this book, the problems encountered in distinguishing proto-agriculture from agriculture are similar in many respects to the difficulties explored in Chapter 5 in distinguishing proto-manufacturing from manufacturing.

2. Domestication and Full-Scale Agricultural Production

Aside from comprising most if not all of the agricultural activities enumerated herein, full-scale agriculture is supposed to include the development of domesticated plants and animals – that is, flora and fauna with a genetic makeup different from their "original" states so that they are more useful for humans. For seed-bearing plants, for instance, domestication can mean larger seeds, compaction of seeds on the plant, less scattering of seeds before harvesting, thinner seed coats, seeds that sprout more quickly or are more resistant to drought or to the impact of weeds, and so forth. Domestication of tubers means, for instance, larger edible parts, earlier maturation, lower content of poisonous or acrid substances, or higher sugar content (Léon, 1977). For animals, domestication means taming, enhancing useful properties such as longer hair (sheep) or greater milk production (cattle), and training to carry out certain tasks (dogs).

In recent years, experimental archaeologists and others have arrived at several important insights. Domestication did not need to be a conscious undertaking and could have been an accidental outcome of various activities, such as harvesting (Rindos, 1984; Anderson, 1991). Moreover, in the words of Jack Harlan (1999), "Domestication of most cereals is relatively simple and straightforward." As evidence, he cited various experiments where certain grasses were fully domesticated in one year and certain rices, in three. For domestication to occur, a genetic variation among wild plants and a culling of those with certain characteristics is necessary. MacNeish (1991:9) discusses an hypothesis advanced by various scholars that most domesticated plants are "open-habitat plants." These plants more readily mutate or mutual strains are more likely to flourish in disturbed soils (e.g., near human habitation), a feature that would have also aided domestication. Further, domestication is not an either/or proposition but rather a matter of degree. Rindos (1984) also argues that domestication must really be considered a coevolutionary process between plants/animals and humans. In any case, domestication was not an exclusive feature of full-scale agriculture but could occur with both proto-plant-production and nomadic-plant-production (see the following discussion).

3. Some Conclusions

The evidence discussed herein suggests that the invention of agriculture was not difficult. The discovery by humans of the seed mechanism for plant growth, in contrast, was a critical technological breakthrough, and it undoubtedly occurred far earlier than 10,000 years ago. But we will never know when or where it took place. We also will not know if proto-plant-production was a straightforward development from this initial insight about seeds because the various techniques used in this subsistence activity might have been discovered separately and accidentally. For the rest of this chapter, I focus primarily on full-scale plant production.

Whereas it is likely that most forms of proto-plant-production increased labor productivity in obtaining food and that, because of seasonality factors, the same can probably be said of nomadic-plant-production, this is not necessarily true of full-scale agriculture. As noted previously, full-scale agriculture appeared to have required much more work than foraging, so we again must face the original question of why foragers, if they were rational, adopted agriculture.

B. Hypothesized Environmental/Geographical Prerequisites of Agriculture

Ecological and climatic conditions have received considerable attention as explanations for the origins or spread of agriculture. The evidence presented herein suggests that their importance is probably much less than commonly believed. I first look at some simple indicators of environmental conditions that are believed favorable to agriculture and then explore some more subtle arguments about biological/geographical determinants.

1. Favorable Environmental Conditions for the Presence of Agriculture

Students of prehistory fall into two opposing camps with regard to the impact of environmental conditions on the origins or spread of agriculture.

Some archaeologists and anthropologists claim that agriculture was more likely to develop in or spread to rich environments with abundant per capita plant resources,[5] and they offer several interesting arguments: Needy societies were not inventive, so only a society living in a rich environment would

---

[5] For instance, various papers in Price and Gebauer (1995).

have had the leisure to experiment with plant production. Further, the benefit/cost ratio of initial agriculture was low, so agriculture could have been worthwhile only where climatic conditions enhanced its benefits (Hayden, 1995a); or where there was great diversity of plant life; or where plant production increased the productivity of foraging, for example, by providing poisons used for fishing (Sauer, 1969: 24). Finally, societies situated in rich environments were more likely to press for increasing food surpluses to finance religious, social, cultural, and political aims (Hayden, 1990). The first two arguments rest on the assumption that the invention of agriculture was extremely difficult, which seems unlikely, given the evidence on proto-plant-production discussed previously; I deal with the third hypothesis in the next section and cast doubt on it as well.

The other group of researchers claims that agriculture was more likely to develop or spread in relatively poor environments – the marginal areas – because the stress on land resources from foraging was higher.[6] Keeley (1995: 261) provides a telling example. In his discussion of the diffusion of the maize–bean agricultural complex, he points to several societies adopting agriculture that lived in poor ecological zones such as Death Valley. At the same time, neighboring tribes that lived in much richer areas and with a higher level of economic development (Carneiro scale), such as the Owens Valley Paiute, were content to practice only proto-agriculture and to rely primarily on gathered foodstuffs.

To test statistically the validity of either approach requires us to develop a measure distinguishing a "rich" or "poor" environment and to determine which conditions for agriculture – climate, soil, and terrain – deserve attention at the time of the transition to agriculture. Several problems arise.

GENERALIZATIONS ABOUT CLIMATE. Unfortunately, we have no global-wide measurements of climate at the time of the transition to agriculture. I am, therefore, assuming that indicators of temperature and rainfall climate today are rough approximations of the climate a long time ago when the transition to agriculture took place. Other indicators, such as the slope of terrain or soil suitability, raise no such difficulties.

A SINGLE INDICATOR. Although this is very difficult, we can circumvent these problems by looking at many different indicators of particular aspects of environmental favorability of agricultural, each scaled in an appropriate fashion.

---

[6] See, for example, Binford (1968) or Cohen (1977a).

SAMPLE. What kind of sample is suitable for examining possible correlations between the importance of agricultural products in their diet and the various environmental indicators? Even under extreme conditions, certain kinds of agriculture could be practiced: irrigation could offset extreme aridity and the herding of reindeer could offset climatic barriers to agriculture in very cold climates. To deal with this problem, I have eliminated from the SCCS all societies with less than 200 millimeters of rainfall per year or with an effective temperature[7] of less than 11° centigrade. Another problem in sample selection arises with seafaring societies that obtained a predominant part of their diet by fishing and hunting for sea mammals. So I have also removed from the sample all societies with more than a 35 percent reliance for subsistence on aquatic resources. This left 135 societies in the SCCS sample, which, in Table 3-1, were then arranged according to their reliance on agriculture (plant production and/or animal husbandry) for their subsistence.

In the table, I use three rainfall indicators: (a) precipitation; (b) evapo-transpiration (the water available to plants for maintenance and growth; i.e., rainfall minus water runoff and the water that percolates into the earth); and (c) the rainfall seasonality.[8] The actual rainfall experienced in a region is of less relevance to agriculture than the water available for agriculture, as measured by evapo-transpiration, but estimating the latter requires knowledge of soil conditions and plant cover. Fortunately, climatologists have made such calculations.

Moving from societies with a total reliance on foraging to total reliance on agriculture, Table 3-1 reveals that the amounts of precipitation and evapo-transpiration show a rise and then a fall as dependency on agriculture increased, while rainfall seasonality shows a fall and then a rise. No linear relationship in either direction is apparent, which is what we would infer from the arguments for both the positive or negative impact of a good climate on agriculture.[9]

The average annual temperature is of less relevance to agriculture than the effective temperature, which can be calculated from data on the average

---

[7] This is a measure of average temperature that also reflects the length of the growing season. It is defined more precisely by Kelly (1995: 66 ff.).

[8] This is the ratio of potential to actual evapo-transpiration, where "potential" is the maximum amount of water that plants in the area can use for maintenance and growth without becoming waterlogged.

[9] The nonlinear relationship could mean that societies living in environments with abundant rainfall had the fortunate choice of relying on both foraging and agriculture, whereas those in less favorable environments were forced to rely on one or the other, but not both, depending on the particular conditions.

Table 3-1. *Conditions for agriculture in a selected sample of tribal and peasant societies*

Percentage of Subsistence from Agriculture (Plant Production and Animal Husbandry)	0 to 5	5 to 25	25 to 55	55 to 75	75 to 95	95 to 100	Entire Sample
Number of societies	14	6	9	45	45	16	135
Rainfall indicators (precipitation and evapo-transpiration in millimeters)							
Annual precipitation	1,063	1,455	1,808	1,755	1,551	1,117	1,530
Annual evapo-transpiration	754	1,205	1,105	1,096	953	824	986
Rainfall seasonality: index	1.76	1.11	1.07	1.42	1.45	1.59	1.45
Temperature indicators (both in centigrade)							
Average temperature	17.4	22.3	22.2	22.9	21.1	21.5	21.5
Effective temperature	16.2	18.6	20.2	20.2	18.6	18.3	18.9
Ecological suitability for crops							
Slope of terrain (4 = steeply dissected; 8 = level to gently undulating)	6.8	8.0	6.9	6.9	6.5	6.5	6.7
Soil suitability (0 = very poor, 8 = very good)	3.9	3.0	4.0	4.4	4.6	4.3	4.3
Climate (for major crops) suitability (0 = impossible for growing, 8 = very good)	6.3	7.2	7.6	7.0	6.7	6.6	6.8
Agricultural potential							
Sum of terrain, soil, and climate suitability (4 = extremely poor; 24 = best possible for agriculture)	16.9	18.2	18.4	17.7	17.5	17.4	17.6
Lowest value of rating for terrain, soil, and climate suitability (0 = lowest; 8 = best for agriculture)	3.7	3.0	3.9	4.2	4.3	4.2	4.1

Note: These indicators are unweighted averages and are discussed in the text. Rainfall seasonality is potential evapo-transpiration divided by actual evapo-transpiration. The sample excludes all societies relying for 35 percent or more of their subsistence on fishing or sea mammals, as well as societies in extreme climatic conditions. Sources and methods are presented in Appendix 3-1.

temperatures in the hottest and coldest months.[10] Both temperature series in Table 3-1 provide little support for those arguing for the importance of environment, since they show no linear relationship with reliance on agriculture for subsistence. Moreover, for three other environmental variables – slope of terrain, soil suitability, and climate – no dramatic differences between the societies with different degrees of reliance on agricultural products for subsistence can also be seen because most of the results are not significantly different from the means of the entire sample. The same can be said for the two combined indicators of these three variables.

The message seems clear: Although the various environmental variables certainly had some impact on the importance of agriculture to subsistence of the preindustrial societies included in the SCCS, they do not appear to have been the key constraints to the adoption or spread of agriculture. The exceptions to this generalization were usually societies in extremely arid or cold conditions, which are not included in the sample. The visual impressions gained from Table 3-1 are confirmed when we attempt to tease out causal relations using a simple regression analysis.[11]

2. Change in Environmental Conditions

A number of scholars have argued the case for the impact of the environment on the origins or adoption of agriculture with an interesting twist. It was not the environment *per se* but, rather, a change in the environment that encouraged agriculture, by creating a stress on land resources. In the 1920s and 1930s, V. Gordon Childe popularized the notion that desiccation in the Near East during a period of several hundred years forced the

---

[10] Although those societies with 0 to 5 percent agricultural subsistence had somewhat lower average and effective temperatures than the other societies in the sample, the temperature differences between the societies in the sample and that of the sample mean are not, with one exception, statistically significant.

[11] More specifically, neither annual evapo-transpiration nor effective temperature provide any statistically significant explanation for percentage reliance on agriculture (plant production and animal husbandry), either together or when combined with the measurements of climate, slope, and soil variables. The summed agricultural potential variable proved no better and, although the minimum indicator variable was positively and significantly correlated with the agricultural subsistence variable, it explained only 10 percent of the variance. Similar experiments with a subsample of societies with less than 45 percent reliance on agriculture for subsistence yielded roughly similar results. A variety of other experiments were attempted but with no more success.

In a previous study (Pryor, 1985a), I used many of the same variables but with less restrictive criteria for eliminating societies living in extreme environmental conditions. That exercise showed a very weak but positive relation between environmental conditions and the presence of agriculture.

inhabitants onto oases, and the resulting resource stress encouraged agriculture, particularly animal husbandry. This hypothesis has been vigorously disputed, but recently Bar-Yosef and Meadow (1995) have argued that the cold, dry spell in the Near East in the period from roughly 10,800 to 10,300 years ago (Younger Dryas period) led to contraction of vegetation belts and smaller yields from natural stands of plants. This change, combined with population pressure and several other factors, forced an increasing reliance on agriculture and the emergence of farming communities. In several other areas and periods, the reliance of agriculture began shortly after similar dry spells (Hayden, 1995a).

But, contrary archaeological evidence is also at hand. For instance, Price, Gebauer, and Keeley (1995) point out that agriculture spread into Europe north of the Alps when the general climate became warmer, wetter, and less variable than it is today. Favorable climatic conditions, however, may have only aided the spread – but not the origin – of agriculture, so the question about causality is still open.[12] Other aspects of this theme are taken up in greater depth when I focus on resource stress as a causal factor. But, at this point, we need to turn to more subtle environmental effects.

3. Biological/Geographical Limitations on Agriculture

Jared Diamond (1999) presents a different and quite interesting perspective on the impact of the environment. He argues that there are only a limited number of edible and productive plant and animal species for humans and, moreover, these sources of human nourishment have a limited geographical distribution. Olsson and Hibbs (forthcoming) develop this argument. As a result of these limitations, agriculture began in just a few places and then diffused outward to other locations, aided by the fact that agriculturalists were militarily more powerful than foragers and forced agriculture on many of the hunting and gathering groups whose territories they conquered or dominated.

---

[12] Another open question is why, if climatic change underlies the origins of agriculture, did agriculture not develop during the Pleistocene, which experienced many climatic changes. Richardson, Boyd, and Bettinger (2001) present evidence that during the late Pleistocene, climates were not just cold, dry, and low in atmospheric carbon dioxide (necessary for photosynthesis), but, most important, their changes were also too variable and abrupt to serve as an impetus to adopt agriculture as a major subsistence activity; whereas during the early Holocene (roughly 11,500 years ago), climates were relatively warmer, wetter, and richer in atmospheric carbon dioxide and their fluctuations were less abrupt.

Two objections can be raised against this intriguing argument. First, although Diamond is undoubtedly correct that high labor productivity could be expected from cultivation of only a very limited number of food plants, this does not mean that agricultural societies could not have arisen from the cultivation of "inferior" crops. For instance, as Diamond himself notes (1997: 100), in the eastern part of the United States, agriculture began about 2500 B.C.E. with the cultivation of such plants as sunflower and goosefoot, and only later did some of these societies adopt maize, which originated from Mesoamerica, as a major staple. Thus, "superior" crops were not necessary for a society to start on the path toward full subsistence dependence on agricultural foodstuffs.

Second, as noted previously, the difference between proto-agriculture and full-scale agriculture is narrow. Despite the obvious diffusion of certain agricultural practices, agriculture could have been independently invented in many more centers than we now know. As shown herein, societies with a limited amount of agriculture existed in quite different environments and utilized quite different native plants. Certainly, the small number of useful and productive plant species that could be domesticated did not constrain gathering, and many of these gathered plants could have been cultivated later as well. Nevertheless, the low productivity of these plants might have limited the full-scale adoption of agriculture, as well as the development of a greater division of labor, higher cultural complexity, and military success, all of which depend on a food surplus that could support nonagriculturalists. Moreover, Diamond is correct that the presence of animals that could be domesticated differed greatly by continent and this, of course, initially constrained the rise of herding in some places, at least until these animals could be introduced into areas that were not their native habitat.

Diamond also argues that agricultural innovations were more likely to spread in an east–west direction than in a north–south direction because in the former, the various societies were more likely to have roughly similar environmental conditions. He uses this observation to explain the faster spread of agriculture in the Eurasian land mass than in Africa. But Africa and the Americas have large east–west distances, over which this diffusion apparently did not take place.

4. Some Conclusions

From comparisons of gross environmental conditions between societies with different degrees of dependency on agriculture for subsistence, it does not appear as though temperature, rainfall, soil conditions, or land slope played a crucial role in the origin or most aspects of the spread of agriculture. Conversely, in certain situations, the change in the climate might have stimulated the spread of agriculture, but many cases can be cited where humans did not adapt their subsistence activities to changing climatic conditions and, as a result, they disappeared.[13] So, a changing climate was neither a necessary nor a sufficient condition for the origin or spread of agriculture. The biological/geographical considerations raised by Diamond tell us little about the origins of agriculture, but they do help us understand its spread.

C. Hypothesized Cultural/Social/Political Conditions as Causes/Prerequisites/Incentives for Agriculture

At the present time, many anthropologists and archaeologists favor the hypothesis relating the origins or spread of agriculture to various social, political, or cultural factors that required the production of a food surplus.[14] Unlike the environmental variables, however, a correlation between such factors and reliance on agriculture for subsistence does not necessarily indicate causation because the direction of the causal arrows may not be clear. Moreover, if a correlation exists, the existence of many important exceptions suggests that the "causal factor" under examination might have been neither a necessary nor a sufficient condition for agriculture. As pointed out in the previous chapter, the *lack* of a correlation suggests that the variable under examination did *not* play a causal role; and, in the following analysis, I find little evidence that any social/political/cultural factors were important factors in the origin or early spread of agriculture.

1. A Cultural Factor: Changes in Mentality

For more than a century, anthropologists and archaeologists have offered a variety of hypotheses based on the notion that the cultures of foraging

---

[13] An oft-cited example is the Viking colony on Greenland around 1000 c.e., which continued its practice of a Scandinavian-type agriculture after the onset of the "Little Ice Age." This type of farming, however, was increasingly unsuitable as the climate became progressively colder. Around the mid-fifteenth century, the colony disappeared, at the same time that the neighboring Inuit communities, which relied for subsistence primarily on fishing and hunting, flourished.

[14] Weisdorf (2003b) has an interesting variation on this theme: namely, that it was the desire for nonfood goods produced by specialists that could be obtained only by exchange of agricultural goods that encouraged agriculture. In the ethnographic literature, however, it is difficult to find any evidence that such a mechanism was important in societies undergoing a transition to agriculture.

and agricultural societies were very different and that a change of mentality, arising for unspecified reasons, must have played a crucial role in the origins or spread of agriculture. Understandably, the supporting evidence has usually been very scanty, but an interesting recent debate brought the issue into prominence once again.

Jacques Cauvin (2000) presents archaeological data to suggest that religious practices (and ideas) in the Near East changed considerably for unknown causes immediately before the rise of agriculture and that this new religion triggered the shift in subsistence practices. Using a comparison of data from forty archaeological sites in the Near East, however, Fuller and Grandjean (2001) reach the opposite conclusion and argue that an agricultural food surplus preceded, rather than followed, a change in religious ideas. Unfortunately, I have been unable to find systematic evidence on this matter drawn from archaeological sites in other areas; the various SCCS series also do not seem to lend themselves easily to a direct test of this hypothesis about the impact of changing ideas.

One highly indirect test, however, seems possible. Because societies with higher levels of cultural complexity had a much more developed division of labor and because the level of economic development (Carneiro scale) was highly correlated with an increasing reliance on agriculture (Table 3-2, Panel B), we might ask whether specialized priests, shamans, or medicine men possessing exclusively owned healing magic arose before or after the emergence of agriculture. Although a series for all of the SCCS societies to test this idea is not currently available, we can use a proxy variable focusing on medical practitioners, which is a specialty relying on "intangible capital" to make a living (see Chapter 2) for societies with less than a 45 percent reliance on agriculture for subsistence. More specifically, my variable designates whether medical practitioners or healers received a fee for their services (1 = no fee; 2 = a small fee; 3 = an economically important fee). The results (Table 3-2, Panel A) show that such fees existed in many foraging societies, although these healers were usually paid in foraged foods and handicrafts rather than agricultural goods or money. Because medical practices were closely connected with religious practices in most of these societies, it seems plausible that professional priests (or freelance shamans or medicine men) were found in many societies that relied completely on foraging for their food. Thus, it does not appear that magical beliefs, religion, or specialized religious practitioners underlay the emergence or spread of agriculture. Unless some reasons can be supplied as to why religious beliefs would suddenly change in a manner to favor agriculture, Cauvin's hypothesis does not inspire confidence.

Table 3-2. *Unweighted averages of social and political variables allegedly related to agriculture*

Variable Number	Description	Range	Percentage of Subsistence from Agriculture						Entire Sample
			0 to 5	5 to 25	25 to 45	45 to 75	75 to 95	95 to 100	
A. My codes									
1–3	Number of societies in sample		14	6	9		NOT		29
1–11	Healers receive a fee for their services	(1 to 3)	2.1	2.2	2.7		CODED		2.3
1–22	Presence of potlatch	(1 to 3)	1.1	1.0	1.1				1.1
1–4	Wealth differences	(1 to 3)	1.6	1.4	1.7				1.6
1–17	Social differentiation	(1 to 3)	1.1	1.4	1.4				1.3
1–10	Slavery presence (at or previous to pinpointed date)	(1 to 3)	1.2	1.1	1.4				1.3
1–7	Taxes or levies by political leaders	(0 to 1)	0.1	0.2	0.2				0.1
1–16	Political centralization	(0 to 4)	0.6	0.7	1.1				0.8
1–14	Territoriality	(0 to 5)	2.4	1.5	2.2				2.2
1–15	Private property in land	(1 to 4)	1.4	1.0	1.9				1.5
B. Codes by others									
	Number of societies in sample		14	6	9	44	40	15	128
	Development index (Carneiro scale)	(0 to 600)	18	26	75	168	297	415	206
	Existence of corporate descent groups	(0 to 1)	0.2	0.2	0.6	0.6	0.8	0.7	0.6
	Social stratification	(1 to 5)	1.1	1.5	1.3	2.3	3.1	3.9	2.5
	Political differentiation	(1 to 4)	1.4	1.7	1.6	2.0	2.6	2.9	2.2

Note: The variable numbers refer to Appendix 2-1, where each variable is explained in detail. The numbers in parentheses are the range of my codes for the particular variable, with the high value indicating an hypothesized favorability for agriculture. The sample excludes all societies in extreme climatic conditions; those relying for 35 percent or more of their subsistence on fishing or sea mammals; and all nomadic herding societies. For the codes of others, the data sources and more details on the variables are described in Appendix 3-1.

2. Social Obligations

A number of anthropologists and archaeologists argue that mounting social ceremonial obligations arising in more complex societies required a food surplus that could be obtained only by agricultural production.[15] More specifically, a socially and politically homogeneous band with few lavish ceremonies or differentiated subgroups had little need to develop a food surplus except to tide it over a lean period. However, if people needed food not just for the subsistence of their families but also to fulfill new social obligations, to cement social alliances, to finance ceremonies or giveaway feasts, to support retainers, to maintain prestige or class status, or to validate high political positions as the "big men," then a more intensive method of food production than foraging might have been needed. For instance, Barbara Bender (1978: 206) argues that "the inquiry into agricultural origins is not, therefore, about intensification *per se*, nor about increased productivity, but about increased production and about why increased demands are made on the economy."

Bender's approach raises problems: It is unclear to me why these increased needs could not have been met with more foraged foodstuffs, especially since, as noted previously, work hours were relatively short in these societies. It is also difficult to find any direct way to test her hypothesis and we must rely on indirect proxies.

At one point, Bender (1975: 8) notes that agricultural societies tended to be organized on a more permanent corporate basis than foraging societies. If this means that they were also more likely to feature corporate kin-group structures,[16] then her idea is testable. The data (Table 3-2, Panel B), however, reveal that corporate kin structures occurred in some societies with little reliance on agriculture (although they were not common) so that this type of social arrangement was not a necessary condition for agriculture. They also appeared in most but by no means all of the societies with a heavier reliance on agriculture, so such structures were not a sufficient condition for this type of subsistence production. Bender's presumed causal relationship does not appear convincing.

3. Competition for Status

Brian Hayden has taken Bender's rather amorphous ideas and made them more rigorous. He argues (1990) that "socioeconomic inequalities and

---

[15] This literature is summarized in a particularly insightful way by Hayden (1990).

[16] That is, descendants of a common ancestor who, as a group, have certain rights (e.g., to land), certain obligations (ceremonial or social), and certain restrictions (e.g., on eligible marriage partners).

competition among complex, economically specialized hunters/gatherers toward the end of the Pleistocene as well as in the Holocene" (11,500 years ago to the present) are the key. More specifically, "the competitive and feasting aspects of economic rivalry among these complex hunters/gatherers [was] the driving force behind food production [agriculture]." Further, competition over certain food resources was destructive of these resources and, hence, maladaptive, especially if the group lived primarily off of animals that have limited offspring and long maturation periods. Overexploitation of cultivated grasses and legumes was less likely.[17] "The eclipse of rigid egalitarianism and sharing that was brought about by the emergence of economic competition (made possible by the effective exploitation of highly productive r-selected [plant and fish] resources) is possibly the most important development in cultural evolution in the last two million years. It can be linked to the emergence of food production, hierarchical societies, craft specialization, slavery, intensive warfare, and many other important cultural traits." Hayden speculates that the first domesticates were not staple crops but rather crops with desirable qualities for feasting – for instance, dog meat, specialty roots, or grain for beer. The available evidence on such matters is slim. It is, however, possible to test his general hypothesis in other ways, and three variables in particular deserve our attention.

FEASTING AND POTLATCHES. Given the ethnographic sources available to me, I found it impossible to code for the importance of feasting in many societies, nor was I able to find any series for feasting compiled by others. Nevertheless, I was able to code for the presence of potlatches (i.e., feasts in which property was given away or destroyed) for the SCCS societies relying on agriculture for less than 45 percent of their subsistence. The results (Table 3-2, Panel A, where 1 = absent; 2 = present but property given away and not destroyed; 3 = property either given away or destroyed) do not support the hypothesis. Among my original sample of fifty-seven SCCS societies, only eight featured potlatches and, of these, six (all on or near the northwest Pacific coast of North America) are not included in Table 3-2 because they relied for 35 percent or more of their subsistence on fishing or sea mammals. The other two societies with potlatches were the Omaha of Nebraska and the Gros Ventre of Wyoming, both of which featured only an attenuated form of this ceremony. Potlatches did not occur in most of the

---

[17] This distinction is between what biologists call K-selected and r-selected species. The former reproduce slowly and devote considerable efforts to raise offspring to maturity (e.g., large animals); the latter reproduce quickly and leave their offspring to fend for themselves (e.g., fish).

societies in the sample and such a ceremony does not seem a likely cause for the origins of agriculture. Some of the research for Chapter 4 also suggests that such giveaway ceremonies to achieve or maintain social status were only infrequently present in most societies with a heavier reliance on agriculture.

SOCIAL DIFFERENTIATION. My codes for wealth differentiation (Table 3-2, Panel A, where 1 = relatively egalitarian; 2 = some differences in wealth; 3 = considerable wealth differences) are, of course, impressionistic. Nevertheless, the results suggest that wealth inequalities increased when a society came to rely on agriculture for more than 25 percent of its subsistence, but that this relationship had many exceptions. My codes for social differentiation (Table 3-2, Panel A, where 1 = egalitarian; 2 = social ranks that are not inherited or fixed; 3 = classes with inherited rank) exclude the presence of slavery. These data reveal an irregular pattern for societies with less than 45 percent reliance on agriculture for subsistence and also do not appear to support the link between social differentiation and agriculture. Finally, my data on slavery either at or before the pinpointed date (where 1 = no slavery; 2 = slaves present, but not extensive, and held primarily by elite; 3 = more extensive holding of slaves) also show no particular trend, at least at these early stages of agriculture. The social stratification codes presented in Panel B of the table (by Murdock and Provost, 1973) are consistent with my coding results in revealing little trend toward social stratification until the society reached a reliance on agriculture for more than 45 percent of its subsistence.[18] Social stratification might have either accompanied or provided an incentive for a greater reliance on agriculture, especially since the food production of subordinates is easier to monitor than in foraging; however, the existence of social stratification in some foraging societies and the lack of such stratification in societies more heavily reliant on agriculture suggest that stratification was neither a necessary nor a sufficient condition for agricultural production.

It is, of course, possible that social differentiation did not appear in those societies with little reliance on agriculture because such a social structure

---

[18] More insight into this relationship between social differentiation and agriculture can be gained by exploring the determinants of social differentiation for societies relying on agriculture for less than 45 percent of their subsistence. A regression calculation shows that the degree of social differentiation was significantly and positively related to its residential fixity and also to the relative importance of fishing in its subsistence. If societies relying on fish and sea mammals for more than 35 percent of their subsistence (e.g., the societies on the northwest Pacific coast of America) are removed from the sample and the regression recalculated, such relationships disappear.

itself spurred a society to move rapidly toward agriculture. This possibility can be investigated by exploring those societies that rely on agriculture for more than 75 percent of their subsistence and examining whether any can be considered egalitarian. In fact, a number can be found: some were nomadic herding societies, but about 8 percent of the societies in this sample of agricultural societies resided in fixed communities and did not have significant social-class inequalities. Thus, social differentiation or the rituals of status validation did not appear a necessary precondition for full-scale agriculture.

POLITICAL DIFFERENTIATION. The social competition hypothesis can be recast in political terms by focusing on political differentiation and the emergence of a political elite. In this respect, my taxation variable (line 7 of Table 3-2, where 0 = no tax or tribute collected by the political leader; 1 = a portion of the food appropriated or given to the leader) and my composite variable for political centralization (line 8 of Table 3-2, which deals with aspects of political power) are particularly relevant. The tax variable reveals no significant trend among societies with less than a 45 percent reliance on agriculture. The composite variable shows a slight jump in political centralization after societies relied on agriculture for more than 25 percent of subsistence. The political differentiation variable manifests an upward trend only among those societies with more than 45 percent of their diet coming from agricultural products.

For the political centralization variable, many exceptions to the trend occur. More specifically, about one in seven of the non-nomadic herding societies relying more than 75 percent on agriculture for subsistence had a very low political centralization (less than a code of 1.5) on a scale from 1 to 4. This means that political centralization was neither a necessary nor a sufficient condition for the emergence of agriculture.

In brief, various aspects of political specialization generally did not emerge until the society had a reliance of at least 45 percent on agricultural products. Hence, political centralization and the need for a food surplus above subsistence needs that it allegedly created cannot account for either the origins of agriculture or its spread. Further, a heavy reliance on agriculture occurred in societies without such centralization.

4. The Existence of a System of Private Property

During the industrial revolution, profit-seeking entrepreneurs would not have invested in buildings and equipment where their ownership was not respected by other individuals or by such institutions as the government or the church. Some make the same type of argument for the neolithic revolution.

As noted in the previous chapter, most foraging societies recognized a group "ownership" of a particular territory, which they were willing to defend by force. Many even recognized private property in land: the foraging Vedda of Sri Lanka, for instance, recognized individual ownership (in the sense of exclusive rights of use) of hills and trees within the band's territory. This was not unusual: other foraging societies in my sample also recognized private ownership of particular fruit trees or fishing spots.

Many Western economists argue that a "change in property rights" was the key explanation for the rise of agriculture. For instance, according to Douglass C. North and Robert Paul Thomas (1977), "[I]t is the incentive change resulting from exclusive property rights that will inevitably create agriculture . . ." They also argue that such exclusive rights prevent over usage of the property, a phenomenon now labeled "the tragedy of the commons." This issue, however, seems overstated because the real issue at stake to prevent over usage is the control of access. Whether it is carried out by the state, the village, the clan, or individuals exercising property rights is of secondary importance.

Nevertheless, some vivid examples illustrating the North and Thomas hypothesis can be easily found. For instance, the !Kung San (Ju/'hansi) in the Kalahari desert in Namibia had a custom labeled "demand sharing" by anthropologists: If one person asked another for a particular article, the latter felt obligated to give it in order not to appear stingy. This transfer was not necessarily a gift because it conferred to the giver the right to request something from the receiver in the future. A related phenomenon was "demand reciprocity," in which one person gave something to another person and then demanded a particular article in return. Demand sharing or demand reciprocity was found in a considerable number of foraging societies, as discussed in the previous chapter. Some anthropologists argue that the custom of demand sharing discouraged the !Kung from working long hours because any accumulated surplus of goods would sooner or later have to be given away. According to Woodburn (1998), some !Kung San who attempted to set up farms were unable to prevent kin from coming to eat up all of the harvested grain, including the seed stock; the Hazda of Tanzania also had this experience.

The evidence against the North–Thomas hypothesis is, however, strong and, according to my data, it seems unlikely that exclusive usufruct rights were either a necessary or a sufficient condition for agriculture. As noted in the previous chapter, all of the foraging societies had such exclusive rights, at least for some articles foraged, produced, or otherwise acquired by individuals or nuclear families. Further, I have not yet found *any* society outside the SCCS sample without some type of exclusive property rights.[19] The big question is where these foraging societies drew the line between mine and thine. Several types of evidence deserve note.

COEXISTENCE. A society could have both agriculture and demand sharing, as shown by two societies in Brazil, the Timbira and Tupinambá (Crocker, 1990: 178, 184; D'Evreux, 1864). In both, the fields were cleared by communal groups, but they considered the individual manioc gardens and their produce as the private property of the individuals who tended them, even though food and other goods were subject to demand sharing.

FOOD INVENTORIES. In high-latitude regions where agricultural products are seasonally harvested, many foraging societies also had private food storage, especially where foodstuffs were gathered only in particular seasons or animals were hunted only in certain months. In such cases, at least for societies in the SCCS sample, all such food caches were considered private property and could not be touched by others except in extreme circumstances.[20]

CHANGE. The line between mine and thine could change when external conditions changed. For instance, when the !Kung San came in contact with Western markets, they became more individualistic and acquisitive within several decades. Instead of pitching their huts in a circle, with their possessions in full view of everyone, they began to build their huts farther from each other, either in a row or scattered, and they stored precious goods in locked trunks where they could not be seen by others (Yellen, 1998). Change in property rights in other societies could occur as a result of changes in group composition. More specifically, because changes in band membership were one way of adapting to fluctuations in weather conditions and were a regular occurrence, it would not have been difficult for those wishing to define property rights in a different way from those in their own band to form separate bands. Yet, other societies rapidly changed toward more exclusive ownership of land when external influences changed.[21]

---

[19] As noted in footnote 7, Chapter 1, certain nonhuman primates have a highly developed sense of private property of their food inventories.

[20] For instance, among the Montagnais of Canada, a starving passerby could use such inventories.

[21] A notable case of change over four decades is that of the Sirionó, as described by Holmberg (1950) and Stearman (1987).

These various examples offer contrary evidence to the hypothesis that private property (exclusive use rights) was a necessary or a sufficient condition for the origin or spread of agriculture. Additional negative evidence is provided in my codes for territoriality and private property, which show an irregular pattern of territoriality and private ownership of land as reliance on agriculture for subsistence increases rather than a clear-cut, one-step jump.

5. A Brief Summary

In some cases, a variety of cultural, social, and political factors might have required a food surplus over and above that necessary for bare subsistence. Further, such a surplus might have been more easily obtained by agricultural production than by foraging. Nevertheless, the hypothesis that such cultural, social, and political factors created demands on production in the society that triggered the emergence of agriculture does not receive general support from my data.

On the other hand, after the point where 25 to 45 percent of subsistence came from agriculture, certain correlations of particular cultural, social, and political factors and greater reliance on agriculture can be found. It is, of course, difficult to determine whether such noneconomic factors caused the spread of agriculture, simply occurred simultaneously, or were the effect of a greater reliance on agriculture. Nevertheless, a sufficient number of exceptions to these correlations can be identified to suggest that these various proposed causal factors were certainly neither necessary nor sufficient conditions for a heavy reliance on agriculture for subsistence. Rather, they either facilitated the adoption of agriculture or were themselves brought about by the increasing importance of agriculture in the society.

The evidence presented also suggests that in most foraging societies, exclusive usufruct rights to certain patches of land and the products therefrom or to food inventories were not unusual. I provide examples where agriculture and demand sharing coexisted and point to evidence showing that the transition to agriculture was not dependent on a particular economic system, defined by clusters of property right and distribution mechanisms. I also note that under certain conditions in particular societies, attitudes toward property rights were quite malleable. Finally, in the previous chapter, I provide evidence that the economic system, defined by various types of property arrangements, also did not appear to have played an important role in the origin or spread of agriculture. In brief, it does not seem likely that the lack of private property rights at a particular time or place served as a serious constraint on the development of agriculture.

D. Hypothesized Impact of Stress on Land Resources

For several decades in the second half of the twentieth century, the hypothesis that the origins and/or spread of agriculture lay in the adaptation of foraging societies to a higher population density and diminishing returns of hunting had many supporters (Cohen, 1977a, 1977b). According to this approach, originally a foraging band could avoid diminishing returns by fissioning, whereby subgroups would hive off and move into unoccupied lands. This process gradually led to a spread of population over much of the globe. At some point within the last 10,000 years, however, most foraging areas were peopled. To offset diminishing returns, hunters and gatherers faced a choice: spend many more hours in foraging; rely on less appetizing foods; turn to fishing (including the hunting of sea mammals); or, finally, increase their reliance on agriculture.

By the 1990s, this resource-stress hypothesis was distinctly a minority viewpoint among anthropologists and archaeologists.[22] To gain a broader

---

[22] Critics advance four arguments against the resource-stress hypothesis:

- *Unaccepted analogy.* Some of the evidence to the hypothesis was based on an analogy with the "broad-spectrum revolution," which occurred 10,000 to 30,000 years ago and represented a shift from the consumption of large, placid animals and easily available plant life to a greater variety of foodstuffs including small animals, dangerous animals difficult to kill, rodents, frogs, snails, crustaceans, other products from the sea, and particular plant foods, all of which required more work hours to obtain or to process. Although such dietary changes suggest that diminishing returns to foraging (aggravated by the extinction of certain megafauna), many researchers argued that this analogy did not hold for the origins or spread of agriculture.
- *Direct evidence.* Several kinds of conflicting evidence are available. If marginal returns in foraging had diminished, people should have been shorter and more malnourished. However, skeletons at these sites where agriculture later developed do not always show such symptoms of increasingly poor nutrition (as summarized by Roosevelt, 1984). By way of contrast, Keeley (1995, 1999) supplies positive evidence, showing that proto-agriculture among a number of Shoshone and Paiute groups was directly related to resource stress. His evidence, however, has been strongly disputed by others (see, for instance, Hayden, 1995) and focuses only on pure foragers.
- *Measurement.* Population density by itself does not indicate a stress on natural plant and animal resources. It is necessary to take into account the natural productivity of the land as well, a defect that several anthropologists (notably Kelly, 1983, 1995; Keeley, 1988) try to repair in the following pages. As I note herein, however, such exercises are fraught with peril.
- *Relative productivities.* Some point out that the average labor productivity of foraging was much higher than in agriculture, so that land stress could not have been involved. But the key point is that the marginal productivity and the point of diminishing returns in foraging is often reached much sooner than in agriculture when population increases. Average productivities are quite irrelevant for the analysis.

perspective, I discuss in this and the following section two related phenomena: evidence for a stress on land resources and sedentarism.

1. Stress on Resources: Potential Food Availability

To focus more sharply on population density, settlement permanence, and stress on terrestrial resources, I omit in the calculations in Table 3-3 all SCCS societies that can be classified as nomadic herding or that relied for more than 15 percent of their subsistence on fishing.

Population density estimates in line 3 of Table 3-3 are rough, particularly for nomadic (but nonherding) societies,[23] but they suggest that whereas population densities were noticeably higher when reliance on agriculture increased from 25 to 45 percent, they were higher by an order of magnitude thereafter. Nevertheless, only one of the societies relying less than 45 percent on agriculture had a population density of more than 0.23 people per square kilometer, while the population densities of societies relying more than 75 percent on agriculture varied widely and, in several cases, were quite low. These results suggest that high population density was a sufficient but not a necessary condition for the origin and spread of agriculture.

Underlying such results was the oft-discussed fact that nomadic foragers found it disadvantageous to have large families, given the difficulty of carrying many small children from place to place. Whether consciously or not, such societies took measures to space children and limit family size, such as sexual abstinence at specified times (e.g., before a hunt or before certain ceremonies), abortion, infanticide, or long nursing periods and the resulting lactational amenorrhea, even after they began to practice some agriculture for subsistence and follow a less nomadic way of life. Therefore, at least during the early stages of agriculture, the stress on land resources, as proxied by population density, appeared to have remained generally low.

A more exact determination of stress on land resources requires calculation of the per capita consumable natural biomass on the territory of the society, an estimate that gives rise to considerable difficulties. It is first necessary to determine the total biomass produced at the specified location of the various SCCS societies. For this purpose, I used Rosenzweig's (1968) formula relating evapo-transpiration to natural biomass production. Since

---

[23] For instance, Murdock and Wilson (1972), whose population density data I use, rate the Timbira of Brazil as having a population density of 1.16 people per km². My reading about this society suggests that this estimate is too high.

Table 3-3. *Demographic and consumption indicators related to agriculture*

	Percentage of Reliance on Agriculture for Subsistence						Entire Sample
	0 to 5	5 to 25	25 to 45	45 to 75	75 to 90	90 to 100	
1. Number of societies in sample	10	4	2	27	40	17	100
Demographic indicators							
2. Fixity of communities	1.0	1.8	4.5	5.0	5.8	5.8	4.9
3. Population density (people per square km)	0.10	0.14	0.69	15.43	69.99	98.41	48.71
Consumption indicators							
4. Natural biomass production (grams/square meter/year)	966	2,923	1,887	2,378	2,000	1,569	1,960
5. Available consumable biomass (grams/square meter/year)	12.7	47.0	19.9	32.8	27.8	20.9	27.0
6. Consumable biomass person per day (an index)	236.6	626.1	51.5	3.8	0.7	0.3	1.00

Note: These averages exclude nomadic herding societies and those societies relying more than 15 percent on fishing and water mammals for subsistence. For fixity of residence (line 2), 1 = migratory; 2 = semi-nomadic (fixed for several months, then migratory); 3 = rotating among 2 or more fixed residences; 4 = semi-sedentary (fixed core, then migratory for a few months); 5 = impermanent (periodically moved); 6 = permanent. Line 6 is calculated from lines 3 and 5 of this table. The sources of data are given in Appendix 3-1.

his formula appears to have a large margin of error, however, we must proceed cautiously; Appendix 3-2 discusses some of the problems in making these calculations. In Table 3-3, line 4 shows that the average SCCS society (nonfishing, non-nomadic herding) lived in an environment producing 1,960 grams of plant growth per square meter per year.

Only a small fraction of this biomass was consumable, however, and the fraction depended on the relative humidity (based in turn on rainfall and temperature) of the environment. In line 5, I use formulae devised by Kelly (1983) that take such factors into account in estimating the amount of above-ground plant biomass edible by humans. Even if the natural biomass estimates are correct, these estimates of available consumable biomass are also subject to error, as discussed in Appendix 3-2.

The final step, shown in line 6, is to divide total consumable biomass by the population density for each society to obtain the consumable biomass per unit of area per person. The result is the biomass potentially available per day for a member of the society in a given area, which is my measure of stress on land resources. Because the measure of natural biomass production is terrestrial, it makes sense to omit societies relying 15 percent or more on fishing for subsistence. For those societies relying on agriculture for less than 45 percent of their subsistence, the results reveal a jagged pattern because the sample of such societies is relatively small and, in addition, three approximations are involved in making the calculation. Therefore, we can focus only on gross differences.[24]

The results suggest a high per capita availability of consumable natural biomass for those societies with 25 percent or less reliance on agriculture for subsistence, considerably less for societies relying 25 to 75 percent on agriculture, and very much less for those societies with more than 75 percent reliance on agriculture. With one exception, all of the societies relying 25 percent or less on agriculture were in environments with an abundance of available consumable biomass.[25] On the other hand, a number of societies with high available consumable biomass per capita had more than a 75 percent reliance on agriculture for subsistence.[26]

---

[24] Appendix 3-2 presents the unsuccessful results I obtained by trying to correlate my measure of land resource stress with other variables that also might be related to it.

[25] The exception was the Aranda of Australia, who registered 5.4 on the index. They relied considerably on tubers and plant roots, which are not included in the estimate of the biomass.

[26] Well-known examples are a number of Indians in the American Great Plains that, before contact with the West, heavily relied on agriculture, although they lived in a relatively rich and sparsely populated area (but see the following discussion). The SCCS sample includes other similar

Such results do not tell us whether the low per capita consumable biomass was a cause or an effect of heavier reliance on agriculture. But they suggest (a) that a low per capita available biomass was a sufficient but not necessary condition for a heavy subsistence reliance on agriculture; and (b) that a high per capita biomass was not a sufficient cause for a low reliance on agriculture. Such conclusions generally parallel the results discussed about population density.

But the argument raises some difficulties, which can be seen from a common criticism of the resource-stress argument that the (average) productivity of foraging was generally much higher than early agriculture. This criticism is, of course, irrelevant because it is the marginal, not the average, productivity that is important (i.e., it is the productivity of the last hour of human labor, not the average of all hours). The marginal productivity of gathering might have been very low, even while the average was high.[27] The calculations in Table 3-3 are also of average, not marginal, quantities, although changes in the averages as we move from societies with less to greater reliance on agriculture present some important clues about the marginal productivities. In brief, my calculations provide suggestive but not conclusive arguments about the relationship between land stress and the origin/spread of agriculture.

2. A Modification

Suitably modified, I believe that the resource-stress argument has merit. In working through its implications, several important factors underlying the origin and spread of agriculture are brought to light.

BENEFITS AND COSTS OF AGRICULTURE. The fact that some amount of agriculture was practiced by some preindustrial societies apparently not suffering from a stress on land resources suggests that we look upon agriculture as one element of a "subsistence portfolio." This means that we should focus attention on attempts to trade off risk, work effort, and return. Too heavy a reliance on one particular food or technique for obtaining food was risky if there were fluctuations in productivity due to natural causes, so that a variety of foods and techniques for obtaining food – including agriculture – lowered

---

examples, for instance, the Barusho of Kashmir, the Yanomamo of Venezuela, the Zuni of Arizona, and the Banen of Cameroon.

[27] It is sometimes claimed that diminishing returns in gathering is considerably greater than in agriculture, but I have never seen any empirical evidence on the matter.

the risk of starvation. Furthermore, if the correlation from year to year between productivities of foraged and cultivated plant foods was low, societies
would be rational to engage in agriculture – even if its marginal productivity
were considerably lower than foraging – in order to lower famine risks.

This benefit–cost calculation can be clearly seen when the external conditions change and can either raise or lower the relative marginal labor
productivities of foraging and agriculture. A well-known example is provided by the Native Americans of the Great Plains, who relied primarily
on agriculture until they obtained horses. Thereafter, they greatly reduced
their reliance on agriculture and turned instead to buffalo hunting – which
had suddenly become much more productive – for a major part of their
subsistence. Another example is provided by the Moriori of the Chatham
Islands (Diamond, 1999: 53-4). These islands were originally colonized by
the Maori, who relied in part on farming. In the succeeding centuries, however, the Moriori abandoned agriculture for hunting and gathering which,
given their much lower population density and the lush environment, provided them with a stable source of subsistence without as much labor as
farming. On the other hand, it is quite possible that dessication in the Near
East 10,000 years ago did lower the marginal productivity of foraging and,
in the absence of measures to reduce the population, a greater emphasis on
agriculture for subsistence was the only way to avoid starvation.

LABOR UTILIZATION. Foraging society had members who were unable to
engage in much hunting and gathering; for instance, women nursing babies,
elderly without sufficient stamina for long hikes, or children. If such societies
remained in any spot for several months, then these members would have
been able to produce some food for their families through agriculture. A
benefit–cost analysis might show that such a use of their time was quite
worthwhile because their marginal productivity, although not high, was
still greater than zero.

The resource-stress argument has other interesting implications for more
advanced agricultural societies.[28] To explore these would, however, take us
too far afield from the general theme of this chapter.

---

[28] For instance, it seems likely that at some point a rising population density would lead to a shift
in both the pattern of crops planted and the pattern of land use. SCCS societies that relied less
than 75 percent on agriculture primarily planted crops that did not require a plow to obtain
high productivity, such as millet, sorghum, maize, dry rice, or root crops. Thereafter, there was a
marked shift toward crops requiring extensive land and the use of a plow. For the percentage of
land used in agriculture, two critical points appear, one after 25 percent reliance on agriculture,
the other after 75 percent reliance (where double-cropping became more common).

The major thrust of the argument should be clear. The data presented herein suggest but do not prove that a stress on land resources is a sufficient but not necessary condition for a shift from foraging to a greater reliance on agriculture (or fishing) for subsistence.

E. Agriculture and Sedentarism

Agricultural production does not require sedentarism; nomadic societies could have carried out plant production in three ways: (1) they could have planted and harvested fields during periods in which they remained in one camp for several months; (2) they could have planted the fields and then periodically returned to tend them; or (3) like the Sirionó of eastern Bolivia (Holmberg, 1950), they could have planted gardens of tubers and maize during one season and then returned many months later to harvest the surviving crop. Because patterns of nomadism and frequency of moves differed considerably among foraging societies, depending in part on seasonality patterns and the richness of the environment (Kelly, 1983, 1995), the types of nomadic-plant-production also differed. In brief, although sedentarism was helpful for agriculture, it was neither a necessary nor a sufficient condition for it.[29] Nevertheless, sedentarism, population density, and a heavy reliance on agriculture had some important interconnections.

If the society relied for subsistence primarily on large game, which reproduce slowly, then nomadism would have been necessary to prevent the overhunting of a given region (Carneiro, 1969). The more a society relied on gathering and/or fishing for subsistence, the less necessary nomadism became, especially since the more rapid reproduction of most plants and fishes meant a more distant point of diminishing returns. Moreover, if the society lived in areas of marked seasonality, then by the time that it had gathered in one place and moved on, the season of plenty would be over and the move would be literally fruitless.

Such considerations suggest that semi-sedentary or settled foraging societies were probably not unusual in the past, assuming that (1) the population of the village remained low or the area was relatively rich, and (2) the domesticated plants were slow-growing and required a certain attention (using various proto-agricultural techniques). For instance, archaeologists have found

---

[29] I should add that it is not even necessary to be a human being to engage in agriculture, since it is also found in the animal world. Hölldobler and Wilson (1990: 527–29; 604–8) discuss how certain species of ants herd aphids to obtain the honeydew they secrete, whereas other species cultivate fungus farms, which they then consume.

small pre-agricultural village sites in Central Europe dating back 25,000 to 30,000 years (Cauvin, 2000). In the Near East from 10,000 to 12,500 years ago, many of the Natufians also lived in pre-agricultural villages, subsisting by gathering wild grains, which they later domesticated.

On average, as shown in line 2 in Table 3-3, the SCCS societies with up to 25 percent reliance on agriculture ranged between fully nomadic and semi-nomadic. The sample has no examples of foraging societies, such as the early Natufians or Owens Valley Paiute in the nineteenth century, who lived in settled communities but had no agriculture. Beyond the point of 25 percent reliance on agriculture, however, settlement fixity increased dramatically in a two-step pattern, although the sample is too small for societies with 25 to 45 percent reliance on agriculture for us to have much confidence in this part of the table. It is noteworthy that several societies with 45 to 75 percent reliance are classified as semi-nomadic or rotating between two or more mixed residences.[30]

A high degree of sedentarism provided the conditions for several positive feedback loops that encouraged an increasing reliance on agriculture. For instance, in settled communities, it was less necessary to limit family size, and an imperceptible change in the population growth rate can have had serious long-term consequences over a millennium. Moreover, if the society engaged in a small amount of agriculture when it became settled, the children (who were useless in hunting or a nuisance in gathering) could be employed tending the crops or watching the herd. Because people did not need to carry all their goods around, sedentarism also meant that it was easier to accumulate wealth and self-reinforcing differences in wealth or status validation rituals could and did arise (as shown in my regression results discussed in footnote 18). Finally, members of sedentary communities could have also engaged in more systematic efforts to domesticate particular plants and animals and to develop new tools and technologies for food procurement, production, and processing. Nondemographic positive feedback loops encouraging greater reliance on agriculture can also be specified in the social and political sphere (Smith, 1973).

Given the high correlation of sedentarism and reliance on agriculture for more than 25 percent of subsistence, it may be more fruitful to attack

---

[30] The most striking exception to the correlation between settlement fixity and reliance on agriculture was the Teda, a Saharan society in Chad rated as semi-nomadic. It relied for more than 75 percent of its subsistence on agriculture (including considerable animal husbandry), but its environmental circumstances were quite special. An additional four societies with 45 to 75 percent reliance on agriculture are rated as semi-nomadic or rotating among two or more fixed residences.

the problem of the spread of agriculture by exploring two issues: Why (and where) did particular societies *not* more fully adopt agriculture when they relied from 5 to 45 percent on agricultural for subsistence and were semi-sedentary. And how were they able to continue the family limitation practices, which they had used in their more nomadic phase, when their residence became more fixed? Unfortunately, these issues must be left for future analysis.

In brief, although permanent settlements in a single place were neither a necessary nor a sufficient condition for heavy reliance on plant agriculture for subsistence, certain mechanisms within fixed communities could have easily led to a heavier stress on land resources and a greater need for food surpluses, both of which could have resulted in an increased dependence on agriculture (or fishing, where that was possible). Of all the variables under examination in this chapter, sedentarism seems the most closely related to the spread of agriculture, but a larger question remains unanswered: Why did sedentarism emerge?

F. Conclusions

Domestication of plants and nomadic agriculture probably developed in all but the most hostile environments. Furthermore, most foraging societies undoubtedly employed some agriculture, or proto-agriculture, as just one of their portfolio of subsistence techniques. The extent to which some foraging societies did resort to deliberate food production for subsistence depended on such factors as the climate, the level of technology, the correlation between agricultural and gathering yields, the availability of particular plants and animals, the labor on hand that could not be used in foraging, and similar factors affecting the ratio of benefits to costs. In sum, the origin of agriculture was not a dramatic event because it was probably independently invented in widely scattered places with different climates and environments, and – as many have argued – the search for its origins or for particular cradles of agriculture does not seem worthwhile.

In contrast to the origins of agriculture, the factors underlying an increasing dependence on agriculture for subsistence in the last 10,000 years were much different and more complicated. Up to now, I have looked for correlations between the relative importance of agriculture in a society's way of life and a number of possible causal variables. In some cases, I found only a low correlation, which means that such a variable can be rejected as a major cause. Many of the alleged causal variables show a rough simultaneity with reliance on agriculture, which makes our task of causal analysis more difficult. Was increased population density a response to agriculture or its cause? Or is this a case of mutual causation? Unfortunately, the traditional statistical methods used by economists to handle such difficulties are inapplicable, but all is not lost.[31]

Instead, I have looked at *exceptions* to the various correlations between suspected causal variables and dependence on agriculture to determine whether a given variable was either necessary or sufficient for the spread of agriculture. The most promising results suggest that a rise in population density, a decline in available consumable biomass, and a greater fixity in the residence pattern of the community were sufficient – although not necessary – conditions for greater reliance on agriculture. In particular, greater sedentarism often set up positive feedback loops (notably through population growth and greater social differentiation) for more dependence on agricultural production for food.

Nevertheless, other causes for greater reliance on agriculture cannot be excluded. For some societies, environmental or climatic changes led to a shift toward agriculture. For other societies, political centralization might have reached the point where it was possible for group leaders to force members to farm and hand over some of their crop. And, finally, for still other societies, social differentiation, combined with competitive feasting and potlatches to validate social status, might have triggered a shift toward more agriculture because food production above subsistence needs was required. Because the cross-cultural data reveal only sufficient, not necessary, conditions for the spread of agriculture, I see no way to support one of these general hypotheses over another.

Of greatest importance, no *single* cause underlay the spread of agriculture in different times, places, and environments (MacNeish, 1991); therefore, generalizing from a small sample of cases is not valid. Because greater sedentarism set in motion positive-feedback mechanisms that in many cases promoted greater dependency on agriculture, it seems more fruitful to explore why certain societies did *not* become more agricultural.

But now a key methodological question must be asked of these results. Because they were gained from a cross-section analysis of different societies at a single pinpointed date, is it legitimate to generalize from them to events

---

[31] One traditional method is the use of simultaneous equation models, but this is not possible for the present problem. First, the data are not sufficiently precise to allow such a technique to be meaningfully employed. Second, the factors influencing the alleged causal variable are also difficult to specify and raise additional simultaneity problems. Third, the determination of inflection points in the various series to determine causation raises other insoluble problems.

occurring over time? The answer is easy: These cross-cultural results provide a plausible but not airtight case about the spread of agriculture. Nevertheless, if some societies within historic time were heavily reliant on agriculture but did not have property X, then the burden of proof that X was a key variable for the origins of agriculture 10,000 years ago lies on those making the argument. More specifically, they must demonstrate that conditions 10,000 years ago were sufficiently different from those observable in the SCCS sample to justify the supposition that causal mechanisms were different. Unfortunately, it seems very difficult if not impossible to make this argument because the archaeological evidence seems too ambiguous and scattered to provide conclusive proof about most of the cultural, social, political, or demographic variables discussed that might have caused a society's increasing reliance on agriculture.

But one conclusion is very clear: namely, that the neolithic and industrial revolutions differed in several major ways that make the analogy between the two extremely misleading. The industrial revolution required major changes in technology with powered machinery replacing hand tools, the factory supplanting the home workshop, and the scale of production (and the corresponding division of labor) increasing dramatically. By way of contrast, the "agricultural revolution" represented no sharp break in technology but emerged as part of an incremental historical process. Initially, the industrial revolution required a particular pattern of property rights, at least where the production was carried out by private individuals, whereas the "agricultural revolution" was implemented under a variety of property arrangements. Initially, the industrial revolution was primarily a deliberate activity undertaken for monetary profit rather than an adjustment to demographic, social, or political changes that influenced the risk/return of various subsistence activities. Moreover, the industrial revolution occurred relatively quickly – in the course of a century or two – in most societies, whereas the shift to a heavy reliance on agriculture probably took millennia, to judge from the many foraging societies in historic time.[32] Thus, "revolution" is an inappropriate concept for understanding either how societies first began to practice agriculture on a small scale or how it eventually came to be their primary source of food.

---

[32] In contrast to agriculture, which emerged in a wide variety of climates, the industrial revolution first occurred in the temperate zone of the northern hemisphere. Nevertheless, it is difficult to discuss climatic prerequisites for manufacturing, at least with a straight face.

PART THREE

AGRICULTURAL SOCIETIES

FOUR

Economic Systems of Agriculturalists

In this chapter, I show that agricultural societies featured four quite distinct economic systems. Each system had readily understandable organizing principles that were unrelated in large part to a variety of environmental, social, and political factors that many have alleged to be important. Despite the great differences between agricultural and foraging economies, most of these general conclusions about their economic systems are similar. On a more specific level, however, their differences were striking. The agriculturalists had a much higher average level of economic development than the foragers and the defining characteristics of their economic systems were also quite different. Moreover, in contrast to the apparent lack of influence of the foraging economic systems on a possible transition to agriculture, the type of agricultural economic system had an important impact on a possible transition to an industry/service economy, a topic discussed in the next chapter.

In the following analysis, I first discuss the sample and the criteria for defining an agricultural economic system. Then, I carry out a cluster analysis to determine the types of systems and examine the most important features of each. An important finding is that the complementarities between different economic institutions and organizations were less strong than in foraging and industrial/service economies, so that the individual societies with the same economic system were dissimilar in some important respects. Finally, I examine the degree to which the four types of economic systems were – or were not – related to various environmental, social, and political variables.

A. The Data Base

1. The Sample

From the SCCS, I originally selected all forty-six of the societies that relied 85 percent or more for their food from their own agricultural production, either plant cultivation or herding. Nevertheless, five of those selected had to be dropped, either because the available ethnographic materials on the economy had too many lacunae or because modern nation-states impinged so much on these communities through land reform or other intrusive institutional and organizational changes that their economic system no longer reflected a primarily preindustrial society.[1]

Table 4-1 presents the entire sample. Although the pinpointed dates of these societies were usually somewhat later than those of the foraging societies, many of the traditional patterns were sufficiently intact to give the results meaning.[2] Roughly half of the societies were located in Asia, with the others situated in Sub-Saharan Africa, Latin America, and the Circum-Mediterranean area.

2. Criteria for Defining an Economic System: Property Relations

As noted in the first chapter, I follow the conventional usage of defining the economic systems in terms of institutions and organizations structuring the property relations and the distribution of goods and services. The indicators for property institutions can be arranged into three groups.

a. Ownership of Land

Several characteristics of land ownership deserve attention. The first is the extent to which fields were "owned" by the community or some large grouping such as a clan (or other sizable kin groups) rather than by individuals or small family groups (nuclear families or small extended families) (4-4).[3]

---

[1] For the Manchu (SCCS #118), insufficient data were available. For the Irish (SCCS #51), Japanese (SCCS #117), Russians (SCCS #54), and Turks (SCCS #47), the central government was too intrusive for key preindustrial institutions and organizations to be maintained.

[2] Of the forty-one societies remaining in my sample, 15 percent were pinpointed at a period before 1900; another 22 percent, between 1900 and 1925; and the remaining 63 percent, after 1925. This means, among other things, that roughly 85 percent of the societies used "modern" money, rather than their indigenous money, for some economic transactions.

[3] The numbers in parentheses refer to the variables explained in detail in Appendices 4-1 and 5-2 and presented in Statistical Appendix Tables SA-4 and SA-5.

Table 4-1. *Agricultural societies used in the sample*

SCCS Number	Society	Location	Date	SCCS Number	Society	Location	Date
11	Kikuyu	Kenya	1920	61	Toda	India	1900
17	Ibo	Nigeria	1935	63	Uttar Pradesh village	India	1945
21	Wolof	Gambia	1950	64	Burusho	Pakistan	1934
23	Tallensi	Ghana	1934	65	Kazakh	Kazakhstan	1885
25	Pastoral Fulani	Niger	1951	66	Khalka	Mongolia	1920
26	Hausa	Nigeria	1900	67	Lolo	China	1910
29	Fur (Darfur)	Sudan	1880	68	Lepcha	Sikkim	1937
34	Masai	Tanzania	1900	69	Garo	India	1955
35	Konso	Ethiopia	1934	71	Burmese village	Burma	1965
36	Somali	Somalia	1900	74	Rhade	Vietnam	1962
37	Amhara	Ethiopia	1953	76	Thai village	Thailand	1955
38	Bogo	Ethiopia	1854	82	Negri Sembilan	Malasia	1958
39	Kenuzi Nubians	Egypt	1900	83	Javanese	Indonesia	1954
43	Egyptian village	Egypt	1950	84	Balinese	Indonesia	1958
48	Gheg	Albania	1910	114	Chinese village	China	1936
50	Basque	Spain	1934	155	Quiché	Guatemala	1930
55	Abkhaz	Georgia	1880	160	Haitian village	Haiti	1935
56	Armenian village	Armenia	1843	163	Yanomamo	Venezuela	1965
57	Kurd	Iraq	1951	171	Inca	Peru	1530
58	Basseri	Iran	1958	172	Aymara	Peru	1940
59	Punjabi (West)	Pakistan	1950				

Note: SCCS = Standard Cross-Cultural Sample. The sample is described in various essays in Barry and Schlegel (1980), and my numbering of societies follows that of the SCCS.

Unfortunately, the distinction between ownership and possession raises difficulties. I define ownership by an individual or a small family group in terms of their claim on a piece of land that was socially enforced. By contrast, possession signifies that an individual or small group was assigned the usage of a piece of land, but its usage could be taken away or reassigned.[4]

Although an individual could have permanent use rights to a piece of land, its uses might have been severely restricted by the community. I have, therefore, coded a second variable to designate the degree to which such use rights were limited, either by the community as a whole or by large corporate kin groups (4-5). Thus, a society could have had individual ownership and yet restricted either the uses of the land or the transfer of such land to others.

Another aspect of land ownership is the degree to which land owners could make their own decisions about when to plow, plant, weed, and harvest (4-12) or whether such decisions were made by the community. Such work coordination was particularly important in nomadic herding societies where all had to move their herds at the same time. In other cases, work coordination was dictated by the exigencies of the irrigation system, or by the necessity of pasturing cattle in contiguous plots of land, or by the sharing of agricultural equipment. In many other societies, however, work coordination had no apparent economic function and seemed a function of particular religious or political needs.

An additional characteristic of ownership institutions is whether usable but idle land was owned by private individuals (or nuclear families) or by larger social units such as extended kin groups or the community as a whole (4-6). In some societies, the community assigned use rights to idle land to anyone; in other societies, all idle land was privately owned.

A final aspect of ownership is the degree to which land could be sold (4-29). This variable, although it was difficult to code, reflected the presence of a market for land.

---

[4] Some peculiar coding problems arose: For instance, among the Garo of Assam, a nuclear family had socially recognized and permanent claims to portions of various fields for a lifetime and paid no rent for their use. Nevertheless, the fields were "formally" owned by "landlords" who did not necessarily farm them but who held a recognized title to them. These titles bestowed prestige to the owners rather than any power over the usage of the land or any right to collect rents from those who used it. Furthermore, the political authorities in the village could assign unused pieces of land to individuals who entered the village. For this society, I considered the land as "privately owned" by those who farmed it.

b. Land Tenancy

For those not directly engaged in farming the land, renting it for agricultural purposes was an important source of income. Two variables capture important aspects of tenancy. The first is a rough estimate of the average rent charged for land, defined in terms of a percentage of the crop (4-7). The second is the ratio of rented land to the total land used in cultivation (4-8).[5]

c. Miscellaneous Aspects of Wealth

One characteristic focuses on the degree to which ownership in people, either as slaves or serfs, was present in the society. Two problems arise in this regard. As I outline in detail in Appendix 4-1, coding for unfree labor gives rise to some serious conceptual problems. Furthermore, although slavery may have been integral to the various societies at a particular point in time, it was often eliminated by Western colonial powers to a much greater extent than among foraging societies. As a result, usually only those societies with relatively early pinpointed dates still retained vestiges of slavery. Nevertheless, using the slavery variable at the pinpointed date (4-10) seemed a more valid procedure than employing a variable indicating whether slavery was present in the previous two centuries, because the institutions of the society adjusted to some degree to the loss of slavery after the intrusion of Western powers.

I also include two variables previously used for the analysis of wealth in foraging societies: namely, the extent of a bride price, which indicates that the marriage rights of one's children served as a component of wealth (4-30), and intangible wealth in the form of healing powers, which served as an important source of income (4-31).

Another ownership variable indicates the rules by which land or cattle in the various societies were inherited. More specifically, I distinguish whether

---

[5] Collection of land rents was a very visible way in which the agricultural surplus (i.e., total production minus the bare minimum of crops needed for the survival of the cultivator and his family) was transferred. I have, however, not used other aspects of the agricultural surplus in the cluster analysis, in major part because of coding difficulties. That is, the "surplus" could have been enjoyed in the form of greater leisure by the cultivator or a higher standard of living for the cultivator's family; or it could have been transferred to land owners, the government, or a religious group. But, most ethnographic accounts do not supply sufficient information to decide how the surplus was being used, except in the case of very visible land rents, taxes, or tithes.

this legacy was divided among all children, among children of one sex, or primarily to one child (4-13).

3. Criteria for Distinguishing Economic Systems: Distribution of Goods and Services

The institutions and organizations structuring the distribution of goods and services can be divided into three groups.

a. Transfers

Food transfers were important to avert starvation when, for some reason, a person's stock of food fell below that necessary to sustain life. Such transfers improved the survival chances of a community unless, of course, all members were suffering food shortfalls at the same time. These transfers could be carried out on a decentralized basis in the form of gifts of aid from relatives and friends; or on a centralized basis, for instance, by political officials, "big men," or church leaders to gain prestige or to accumulate obligations by others. Food transfers could also occur for less urgent reasons, for instance, to show hospitality or friendship.

The extent of food sharing is extremely difficult to code because many early ethnographers paid little attention to this phenomenon or to whether such sharing represented a form of reciprocity or was a one-way gift.[6] Although I include such sharing in my list of variables (4-32), I do not have a great deal of confidence in the codings of many of the societies.[7] Food could also be shared by being transferred from political leaders or "big men" to those in need. These centric transfers proved much easier to code and are also included in the calculations (4-14).

A different type of sharing was the degree of mutual aid among agriculturalists – that is, the degree to which they exchanged labor services with each other (4-11). In these practices, land ownership is irrelevant. As Netting (1990) emphasizes, communal land did not imply communal work groups or mutual aid; furthermore, owners of individual pieces of land could cooperate with each other on most tasks.

---

[6] An exception is a quantitative analysis of various forms of sharing in an isolated Eskimo village by Pryor and Graburn (1980).

[7] Unfortunately, I could not test Hayden's hypotheses (1995) that food sharing decreased as the individual variation in food production due to random elements decreased (e.g., episodes of unsuccessful foraging or agriculture) and as variations due to individual effort and skill increased. He also conjectures that as the agricultural surplus increased, the frequency of one-way food sharing (i.e., gifts not requiring an immediate return) decreased.

b. Market Transactions for Goods, Labor, and Loans

Goods and services can, of course, also be distributed through markets and it is important to distinguish various types of such mechanisms. One variable deals with inter-community trade for goods: the relative importance of the exchange of goods (as a percent of income) with outside communities (4-15). The other variable focuses on intra-community trade: the relative importance of exchange of goods produced within the community with other members of the community (4-16). Both variables are coded in terms of an estimate of their ratio to total production of goods.

Two similar variables can be coded for the labor market. One variable is inter-community labor exchanges, in which men and women from one community obtained employment in other communities for shorter or longer periods (4-17). The other variable is intra-community labor exchanges, in which various members of a community worked for wages (defined in some manner) for other members of the same community (4-18). The importance of both types of labor was estimated in terms of the total labor force.

Finally, I include a variable to assess the degree to which a society had some type of market for property or wealth. More specifically, I have coded the presence of an interest rate for production loans or for both production and consumption loans (4-19).

c. Wealth Related to Distribution

The distribution of wealth is an indirect indicator of both the distribution of income and the degree to which the society attempted to level economic opportunities, especially by transfers of goods to low-income members of the population (4-20). The more unequal the distribution of wealth, the less likely intra-community transfers were important.[8]

The relative wealth of the political leaders of the community is also of interest (4-21). If such wealth was considerably greater, it could indicate either that the political leaders used their positions to gain wealth (by taxing the villagers and keeping part of the receipts for their own use) or, less likely, that the community voluntarily chose to rely for its leadership on its wealthiest members. Finally, I include a closely related variable: namely,

---

[8] Of course, any estimate of the distribution of wealth requires a subjective appraisal of primarily qualitative information, but if the ethnographer notes that land farmed by the wealthiest members was only two or three times greater than that of the poorest members of the community, it is safe to say that the distribution of wealth was much more equal than if this ratio were twenty to one.

the degree to which political leaders taxed the population, either to redistribute these revenues back to the community or to keep them for themselves (4-33).

B. The Types of Economic Systems

In this section, I carry out the cluster analysis using the twenty-two variables discussed previously that describe various institutions and organizations of the agricultural economies in the sample. The results reveal four distinct groups of economies. As also for foragers, both the economic systems and many of the specific institutions and organizations were significantly related to the level of economic development. To isolate those characteristics that define the economic system, it is necessary to take the development level into account, which I carry out using the same regression technique as that employed in Chapter 2.[9] After describing each type of economic system, I then compare my classification with that of others to provide additional perspective.

1. General Results

The MDL analysis indicated that four clusters were optimal in analyzing the sample.[10] A problem arises, however, because the clusters are less tightly packed than for the other three cluster analyses (i.e., foragers, developing market economies, and advanced market economies) described in this book.[11] This has several important implications:

INSTITUTIONAL CONSTRAINTS. The agricultural economic systems provide fewer constraints on the mix of institutions and organizations than in the other three cases. In other words, in agricultural economies, the "logic of

---

[9] More specifically, to determine whether the type of economic system can be explained by a particular institutional indicator, I calculated regressions of the following type:

$$EcSys = a + b\ DevLev + c\ I,$$

where EcSys is a dummy variable (equal to 1 if the society had the specified economic system, equal to 0 if it didn't); DevLev is the level of economic development (variable 2-6); I is the indicator under examination; and a, b, and c are the calculated regression coefficients. For twenty-two indicators and four economic systems, this required calculating eighty-eight regressions. Because the variable to be explained is binary, I used a probit-regression technique.

[10] I describe this type of analysis in Chapter 1.

[11] More specifically, the cluster analysis reduced the variance of the distances between each point and every other point by only 30 percent.

institutions," which concerns the complementarities between institutions and organizations, was less binding.

ROBUSTNESS. The results of the cluster analysis are less robust. That is, the composition of the clusters might vary somewhat more when particular characteristics are added or subtracted from the sample used in the estimates.

BORDERLINE CASES AND CLEANING THE SAMPLE. It might seem likely that in agriculture, more societies would lie close to the borderline with other clusters and would have to be eliminated from the analysis of systemic characteristics.[12] This did not occur, however, which suggests that the combination of institutional variables I have used has sufficient robustness that reliance can be placed on the results.

Table 4-2 summarizes the major results of the cluster analysis. Before turning to an examination of the individual economic systems, three general observations are relevant.

The average levels of economic development of four types of economic systems formed a visible scale, with the development levels significantly lower for the first two and significantly higher for the last one. Nevertheless, the range on the development levels was large, so that the societies with each type of economic system had considerable overlap on the development scale with societies having other types of systems.[13]

Moreover, a considerable number of the institutional variables also showed a significant relation to the level of economic development, as shown by the development elasticities.[14] As we might expect, four of the five property institutions were positively and significantly related to the development level, as were both of the tenancy variables. Moreover, three of the four market variables were also significantly and positively related to the level of economic development, as were wealth inequalities.

Finally, several of the twenty-two institutional and organizational variables defining the different types of agricultural economic systems were also related to important factors in increasing the possibility of an early date of industrialization, a subject discussed in the following chapter.

---

[12] More specifically, using the technique described in footnote 14 of Chapter 2, I had to eliminate four societies from my calculation of the average characteristics of each system. This number is the same as in the case of the foraging societies; for the advanced market economies, for which my sample was half as large, I had to eliminate half as many.

[13] More specifically, the average standard deviation of the four types of economic systems was 115.

[14] Similar to the procedure followed in Chapter 2, I included all of the forty-one societies in this calculation.

Table 4-2. *Defining characteristics of agricultural economic systems*

Variable Number	Description	Range	Development Elasticity	Average Scores				Total Sample
				Hd+	Eg	IF	SM	
Number of societies in sample				8	11	5	12	36
5-7	Development level (Carneiro scale)	(0–600)		188⁻	255⁻?	282	506⁺	325
Averages of property institutions								
4-4	Field ownership: communal to individual	(0–4)	+0.23	**1.00**⁻	**3.55**⁺	3.60	4.00	3.16
4-5	Individual use rights: bounded to absolute	(0–3)	+0.19	**0.63**⁻	**2.50**⁺	**2.70**⁺?	2.63	2.15
4-12	Extent of work coordination	(0–2)	−0.15	0.91	0.96	1.13	0.91	1.11
4-6	Individual ownership of "empty land"	(0–2)	+0.18	**0.69**⁻	1.30	1.40	1.96	1.39
4-29	Extent of land sales	(1–3)	+0.21	**0.31**⁻	**1.41**⁺	1.20	1.50	1.16
4-7	Rate of rent	(1–4)	+0.38	1.06	**1.32**⁻	**2.80**⁺	**3.00**⁺	2.00
4-8	Extent of tenancy	(1–4)	+0.34	**1.06**⁻?	**1.32**⁻?	2.13	2.63	1.78
4-10	Extent of slavery	(1–3)	−0.00	1.06	**1.00**⁻	**2.30**⁺	**1.00**⁻	1.22
4-30	Extent of bride price	(1–3)	+0.01	1.86	1.88	**2.30**⁺	1.50	1.84
4-31	Importance of intangible wealth	(1–3)	+0.08	2.50	2.50	2.33	2.45	2.48
4-13	Inheritance: all children or primogeniture	(0–3)	−0.12	1.88	1.68	2.10	1.54	1.73

Averages of distribution institutions

4-32	Extent of food sharing	(1–3)	+0.04	1.92	1.73	1.63	1.83	1.76
4-14	Extent of central redistribution of food	(1–3)	−0.07	1.50	1.27	1.38	1.46	1.42
4-11	Extent of mutual aid	(0–1)	**−0.12**	0.64	0.67	**0.17**$^{-?}$	0.50	0.59
4-15	Extent of inter-community trade	(1–3)	+0.05	2.63	**2.14**$^{-}$	2.50	**2.96**$^{+}$	2.58
4-16	Extent of intra-community trade	(1–3)	**+0.30**	1.06	1.59	1.83	2.21	1.74
4-17	Wage labor outside community	(1–3)	+0.15	1.75	1.50	1.75	2.00	1.74
4-18	Wage labor inside community	(1–3)	**+0.31**	1.56	**1.36**$^{-}$	1.80	**2.79**$^{+}$	1.92
4-19	Extent of interest on loans	(1–3)	**+0.22**	1.92	2.18	2.67	2.46	2.24
4-20	Inequality of wealth	(1–3)	**+0.14**	**2.81**$^{+}$	**2.23**$^{-}$	2.75	2.83	2.63
4-21	Relative wealth: political leaders	(1–2)	**+0.12**$^{?}$	1.56	1.68	1.63	1.67	1.63
4-33	Extent of taxation	(1–4)	+0.15	2.00	1.91	2.00	3.27	2.43

Note: Hd+ = herding-plus system; Eg = egalitarian farming system; IF = individualistic farming system; SM = semi-marketized farming system. The development elasticity indicates the percentage change in the indicator under examination to a 1 percent change in the level of economic development. For all the values in the table, boldface indicates statistical significance; if there is no question mark in the superscript, the level of significance is 0.05; otherwise, it is 0.10. The significance tests for the average scores are made when the development level is held constant (a procedure explained in the text) and, in the superscript, the sign indicates the direction of significance.

These labels for the economic systems are explained in the text. The individual codings, as well as their sources, are described in greater detail in Appendix 4-1. The variable number refers to the number of the variable in the Appendix and also in Statistical Appendix Tables SA-4 and SA-5, which give the values for the different societies and indicators.

2. The Herding-Plus System

The economic system (cluster) I label as "herding-plus" contains seven of the eight societies in the sample where herding provided more than 65 percent of subsistence.[15] It should not be surprising that individuals in these societies had significantly less ownership of individual pieces of land than the other societies in the sample, even while the community as a whole often had claims on certain land along their routes of migration. But, the small Inca community in the Andes also had similarly low ratings on a number of the characteristics of individual ownership and were part of this cluster, even though their economy was oriented primarily toward crop production. Such a result suggests that other crop-producing societies outside my sample might also have had a herding-plus economic system.

Given the uncertainties in herding and the possibility that a person's herds might be wiped out in a day from wild animals, disease, or other dangers, the societies with this type of economic system also had greater wealth inequalities. For different reasons, wealth in the Inca communities was also highly unequally distributed.

3. Types of Crop-Producing Economic Systems

The cluster analysis isolates three types of agricultural economic systems where the various societies relied primarily on crop production.

a. The Egalitarian Farming System

The egalitarian farming societies were distributed widely over the globe. Even when their relatively low level of economic development was factored out, they showed significantly less inequalities of wealth, less tenancy, less external trade with other communities, and less wage labor within the community. As I show herein, they also had significantly less social inequalities.[16]

---

[15] The Bogo of Ethiopia were the only herding society that did not have this type of economic system. Although at certain seasons, some of the Bogo undertook migrations, they should be considered as predominantly stationary herders because they lived primarily in large permanent villages (4-25). All of the societies classified as having a herding-plus economic system had a much higher degree of nomadism.

[16] Although the degree of field ownership and individual use rights of societies with an egalitarian farming system were roughly the same as the other plant-producing societies, they were significantly higher in this dimension when the impact of the level of development was factored out, a statistical artifact arising from the fact that the regression was heavily influenced by the extremely low degree of individual ownership by the societies with a herding-plus economic system.

b. The Semi-Marketized Farming System

The societies with this type of economic system were also widely distributed. Factoring out the impact of the level of economic development, they had significantly more trade with other communities, more wage labor within the community, and higher rents on land than other societies in the sample. They also had significantly less slavery, a function both of their greater contact with the West and the lesser need for unfree labor because the land owners could extract a surplus from their land by leasing it out at relatively high rents. Some characteristics of their economic system – for instance, greater individual ownership of fields, greater individual ownership of "empty land," greater tenancy, and higher taxes – were a function of their higher average level of economic development, not their economic system.

c. The Individualistic Farming System

Of the five societies classified as having an individualistic farming system, four were in Africa and the fifth was located in what is now a breakaway province of the Republic of Georgia. Factoring out the level of economic development, these societies have relatively few distinguishing characteristics. They did have significantly more slavery and less mutual aid between families – two characteristics that, I conjecture, were related. They also manifested higher absolute use rights to the land and higher rents on the land, even though their land scarcity – at least, as measured by population density – was not out of line with what could be predicted from their level of economic development. I argue herein that the societies with this type of economic system were marked by significantly more political centralization and both internal and external warfare, characteristics that made them more brittle.

4. Possible Biases in the Results

Because of the methods employed in selecting societies for the SCCS, certain areas of the world are not represented in my sample. That is, Murdock and White (1969) selected for the SCCS only one society from each culture area they isolated, and if they happened to choose a foraging society, my sample would inevitably lack an agricultural society for that area. Although this might have influenced the relative number of societies in each cluster, it is difficult to see how this could have affected the typology of four economic systems that emerged.

The SCCS does not include certain types of agricultural societies. For example, plantation economies where the major production units were large farms cultivated exclusively by wage laborers or slaves (see Pryor, 1982b) are not represented. Perhaps some of these societies, had they been included in my sample, would have formed a separate cluster. In addition, as noted previously, I have excluded all societies in the SCCS with less than 85 percent reliance on crop production and herding for their food so as to focus on relatively pure agricultural societies. As a result, those with an admixture of agriculture and foraging are also not represented, a reason why none of the societies in the sample had a full-blown "big-man" system of distribution.

Finally, as discussed in previous chapters, I focus primarily on local communities in analyzing the economic systems of preindustrial societies. Underlying my research design are two considerations. On a theoretical level, I follow Netting's argument (1990: 60) that "political centralization under a chiefdom or state regime contributes little directly to the organization of production, though government's role in military and defensive activities, enforcing tributary obligations, and promoting regional market exchange affect the farm household." By "organization of production," he seemed to include property rights and distribution. On a practical level, it turned out to be very difficult to assess the share of supracommunity governmental organs in the tax receipts or labor services. Nevertheless, in a later section of this chapter, I briefly investigate how several variables reflecting the centralization of the political system (including higher levels of government) correlate with the economic system. With one important exception, these variables do not show much relation to the economic systems.[17]

In brief, my sample does not represent all the agricultural societies in history that have ever existed, nor is it meant to. Rather, my purpose has been to study a range of relatively pure agricultural societies, to isolate some important economic systems, thereby constructing a preliminary framework for understanding agricultural economies in general. Equipped with such a scaffolding, we can gain perspective on those agricultural societies not represented in the sample without being overwhelmed by a tsunami of ethnographic and historical facts.

---

[17] One bias must be noted, however. In states or regions ruled by powerful chiefs, some activities of the central government and of overall political leaders are not reflected in my codes. For instance, even though the overall leader of the society might have been fabulously wealthy, local leaders of a community might not have been much richer than the average person.

5. System Labels: Mine and Others

I have tried to label the four economic systems according to their most prominent features. It is useful, however, to compare briefly my typology to classifications proposed by others, in particular, Marxists.[18]

The "Germanic mode of production" (Marx, 1953) most closely resembles what I call egalitarian farming societies. A major difference, however, is that many of the societies with this type of economic system in my sample were embedded in a more embracing polity – often a colonial power – even though the influence of that higher level of government on the community's economy was often slight, whereas Marx focused primarily on acephalous societies.

The concept of "feudalism" raises much more serious problems. For Marxists, according to Stanislav Andreski (1964: 401–2), the concept of feudalism "becomes an absolving ocean in which virtually any society may receive its baptism." After wading through several dozen definitions of the concept, I concluded in an earlier analysis (1980b: 57) that it is "so vague and loaded with so many conflicting connotations that it may be best to avoid the term altogether," a judgment I have since found no reason to retract.

If we define "feudalism" in terms of a military aristocracy organized through a system of vassalage to a sovereign, then such a political arrangement could certainly occur among the societies with semi-marketized or individualistic systems, especially if the impact of such a political arrangement manifested itself at the village level primarily in the collection of taxes. If we define feudalism in terms of a high rate of tenancy, a use of extensive unfree labor, and relatively little inter-community trade, then feudal societies would not fit easily into any of the four clusters, a function of the fact, as noted herein, that relatively few societies in my sample had extensive unfree labor. Finally, if we define feudalism in terms of a "natural" economy with relatively little commercial exchange within or between communities, the egalitarian and individualistic farming societies would be relevant. Because "feudalism" in Western Europe reflected these three sets of characteristics in different proportions at different times, the problem of finding a correspondence with my categories should be evident.

Finding a correspondence with the "Asian mode of production" raises yet other difficulties. In such societies, according to most Marxists, the key is

---

[18] I have selected the Marxist schema because it is often employed, not because I believe it to be particularly rigorous or useful (Pryor, 1982a). Some notion of the vagueness of the terminology can be seen in the dispute between Tökai (1979) and other Marxists about whether Tokugawa, Japan, represented a feudal society or some variant of the Asian mode of production.

irrigation, with a central government directing a major section of the economy by means of its control of the irrigation systems. Although 60 percent of the societies in my sample featured irrigation, most of them would not fit such a definition, for the irrigation waters came from wells or from rivers (e.g., the Nile) whose waters were ample for all users, or from relatively short rivers whose waters were not shared with other communities. The remaining societies with irrigation divided river waters with other villages through an elaborate system of inter-community bargaining, combined with schedules and enforcement mechanisms for allocating the allotted waters.

As Netting (1990: 55) notes, "Inter-village cooperation in irrigation does not presuppose central administration, and systems involving high capital investment of large-scale engineering seem to have followed from the prior existence of a state rather than contributing to its formation." In some of the societies in the sample, the use of irrigation waters seems to have been at least partially regulated by jurisdictions higher than that of a single village – for instance, the Incas of Peru around Cuzco, the Barusho (Hunzakut) of northeastern Pakistan, the Chinese village of Kaixiangong, and, to a certain extent, the Negri Sembilan of Malaysia. It is worth noting, however, that according to results of the cluster analysis, these four societies did not have the same economic system. In brief, the "Asian mode of production," with its exclusive focus on irrigation directed by a central authority over all villages, is not represented in my sample except, perhaps, with the exception of the Barusho.

C. Possible Determinants of the Types of Economic Systems: Demography and Environment

In the following discussion, I investigate the causal role of two relatively exogenous factors, demography and environment, on the economic system; in the subsequent section I examine three more endogenous variables that might have also been important. As in Chapter 2, I approach this problem by examining correlations between a variety of variables and the economic system, factoring out the impact of the level of economic development.[19] If

---

[19] In all cases, I have calculated ordinary least-square regressions of the following sort:

$$I = a + b \, \text{DevLev} + c \, \text{EcSys},$$

where I = indicator, DevLev = level of economic development; EcSys = economic system, and a, b, and c are the calculated regression coefficients. I used this regression form because it is unclear in which direction causality runs, and this regression form is more familiar than the probit-specification used previously.

the variable is not significantly related to the economic system, then a causal relationship can be ruled out; if the relationship is statistically significant, then I try to determine whether the variable under examination is the cause of the system, or an effect, or neither. The relevant data are presented in Table 4-3.

1. Demographic Variables

The societies with a herding-plus economic system were nomadic, with one major exception discussed previously. It is, therefore, not surprising that they had both a lower population density and a smaller community size than other societies in the sample. Obviously, neither density nor community size were determinants of the system.

The significantly higher population density of the societies with a semi-marketized system did have an important influence on the characteristics of the system. For an explanation, it is useful to turn to the open resource hypothesis developed at the turn of the twentieth century by the Dutch anthropologist Herman Nieboer (1971). "Open resources" could be found in low-density areas where land for crop production was easy to obtain and relatively little capital or complex technological knowledge was necessary for agricultural production. In such a situation, "every able-bodied man can, by taking a piece of land into cultivation, provide for himself. Hence it follows that nobody voluntarily services another; he who wants a labourer must subject him, and this subjection will often assume the character of slavery" (p. 298). In analyzing this hypothesis, Evsey Domar (1970) argued that of the "three elements of agriculture – free land, free peasants, and nonworking landowners – any two elements but *never all three can exist simultaneously*. The combination to be found in reality will depend on the behavior of political factors."

The societies with a semi-marketized system had higher tenancy and no unfree labor; in previous centuries, they had unfree labor (4-9) but to a lower degree than the other types of economic systems. Because their land was individually owned and sufficiently scarce that those without land were forced to rent it, land owners could extract a surplus without using unfree labor, a result quite consistent with the Nieboer–Domar hypothesis.

Although my sample does not have a sufficient number of societies with unfree labor to prove this hypothesis, my data are suitable for exploring one important implication: namely, that slavery was not an inevitable evolutionary step as the level of economic development increased. Both of my series on slavery (4-9 and 4-10) show a slight increase and later a slight decrease

Table 4-3. *Possible determinants of agricultural economic systems: demography and environment*

Variable Number	Description	Range	Development Elasticity	Average Scores					Total Sample
				Hd+	Eg	IF	SM		
Development level (Carneiro scale)		(0–600)		**188**	**255**	282	**506**		325
Demographic variables									
5-18	Density (population/square mile)	unbounded	**+0.25**	**3.63**$^{-?}$	4.64	4.80	**6.25**$^{+?}$		4.95
4-25	Average community size	(1–9)	**+0.53**	**2.56**$^-$	**6.86**$^+$	6.20	8.00		6.24
Climate variables									
5-7	Precipitation (mm)	unbounded	−0.24	**826**$^{+?}$	1,523	960	1,201		1,159
5-8	Actual evapo-transpiration (mm)	unbounded	−0.10	524	914	646	976		797
5-9	Rainfall seasonality	unbounded	−0.08	5.38	1.93	1.25	1.42		2.57
5-10	Effective temperature (°C)	unbounded	−0.05	**15.2**$^{-?}$	18.3	16.7	17.9		17.3
5-11	Altitude (meters)	unbounded	−0.61	**1,710**$^+$	494	711	452		793
Farming variables									
5-12	Slope of terrain (steep = 4, level = 8)	(4–8)	−0.01	6.38	6.27	5.60	6.75		6.41
5-13	Soil quality for farming (0 = poor)	(0–8)	+0.08	4.38	3.73	3.60	4.25		4.08
5-14	Suitability of climate for major crops (0 = very poor; 8 = very good)	(0–8)	+0.03	5.25	6.55	6.80	6.42		6.22
5-15	Famine threat (1 = low; 4 = high)	(1–4)	−0.01	2.80	2.84	2.92	2.34		2.67
4-23	Irrigation (0 = absent; 1 = considerable)	(0–1)	**+0.23**	0.25	0.59	0.40	0.92		0.58
5-4	Animal husbandry ratio	(0–1)	−0.18	**0.78**$^+$	**0.22**$^-$	0.48	0.22		0.38

Agricultural potential

5-16	Sum of suitability of terrain, soil, and climate (4 = extremely poor; 24 = best for agriculture)	(4–24)	+0.02	16.0	16.5	16.0	17.4	16.7
5-17	Lowest value of rating for terrain, soil, and climate suitability (0 = lowest; 8 = best for agriculture)	(0–8)	+0.06	4.00	3.55	3.40	3.92	3.78

Note: Hd+ = herding-plus system; Eg = egalitarian farming system; IF = individualistic farming system; SM = semi-marketized farming system. The development elasticity indicates the percentage change in the indicator under examination to a 1 percent change in the level of economic development. For all the values in the table, boldface indicates statistical significance; if there is no question mark in the superscript, the level of significance is 0.05; otherwise, it is 0.10. The significance tests for the average scores are made when the development level is held constant (a procedure explained in the text) and, in the superscript, the sign indicates the direction of significance.

These labels for the economic systems are explained in the text. The individual codings, as well as their sources, are described in greater detail in Appendix 4-1. The variable number refers to the number of the variable in the Appendix and also in Statistical Appendix Tables SA-4 and SA-5, which gives the values for the different societies and indicators.

in slavery as the average level of economic development rises. Contrary to classic Marxist theory, however, my data on slavery show no significant relationship, either lineal or quadratic, with the level of economic development. In the range of development levels where slavery appeared in some societies, many did not have slavery, either at the pinpointed date or in the previous two centuries before Western colonial powers had banned slavery. I have also analyzed such results elsewhere on somewhat different grounds, with a different data set and at greater length (Pryor, 1977a). In any case, as population density grew, the distribution of land became increasingly commercialized, and unfree labor, if it ever existed, became increasingly less necessary for producing income for land owners.

Community size did not greatly differ between the societies concentrating on crop production with the three different types of economic systems.[20] The significant relation between community size and the egalitarian economic system is merely a statistical artifact reflecting the sharp differences between the three crop-producing economic systems and the societies with a herding-plus system. Both higher population densities and larger community were, however, significantly associated with higher levels of economic development.

2. Environmental Variables

I use three rainfall indicators: precipitation, evapo-transpiration, and rainfall seasonality.[21] The actual precipitation experienced in a region is of less relevance than the water actually available for agriculture, as measured by evapo-transpiration. Calculation of the latter requires knowledge of soil conditions and plant cover; fortunately, climatologists have taken great pains

---

[20] When I calculated regressions similar to those underlying Table 4-2 but without the societies with a herding-plus economic system for variable 4-25, I found no significant differences between the three types of economic systems.

   The relationship among the level of economic development, community size, and density discussed at the end of the paragraph was calculated in a regression with the level of economic development as the dependent variable and with population density and village size as the explanatory variables. The coefficient of determination is 0.42, and the calculated coefficients for both explanatory variables are statistically significant at the 0.05 level.

[21] Roughly speaking, evapo-transpiration is the water available to plants for maintenance and growth (i.e., rainfall minus the water runoff and the water that percolates into the earth). Rainfall seasonality is the ratio of potential to actual transpiration, where potential evapo-transpiration is the maximum amount of water that plants in the area can use for maintenance and growth without becoming waterlogged.

to make such estimates. Effective temperature is more relevant for farming than is average temperature because it reflects the length of the growing season.[22] The various farming variables should be self-explanatory and the variables indicating agricultural potential are composite variables using data for three of the farming variables.

The societies with a herding-plus economic system were found in significantly drier and colder locations and at higher altitudes than the other societies in my sample. These sites were less suitable for crop production. The three types of economic systems with societies focusing primarily on crop production did not significantly differ from each other with regard to all five climate variables, all the farming variables (except for the share of animal husbandry), and the two composite variables for agricultural potential. In brief, we cannot explain the presence of these three economic systems by pointing to any particular feature of their environment.

D. Possible Determinants of the Types of Economic Systems: Other Factors

1. Cultural Diffusion

Anthropologists usually speak of cultural diffusion in terms of the transplantation of particular characteristics or technologies. Some even go further and suggest that one society could have a sufficient impact on another (through conquest or extensive contact) to influence its institutions and economic system. This phenomenon can be examined from several viewpoints.

From a geographical perspective, if particular types of economic systems diffuse, societies located close to each other would be more likely to have the same economic system. However, when the societies with each economic system are plotted on a map (a feature of many cluster-analysis computer programs), such bunching does not seem apparent. If we divide the world into four regions (Sub-Saharan Africa, Circum-Mediterranean and West Asia, East Asia, and the Americas) and use a simple chi-square test, we find that the distribution of economic systems among these four areas shows no significant deviation from what the overall distribution of societies in these

---

[22] More specifically, it is calculated with a formula that takes into account the temperature in the hottest and coldest months to determine the impact of seasonal temperature fluctuations. Kelly (1995: 66) discusses this measure at greater length.

areas would lead us to suspect. In brief, cultural diffusion, at least from a geographical perspective, was not present.

From a temporal perspective, however, the situation was much different. The West had several important influences on these agricultural societies: "external trade" (i.e., the exchange of goods with other communities, particularly urban centers offering modern goods) increased; certain institutions of servitude, such as slavery, were forcibly eliminated; and wage labor outside the community to obtain "modern money"assumed greater importance. Furthermore, the later the pinpointed observation date of the community, the longer such processes had time to work themselves out.

It seems likely, therefore, that those societies with a semi-marketized economic system were pinpointed at a more recent date than other societies and the societies with a herding-plus or egalitarian systems, at an earlier date. These conjectures are confirmed by the data.[23] This means that my sample is biased in the sense that it is not representative of all of the agricultural societies that have ever existed. Nevertheless, such results should not have much of an impact on the distinguishing characteristics of the individual types of economic systems.

2. Political Variables

Table 4-4 provides the starting point for exploring the role of political institutions as determinants or, at least, as correlates of agricultural economic systems. I focus particularly on warfare and on political centralization, which is a composite variable to measure various aspects of the power of the leader.[24]

When the impact of the development level was factored out, the individualistic farming system had significantly higher warfare, both external and internal (civil war), and a relatively high degree of political centralization (missing significance at the 0.10 level by just a shade). In a sense, we are

---

[23] More specifically, I used the pinpointed date as the explanatory variable and the economic system as the variable to be explained and regressed this against the date. To avoid influencing the results by extreme values of the dates, I recoded them: before 1825 = 1; 1825 to 1874 = 2; 1875 to 1924 = 3; 1925 and thereafter = 4. The herding-plus and the egalitarian economic systems were significantly and inversely related to the dates; the semi-marketized economic system was significantly and positively related to the pinpointed dates. It is noteworthy that the pinpointed dates had no significant relationship with the relative level of economic development.

[24] More specifically, it is an unweighted average of five variables: the relative wealth of the local political leader, his relative power, the manner of his selection (i.e., through consensus or inheritance), the elaborateness of the local political hierarchy, and the level of village sovereignty (i.e., whether the village was self-ruling or whether it was subordinate to higher political units).

Table 4-4. *Possible determinants of agricultural economic systems: other variables*

Variable Number	Description	Range	Development Elasticity	Average Scores				
				Hd+	Eg	IF	SM	Total
Development level (Carneiro scale)		(0–600)		**188**	**255**	**282**	**506**	325
Political variables								
4-24	Extent of local political centralization	(0–4)	**+0.42**	1.69	1.66	2.41	**2.06**⁻?	1.90
5-19	Extent of internal warfare	(1–17)	+0.08	11.00	**6.1**⁻?	**15.7**⁺?	10.40	9.80
5-20	Extent of external warfare	(1–17)	+0.15	10.10	6.20	**15.8**⁺	7.80	9.20
5-21	War for land (low to high)	(0–1)	−0.01	0.50	0.18	0.33	0.42	0.34
Social variables								
5-24	Presence of corporate lineage groups	(0–1)	**−0.14**	0.88	1.00	1.00	0.67	0.86
5-25	Postmarital residence (matrilocal = 1; patrilocal = 4)	(1–4)	−0.09	4.00	3.45	4.00	3.00	3.43
5-26	Presence of polygyny (low to high)	(1–4)	−0.06	3.13	3.27	3.20	**2.58**⁻?	3.00
5-27	Extent of cousin marriage (low to high)	(0–5)	−0.11	3.75	**4.45**⁺	1.67	2.18	3.32
4-22	Social inequalities of free population	(1–3)	**+0.19**	2.31	**2.00**⁻	**2.80**⁺	2.58	2.36
5-23	Percentage of subsistence production by women	(0–1)	−0.09	0.36	0.39	**0.20**⁻	**0.28**⁻	0.32
5-22	Male dominance (low to high)	(1–3)	**−0.09**?	2.38	1.88	2.00	2.10	2.10
Economic variables								
4-26	Capital intensity of production	(0–4)	+0.15	**3.88**⁺	**2.36**⁻	3.80	3.25	3.22
4-27	Extent of fixed rents on land (low to high)	(0–4)	**+0.52**	0.50	**0.64**⁻	**2.88**⁺	**2.92**⁺	1.60
4-28	Extent of gambling	(1–3)	**+0.23**	1.19	1.20	1.83	1.83	1.47

Note: Hd+ = herding-plus system; Eg = egalitarian farming system; IF = individualistic farming system; SM = semi-marketized farming system. The development elasticity indicates the percentage change in the indicator under examination to a 1 percent change in the level of economic development. For all the values in the table, boldface indicates statistical significance; if there is no question mark in the superscript, the level of significance is 0.05; otherwise, it is 0.10. The significance tests for the average scores are made when the development level is held constant (a procedure explained in the text) and, in the superscript, the sign indicates the direction of significance.

These labels for the economic systems are explained in the text. The individual codings, as well as their sources, are described in greater detail in Appendix 4-1. The variable number refers to the number of the variable in the Appendix and also in Statistical Appendix Tables SA-4 and SA-5, which gives the values for the different societies and indicators.

dealing with a tautology because a major reason for centralizing political authority was to fight wars. It is noteworthy, however, that the motive for these external wars was not necessarily to gain land (5-21) but rather to obtain booty, women, tribute, and renown. As noted herein, societies with this economic system also had a significantly higher degree of social inequality. Such features suggest that these societies were relatively brittle and that they might partly explain why the sample contained half as many societies with this type of economic system as the other two types of economic systems oriented toward crop production. Their significantly less mutual aid in farming (Table 4-2) was undoubtedly related to these political and social features as well.

By way of contrast, the societies with an egalitarian economic system had significantly less internal warfare and the societies with a semi-marketized system had significantly less political centralization when the impact of the level of economic development was factored out. In this latter case, the greater emphasis on market activities seemed to overbalance the necessity for (or interest in) powerful political leaders.

Although the correlations noted in the table provide a more rounded picture of the four types of economic systems, it is difficult to imagine a mechanism by which they could be considered as determinants of the system, at least for the societies in my sample. Rather, the political and economic characteristics of these economic systems were more likely to have emerged together.

The lack of any significant relation between three of the four types of economic systems and the level of political centralization to the economic system should not mask the fact that the functions of the political leadership in the various types of economic systems were quite different. In the herding societies, the political leadership in the community, as well as supracommunity political leaders, often coordinated the routes and schedules of the seasonal migrations. In semi-marketized systems, the political leadership focused more attention on adjudicating contract disputes and land-ownership rights. In those societies with slavery, the political leadership was more concerned with the use of coercion to enforce the slave system and keeping the system together. In societies with an egalitarian system, governmental roles were more diffuse. In very few societies did the centralized political authorities centrally direct production, except to extract certain types of tribute-in-kind from particular communities or maintain irrigation. For instance, the famous roads of the Incas were built primarily to increase the tribute from subordinate villages and facilitate its delivery. Otherwise, the villages were left to rule themselves and govern their economy.[25]

3. Social Variables

The literature in anthropology places enormous stress on social structure and its importance for distinguishing different types of societies, in major part because these kinship factors organized people's life cycle and determined to a considerable extent their access to the wherewithal for subsistence. Once we turn from analysis of the economy to the economic system, however, the importance of the social structure becomes more problematic.

As we would expect, social inequalities of the free population were significantly lower among the societies with an egalitarian economic system and significantly higher among the societies with an individualistic system (which also had a higher incidence of slavery). Table 4-4 also shows several other significant correlations. Nevertheless, it seems unlikely that these scattered social relations were important determinants of the economic system. For instance, the societies with a semi-marketized economic system had less polygyny and the societies with an egalitarian system had more flexibility in cross-cousin marriages; but, the contribution of these such factors to the emergence of the economic system is, to say the least, obscure.

4. Economic Factors

Table 4-4 includes three economic variables that were not determinants of the economic system but might have been related to the functioning of the economy.

---

[25] In certain times and places, the governments of agricultural societies – usually with relatively commercialized economies – also took measures to maintain adequate food supplies. Sometimes the preferred policies were those encouraging markets. For instance, in eighteenth-century Japan, the government maintained national markets for grain and took measures to reduce transportation and transaction costs in using such markets. In other cases, more direct interventions using state granaries were employed. Such a system had ancient roots (undoubtedly much further back in time than the system devised by Joseph for the Pharaoh) and was particularly well developed in eighteenth-century China, where the government used this stored grain both to supply food during famines and to control price fluctuations (various essays in Will and Wong, 1991). Unfortunately, the extent to which any of these measures had a marked influence on the economic system of the various communities is unknown, although in most cases it seems unlikely that the impact was very great.

Capital intensity of production included both cattle and equipment for crop production. It depended in part on physical factors, such as the availability of rivers for irrigation or the hilliness of the terrain, or on the suitability of cultivation of certain grains, which lent themselves to plow agriculture (e.g., wheat), in contrast to certain root crops that did not require so much use of the plow (a proposition discussed by Pryor, 1985b). It also depended on whether the political leaders had the means to coerce people into creating such capital (e.g., irrigation systems).

Obviously, the societies with a herding-plus system had a significantly higher degree of capital intensity because of the importance of flocks for their subsistence. The societies with an egalitarian system had a significantly lower degree of capital intensity, which, of course, was related to their lower level of economic development. Once a certain average level of economic development is achieved, however, this relationship with capital intensity no longer seemed to hold, a result I find puzzling.

The other two economic variables are related to economic risks borne by members of the society. Share rents (sharecropping) or labor rents divide the risks of a poor crop between the renter and the land owner, whereas a fixed rent places the risk of a poor crop entirely on the shoulders of the renter. The societies with an egalitarian system were significantly more likely to have share rents, whereas crop-producing societies with the other two types of economic systems were significantly more likely to have fixed rents.

One measure of attitudes toward risk is the incidence of gambling. As noted in Chapter 2, this economic activity was found in a number of foraging societies. It was, however, relatively infrequent in agricultural societies, perhaps because gambling losses could have had more severe consequences. That is, in foraging societies, a person who lost in gambling could go out and forage more food or, perhaps, borrow food from others because these societies featured much greater food sharing (a feature minimizing production risk) than agricultural societies. In the latter societies, by way of contrast, gambling losses could result in a loss of herds or seed stock, so that a family would fall below the minimum level necessary to sustain itself in the next year – a serious matter in a situation where it was more difficult to borrow food.[26] Once the level of economic development is factored out, the incidence of gambling was not significantly different in any type of economic

---

[26] It is sometimes argued that foragers had much more leisure time than agriculturalists. As a colleague has suggested, if this were true, then they would have had more time to gamble. Although this conjecture may have been true for the Hazda (of Tanzania), it did not hold for the !Kung (of the Kalahari desert).

system. Such results, which reflect a tolerance for risk, suggests that the difference in the frequency of fixed rents was not due to any different attitudes toward risk.

E. Systemic Change in Agricultural Economic Systems

Two kinds of changes warrant brief discussion: namely, changes from one agricultural economic system to another, and changes in the focus of production either from agriculture back to foraging or from agriculture to industry.

1. From One Agricultural System to Another

For many of the societies in the sample – or, for that matter, for most agricultural economies in general – we do not have a very clear picture of how the economic system evolved. One notable exception is Haiti, where we know that between 1850 and 1934, average farm size in the peasant economy of Haiti shrank greatly (due to increasing population), land holdings became more splintered, and the extended-family compound became less common. From additional information, we can make some inferences about changes in its economic system. Nevertheless, because the historical records of most of the other societies in the sample are not sufficient to provide much systematic evidence to make useful generalizations, we must be content with isolated narratives, of which the rise and fall of feudalism in Europe is the most documented case. Various case studies suggest a variety of causes underlying such systemic changes, of which several deserve particular mention.

DEMOGRAPHIC FACTORS. From the previous discussion, it seems highly likely that in certain circumstances, increasing population density played a critical role in pushing agricultural societies toward a more marketized economic system. For instance, from the beginning of the nineteenth century to the end of the twentieth century, as the population density increased, the society of the Haitian countryside appeared to move from an individualistic economic system based on slave plantations to an incipient egalitarian system and then, as the population density continued to rise and as landlords acquired more and more of the land, to a semi-marketized system. But, population density was not necessarily the key aspect in other societies. As Postan and Hatcher (1985) point out, increasing population density and growing exports in Eastern Europe during the fifteenth and sixteenth centuries were accompanied by the introduction of serfdom, not a semi-marketized economic system.

POLITICAL FACTORS. External conquest often led to dramatic systemic changes – for instance, the changes occurring in England after the Norman invasion. But, internal conquest – the use of force by domestic groups – could also account for changes in the economic system: for instance, the enserfment of the free peasantry in Eastern Europe. Even the threat of conquest has had a systemic impact: In the early Middle Ages in Europe, the fear of marauders from without provided an incentive to relinquish land rights to a domestic political leader for protection.

PRODUCTION SHOCKS. If farmers experienced a crop failure and were not helped through the crisis by some type of redistribution of community food resources, they would have to pledge their lands to obtain food. The inability to repay such debts could have led to both a centralization of land ownership or even, in more extreme cases, a systemic change, which might have been the case of Iceland during the Middle Ages. Of course, if there were institutions facilitating debt forgiveness (e.g., the year of the Jubilee among the ancient Hebrews), then the tendency for money lenders to accumulate more and more land might have been mitigated.

TECHNOLOGY SHOCKS. The role of technological changes has often been misinterpreted because the mere availability of a new technology does not mean that it would have been adopted. Under certain conditions, however, agricultural innovations – new crops, farming techniques, tools, or sources of power – could trigger a shift from one type of agricultural system to another. This might occur, for instance, by the creation of a surplus, which would encourage more commercialization. On the other hand, such technological changes might not be adopted if, for instance, the existing system relied on unfree labor and those actually carrying out the farming had no incentive to introduce such changes because the gains would have been taken away from them.

CLASS STRUGGLE. According to Robert Brenner (1985: 213), demographic and commercial trends "acquire their economic significance for distribution of income and development of the productive forces only in connection with specific, historically developed systems of social-property relations and given balances of class forces." Under different property structures and a different balance of power, similar demographic or commercial trends – with their associated patterns of factor prices – could lead to much different results, at least in societies where landlords were important.

This means that we cannot focus just on dramatic revolutionary events, such as the sudden overthrow of the slave plantation system that occurred in Haiti. Rather, we must take into account more protracted struggles, such as that between the serfs and lords in late medieval Europe (various essays in Aston and Philpin, 1985). Interpretative problems arise because, within many preindustrial agricultural communities outside of Europe, social groups based on gender, age, kinship, or occupation were often much more socially relevant than social class for understanding the operations of the economic system. Moreover, as many anthropologists have pointed out, agricultural communities often took special measures to dampen or diffuse group conflicts. Thus, even in the most rigidly stratified communities, such as the Indian village of Senapur in Uttar Pradesh in my sample, the class or caste struggle was covert rather than open. At any given time, this conflict often focused on very small issues, not easily caught in the snapshots used in cross-sectional analyses. As a result, for many areas of the world we have relatively little comparable information on how the community economic systems were transformed as a result of inter-group conflicts about existing property relations, even though such struggles may have been the most stimuli for major systemic transformations.

2. Changes in the Focus of Production

In Chapter 3, I examine the "progressive" transition from foraging to agriculture, and in Chapter 5, I analyze a similar progressive transition from agriculture to industry. But a "regressive" transition deserves brief mention at this point: namely, from agriculture back to foraging.

As many have discussed, the introduction of the horse to the American West represented a major technological innovation by making it possible to live by gathering and by hunting buffalo rather than by agriculture. As a result, many groups of Plains Indians turned away from farming to foraging. A less-known example is that of the Moriori of Chatham Island in the South Pacific. They were originally Maori and may have relied primarily on farming. After landing on an island with a very rich foraging base, however, they abandoned agriculture and became foragers (Diamond, 1999: 54 ff). In this case, the demographic mechanism discussed previously was working in reverse; to maintain a low population density, they employed such means as castrating some male children.

F. A Brief Summary

Using a worldwide sample of forty-one agriculture communities and employing a cluster analysis of twenty-two institutions or organizations relating
to property relations and the distribution of goods and services, I isolate four
basic types of economic systems: herding-plus, egalitarian, individualistic,
and semi-marketized. Although in several cases external variables had some
impact on certain systemic characteristics of these societies (e.g., the high
land density of the societies with a semi-marketized system, the centralized
political system of the societies with an individualistic system), other features
of their physical environment, geographical location, or social or political
structure did not appear to determine the economic system. This result, of
course, is dramatically at odds with a common assumption among many
anthropologists that particular social structures were the key causal forces
in determining how the economy functioned and that the economic system
was merely an epiphenomenon unworthy of study in its own right.

The delineation of agricultural economic systems provides us with a
broader perspective of preindustrial agricultural societies to bring to case
studies of individual communities so that we are not overwhelmed by isolated facts. The isolation of the four economic systems provides a useful
framework for analyzing a variety of economic activities and for separating
those features of the economy that are common to all agricultural societies
or that are common only among those economies with the same economic
system from those features that are unique to particular societies.

The societies with a herding-plus system have been generally (but not
always) found among societies with relatively low levels of economic development. Holding their development level constant, they featured group
rather than individual ownership of land, low tenancy, small communities,
low population densities, and high inequalities of wealth (but not social
inequalities). Although primarily herders, this group included one settled
crop-producing society that shared many of these characteristics.

Societies at the middle level of economic development were likely to have
one of two economic systems. Holding the level of development constant, the
societies with an egalitarian economic system had no slavery, little tenancy,
low inequalities of wealth and low social inequalities, a relatively low amount
of trade with other communities, and less internal strife. They also had the
lowest average level of economic development of the three economic systems
focused on crop production. Holding the level of development constant, the
societies with an individualistic system appeared the least stable. They had
significantly less mutual aid, high fixed land rents, high social inequalities,

greater internal and external warfare, and, in most cases, greater political centralization.

The societies with a semi-marketized system were generally found at the highest levels of economic development. Holding their development level constant, they featured more trade with other communities, more wage labor within the community and less slavery, high fixed land rents, a high population density, and, for its level of development, a low degree of political centralization. On average, these societies also had a much higher level of economic development than the other societies.

The cluster analysis also explains less of the differences between these agricultural societies than the other types of economic systems explored in this study. This means that the complementarities among institutions were less strong, so that the logic of institutions leads us to greater uncertainty about the exact delineation of these systems.

This chapter could not resolve several basic issues. The far distant pasts of most of these agricultural societies are lost in the mists of history and, because the search for outside determinants of various types of economic systems was unsuccessful, we cannot know how these systems originated. Further, the impact of these types of economic systems on economic performance could not be determined because of lack of suitable macroeconomic data for the analysis. This topic, instead, must be approached through case studies, a type of research beyond the scope of this book. Finally, I have left unanswered how and why some of these societies evolved into industrial/ service economies, whereas others did not. This is the focus of the next chapter.

FIVE

From Agriculture to Industry

Although economic historians have intensely discussed the ultimate causes of the industrial revolution for more than a century, they have found little agreement. Was it differential population growth that changed the land-labor ratio and wages? Or the modernization of traditional rural society by land enclosures? Or the growth of foreign trade through colonial expansion? Or the overthrow of absolutist regimes and the reduction of uncertainty of property rights? Or the rise in urbanization and literacy? Or the increase in a nation's economic infrastructure?

It is not my intention to deal in this chapter with the industrial revolution in its entirety but rather to focus on one small part of the issue. In the previous chapter, I touched briefly on certain aspects of the systemic change of agricultural economic systems. In this chapter, I explore at greater length a critical aspect of these dynamic systemic elements: namely, the extent to which, in past centuries, the type of agricultural economic system aided or hindered the transformation to an industrial/service economy. Thus, many of the issues raised previously – for instance, the impact of the growth of the Atlantic trade – cannot be handled. The role of intermediaries between the farmers and the urban sector – for instance, small shopkeepers, traveling merchants, and financiers – is also left undiscussed. Nevertheless, we cannot avoid facing certain problems arising from the complexity of the causal connections between agriculture and manufacturing and the difficulties in pinning down the multifaceted nature of industrialization.

According to E. L. Jones and S. J. Woolf (1969: 1), "One of the less palatable lessons of history is that technically advanced and physically productive agricultures do not inevitably bring along a sustained growth in per capita real income, much less promote industrialization." They use ancient China, Rome, and the Mayans as examples to argue their case. But, this immediately raises the issue of whether the agricultural sector is at all relevant for the transition to manufacturing. At least in theory, the agricultural sector may have little to do with industrialization because a nation can always follow a dualistic pattern of development; that is, it might export the products of its urban sector for agricultural products from other countries, thereby ignoring its own agricultural sector except as a pool of labor. European industrialization in the eighteenth and nineteenth centuries did not feature such a pattern of dualism; but, in the twentieth century, examples include states such as Hong Kong and Singapore, which had almost no agricultural sectors at all. More common cases of dualism include cases where the agricultural sector was neglected and the new factories were located in the towns so that income differences between urban and rural areas widened dramatically.[1]

Unfortunately, industrialization cannot be easily carried out by examining individual communities, which has been the major unit of analysis in the previous chapters. Instead, it is necessary to focus on the entire agricultural economy of a country and to use a sample of nations, rather than communities, for the empirical comparisons. Unlike the previous chapters, however, we are no longer confined to a cross section of societies or nations at a single point in time because we have sufficient data to look at the role of agriculture in industrialization as an historical process.

Consideration of such broad issues requires some initial attention to several key definitions.[2] Then, I explore several crucial characteristics of the rural sector of countries that were the earliest to industrialize: namely, widespread literacy, high agricultural productivity, considerable marketization of the countryside, and land-tenure arrangements encouraging entrepreneurial attitudes. These results, in turn, allow a focused discussion of those features of community agricultural economic systems discussed in the previous chapter that would be related to these national characteristics. More specifically, of the four agricultural systems defined in the previous chapter, the societies with semi-marketized economic systems were (and are) most likely

---

[1] In recent years, development economists have focused considerable analytic efforts on investigating the relationship between the growth of agricultural and industrial production. For instance, Hwa (1988) uses a large cross-section of evidence from the post-World War II period to demonstrate a positive correlation (although the direction of causality is unclear) in growth of these two sectors. And, of course, there is a certain complementarity between agriculture and manufacturing in that rural manufacturing can take advantage of off-peak economic activity in agriculture and urban workers in many areas can temporarily leave their work to help with the harvest. Despite this general correlation between agricultural and manufacturing growth, the arguments in the text still apply.

[2] One additional methodological issue is discussed in Appendix 5-1: namely, whether my primary focus on industrialization in Europe biases my conclusions.

to manifest those rural characteristics most favorable for industrialization. Such an approach, which focuses primarily on rural institutions, sidesteps issues about the "prime causes" of industrialization to highlight the contributions of the agricultural economic system.[3]

A. Distinguishing Manufacturing, Proto-Manufacturing, and the Industrialization Threshold

1. Definition of Some Relevant Concepts

In exploring the transition from foraging to agriculture in Chapter 3, it proved necessary to distinguish agriculture from proto-agriculture. At this point, it is necessary to differentiate manufacturing from proto-manufacturing.

In a very general sense, *industry* is the processing of raw materials to make goods whose possession will, in turn, be transferred or sold to others. *Craft work* is industrial production carried out at home or in small workshops with simple hand tools or human-powered machinery. By way of contrast, *manufacturing* is industrial production carried out in centralized sites using considerable machinery powered by some source external to the immediate workplace. Finally, *proto-manufacturing* includes many forms of industry between craft work and manufacturing – for instance, small-scale flour mills, glass production, or brick-making – which use some external sources of power but have only a relatively small labor force at a single location, or

---

[3] My focus on the impact of the agricultural sector in the industrialization process means that I do not deal with the critical role of the state (e.g., in setting tariff rates or promoting industry), the urban sector in general, new inventions, or underlying economic factors such as resource endowment, comparative advantage, or first-mover advantages. These omissions should not be interpreted to mean that I believe industrialization was agricultural-led, as opposed to technology- or state-led. In Appendix 5-3, however, I do explore briefly whether a change in general economic values in the various nations was a necessary condition for their industrialization.

In the following discussion, I also deliberately avoid talking about "feudalism" and "capitalism." According to Richard Grassby (1999: 63), "Capitalism can be defined in terms of the market economy, the growth of financial markets, and consumerism, all of which clearly preceded industrialization. And most of the characteristics associated with it [capitalism], including those of modernity, were clearly a consequence of the Industrial Revolution . . . Ironically, the literature has always focused on the transition from feudalism, not on the transition to industrialization." Although many, such as Karl Marx, considered factory production as the paradigmatic capitalist production form, of course, such factories can be cooperatively or communally owned and industrialization can follow a socialist path.

certain textile "factories," which employ a large, supervised labor force but make relatively little use of external sources of power. Proto-manufacturing also includes the putting-out system, where a coordinator supplies inputs to a large number of home workers (e.g., wool to make yarn) and then sells or transfers the product to others.[4] In the eighteenth century, most proto-manufacturing took place in rural or semi-rural areas for three reasons: to be closer to the sources of raw materials, to take advantage of a cheaper and readily available labor supply, and to avoid guild restrictions. Considerable controversy about proto-manufacturing has arisen among economic historians, and I deal with many of these issues later in this chapter when discussing various aspects of marketization of the rural sector.

Finally, an economy is *industrializing* when the volume of manufacturing production, the share of the labor force employed in that sector, and labor productivity in manufacturing are all rising.[5] According to this definition, the presence of a free labor force or of markets is not necessary. It would include the growth of factories employing either slaves (e.g., the sugar mills in the eighteenth-century Caribbean lands or the urban factories in the U.S. pre-Civil War South[6]) or serfs (e.g., the mills and mines in eighteenth-century Russia and other Eastern European lands).

Although markets may aid industrialization, they are neither a necessary nor a sufficient condition for the growth of manufacturing because markets have existed throughout history where industrialization did not occur. Nevertheless, in the eighteenth and nineteenth centuries, as I show herein, a high degree of marketization was strongly correlated with industrialization. To confuse matters, some Marxist nations, such as North Vietnam

---

[4] The economic history literature generally employs the term "proto-industry" for such production arrangements and its meaning has shifted somewhat since it was introduced. My concept of proto-manufacturing includes production exclusively intended for local markets and located in either rural or urban areas, whereas the term *proto-industry* often does not. A number of other terms related to proto-manufacturing are also in usage: "industrialization before industrialization" (Kriedte et al., 1981), cottage industry, domestic industry, rural industry, rural handicrafts (used loosely), and (for Russia) *kustar* industry. My concept is tailored to Paul Bairoch's usage, which is used in my estimates of the threshold of industrialization.

 Although proto-manufacturing was carried out very often in the home (or its outbuildings), it does not include production carried out by a family for its own use. It also does not include the work of many small shopkeepers unless they manufactured goods for sale.

[5] This seemingly mundane definition of industrialization is not standard. For instance, Charles Tilly (1982) argues that industrialization consists of the creation of a significant proletariat (i.e., wage laborers without land or other capital) carrying out industrial work in *any* type of workshop. Thus, he would argue that the proto-factories in rural Europe represented an early form of industrialization, albeit without a concentration of capital.

[6] These factories and their impact are analyzed by Goldin (1976).

and North Korea, began industrializing in the second half of the twentieth century without extensive markets in the context of a centrally planned economy, at least between factories.[7] To keep the discussion in this chapter straightforward, however, I defer discussion of these nonmarket cases until Chapter 8.

Several immediate implications of these definitions deserve mention. Industry is not a recent phenomenon: In the form of craft work, it has been present to a limited extent in many foraging and agricultural societies. Moreover, throughout history, industry has not been tied to urban areas. Finally, craft work did not inevitably lead to proto-manufacturing and, as I discuss herein, proto-manufacturing did not inevitably lead to manufacturing.

2. Dating the Threshold of Industrialization

Although the *industrial revolution* is a common term representing some arbitrary point or span of time in which this process occurred, it raises some obvious problems of historical dating. For instance, various economic historians have dated the industrial revolution in England to as early as the last decades of the seventeenth century or as late as the first decades of the nineteenth century; most, however, seem to place it as occurring between 1750 and 1815. For my purposes, a more useful term is the *industrialization threshold*. This represents the point at which manufacturing production in a nation passed a certain level, which I place as the per capita level of manufacturing production in England in 1778; this date represents a rough average of the various dates for the industrial revolution in England that I have found in the literature. Using Paul Bairoch's (1982) estimates of manufacturing in different nations since the seventeenth century, I have calculated the date of this threshold for other nations in the sample. If I had selected another level of per capita manufacturing production, the dates of the threshold of industrialization in other countries would have changed, but the rank order would remain roughly the same and the conclusions drawn from the regression experiments described herein would not be significantly different.[8]

---

[7] Of course, at the last link of the manufacturing chain, the goods were sold to customers but usually at fixed prices, and important nonprice rationing mechanisms were in place. In such cases, the prices were more of an accounting device than an economic instrument.

[8] Reynolds (1985) has proposed an alternative concept for dating the industrial revolution: namely, the "turning point," which occurs when per capita GDP starts an uneven rise and does not return to its original level. This measure is difficult to apply and, moreover, leads to some counterintuitive results. For instance, Chile experienced a turning point in 1840 and Thailand in 1850. W. W.

B. The Impact of Rural Literacy and Agricultural Productivity on Industrialization

1. The State of the Debate

The proposition that literacy was a vital prerequisite for industrialization at an early date rests on three arguments (Mokyr, 2002): (a) The eighteenth and nineteenth centuries witnessed an explosive increase of technological literature, farmer's almanacs, and encyclopedias of production techniques, all written in the vernacular (Mokyr, 2002). As a result, literacy suddenly began to have an economic payoff. (b) A growing manufacturing sector required access by many people, especially those who wished to become entrepreneurs, to the expanding knowledge base underlying the new technologies that were being introduced. Moreover, literacy permitted those in the rural sector both to join an urban entrepreneurial group and to offer themselves as workers who did not need minute oral instructions. (c) For manufacturers to achieve the economies of scale necessary for profitable competition against craft workers, they had to have fairly wide markets for their products. This, in turn, required a certain degree of commercialization, which necessitated some level of general literacy because any extensive buying and selling required trading accounts to be kept and contracts to be drawn up and signed. In the next section, I examine the commercialization argument in greater detail, but in this discussion, I focus on literacy.

For many decades, economic historians have been concerned about the empirical evidence showing the causal role of the relevance of literacy for explaining the industrial revolution in Europe. Certainly, a simple linkage is difficult to find, especially because, in the eighteenth century, few occupations made a direct use of literacy. Sanderson (1972), for instance, presents evidence that in the Lancaster area of England, literacy was not needed for most new jobs created in the early stages of industrialization and, moreover, that the correlation between literacy and wages, while positive, was low. Certainly, many urban workers in repetitive, unskilled work did not need to be literate, especially if they had served an apprenticeship. The share of workers in manufacturing who needed to be able to read, at least for advancement if not for their entry-level positions, is far from clear.[9] Nevertheless, in the

---

Rostow's (1960) concept of takeoff is yet another approach and, as Reynolds points out, leads to much later dates than his.

[9] In a recent econometric analysis, for instance, Allen (2003) finds that literacy played little role in the rise of agricultural productivity in Europe in the years between 1400 and 1800.

long run, the level of literacy did increase during the industrial revolution, even though in certain short periods and in certain nations it did not (e.g., in the United Kingdom, literacy actually fell somewhat during the second half of the seventeenth century). Such evidence points to the difficulties in separating cause and effect in discussing the relationship between rising literacy and manufacturing production (Mokyr, 1985b).

This debate about the role of literacy has also raged among development economists. In the early 1960s, for instance, Mary Jean Bowman and C. Arnold Anderson (1963) used cross-section evidence for the 1950s to suggest that no country with a low average literacy rate could expect a per capita income of more than $2,150 (converted to 2000 prices) and that significant economic growth required higher levels of literacy. They were implicitly emphasizing the importance of literacy in the countryside, because the overwhelming majority of the population in poor countries lived in rural areas. Two objections were immediately leveled against them. First, such a correlation could not distinguish between literacy as a cause or an effect of industrialization. Second, the measurement of literacy is extremely slippery and economic historians have had to use such imperfect indicators as whether people could sign marriage registers.

Because literacy was correlated with two other variables related to industrialization – namely, urbanization and high labor productivity in agriculture – many suggest that this emphasis on the crucial role of literacy is misplaced. Some argue that urbanization was really the key variable and that both higher literacy and greater commercialization were the result of the creation of urban centers. According to this approach, greater urbanization permitted a faster spread of ideas and provided the necessary infrastructure for industrialization to occur, such as banks, legal institutions, and transportation facilities. Urbanization also forged a closer geographical connection between the suppliers and demanders of investment capital.

Yet, others claim that the key variable was agricultural productivity because it brought about both greater urbanization and literacy. More specifically, higher agricultural productivity meant that a smaller labor force was needed to produce food for subsistence, thus releasing a larger labor force for other activities, including manufacturing. Moreover, higher agricultural productivity would have meant that more resources could be utilized for education (especially in the countryside), which would suggest that higher literacy was a function of higher agricultural productivity and not the reverse.[10]

---

[10] Allen (2003) provides an interesting twist to these arguments with econometric evidence that the major impact of higher agricultural productivity was a change in the sectoral structure of

2. Tests of the Hypotheses

Which of three related explanatory variables for industrialization was the most important: urbanization, agricultural productivity, or rural literacy? Some relevant data are presented in Table 5-1 and two problems of their analysis arise: First, it is difficult to sort out cause and effect because these variables were interrelated.[11] Second, comparable data on agricultural productivity are not available; however, because agriculture was by far the largest sector in all these economies, per capita GDP serves as a good proxy.

Turning first to the index of per capita GDP (where the world average in 1820 = 100), the table reveals that most of the nations industrializing before 1914 had a per capita GDP in 1820 considerably above the world average. Notable exceptions, however, were Australia, Japan, and Russia – three nations in which the state and/or foreign investors played crucial roles in the industrialization process. Moreover, the date of the threshold of industrialization was significantly related to the per capita GDP in 1820.[12] More specifically, the higher the level of per capita GDP (or agricultural productivity) in 1820, the earlier the date of the threshold of industrialization.

The correlation between agricultural productivity and industrialization, however, was only a general tendency and admitted many exceptions

---

the economy and that it was not so much a cause of greater productivity in manufacturing as it was a response to it.

[11] Using just the sixteen OECD countries for which data for all three variables are available, and using per capita GDP as a proxy for agricultural productivity, the matrix of uncorrected correlation coefficients (R) is:

	Per Capita GDP	Urbanization	Literacy Variables
Per Capita GDP	1.0000		
Urbanization	0.6724	1.0000	
Literacy over 50 percent	0.4901	0.1678	1.0000

[12] Letting TI = date of threshold of industrialization and YCap = GDP/capita in 1820, we have the following ordinary least-squares relationships for the entire sample (standard errors in parentheses; statistical significance at the 0.05 level marked with an asterisk):

$$(1)\ TI = 1942^* - 0.457^*\ YCap \quad R^2 = 0.4035$$
$$\quad\quad (23)\quad (0.135) \quad\quad\quad n = 19$$

and when Australia, Canada, and Japan (for which literacy data are not available) are excluded from the sample:

$$(2)\ TI = 1937^* - 0.437^*\ YCap \quad R^2 = 0.2831$$
$$\quad\quad (34)\quad (0.186) \quad\quad\quad n = 16$$

The significant relationship between per capita GDP and the threshold of industrialization in equation 1 also holds, although to a lesser degree, when England is removed from the sample; in equation 2 it does not.

Table 5-1. *Literacy, per capita GDP, and urbanization in nations industrializing before 1914*

Country	Date of Threshold of Industrialization	Adult Literacy in 1800		Index of Per Capita GDP in 1820; World Average = 100	Urbanization Rate in 1800
		Greater than 70 Percent	Between 50 and 70 Percent		
England	1778	0	1	256	20.8%
Switzerland	1817	1	0	192	6.9
Belgium	1823	0	1	198	21.7
United States	1825	1	0	188	5.6
France	1835	0	1	184	12.9
Germany	1852	1	0	159	9.4
Sweden	1852	1	0	180	5.5
Norway	1873	1	0	166	6.0
Austro-Hungary	1876	0	1	183	7.9
Finland	1876	1	0	117	1.3
Netherlands	1881	1	0	273	34.1
Spain	1881	0	0	159	19.5
Denmark	1885	1	0	191	13.3
Italy	1887	0	0	167	21.9
Canada	1888	—	—	134	—
Russia	1899	0	0	103	5.0
Japan	1902	—	—	100	—
Australia	1904	—	—	78	—
Portugal	1907	0	0	144	15.2

Note: A dash indicates no data are available. For the literacy data, 1 indicates yes, 0 indicates no. If both are zero, literacy was below 50 percent of the adult population. This date of the threshold of industrialization is set as the year when various countries reached the level of per capita manufacturing production achieved in England in 1778; it is based on calculations by Bairoch (1982). Sources and detailed methods for estimating the data in this table are explained in Appendix 5-4.

because, as noted previously, high agricultural productivity was neither a necessary nor a sufficient condition for industrialization. For instance, the Netherlands had a high relative per capita GDP (and literacy), and yet it reached the industrialization threshold belatedly (see the following discussion), whereas Germany and Russia industrialized at a much earlier date than their relative levels of economic development would lead us to expect.

The relationship between literacy and the date of the threshold of industrialization is also statistically significant and in the expected direction: The higher the literacy in 1800, the earlier the threshold of industrialization was reached.[13] This relationship, as measured by the coefficient of determination, is also somewhat higher than that using the index of per capita GDP alone, which suggests that literacy played a more important role. This conclusion becomes even more apparent when England is removed from the sample.[14]

This statistical relationship between literacy and the date of the industrialization threshold is sufficiently strong to warrant more detailed investigation about what my literacy variable is measuring. Because the population was predominantly rural in most of the countries, differences in national literacy

---

[13] Using the terminology in the previous footnote and letting $L_1 =$ greater than 70 percent literate and $L_2 = 50$–70 percent literate, the OLS regression result is:

$$TI = 1894^* - 35.9^*L_1 - 65.5^*L_2 \quad R^2 = 0.4645$$
$$(13) \quad (16.9) \quad (19.5) \quad n = 16$$

This relationship also holds when England is removed from the sample ($R^2 = 0.4271$).

[14] This conclusion is buttressed by the fact that one standard deviation difference from the mean of the education variables had a greater impact on the date of the threshold of industrialization than one standard deviation of the GDP index. The latter result is particularly apparent when England is removed from the sample. The relevant values for this exercise are:

	With England		Excluding England	
	Average	Standard Deviation	Average	Standard Deviation
GDP per capita index	179	43	174	39
Urbanization	12.9%	8.7%	12.4%	8.8%
Literacy > 70 percent	0.50	0.52	0.52	0.52
Literacy 50–70 percent	0.25	0.45	0.20	0.41

Certain problems of interpretation of the standard deviations arise, of course, because the GDP variable is continuous, whereas the literacy variables are discrete.

One contrary piece of evidence to the proposition that higher literacy encouraged faster economic growth also deserves mention. A cluster analysis for the developing countries of the world in 1990 (Appendix 6-8) shows that although those nations with the type of economic system with the fastest growth also had workers with the most education, this characteristic was more a function of the level of economic development than of the system *per se*.

rates primarily reflected literacy in the rural population; and, as indicated previously, knowledge of the growing technical literature was a ladder by which rural workers could climb out of agriculture and into urban production. But, this literacy variable might have also mirrored a growing desire to read the scriptures (a result of the Protestant Reformation) or else it reflected the impact of the Enlightenment. The latter emphasized the spreading of formal knowledge, so that the ability of individual farmers to read and write was less important than the belief of individuals and of local governmental authorities that formal knowledge of various types was important in and of itself and worthy of special encouragement.

By way of contrast, urbanization alone was not statistically related to the date of the threshold of industrialization.[15] Nor was urbanization related to literacy, which strongly suggests that rural literacy, not urbanization, was the key factor in promoting industrialization. Urbanization was, however, positively and significantly related to the per capita GDP. We would expect such a relationship because higher agricultural productivity meant that a lower share of the labor force was needed to feed the nation.

When trying to explain the date of the threshold of industrialization using all three of the variables, we run into problems arising from the intercorrelations among the three explanatory variables (multicollinearity), so that none of the calculated coefficients is statistically significant. When literacy and urbanization, which were not significantly related to each other, are used in the regression analysis, the results show that higher literacy rates brought a nation to the industrialization threshold earlier, whereas urbanization had no impact.[16] When just per capita GDP and the literacy variables are used for the tests, only the literacy variables are statistically significant (both with

---

[15] The OLS regression result is (standard errors in parentheses, statistical significance at the 0.05 level marked with an asterisk):

$$TI = 1860^* - 7.73 \text{ urbanization (U)} \quad R^2 = 0.0004$$
$$(16) \ (107.59) \qquad\qquad\qquad n = 16$$

[16] Using the terminology in the previous footnotes, these OLS relationships are:

(1) $TI = 1895^* - 364L_1 - 65.4^*L_2 - 9.67U$ $R^2 = 0.4650$
       $(20) \quad (18.2) \quad (20.3) \quad (89.6)$ $n = 16$

(2) $TI = 1966^* - 0.780^*YCap + 249^*U$ $R^2 = 0.4924$
       $(32) \quad (0.220) \qquad (107)$ $n = 16$

(3) $TI = 1922^* - 0.195YCap - 28.1L_1 - 53.4^*L_2$ $R^2 = 0.5050$
       $(32) \quad (0.196) \qquad (18.7) \quad (23.0)$ $n = 16$

(4) Excluding England
     $TI = 1898^* - 0.0279YCap - 34.8^*L_1 - 47.6^*L_2$ $R^2 = 0.4281$
       $(30) \quad (0.1928) \qquad (16.8) \quad (20.6)$ $n = 15$

and without the inclusion of England). Because the signs of the calculated coefficients are in the right direction, this suggests that – although problems of intercorrelations prevent great weight being placed on such results – the literacy variables proved to be more strongly related to the industrialization threshold than did the agricultural productivity proxy (which is somewhat related to the literacy variables).

Up to now, I have implicitly assumed that the correlations between particular variables and the threshhold of industrialization point to causal relationships. In major part, this is because for most countries the hypothesized causal variables are measured at a point in time before the industrialization threshold was reached.

In brief, for countries industrializing before World War I, a high rate of rural literacy in 1820 appears to have been an important factor for explaining when the threshold of industrialization was reached. The statistical results also suggest that such literacy was also a more important causal factor than high agricultural productivity or urbanization. Thus, these results corroborate a conjecture about early industrialization which, although not novel (see, for example, Sanderson, 1972: 89), has not been put to such a test.[17]

If we follow this causal relation between literacy and industrialization farther down the trail, we face the issue of why certain nations invested more in education than others. In this regard, Galor, Moav, and Vollrath (2003) argue that the more unequal the ownership of land, the lower were the public expenditures on education.[18] In part, this was because large land

---

Like equations (3) and (4), equations (1) and (2) obtain roughly the same results when England is removed from the sample. Note that because of multicollinearity, the urbanization variable in equation (2) has the "wrong" sign. When just per capita GDP and the urbanization variables are used, the correlation between the explanatory variables is too high (multicollinearity) for the results to be meaningful.

[17] As noted herein, Allen (2003) finds that literacy had little impact on economic development. He was, however, dealing with an earlier period and was not focusing on industrialization, so that our results are not necessarily inconsistent.

[18] Their data for U.S. states in 1920 support the proposition of the inverse relation between land concentration and education expenditures, as does a comparison of nations throughout the world by Deininger and Squire (1988) for the period from 1960 to 1990. For 1900, however, the Galor–Moav–Vollrath data do not support the hypothesis, in major part (according to a communication from Dietz Galor) because education expenditures in that year were mostly for primary education, which was roughly the same in all states. By the 1920s, the various states differed considerably in expenditures on secondary education, which is picked up in their regressions. The differences between nations in 1859 were for primary education, so the inverse relationship between land concentration and education again holds.

Others have also argued this inverse relationship between land inequality and literacy (or expenditures on education) – for instance, Sokoloff and Engerman (2000). Wright (1986: 79) argues that the U.S. South underinvested in public education because the farm owners, who

owners, who dominated decisions on taxation and public expenditures, did not believe that education would greatly enhance agricultural productivity and, moreover, they also wanted to keep the workers on the land by not providing them with a useful urban skill.

Two other shards of evidence support this intriguing hypothesis. Using data from Morris and Adelman (1988) for 1850, my regressions reveal a statistically significant and expected inverse relationship between literacy and land inequality, not just for a sample of twelve European nations, but also for their full sample of twenty-three nations throughout the world.[19] Moreover, in a cluster analysis of the economic systems of developing nations in 1990 (Appendix 6-8), the nations having the type of economic system with the highest and fastest growing per capita GDP had both a higher level of education and a lower inequality of land ownership than the other nations in the sample; although, when the impact of the level of development is factored out, only the indicator for the distribution of land ownership is statistically significant.

One last thread to the agricultural productivity argument needs to be tied. A previous generation of economic historians argued that an "agricultural revolution" needed to precede an industrial revolution. Leaving aside issues concerning spurts in agricultural productivity that occurred at different times in the millennium before industrialization, it seems clear that if agricultural productivity had achieved a relatively high level of productivity by the time industrialization began, a further leap in agricultural productivity before the manufacturing sector took off would not have been necessary. By way of contrast, those countries with relatively low agricultural productivity, however, would have been more likely to experience a rapid increase of such productivity in the quarter-century or so preceding the date of the threshold of industrialization. In Appendix 5-2, I show that this hypothesis receives considerable empirical support and review some of the literature on this topic.

Turning to the individual characteristics of the agricultural economic systems in the various communities delineated in the previous chapter, no data are available on literacy. Nevertheless, it seems likely that those living in communities with considerable wage labor and trade outside the community

---

    would pay a considerable portion of the tax, would not be able to capture the returns for such schooling because the recipients would leave the rural areas for the cities.

[19] For Europe, the relationship also held when per capita income and urbanization were added to the sample. For the worldwide sample, the inverse relationship was statistically significant only when controlling for per capita GDP.

would have had the greatest incentives to learn to read and write. According to the data in Table 4-2, the societies with a semi-marketized economic system had both the greatest relative volume of trade with other communities and the greatest share of members working outside the community, so they most likely would also have had the highest rates of literacy.

C. Marketization

Marketization of the agricultural sector – the penetration of markets into the rural economy – was neither a necessary nor a sufficient condition for industrialization because, as noted in the introduction, the urban sector could have received its food through foreign trade, rather than from its own countryside.[20] Moreover, governments could have also aided the development of manufacturing without having much impact on rural markets through export or investment subsidies, monopoly privileges and high tariffs, or construction of transportation infrastructure for foreign trade. Nevertheless, for a variety of reasons discussed herein, it seems highly likely that marketization of the rural sector was (and is) a very favorable factor for industrialization.

Several prerequisites were necessary for rural marketization: For instance, extractions from agriculture – such as taxes collected by the state, tithes by the church, and rents from landlords – had to be sufficiently low and agricultural productivity sufficiently high to leave the rural population discretionary income for the purchase of goods and services.[21] Moreover, the crops

---

[20] I do not use alternative terms, such as *agrarian capitalism*, because marketization focuses on a broader set of phenomena and is not tied to one particular type of commercial infrastructure. Agrarian capitalism usually refers to market-oriented agricultural production by large farms relying on hired labor. But I want to examine not just the market for goods but also the markets for labor, capital, and land. Furthermore, in many countries in the eighteenth and nineteenth centuries, the marketing of agricultural products was also partly carried out by smallholders, who devoted only part of their efforts to market production and who did not rely on any hired labor. The real question is the degree of market penetration necessary for industrialization to occur, rather than who actually carried out marketing activities. Of course, it might be argued that greater marketization occurred when the large farms accounted for most of the produce sold; but, this is far from obvious, even for export production where smallholders often sold their crops to middlemen for export (e.g., cotton farmers in the U.S. southern states).

[21] Some have taken this argument further and argued that population pressure on the land could not have been sufficiently high that very high land rents were extracted – a conjecture that, as shown herein, is not validated by the data.

Unfortunately, the total amount of collective extractions during the early years of industrialization in Europe is not known with any exactitude, except for certain taxes. Nevertheless, the available evidence is sometimes surprising. Mathias and O'Brien (1976) estimate that at the beginning of the eighteenth century, total central governmental taxes (i.e., extractions other

also had to be sufficiently nonperishable to be sent to urban markets, and the country in question had to have adequate waterways for transport because land transportation was usually extremely costly. A modicum of law and order had also to prevail, provided either through a central government or an intricate system of private institutions, so that contracts and private property were secure. I first address the question of marketization directly and then turn to a special aspect of this phenomenon associated with proto-manufacturing.

1. The Penetration of Markets as a Factor Underlying Early Industrialization

The proposition that a certain marketization of the rural economy was important for industrialization rests on one or more of five major arguments. (a) Development of markets for agricultural products was important in creating a complementary market in rural areas for manufactured goods, especially because manufacturers could achieve the economies of scale necessary to make their goods affordable only by selling large quantities of them. (b) Further development of markets for the exchange of agricultural and manufactured goods led eventually to the creation of the financial, legal, and transportation infrastructures necessary for manufacturing. (c) A market for labor also had to develop for manufacturers to obtain a work force. (d) The profits from domestic commerce was necessary for financing early manufacturing. (e) A market for land provided easier access to capital for investment because land could be mortgaged or used as security for a loan to finance manufacturing activities. Each of these propositions is controversial and has both strong supporters and opponents.

In the following discussion, I explore this relationship among markets, trade, and industrialization in those nations that reached the threshold of industrialization before 1914. In particular, I explore the empirical question of whether an upsurge in rural market activity actually preceded industrialization.

than local taxes and tithes) as a share of total commodity production (services not included) were higher in England than in France (17 and 11 percent, respectively). By the end of the century, the tax share had risen considerably in the former country (reaching 24 percent) while remaining roughly constant in the latter. This widening spread can also be seen when taxes are converted to wheat equivalents. Although it is often claimed that taxes were much more regressive in France than in England, because the bourgeois and noble land owners were often relieved of certain land taxes in France, Mathias and O'Brien show that total taxes might possibly have been more progressive in the France. It does not seem likely, however, that the wealthy in either country were sufficiently burdened by taxes to reduce dramatically the potential funds for investment.

Table 5-2 presents two sets of measures designed to disentangle the issue of whether markets and trade preceded or followed industrialization. The first set, coded by Adelman and Morris (1978; see also Morris and Adelman, 1988), shows the penetration of markets for goods, labor, capital, and land in twenty-four countries in 1850. Although it would have been desirable to have such data for 1800 as well, they are not available. The second set presents the average annual growth of per capita exports and GDP in constant prices in the quarter-century preceding and following the threshold of industrialization. In almost all cases, such exports were tied to rural marketization because, for the most part, they consisted either of agricultural products or manufactured goods using agricultural raw materials.

According to the marketization hypothesis, industrialization occurred earlier in those countries where market activities were greater. Such a proposition receives impressive support: all five indicators are significantly and inversely related to the date of the threshold of industrialization. The degree of statistical fit (coefficient of determination) is highest for the composite market variable, next highest for the capital and goods markets, and lowest for the labor and land markets.

Because greater manufacturing meant more market penetration, a better test is to look only at those nations industrializing after 1850. In these cases, only the high penetration of composite markets, capital markets, and goods markets lead to significantly earlier dates for the threshold of industrialization, with the capital market showing the highest explanatory power (the penetration of the labor and land markets were not statistically significant at all).[22] Many of the factors underlying these various types of market penetration are difficult to isolate, especially because they seemed to vary from country to country.

The foreign trade data reveal that before the date of the threshold of industrialization was reached, exports were increasing as a share of GDP in roughly 70 percent of the countries industrializing before 1914. After the industrialization threshold was passed, the same increasing export/GDP ratio can be observed in roughly the same percentage of these nations. In slightly

---

[22] The OLS regressions for these three markets are (with standard errors in parentheses and an asterisk designating statistical significance at the 0.05 level):

(1) $TI = 1937^* - 11.1^*\ GMP$ $R^2 = 0.2129$ TI = date of threshold of industrialization
      (17)   (5.4) $n = 17$ GMP = goods market penetration
(2) $TI = 1942^* - 14.8^*\ CMP$ $R^2 = 0.5085$ CMP = capital markets penetration
      (11)   (3.8) $n = 16$ CMVP = composite market variable
(3) $TI = 1957^* - 17.3^*\ CMVP$ $R^2 = 0.4355$ penetration
      (16)   (4.9) $n = 17$

Table 5-2. *Market penetration indicators*

Country	Date of Threshold of Industrialization	Market Penetration in 1850 Scaled 1 to 10					Per Capita Growth Date of Industrialization Threshold			
		Goods	Labor	Capital	Land	All	25 Years Before		25 Years After	
							Exports	GDP	Exports	GDP
England	1778	7.8	7.8	6.4	7.0	7.4	+0.3%	+0.1%	+5.2%	+0.3%
Switzerland	1817	6.6	5.5	4.6	7.0	5.8	—	—	—	—
Belgium	1823	7.8	7.8	6.4	7.0	7.4	—	+0.3	+4.1[e]	+0.5
United States	1825	7.8	7.8	6.4	7.0	7.1	-2.3	+0.4	+0.5	+1.2
France	1835	6.6	7.8	4.6	7.0	6.6	+6.9[a]	+1.3[a]	+3.9	+0.9
Germany	1852	4.4	5.5	4.6	7.0	5.0	+1.0[b]	—	+4.3	+1.1
Sweden	1852	2.1	5.5	4.6	4.0	4.2	+1.5[a]	—	+4.1	+2.3
Norway	1873	2.1	5.5	1.0	1.0	2.3	—	—	+1.6	+0.9
Austria	1876	—	—	—	—	—	+2.6	+0.7	+1.3	+1.6
Finland	1876	—	—	—	—	—	+3.3	+2.0	+1.5	+1.5
Netherlands	1881	6.6	5.5	4.6	7.0	5.8	+3.2	+1.0	+0.6	+0.6
Spain	1881	2.1	5.5	4.6	4.0	3.9	+3.6	+1.5	+1.5	+0.4
Denmark	1885	2.1	5.5	1.0	4.0	3.1	+3.4	+1.1	+3.4	+2.0
Italy	1887	4.4	5.5	4.6	4.0	4.4	+1.7	+0.1	+2.6	+1.4

Canada	1889	2.1	5.5	4.6	4.0	3.9	−0.0[f]	+2.5[f]	+2.9[g]	+2.0[g]
Russia	1899	3.3	1.0	1.0	1.0	1.3	+0.2[c]	+2.5[c]	+2.5[c]	+0.6[c]
Japan	1902	4.4	3.3	—	1.0	2.6	+6.8	+2.1	+5.9	+1.1
Australia	1904	3.3	3.3	2.8	1.0	2.6	+1.6	−0.7	+0.8[d]	+2.4[d]
Portugal	1907	—	—	—	—	—	−1.4	+0.8	—	—
New Zealand	1913	2.1	3.3	1.0	1.0	1.5	—	—	—	—
For comparison purposes										
Brazil	1953	3.3	1.0	1.0	4.0	2.1	−0.5	2.2	3.4	3.8
India	1976	2.1	5.5	1.0	4.0	2.9	+0.5	1.4	6.3	3.2
Argentina	>1950	1.0	5.5	1.0	4.0	2.6	—	—	—	—
Burma	>1950	2.1	5.5	1.0	1.0	2.1	—	—	—	—
China	>1950	1.0	3.3	1.0	4.0	2.1	—	—	—	—
Egypt	>1950	1.0	1.0	1.0	1.0	0.7	—	—	—	—

Note: A dash indicates that data are not available. Data on market penetration for individual markets come from Adelman and Morris (1978); and the composite market penetration variable from Morris and Adelman (1988), where individual markets are weighted by scores derived from a principle component analysis. All growth rates are calculated by fitting an exponential curve to the series to minimize endpoint problems. Data sources and methods for the export and GDP data are presented in Appendix 5-5.

In some cases, data were unavailable for the quarter-century before or after the threshold of industrialization, so shorter periods had to be used: a = 20 years; b = 16 years; c = 14 years; d = 9 years; e = 17 years; f = 22 years; g = 24 years. For Austria, the date of the industrialization threshold and also exports refers to the entire Austro-Hungarian Empire, but GDP and agricultural growth rates are only for the Austrian half of the empire.

more than half of these countries, the growth of per capita exports also accelerated. The nations where exports did not grow much faster than the GDP were a mixed lot. The United States and Canada were large in area and, in these cases, it seems likely that high internal transportation costs adversely affected exports. I also have the impression that the rural sectors of England and Portugal were already relatively marketized more than a quarter-century before these nations reached the industrialization threshold.

The exact way in which rural marketization encouraged industrialization in various countries is a matter of fierce debate among economic historians, and it is difficult to draw many generalizations. Not only are the historical facts in dispute, but also the process of industrialization varied considerably from country to country. Although the regression results reported herein suggest a relationship between market penetration and early industrialization, we should also briefly consider some scenarios in which marketization either did not aid industrialization or did so in ways that run against the conventional wisdom.

If marketization focused exclusively on the export of agricultural products, then manufacturing might have been actively discouraged. It is often argued, for instance, that the existence of expanding markets for Portuguese or Danish agricultural exports, particularly in England, delayed industrialization in these nations. By way of contrast, if a relatively larger share of a nation's population had some education in skills useful for factory work so that the nation had a comparative advantage in its manufacturing exports, then both domestic and foreign trade in manufactured goods would have risen and, at the same time, rural production of raw materials for such production would have been encouraged as well.[23]

It is also claimed that colonial outlets encouraged both trade and industrialization. It should be noted, however, that excepting England, France, Spain, Portugal, and the Netherlands, none of the other countries in the table had important colonies.[24] Paul Bairoch (1993: 77–78) notes that in the nineteenth century, these five colonial countries had slower rates of

---

[23] Galor (2003) argues that the fertility rate would also fall, as these educated workers would use their family resources to educate a small number of children, rather than spread such funds over a larger number of children (i.e., focusing on the quality, not the quantity, of offspring). These more highly educated children would, in turn, be more employable in the new factories.

[24] Although Belgium and Germany had colonies, their role as a market for exports was minuscule. Some claim that Australia, Canada, New Zealand, Russia, and the United States were experiencing "internal colonization," but this seems a phenomenon of a different order.

GDP and manufacturing growth than nations such as Belgium, Germany, Sweden, Switzerland, and the United States, which did not have colonies.

Many believe that the growth of trade, even of agricultural products, aided industrialization by providing for a source of finance for the new factories, but three counterarguments should be noted, as follows:

- Merchant capital was not necessarily the main source of financing investments in the manufacturing sector. Moreover, as the industrial revolution advanced, many "new towns" with a manufacturing base rapidly eclipsed the old urban commercial centers, an unexpected development if merchant capital was crucial to manufacturing. (It must be noted, however, that many of these new towns were former proto-manufacturing centers.) Nevertheless, until economic historians disentangle the varied sources of finance of the new manufacturing industries for most countries industrializing before 1914, the exact role of merchant capital must remain uncertain.
- In the early years of industrialization, building and equipping a factory did not necessarily require a large investment (Neale, 1975).[25]
- Although the total profits from foreign trade in certain countries such as England were high, this does not necessarily mean that such income actually flowed into the manufacturing sector. Instead, these profits might have been spent in riotous living or in luxurious estates. Moreover, in some countries alternative sources of investment finance were available; for instance, in England, land owners and aristocrats invested (and participated) substantially in crucial manufacturing sectors in some countries, although rural sources of finance did not seem universal. Unfortunately, we have no exact accounting of the source of investment funds in most countries, although in England, at least, it seems likely that a considerable share was privately raised among the friends of the manufacturer, who were not necessarily merchants or merchant bankers.

It is also important to note that the existence of relatively free markets did not mean that manufacturing would necessarily be encouraged. In Europe, for instance, the Netherlands was highly marketized (and also had a high level of literacy and a sophisticated financial system), yet this "first modern economy" was a relatively late industrializer, due to a variety of

---

[25] Although capital requirements for factories tended to rise in the nineteenth century, much new industry in nations beginning industrialization in the twentieth century was still highly labor-intensive and required relatively little physical capital.

barriers and disincentives (discussed in detail by de Vries and van der Woude, 1997). Another case is China, which for some centuries had relatively free factor markets for land, labor, and capital and a moderately commercialized economy, with money, public and private proto-factories in certain localities, an impressive transport infrastructure (particularly canals), extensive trade networks, and a comparatively stable institutional framework for carrying out trade and production (Chao, 1982). Yet, overall market penetration, as shown in Table 5-2, was not particularly great in 1850 and China did not industrialize until the twentieth century, in large measure under the aegis of a communist government.

In brief, the foregoing discussion suggests that those agricultural economic systems that were relatively more marketized had a higher probability of industrializing at an earlier date than nonmarketized nations, other factors remaining the same. Turning to the defining characteristics of the four agricultural economic systems (Table 4-2), the semi-marketized communities were significantly more likely to have two crucial markets than other types of agricultural systems: namely, wage labor inside the community and inter-community trade of goods. Moreover, their significantly higher land rents also provided a concentration of capital that could be useful for financing new industries (the type of rent, however, makes a difference, a phenomenon discussed in the next section). No other type of agricultural economic system significantly had those characteristics indicating a high penetration of markets.

For the (non-Marxist) developing countries in 1990, we have no good indicator of marketization with which to compare the nineteenth-century data in Table 5-2. Nevertheless, a cluster analysis of economic institutions in these nations (Appendix 6-8) shows that those nations with the type of economic system with the fastest growth have a number of characteristic fostering market activities – for instance, significantly less product market regulations, lower barriers to starting new businesses, and greater freedom to set their own prices.

2. Proto-Manufacturing as a Type of Marketization: A Semi-Digression

At first sight, the idea that proto-manufacturing was a necessary first step to industrialization is appealing. Starting from an influential essay by Franklin F. Mendels (1972), various economic historians have provided a grab-bag of reasons to support this proposition. For instance, proto-manufacturing created both a means by which merchants could accumulate capital and the managerial experience necessary for industrialization; moreover, it also provided the nucleus of a disciplined proletariat available for manufacturing. And, different case studies (e.g., those collected in Deyon, 1982) show quite convincingly that various European countries industrializing in the nineteenth century went through a proto-manufacturing stage (although, of course, a low level of proto-manufacturing existed in earlier centuries as well).

It is often argued that the destruction of feudalism was necessary for capitalism and industrialization to develop, but proto-manufacturing and serfdom were evidently compatible. For instance, in many regions east of the Elbe in the eighteenth and early nineteenth centuries, serfdom seemed to have easily coexisted with both proto-manufacturing in the countryside and commerce in the towns. In Russia and Bohemia in the eighteenth century, for instance, large land owners set up on their estates proto-manufacturing enterprises manned by serfs (Myška, 1996).[26] It seems likely that in both countries, the serf-holders viewed these enterprises as an opportunity to utilize their labor force more fully during the winter. Some have argued that serfdom bred attitudes incompatible with employment in urban factories.[27] We can, however, infer from the case of Russia, which reached the threshold of industrialization less than four decades after the emancipation of the serfs, that such attitudes can be suitably modified (see also the following discussion).

But, precedence in time does not necessarily indicate causality, and proto-manufacturing might have merely reflected the fact that rising agricultural productivity had created a sufficient food surplus for a noticeable part of the rural labor force to be engaged in nonagricultural activities. Moreover, later case studies from various European countries (e.g., those summarized by Ogilvie and Cerman, 1996a, 1996b) have discredited many of

---

[26] Although Peter the Great's efforts to create certain industries are said to have strengthened serfdom in particular respects, some historians, such as R. L. Rudolph (1982), argue that the system quickly mutated after Peter and that "the serf system in many ways served to promote proto-industrialization [i.e., proto-manufacturing] with the development of networks of trade and transport, the creation of a market for proto-industrial and agricultural commodities, the encouragement of labor skills, and the inducement to peasants to initiate proto-industry and to take up extra-agricultural employment."

[27] "The institution of labor services [before emancipation in Russia] bred mendacity and deception. The serf-entrepreneurs had many excellent reasons to deceive their owners. The legal uncertainty with regard to peasants' property rights was hardly designed to educate the mass of the population in the spirit of respect for contractual obligations" (Gerschenkron, 1966: 48). The previously mentioned factories in the U. S. South that, before the Civil War, employed slaves might also serve as a counterexample to Gerschenkron's contention (Goldin, 1976).

the hypothesized causal links between proto-manufacturing and subsequent industrialization.

Without doubt, in some regions manufacturing did emerge from proto-manufacturing, and in other regions manufacturing and proto-manufacturing coexisted. Yet, in still other cases, proto-manufacturing flowered and then wilted, and the region returned to agriculture.[28] More specifically, in some countries industrial production, which had moved to the countryside in the eighteenth century, moved to the towns in the nineteenth (Tilly, 1982). This allowed those providing the capital for such manufacturing to take closer control of the productive process and/or to move production toward new sources of power. As a result, proto-manufacturing declined in the countryside, which began to specialize more on agriculture again. Furthermore, people employed in the rural proto-factories, such as landless workers or underemployed family members, did not necessarily become wage workers in urban factories, which drew much of their labor force from other sectors of the economy. Moreover, the entrepreneurial class of urban manufacturing did not necessarily emerge from the merchant bourgeoisie directing such proto-manufacturing in the rural areas. Finally, in the second half of the twentieth century, proto-manufacturing might not have been crucial in the industrialization process and, in many cases, the most important leap seemed to be from craft work to manufacturing without the intermediate step of proto-manufacturing.[29] These considerations suggest, according to Robert Duplessis (1997: 207) that "proto-industrialization bore a contingent rather than a necessary relationship with later industrial development; and any specific rural region was as likely to return to an agricultural vocation as to see the rise of mechanized factories."

Although proto-manufacturing did not appear to have played a direct role in industrialization in most countries, in the eighteenth and early nineteenth centuries it appears to have fostered marketization of the countryside, which I argue herein encouraged industrialization. Thus, proto-manufacturing – however transitory – was one part of a much broader set of market activities that provided a favorable environment for manufacturing to take root.

---

[28] S. P. S. Ho (1982) presents a model in which such a reversion to agricultural production would not necessarily represent any intrinsic weakness of proto-manufacturing but could be caused by a change in factor proportions and/or relative prices of agricultural and proto-manufactured goods, occasioned by trade or population growth.

[29] Many Caribbean islands, which featured considerable craft work and proto-manufacturing (particularly sugar mills) in the eighteenth century, had not yet industrialized by the twentieth century, additional evidence that manufacturing does not necessarily emerge from proto-manufacturing.

D. The Impact of Land-Tenure Arrangements on Industrialization

As argued previously, land-tenure arrangements and concentration of land ownership had an impact on literacy, which, in turn, facilitated and fostered industrialization. In an interesting econometric study, Allen (2003) finds no statistically significant impact of land enclosures on agricultural productivity and economic development. My focus on land-tenure arrangements deals with a broader set of influences on agricultural productivity and industrialization, especially those encouraging individual decision-making and a long-term perspective. Two other important institutions would have been useful to examine in addition to land-tenure arrangements: namely, security of property rights and availability of finance for agricultural investment, but suitable data could not be located. For determining the land-tenure variable, the following factors appeared important.

DECISION-MAKING AUTONOMY. In tenure arrangements where community leaders or customs determined key production decisions – such as when, where, and what to plant or when to weed and harvest – farmers would be unlikely to develop habits of independent decision-making or entrepreneurial attitudes that would be useful in an urban manufacturing environment. This suggests, for instance, that communally directed open-field agriculture in the eighteenth and nineteenth centuries was not conducive to industrialization.[30] On the other hand, if suitably trained, such farm workers might make a docile industrial proletariat.

FREE LABOR. As noted previously, some argue that useful habits and attitudes for industrialization were unlikely to develop among serf or slave laborers. Moreover, many believe that industrialization was discouraged by barriers to mobility from the countryside. For instance, in Russia after the emancipation, peasants were still not "free laborers" because they could not permanently leave their village without giving up land rights, paying a high fee, and receiving permission from village authorities (Gerschenkron, 1966: 120). If they temporarily worked outside the community, they could also

---

[30] Robert Allen (1999) presents evidence that some types of open-field agriculture, which were not communally directed and allowed for individual decision-making, exhibited in certain periods the same rise in productivity as other kinds of farming. Various papers on the impact of enclosures in Grantham and Leonard (1989) show the wide range of opinion about the economic impact of land enclosures.

be called back at any moment. Nevertheless, as I previously suggested, these arguments are overdrawn because, despite these handicaps, Russia reached the threshold of industrialization relatively quickly after the emancipation of the serfs.

SECURE TENANCY. Useful habits and attitudes for industrial and/or urban life seemed also unlikely to develop where farmers had insecure tenancies, either because exclusive claims to farmland were not protected by the community or because the land owners offered only short-run tenancies. This is because such farmers had to focus their attention on immediate outcomes and did not have incentives for investment or the exploration of new production techniques, both of which favor the industrialization process. The situation, of course, was quite different among farmers who owned their land or who had secure, long-run tenancies without unduly high rents.

MODERATE-SIZED AND VIABLE FARMS. If farms were too small to support a family adequately or too fragmented for efficient farming, or if the soil was poor or the climate harsh, then the ensuing rural poverty could have had two adverse impacts on industrialization. First, the rural sector would not have the discretionary income to purchase manufactured goods. Second, the farmer's attention would focus on overcoming short-run difficulties rather than on long-term investment in physical and human capital. However, rural poverty also provided a ready labor force for proto-manufacturing and possibly a transition into manufacturing.

MODERATE INEQUALITIES OF LAND OWNERSHIP. High inequalities in land holdings could permit the accumulation of considerable wealth to finance the new factories or infrastructure necessary for industrialization.[31] Two powerful counterarguments can be raised. High inequalities of land ownership could have also encouraged a complete disdain for risky investing in industry or engaging in economic activities with only a long-run payoff, a situation reflected (parodied?) in Ivan Goncharov's nineteenth-century novel *Oblomov* about a Russian aristocrat and land owner too lazy to get out of bed and manage his estate. Furthermore, as previously noted, higher land concentration led to lower public expenditures on education.

---

[31] R. S. Neale (1975) notes that in England in the eighteenth century, large land owners and aristocracy acted as significant sources of finance in crucial sectors such as mineral extraction, timber production, and iron manufacture; their funds also constituted the bulk of investment in the turnpike system; and they contributed about one third of the investment in canal construction.

COMMERCIALIZATION OF LAND-TENURE ARRANGEMENTS. If landlord, tenant, and hired agricultural workers had contracted with each other in a strictly businesslike manner, with relatively little emphasis on traditional rights and privileges, this transformation of land-tenure arrangements to a more commercial basis might have been conducive to industrialization.

HIGH LAND DENSITY. From the reasoning underlying the Nieboer–Domar hypothesis discussed in the previous chapter, commercialization of land tenure was most likely to be found where population densities were high. High land densities were also related to higher commercialization.[32] These considerations, however, run counter to the conjecture offered earlier in this chapter that very high land densities would lead to high land rents and little discretionary income for farmers to buy urban goods.

FIXED LAND RENTS. With fixed land rents, the tenant receives all of the production left over after paying the rent and this, in turn, encourages entrepreneurial activities by the renters. By way of contrast, sharecropping or a system of required labor days acts as a tax on the labor of the renters because renters receive only a part of the rewards for agricultural improvements that they make.

None of the various factors listed herein seem completely convincing, and some even support an alternative hypothesis that the key issue was not the land-tenure arrangements but rather the availability of an inexpensive and disciplined labor force for manufacturing production. Nevertheless, these various conjectures about land tenure are sufficiently intriguing to warrant empirical exploration. For this purpose, I again draw on data by Morris and Adelman (1988) on certain aspects of tenure arrangements and ownership inequalities in twenty-three nations in 1850, simplifying their coding by coding the various values of their two variables according to whether the arrangements encouraged early industrialization according to the considerations listed herein.

Using the data in Table 5-3 and calculating a simple linear regression for the countries with a threshold of industrialization before 1914, we find, as expected, that higher population densities and favorableness of land-tenure arrangements were significantly associated with earlier dates of industrialization, whereas the land concentration variable shows no statistically significant relationship (no matter what alternative codings I tried). The influence of land concentration thus appears to have been indirect – that is, through

---

[32] The data come from Tables 5-2 and 5-3.

Table 5-3. *Land tenure, ownership, and population density in 1850*

	Threshold of Industrialization	Land				Threshold of Industrialization	Land		
		Density	Tenure	Concentration			Density	Tenure	Concentration
England	1778	90.9	1	1	Canada	1889	0.5	1	0
Switzerland	1817	108.8	1	0	Russia	1899	5.9	0	1
Belgium	1823	154.9	1	0	Japan	1902	72.9	1	0
U.S.	1825	4.9	1	0	Australia	1904	0.3	0	0
France	1835	68.2	1	1	New Zealand	1913	0.3	0	0
Germany	1852	98.9	1	0	Argentina	1950	1.5	0	0
Sweden	1852	9.2	1	0	Brazil	1950	0.8	0	0
Norway	1873	5.2	0	0	Burma	1950	20.8	0	0
Netherlands	1881	95.5	1	0	China	1950	100.3	1	0
Spain	1881	57.6	0	1	Egypt	1950	89.6	1	1
Denmark	1885	36.3	1	0	India	1950	57.3	0	0
Italy	1887	97.8	0	1					

Note: Land density is population per square kilometer of "standard farmland," which is an estimate of land suitable for cultivation, taking into account climate, rainfall, and possibilities for double-cropping. These data come from Morris and Adelman (1988: Table A-14).

Land tenure = 0 if most farmers worked for large estates or latifundia, either as unfree labor, hired labor, or tenants with short-term leases; or if they had a claim to land but their farming was subject to communal controls; or if they had short tenancies with little security and little recompense for improvement. Land tenure = 1 if most cultivated land was cultivated by independent farmers or farmers with relatively fixed tenures of variable lengths who were compensated for improvements. These data come from Morris and Adelman (1988: Table A-37).

Land concentration = 0 if most land was communally owned, or owned by smallholders with extreme parcelization or fragmentation; or if there was very high inequality of land holdings. Land concentration = 1 if land holdings were small but compact or if medium size with medium to high inequality of holdings. These data come from Morris and Adelman (1988: Table A-37).

its impact on education – rather than direct.[33] If both population density and favorableness of land-tenure arrangements are entered into the equation together, only the former proves statistically significant. Moreover, the addition of the land concentration variable does not change this result.[34]

Given the approximate nature of the land-tenure variable and the relatively small sample sizes, such results must be considered as tentative; nevertheless, they suggest that the hypothesis linking land tenure to the date of the threshold of industrialization has some validity, even though many exceptions to this relationship can be found. For instance, Russia in the nineteenth century appeared particularly unsuitable for industrialization, even after the emancipation of the serfs in 1861 because, as noted previously, mobility between the countryside and the city was limited and rural poverty was widespread. Yet, under considerable state guidance, industrial development proceeded rapidly, so that by the last decade of the nineteenth century, workers in mining and manufacturing (including crafts) constituted 14 percent of the labor force (Mitchell, 1998). In other countries as well, compensatory state policies and/or changes in the initial land-tenure arrangements offset the adverse impact of the initial land-tenure situation. Nevertheless, for those countries reaching the industrialization threshold after 1850, land tenure and ownership institutions in 1850 set up conditions that had an impact on the industrialization process in the second half of the nineteenth century and the first half of the twentieth century.[35]

Turning to the individual characteristics of the four agricultural economic systems discussed in the previous chapter, several factors must be taken into account. As the level of economic development rose, the various communities were more likely to be individually owned land and, moreover, to have fewer restrictions on the ways in which that land could be used. Because the

---

[33] Some contrary evidence that the impact was direct is provided by a cluster analysis of developing countries in 1990 (Appendix 6-8). Those societies with the type of economic system exhibiting the fastest growth had a significantly greater degree of equality of land holdings.

[34] The following ordinary least-squares regressions can be calculated (where TI = date of threshold of industrialization, Den = population density variable, and Ten = land tenure variable). Standard errors are placed in parentheses and an asterisk indicates statistical significance at the 0.05 level.

(1) TI = 1899* − 0.24 Den − 34.5* Ten $R^2 = 0.4070$ All countries reaching TI
     (14)   (0.17)   (17.2) $n = 17$ before 1914

(2) TI = 1921* − 0.09 Den − 57.7* Ten $R^2 = 0.3977$ All countries in sample
     (14)   (0.20)   (18.8) $N = 23$

When subsamples from smaller time periods are selected, these results are not very robust.

[35] Countries attaining the industrialization threshold after 1850 also appeared to begin manufacturing in urban areas, in contrast to those nations reaching the industrialization threshold earlier. Although this phenomenon can, in part, be traced to the fall in transportation costs, it also lessened the influence of agricultural institutions on industrialization.

societies with the semi-marketized economic system had the highest level of economic development, they were more likely to have these institutions. Moreover, Tables 4-2 and 4-3 also show that the semi-marketized societies also had both significantly higher land rents, a higher incidence of fixed rents, and less unfree labor, all conducive, according to the previous argument, for industrialization at an earlier date.

E. Summary

Although certain rough generalizations can be drawn about the process of industrialization, exceptions abound for any hypothesis advanced and, as Adelman and Morris (1980: 2) note, "historical experience provides no single path, model, or pattern of industrialization." Nevertheless, a nation was more predisposed for early industrialization if its rural sector was characterized by the following conditions:

- The rural population had a significant share of literate people and labor productivity in agriculture was relatively high.
- The rural sector was penetrated by markets for goods, labor, land, and capital, at least for those nations where the government did not play a highly active role in the industrialization process.
- The land was cultivated either by the owner or by a person holding secure tenures, who could make key economic decisions without a great deal of community interference. This means that agriculture was not dominated by large estates or latifundia or by large farms with unfree labor.

These are not, of course, original ideas, although I believe that my approach has made them more robust. Nevertheless, it should again be emphasized that industrialization required other conditions that lay outside of the agricultural sector. For instance, the government had to ensure domestic order and enforceable contracts, and either public authorities or the private sector had to supply the country with a transportation, commercial, and financial infrastructure suitable for manufacturing production and the trade of manufactured products.[36]

The purpose of my analysis is to determine which of the four different types of agricultural economic systems would have been most likely to

---

[36] Of course, the government must also be limited in the amount that it can extract from the population in the form of taxes. Unfortunately, it is difficult to specify the optimal point. Mathias and O'Brien (1976) provide evidence that in the eighteenth century in England, the burden of taxation was greater than in France. Moreover, church tithes were also higher (Cooper, 1985: 169). Yet, despite these extractions, England reached the industrialization threshold more than a half-century before France.

favor an early transition to manufacturing – herding-plus, egalitarian, individualized, or semi-marketized. On all counts, the comparisons of national characteristics of early industrializers with the characteristics of the different agricultural economic systems in communities (Tables 4-1 and 4-2) suggest that the societies with a semi-marketized economic system were most likely to have had those characteristics favorable for early industrialization. More specifically, these societies had the highest agricultural productivity and the greatest incentives to become literate, they were more likely to have markets allocating goods, services, and labor, and they were also more likely to have individually owned fields with fewer communal restrictions and high fixed rents on the land. Nevertheless, the delayed industrialization of the Netherlands, which scored favorably on all these criteria, also indicates that the agricultural economic system alone is not sufficient to explain the transition to manufacturing. In reviewing the characteristics of the societies with other types of economic systems, none of the others had these preconditions for industrialization possessed by societies with a semi-marketized economic system.

Such results suggest that, contrary to its role in the transition from foraging to agriculture, the economic system did play an important role in the transition from agriculture to industry. Of course, many semi-marketized societies and states never made this transition, which means that a semi-marketized economic system was a necessary but not a sufficient condition for industrialization.

Moreover, these results also suggest that if the economic system of an agricultural society does not first change into a semi-marketized system, its chances for industrialization are considerably reduced. Of course, the faster-than-expected industrialization of Russia after the emancipation of the serfs also indicates that nations with these other agricultural economic systems are not inevitably doomed to economic backwardness. Nevertheless, the generalizations I draw about the influence of the different types of agricultural economic systems on industrialization are based on probabilities. What the analysis in this chapter has traced is simply the most probable path of industrialization.

The transition from agriculture to manufacturing contrasts in other respects with the transition from foraging to agriculture discussed in Chapter 3. The transition to industry required major changes in technology; the transition to agriculture represented no sharp technological break. Initially, the former was primarily a deliberate activity undertaken for monetary profit or national power, whereas the latter was an adjustment to demographic, social, or political changes. The former occurred in a relatively short period of time; the latter, over many centuries.

PART FOUR

INDUSTRIAL/SERVICE SOCIETIES

SIX

Advanced Market Economic Systems

In this chapter, I focus on economic systems of the industrialized OECD nations. These might seem simpler to analyze than foraging and agricultural economies, because we can draw upon more plentiful and standardized information. But, the complexity of these advanced economic systems also raises difficulties that were not necessary to confront in previous chapters.

The discussion begins with a cluster analysis to define the types of economic systems, using readily available data on forty different institutions and organizations. Although the results are not startling, they do confirm our intuitions, as well as the conclusions of several other studies using many fewer indicators. I then analyze the impact of these economic systems on the functioning of the economy, a task not possible for foraging and agricultural systems because of the lack of suitable data. Finally, I look at various political, ideological, social, and cultural correlations that might indicate why these countries adopted their current economic systems. In the following chapter, I examine how these advanced market systems have evolved over time and where they are heading.

A. Defining the Economic Systems

1. Data and Statistical Technique

We face a kaleidoscope of classifications and approaches when looking at the literature on economic systems of advanced market economies. A possible alternative to the cluster analysis used in previous chapters is a factor analysis to derive "ideal types," but because all of the OECD nations had mixed economies, this did not prove fruitful.[1] I continue, therefore, to apply the same statistical methods as in previous chapters.

For the data on economic institutions and organizations, I draw upon three different types of indicators: Some of these forty indicators are derived from the laws defining the institutions (e.g., various types of government regulations or creditor rights); others, from statistics about their activities (e.g., centralization of banks or the percentage of workers covered by collective-bargaining contracts); while still others, from expert opinion (e.g., the level of the economy at which wages are most often bargained or the competitiveness of the economic environment). The summary data in Table 6-1 also specify which of the three types of indicators is involved.[2] Whenever possible, I also tried to collect these indicators for 1990, the year before the Maastricht agreement was signed, because the homogenization of European economic institutions allegedly accelerated thereafter.

These indicators (discussed in detail in Appendix 6-2) are grouped into five categories: (a) those reporting the ways in which the product market functioned in the different countries (twelve indicators); (b) those describing aspects of the labor market and various types of labor institutions (eight indicators); (c) those referring to various characteristics of enterprises and the system of production (six indicators); (d) those detailing the relative importance of different types of direct governmental activities (seven indicators); and, finally, (e) those reporting particular aspects of the financial system (seven indicators). Some of these indicators overlap in certain respects, but all reflect what I believe to be crucial aspects of the property and distribution institutions of the societies.

2. The Results

Chart 6-1 presents the results of a cluster analysis when different numbers of clusters are specified.[3] I must emphasize that these are not subjective

---

[1] Appendix 6-1 provides details of the factor analysis underlying this experiment.

[2] The development of these indicators has been carried out principally by four teams: a primarily Harvard-based team composed of a shifting combination of Juan Botero, Simeon Djankov, Rafael La Porta, Florencio Lopez-de-Silanes, Andrei Shleifer, and Robert W. Vishny; a World Bank team composed of Daniel Kaufmann, Aart Kraay, M. Mastruzzi, and Pablo Zoldo-Lobatón; an OECD team of Giuseppe Nicoletti, Stefano Scarpetta, and Olivier Boylaud; and an independent team of Peter A. Hall and David Soskice. My intellectual debt to them should be readily apparent.

[3] As in previous chapters, I instructed the program to iterate two hundred times and then averaged the results of one hundred such calculations. I then repeated this procedure ten times (for the four clusters case, twenty-five times) and averaged the results of these runs. For each column,

judgments on my part but rather the results of the statistical analysis. From these calculations, we can draw several important conclusions.

CLUSTER PERMANENCE. Three clusters – namely, those consisting primarily of Southern European, Western European, and Nordic nations – appear relatively consistent when four to six clusters are specified. The cluster consisting primarily of Anglo-Saxon nations (hereafter the Anglo-Saxon-plus, or AS+, group) was the least homogeneous, with two of the nations (Switzerland and Japan) hiving off when five clusters were specified and then breaking up into two separate groups when six clusters were calculated.

CLUSTER BOUNDARIES. Of the twenty-one countries, three appeared to have irregular patterns in Chart 6-1. France, which was questionably in the Western European group in the four-cluster calculations, moved from the Western European cluster to the Southern European cluster; similarly, Switzerland, which was also a questionable member of the AS+ group in the four-cluster group, moved to the Western European cluster and finally to a separate cluster. This suggests that these two "wandering nations" laid close to the boundaries of the respective clusters – that is, away from the "core nations" forming each cluster; for this reason, I omit these two nations in the calculation of the averages for each system. A different kind of boundary problem arises with the economic system of Japan, which appeared solidly in the core of the AS+ nations when three and four clusters are specified, but broke off from them thereafter to form a separate cluster and then to join Switzerland in yet another cluster in the six-cluster calculation.

LEVELS OF SIMILARITY. The case of Japan, which is often considered to have an economic system very different from that of the United States or other AS+ nations, illustrates another feature of the cluster boundaries. As the prespecified number of separate clusters increases, the criteria for forming a cluster become ever tighter (as shown in Chart 1-1 for cluster S). What Chart 6-1 tells us is that, when considering only a few major criteria, Japan is most similar to the AS+ nations, but if we define economic systems in more institutional detail, then it must be considered as very different.

I then placed each country in the cluster where it most often appeared, designating with a question mark those cases where it did not appear in its most common cluster in less than 70 percent of the runs. Except for the calculations with five clusters, the various countries were found over 90 percent of the runs in the particular clusters specified in Chart 6-1.

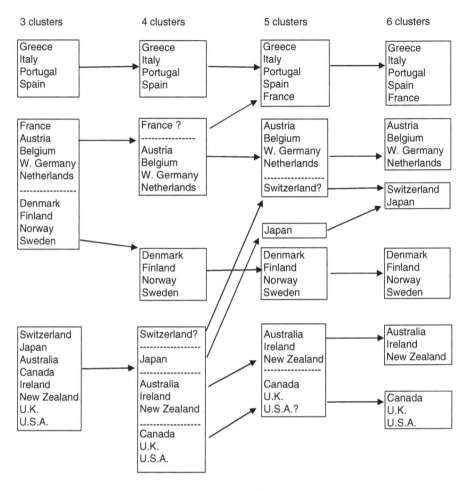

A question mark indicates that less than 70 percent of the cluster runs placed the country in that particular grouping.

Chart 6-1. Results of the cluster analysis for industrialized market economies.

INTERPRETATIONS. The clusters indicate the pattern of institutions that appear together in a group of countries and, as indicated in Chapter 1, I interpret the clusters as distinguishing different economic systems. The problem of separating the impacts of the level of economic development from the economic system also arises because the Southern European cluster of nations has a significantly lower average per capita GDP (in 1990 dollars) than the other nations in the sample. Although we need not at this point determine the direction of causation between the economic system and per capita GDP, the per capita GDP must serve as a control variable at all steps of the analysis, as in previous chapters. Using the MDL calculation, we can also determine that the optimal of clusters – or distinct economic systems – for our analysis is four.

To determine whether the composition of these clusters is robust, I made a similar calculation, but with only thirty indicators, and obtained essentially the same results.[4] When I reduced the number of indicators to eleven, about 75 percent of the countries appeared in the same clusters as in Chart 6-1.[5] In sum, the results appear robust and, moreover, forty indicators were useful for completeness even if they were not necessary to obtain the same results.

The composition of the four clusters is not surprising, and it is worth noting that other economists have recently come up with roughly the same groupings of nations. For instance, Jelle Visser (2001), who focused primarily on different models of industrial relations, distinguished four distinct types (i.e., Nordic corporatism, Western European social partnership, Anglo-Saxon pluralism, and Latin confrontation). Soskice (1999) and Kitschelt et al. (1999b) also arrived at quite similar groupings of nations; both placed emphasis on how the firm interacts with the rest of the economy, particularly with regard to the coordination of production, vocational training, and industrial relations. Soskice focused particularly on four criteria (i.e., the system of industrial relations, the financial system, the education and training system, and the system regulating inter-company relations); Kitschelt paid more attention to the coordination of production and the system of industrial relations.[6] In carrying out a cluster analysis based on a wide number

---

[4] To make this test more difficult, I also estimated a number of the indicators in a somewhat different way.

[5] I also calculated two other tests of robustness. One was a variance test, which started with the variance of the multidimensional distance between countries using the forty indicators and then compared this with the multidimensional variance between countries within the same cluster. For four clusters, the variance is reduced 41.5 percent; for six clusters, 53.8 percent.

A second test was making twenty-five runs and determining the percentage of times a given nation was placed in the cluster where it most often occurred (shown in Table 6-1). For the entire sample in these different runs, the various nations always appeared in the same cluster 93.9 percent of the time. Omitting France and Switzerland (the two "wanderer nations"), this rose to 97.7 percent.

[6] More specifically, both start with Soskice's distinction between nations with coordinated market economies and those with liberal market economies. The latter group includes Britain, Canada, Ireland, U.S., Australia, and New Zealand, although the authors note that the latter two nations have special characteristics that do not fit nicely into their schema. In the former group, they distinguish between those economies coordinated through industries and those coordinated through groups of companies across industries (e.g., the keiretsu of Japan and chaebol of Korea). Kitschelt and his colleagues also differentiate between those countries coordinated at the national level (Nordic countries) and those coordinated at the sectoral level (some Western European

Table 6-1. *Defining average characteristics of four industrial economic systems in 1990*

| Features | | Indicator | Range | Devel. Elasticity | Economic Systems | | | | |
A	B				Southern European	AS+	Nordic	Western European	Total Sample
Product market									
L	D	Regulation of product market	0.6–3.1*	−0.40	2.800+	1.086	2.100	2.000	1.876
L	P	Protection of patent rights	0–1	+0.66	0.599	0.698	0.702	0.805	0.707
L	P	Good legal environment for markets	0–1	+0.19	0.747−	0.846	0.882	0.880	0.842
LS	PD	Barriers to starting new businesses	0 upward	−2.21?	0.542+	0.074−	0.104	0.321+?	0.237
LSX	P	Social partnership of capital and labor	0–1	+1.16	0.313	0.371−?	0.852+?	0.777	0.548
S	D	Ratio of government subsidies to GDP	0–1	−1.04	0.028	0.017	0.032	0.028	0.024
S	D	Intersectoral grants for R & D	0–1	−0.36	0.366	0.261	0.290	0.304	0.296
S	D	Foreign trade barriers	0–1	−0.25	0.621	0.703	0.501	0.693	0.636
XL	D	Freedom to set prices	0–1	+0.52	0.539	0.748+	0.650	0.637	0.663
X	D	Product market competition	0–1	+0.08	0.700	0.726	0.654−?	0.758	0.713
X	D	Effectiveness of antitrust laws	0–1	+0.22?	0.436	0.529+?	0.471	0.516	0.493
X	PD	Presence of business clusters	0–1	+0.54	0.513	0.626	0.650	0.663	0.616
Labor market									
S	D	Coverage of collect. barg. agreements	0–1	−1.20	0.797+	0.459−	0.673	0.888+	0.663
L	D	Centralization of largest peak union org.	0–1	−0.62	0.476	0.367	0.464	0.607	0.457
L	D	Power of work-place representatives	0–1	−0.48*	0.250	0.036	0.125	0.188	0.138
L	D	Legal protection: workers, employment	0–1	−0.63	0.662	0.362−	0.418	0.485	0.464
L	D	Legal protection: labor bargaining rights	0–1	−0.82	0.698+	0.331	0.444	0.384	0.452
X	D	Coordination of wage negotiations	0–1	−0.84*	0.417	0.292−?	0.688	0.750	0.520
XS	D	Strength of vocational training system	0–1	+3.88*	0.500	0.000−	0.938+	0.750	0.500
X	D	Level of economy where wages bargained	0–1	−0.12*	0.385	0.323−?	0.750+	0.594	0.482
Production and business sector									
S	P	Widespread firm ownership	0–1	+1.14*	0.000−?	0.557+	0.200	0.100−?	0.267
S	P	Importance of large manufacturing firms	0–1	+1.26	0.203	0.427	0.344	0.409	0.364

164

#	A	B	Feature	Range	Development elasticity					
3	L	P	Power of peak organizations	0–1	-1.07^*	0.476	0.245^{-}	$\mathbf{0.857^{+}}$	0.464	0.468
4	L	P	Shareholder rights	0–1	$+0.45$	$\mathbf{0.250^{-}}$	0.771^{+}	0.500	$\mathbf{0.250^{-}}$	0.476
5	L	P	Creditor rights	0–1	-0.07	0.500	0.400	0.550	0.650	0.486
6	L	P	Significant worker role in firm decisions	0–1	-1.12^*	0.283	$\mathbf{0.000^{-}}$	$\mathbf{0.650^{+}}$	0.533	0.298

Government sector

#	A	B	Feature	Range	Development elasticity					
1	S	PD	Govt. direct share of fixed investment	0–1	-0.21	0.152	0.139	0.133	0.114	0.137
2	S	D	Govt. share of total consumption	0–1	$+0.31$	0.197	0.217	$\mathbf{0.317^{+}}$	0.222	0.233
3	S	D	Ratio of govt. domestic transfers to GDP	0–1	$+0.13$	0.149	$\mathbf{0.127^{-}}$	0.198	$\mathbf{0.221^{+}}$	0.167
4	S	P	Direct govt. share of total employment	0–1	$+0.34$	0.149	$\mathbf{0.142^{-?}}$	$\mathbf{0.316^{+}}$	0.155	0.181
5	S	P	State enterprise share of total employment	0–1	-0.93	0.036	0.023	0.043	0.043	0.036
6	S	D	Share of R & D in government sector	0–1	$\mathbf{-1.66}$	0.273	0.204	0.152	0.114	0.184
7	L	D	Coverage of social security system	0–1	-0.02	2.248	2.106	$\mathbf{2.560^{+}}$	1.950	2.206

Financial sector

#	A	B	Feature	Range	Development elasticity					
1	L	D	Central bank independence	0–1	$\mathbf{+0.99}$	0.330	0.498	0.406	$\mathbf{0.604^{+?}}$	0.479
2	L	PD	Restriction on bank activities	0–1	-0.09	0.354	0.393	0.313	0.250	0.317
3	L	D	Openness of external capital flow	0–4	$\mathbf{+3.48}$	3.225	3.429	3.525	3.750	3.490
4	S	PD	Comprehensiveness of accounting rpts.	0–1	$\mathbf{+0.49}$	0.603	0.802	0.822	$\mathbf{0.669^{-?}}$	0.736
5	S	P	Bank concentration	0–1	-0.72	$\mathbf{0.550^{-}}$	0.611	$\mathbf{0.827^{+}}$	0.653	0.638
6	S	D	Relative size of financial system	0 upward.*	$\mathbf{+1.01}$	0.812	1.186	0.835	1.210	1.101
7	S	D	Stock market activity/bank activity	0 upward.	$+0.34$	$\mathbf{0.074^{-}}$	$\mathbf{0.671^{+?}}$	0.280	$\mathbf{0.188^{-?}}$	0.367
			Per capita GDP (1990 dollars)			$\mathbf{12342}$	17149	17870	17507	16696

Notes: Features: Column A designates whether the indicator is based on legal definitions (L), statistics (S), expert (X), or some combination thereof. Column B designates whether the indicator refers primarily to property (P) or distribution (D). *Range:* An asterisk designates that the range is not absolute but is based on the highest and lowest recorded values. *Development elasticity* designates the percentage change of the indicator resulting from a 1 percent change in the per capita GDP; and a rough estimate is designated with an asterisk. The second through fifth data columns present averages (excluding France and Switzerland). The level of significance is determined when per capita income is held constant, and the sign of the coefficient in this regression is designated in a superscript. A statistically significant result at the 0.05 level is boldface, with a question mark placed as a superscript if the level of significance is 0.10. Sources and exact meaning of the data are discussed in Appendix 6-2; the actual data are presented in Statistical Appendix SA-6.

of indicators of governmental regulation of (and intervention in) product and labor markets, Nicoletti, Scarpetta, and Boylaud (2000) also derived roughly the same grouping of countries as that shown in the chart. The prosaic results of my cluster analysis, however, give us greater confidence in the outcome of the analysis of foraging and agricultural societies, with which we have less familiarity.

3. Special Characteristics of the Four Individual Economic Systems

Table 6-1 presents data on the forty institutional characteristics used to define the types of economic systems. There is no need to try the patience of the reader by describing each characteristic in detail; in Appendix 6-2, I carry out this task and also indicate the relevant sources of the underlying data.

To clarify the role of the level of economic development on the economic system, two types of comparisons are useful. The first test, shown in the first data column, is a simple income elasticity – that is, the percentage change in the numerical value of the indicator associated with a 1 percent change in per capita GDP.[7] For instance, the degree of protection of patent rights is significantly and positively related to the level of economic development, whereas, by contrast, the degree of regulation of the product market is not.

The second test of the role of the level of economic development, shown in the second through fifth data columns, presents the average values for each indicator among the nations sharing a particular type of economic system. I have also determined if this value is significantly different from the other nations in the sample when holding the level of per capita GDP constant.[8] Statistically significant results for the economic system variable

nations, such as Belgium, Germany, and Switzerland). For particular purposes, Soskice has also distinguished between Western European and Southern European economies, placing France toward the latter group.

[7] In order to use the entire sample, the "borderline" nations are included in these calculations. Such a calculation, of course, tells us nothing about the direction of causation.

[8] More specifically, to determine whether the type of economic system can be explained by a particular institutional indicator, I calculated regressions of the following type:

$$EcSys = a + b \, DevLev + c \, I,$$

where EcSys is a dummy variable that is equal to 1 if the society has the specified economic system and equal to 0 if it doesn't; DevLev is the level of economic development, I is the indicator under examination; and a, b, and c are the calculated regression coefficients. For forty indicators and four economic systems, this required calculating 160 regressions. Because the variable to be explained is equal to either 1 or 0, I used a probit-regression technique.

at the 0.05 level from the regressions underlying this exercise are shown in boldface, with the sign of the calculated coefficient shown in the superscript; a question mark in the superscript distinguishes significance at the 0.10 level from the 0.05 level. Thus, significantly more workers in the Southern European nations belonged to labor unions, whereas among the AS+ nations, significantly fewer belonged.

Finally, in the last data column, I present the average value of the indicator for the entire sample. This provides more perspective on the particular values for the individual systems.

In major respects, the AS+ economic system embodied the characteristics of a traditional liberal market economy, with organized labor in a relatively weak position. Controlling for per capita GDP, the countries with this type of economic system had significantly fewer barriers to starting new enterprises, greater freedom of firms to set their own prices, a smaller share of workers belonging to labor unions, less legal protection against job loss and fewer safeguards for collective bargaining, more widespread firm ownership, a weaker system of vocational education, fewer national organizations representing employers, greater protection of shareholder rights, little role of workers in firm decision-making, and a lower ratio of government transfer expenditures to the GDP. Less certain characteristics (the significance level is 0.10) included a less apparent social partnership between management and labor, more effective antitrust laws, less coordination of wage negotiations (which were more likely to be carried out at the enterprise level), a smaller share of total employment by the government, and more financing of enterprise investment through the stock market rather than banks.

The results show what we already know, that the Nordic economic system was, in may ways, the opposite of the AS+ system, particularly with regard to the economic role of the government. Among the statistically significant characteristics of these economies were a greater strength of the vocational system, bargaining of wages at the national or industrial level, greater power of national employer organizations, a higher share of government consumption expenditures in the GDP (i.e., government expenditures excluding transfers, subsidies, and investment), a larger share of total employment by the government, greater coverage of the social security system, and a higher concentration of banking activity. At a lower level of statistical confidence, the nations with the Nordic economic system had a greater social partnership of capital and labor and less competition in the product market.

The Western European economic system reflected a different type of ordered market economy. When the level of economic development is factored out, a larger share of workers in these countries belonged to labor unions, minority stockholders had fewer rights, and government transfers were a higher ratio to the GDP. Other less certain characteristics were a greater social partnership of capital and labor, less widespread firm ownership, higher central-bank independence, less comprehensive accounting standards, and a smaller share of industrial investment financed through the stock market.

Finally, the Southern European economic system revealed yet another admixture of characteristics, some related to a lower average level of economic development of the various nations, others unique to this group of countries. When the per capita GDP is held constant, we find that these nations had more regulation of the product market, a more unfavorable legal environment for markets, more barriers to starting new businesses, more legal protection against job loss and more safeguards for collective bargaining, a smaller share of workers belonging to labor unions, fewer stockholder rights, and less concentration of banking activities.

By and large, the major results of this statistical exercise should not be surprising to those familiar with the economies of the OECD nations. As I show in the next chapter, many of the institutional characteristics defining the particular types of economic systems have been changing over time. For instance, since 1990, peak employer organizations in the United States may have been becoming stronger (e.g., the Business Roundtable), while in some European nations they were becoming weaker.

These results also raise the critical question of the impact of these institutional differences on the performance of the economy, a topic discussed in the following section. But, before turning to this question, it is useful to note two unexpected findings.

SIZE OF THE GOVERNMENT SECTOR. The government, of course, played an important causal role in many of these institutional indicators. Nevertheless, the seven indicators for the size of the government sector turned out to be no more likely to distinguish the types of economic systems than the other four classes of indicators. This suggests that the traditional focus on the size of the government sector as an exclusive means of categorizing an economic system is misplaced, and that we must pay just as much attention to other economic institutions. It is quite possible, however, that the political and social forces influencing the size and type of government sector were also important in structuring the economic institutions outside the government sector.

UNIMPORTANT INDICATORS. A number of the indicators, which I had assumed would differentiate between the economic systems, did not play such a role. Among others, these included patent protection, the ratio of government subsidies to the GDP, barriers to foreign trade, the presence of "business clusters" (groups of separately owned businesses in different industries operating together), centralization of umbrella labor organizations ("peak labor unions"), the power of union representatives in the work place, the relative share of employment in large manufacturing firms, creditor rights, the government's direct share of fixed investment, the employment share of state-owned enterprises, the share of R & D carried out by the government, restrictions on bank activities, and openness of external capital flows.

In brief, this statistical investigation confirms in a systematic fashion what we intuitively know about the economic systems of the OECD nations from our general reading of the literature. One caveat, however, deserves emphasis. The foregoing discussion focuses on averages of nations with the same type of economic system. Although all nations with the same system were similar in some respects, this is not true in all respects; and, of course, within the four main groupings, the economic system of each nation had its own unique features. More specifically, if we wish to gain greater understanding of the economic system of France or Netherlands, we must not focus our attention just on the results of Chart 6-1 and Table 6-1 but rather look at the very special features of each economy. For France, for instance, this would mean looking at the legacies of its indicative planning system and the peculiar aspects of its labor unions; for the Netherlands, this would mean that we must understand the operations of its tripartite government/industry/labor union commissions that have helped to guide government policy. In brief, my approach focuses on the most general aspects of the economic system, rather than the specific details of the individual economies.

B. Economic Performance and Economic Systems

The performance of the economy is an effect of the economic system and a cause for systemic change. In trying to isolate the determinants of these systems, it is useful to explore these relationships by examining the economic performance of the four systems.

A possible starting point comes from the study of the origins of individual institutions. Of the many explanations of institutional origins, the one most tightly connected to standard economic theory is the benefit/cost approach: Institutions are created whenever their social benefits exceed their social costs. Such an approach, however, has three major shortcomings: (1) It assumes that economic institutions exist to promote economic efficiency or some other performance criteria. This seems at odds with what we know about the real world, where long-lasting economic institutions in many countries are often a source of considerable economy-wide inefficiencies. (2) It assumes that the costs and benefits fall on "the people" as a whole. In many cases, however, politically powerful individuals create such institutions to reap great benefits for themselves, while the rest of the population bears the costs. (3) Finally, it assumes that the relative benefits and costs of institutions are visible and understandable and that people are sufficiently rational to base their decisions on such considerations. If these conditions do not hold, it is unlikely that people would "choose institutions" in a systematic manner or that we could verify the benefit/cost hypothesis.

Many of the same objections can be made to the benefit/cost approach of an entire configuration of institutions – that is, of the economic system. Nevertheless, certain economic benefits of the system – namely, particular performance indicators – can be measured, even though the full human costs of the system cannot. The question now is whether we can explain why nations have particular economic systems by their measurable differences in performance.

1. Direct Economic Considerations

At this point, I offer two conjectures. First, if the major institutions of an economic system were specifically designed to achieve certain economic outcomes, it is quite possible that such an economic system would be significantly different from others. In this regard, the income redistribution system, whereby the government transfers income from one group to another, comes immediately to mind. Second, if a particular type of economic performance is relatively apparent to all, then in a set of functioning democracies it would seem unlikely that major performance differences between nations with different economic systems would persist for very long. All of the OECD nations in my sample have been democracies, at least in the last few decades of the twentieth century. According to this argument, considerable political pressure would build up in such a political system to change an underperforming economic system. Two exceptions to this conjecture are immediately apparent: the system might maintain its inertia if changing one institution required changing many other institutions as well; or if, as noted previously, poor performance was due to institutions and mechanisms that were difficult for citizens to understand.[9]

Panel A of Table 6-2, which is set up much like the previous table, shows one instance of a very visible impact of the economic system: namely, its impact on income distribution. This indicator is not related to the level of economic development (the first data column), so the comparison of systems is less difficult. When we look at income inequality in terms of the ratio of incomes at the 20th and 80th percentile to the median income, it is apparent that the direct distribution of incomes before taxes and transfers (more precisely, factor incomes) was not significantly different between three of the four economic systems, but the AS+ had significantly higher relative factor incomes in the upper part of the income distribution. By contrast, the distribution of income after taxes and transfers (disposable personal income) was significantly more unequal in the AS+ nations and significantly more equal in the Nordic countries. In the Western European nations, the ratio of income of those in the 20th percentile to the median shows significantly greater equality than the other nations when the impact of per capita income is factored out.[10] The extent of the redistribution of income through the fiscal system in each economic system can be measured by comparing the percentile ratios for the two concepts of income. Such an exercise shows that fiscal redistribution of income was particularly important in the Western European and Nordic economic systems.

Panel B of Table 6-2 presents four common macroeconomic performance indicators, which are generally believed to reflect the well-being of a large part of the population, a sentiment endlessly repeated by leading politicians

---

[9] Any economic outcome can have several possible causes, for instance, random events, particular governmental policies, or the impact of particular economic institutions. As a causal factor, the economic system can buffer the impact of random events; it can directly influence outcomes by channeling economic activity in a particular direction; it can reinforce or dampen tendencies toward change arising from forces outside the system; or it can act indirectly by facilitating or obstructing governmental economic policies. Such considerations lead to statistical nightmares, as illustrated by the enormous statistical difficulties in determining whether the size of government really affects the economic growth rate. Slemrod (1995) has a lucid discussion of these problems. Lindert (2004a:17, 2004b: 82–99) shows how many of these difficulties can be overcome and demonstrates that the relative importance of social transfers in OECD nations have apparently had little impact on GDP growth rates in the latter decades of the twentieth century. If economists have difficulty in understanding the impact of the economic system, then others may be excused for their confusion.

[10] These conclusions also hold when other percentile ratios and other measures of income distribution (gini coefficients and Atkinson ratios) are used.

Table 6-2. *Average values of economic performance indicators for OECD countries*

		Economic System				
	Development Elasticity	Southern European	AS+	Nordic	Western European	Total Sample
Panel A: Income distribution around 1990: Ratios of incomes at specified percentiles						
20th to 50th percentile						
Factor income	−1.23	n.a.	0.389	0.269	0.379	0.384
Disposable personal income	+0.03	0.624	0.590^{-}	0.700^{+}	$0.695^{+?}$	0.654
80th to 50th percentile						
Factor income	−0.09	n.a.	1.758^{+}	1.609	1.625	1.661
Disposable personal income	−0.11	1.544	1.601^{+}	1.341^{-}	1.428	1.479
Panel B: Macroeconomic indicators: Average annual rates, 1980–2000						
GDP per capita	−0.35	1.99%	2.27%	1.80%	1.89%	1.95%
GDP per worker	−0.44	1.59	1.78	2.16	1.70	1.73
Unemployment rate	**−1.20**	10.68	7.66	6.18	6.79	7.65
Inflation rate	**−1.85**	9.30^{+}	3.54	4.03	2.47	3.47

Note: Development elasticity designates the percentage change of the variable associated with a 1 percent change in the per capita GDP. In the second through fifth data columns, the tests of statistical significance are made by calculating ordinary least-squares regressions of the following type:

$$\text{Indicator} = a + b\,Ycap + c\,EcSys,$$

where Ycap is per capita GDP, EcSys is a dummy variable with a value of 1 for a particular economic system and a value of 0 for all other economic systems; and a, b, and c are calculated coefficients. France and Switzerland are excluded from these calculations (but not the calculation of the elasticities).

I estimated the income distribution statistics from data sets of the Luxembourg Income Study <www.lisproject.org>. In these calculations, data are missing for Japan, New Zealand, Greece, and Portugal, which means that for the Southern European system, only two countries are included and, therefore, the results should be carefully interpreted.

Appendix 6-3 discusses the sources of data for the other macroeconomic indicators.

of all ideological stripes. These indicators cover the period 1980 through 2000, thus spanning the year (1990) for which the systems were determined.

The data in the first column show that both the unemployment and inflation rates were lower in those countries with a higher level of per capita GDP. When the 1990 level of per capita GDP is held constant, the data reveal that, with one exception, the differences between the performance levels of the economic systems were not statistically significant for any of the performance indicators. For the rate of per capita GDP growth, I reran the regressions holding not just per capita GDP in the initial year constant, but also the average years of education of those in the labor force in the initial year and the ratio of gross capital investment to the GDP from 1975 through 1995 (to account for lags in the impact of investment). These three variables, according to Levine and Renelt (1992), constitute the minimum required for testing growth models.[12] The results, however, were the same as before and showed that the economic system appeared to have no impact on growth rates, at least with the control variables I have specified.

The single exception to the apparent unimportance of the economic system of the OECD countries in explaining macroeconomic behavior was the rate of inflation, which was significantly higher in the Southern European nations. In part, the weaker fiscal disciplines of these Southern European nations, which underlay this inflation, can be attributed to the lack of the central bank's policymaking independence from the ministry of finance (as shown by the first financial indicator in Table 6-1). To prevent tut-tutting, I might add that inflation – unless it is extremely severe – has not usually had an adverse impact on either growth or unemployment in my sample of OECD nations.

The seeming unimportance of the economic system on economic growth and unemployment in the OECD countries does not necessarily hold for all types of economic systems. As shown in the following chapters, the economic system of developing market economies and also of Marxist regimes did have an important impact on economic growth. At this point, it should also be noted that the apparent lack of impact of economic system on certain macroeconomic indicators among the OECD nations also did not provide any incentive for any of these countries to change its economic system, a topic discussed at greater length in the next chapter.

---

[12] Rodrik, Subramanian, and Trebbi (2002) present various regressions showing that to explain economic growth, geographical and trade variables have little explanatory power when institutional variables are also included. Given the relatively small size of my sample, I have, therefore, omitted such variables in my regression exploring the other determinants of economic growth.

2. Other Performance Indicators

The performance of an economic system can, of course, be rated on many indicators other than those discussed herein. In this section, I very briefly consider four indicators of a quite different type: class struggle, health, pollution, and innovations.[13]

CLASS STRUGGLE. To explore whether certain economic systems lead to more overt conflict between capital and labor, I use three proxies for class struggle in the period from 1988 through 1992: the days of work lost in strikes in the manufacturing sector as a percentage of total work days, days of absenteeism per manufacturing worker per year, and days of work lost per worker per year because of claimed illness (which partly overlaps with the second indicator). When we hold the level of per capita income constant, the Southern European countries had significantly higher strike days per worker. At a lower level of statistical significance, the Nordic nations had greater absenteeism, in contrast to the AS+ nations, which had less.[14] One indirect indicator of class struggle, because it may reflect employer negligence toward workers, is the rate of industrial accidents, as measured either by days of work lost or by fatalities. When the impact of per capita GDP is held constant, the accident rates for the four economic systems did not significantly differ from 1988 through 1992. Such mixed results suggest either that the class-struggle indicators were not tied to the economic system in any consistent manner or that strikes and absenteeism were substitutes for each other.

HEALTH STATUS. Three indicators of health in the 1988–92 period are readily available: life expectancy, infant mortality, and low birth weights. When we hold per capita GDP constant, the Nordic nations have significantly fewer babies with low birth weights, which is probably a function of their higher governmental health expenditures. At a lower level of statistical significance, the AS+ nations had more babies with low birth weights. For the other two

---

[13] The sources of all data used in this and the following paragraph are discussed in Appendix 6-4. The statistical analysis is carried out in the same manner as in Table 6-2, with per capita GDP held constant.

[14] Statistical experiments using an income distribution variable (the ratio of incomes in the 80th to the 20th percentile) suggest that in the case of strike days lost, this income ratio may have served as the most direct cause, so that the economic system was only an indirect cause. When I specify "possibly" in the text, I mean that the calculated regression coefficient is statistically significant, but only at the 0.10 level. Absenteeism is also influenced by nonsystemic factors. For instance, if a high percentage of both parents are in the labor force, absenteeism may reflect the necessity to tend a sick child rather than worker resistance to management.

indicators, however, no statistically significant differences between the economic systems could be found.

POLLUTION. The control of pollution is another success criterion of an economic system, and I focus on three types of air pollution for which data for the 1988–92 period are readily available: namely, sulfur oxides, nitrogen oxides, and carbon monoxide. Statistical calculations to determine the role of the economic system yield mixed results and depend on the control variables. If we hold both per capita GDP and population density constant, however, none of the economic systems has significantly different pollution rates from the others.[15] If we look at pollution restrictions using observer data (namely, surveys of business people [Nicoletti and Pryor, forthcoming] and hold per capita GDP constant, the Western European nations had significantly more pollution regulations. Nevertheless, the relation between economic system and actual pollution, once population density and the level of development are taken into account, appears weak.

INNOVATION. One of the major arguments for the alleged superiority of the AS+ economic system is that it is more encouraging of innovation. A proxy for such activity is the average number of new patents per capita in the 1988–92 period. When we hold per capita GDP constant, no statistically significant differences between the economic systems can be found.[16]

Of the four kinds of performance criteria discussed, the economic system had a significant impact on only two indicators: namely, strike days and low birth weight.[17] Such disappointing results may arise either because the

---

[15] When I used only per capita GDP as the control variable, the AS+ countries had significantly higher emissions of sulfur oxides and carbon monoxide, whereas the Western European nations had significantly lower emissions for sulfur oxides.

[16] Appendix 6-4 discusses how I partly circumvented comparability problems of the international patent statistics.

[17] I also tried a number of other statistical experiments – for instance, using the indicator bravely devised by Afonso, Schuknecht, and Tanzi (2003) to measure the performance of governmental administration in 1990. It is composed of four equally weighted indices measuring corruption, red tape, quality of the judiciary, and the size of the shadow economy. When we use their data for 1990 and hold per capita GDP constant, the Southern European countries score significantly worse than the other countries, whereas the Nordic countries possibly score higher. I suspect, however, that such results are due more to differences in the social capital and interpersonal trust than to the economic system per se. I also regressed the systems variables against several of their measures of efficiency of the government sector for 2000 but found little of interest. Using survey data on governmental corruption (Mocan, 2004), I found no significant difference between the four economic systems.

performance indicators are not very satisfactory or because very specific institutions, such as government health services, had the most important impact on performance. In this latter case, the economic system embraces too many institutions to capture such a specific impact.

3. Some General Considerations

Unraveling the quite different roles that particular institutions may play within a given economic system provides a useful perspective to understanding the impact of the economic system on performance.

CRITICAL IMPORTANCE OF ONE OR SEVERAL INSTITUTIONS. The economic performance of a nation may depend on a few institutions rather than on the economic system as a whole. For instance, an enormous amount of scholarly energy has been devoted to isolating those few institutions that directly account for differences in the rate of economic growth. For such analyses, Acemoglu, Johnson, and Robinson (2004) place great emphasis on security of property rights. They and others also stress the importance of the availability of finance and other features of the financial system.[18] Another example is provided by Timur Kuran (2003) who, in a fascinating essay, argues that the Middle East became economically underdeveloped about a millennium ago because of the influence of three interlocking institutions: the Islamic law of inheritance, the absence in Islamic law of the concept of a corporation, and the existence of the *waqf* (a charitable foundation), which locked vast resources into unproductive organizations. Whether the logic of institutions ties these three institutions to other economic institutions remains to be seen.

VARIATIONS IN RELATIVE PERFORMANCE OF ECONOMIC SYSTEMS. This can be seen most clearly by looking at performance data over time. For instance, the data underlying Table 6-2 show that, on average, the AS+ nations had higher average growth of per capita GDP during the 1980s and 1990s than the Western European nations; but, in the 1950s and 1960s, the reverse was

---

[18] This literature is reviewed by Beck, Demirgç-Kunt, and Levine (2003), who trace the origin of these financial structures and institutions to the type of legal system. But, other possible property institutions unrelated to finance, such as the presence of certain types of joint stock companies, come readily to mind. Recently, Glaeser et al. (2004) have also provided some interesting evidence challenging the conventional wisdom that property institutions have a great influence on economic growth.

true.[19] A different kind of variation can also occur at a single point in time among the nations with the same economic system. For instance, although the data between 1980 and 2000 show the average unemployment rate in the Nordic countries to be roughly the same as that of other nations, this rate was about twice as high in Denmark and Finland as in Norway and Sweden.

INTERACTIONS BETWEEN ECONOMIC EVENTS (SHOCKS), INSTITUTIONS, AND OUTCOMES. A number of economists have emphasized that the economic environment in the 1950s and 1960s was much different than it was in the 1980s and 1990s, when unemployment rose in certain countries with particular labor market institutions.[20] For instance, countries whose institutions favored rising monetary wages, laws raising the costs to employers of releasing workers, or high and long-lasting payments to the unemployed are more likely to experience higher long-term unemployment when shocks – such as falling productivity, rising inflation, and rising real interest rates – hit the economy, which they did in the last quarter of the twentieth century. And, of course, economists have invoked these arguments to explain why unemployment rates in many European nations increased so greatly in the same period. In brief, changes in the economic environment interacted with particular labor market institutions, which, in turn, affected other economic outcomes in ways that depended on the configuration of these institutions. It might be added that some of these labor market institutions are not included in my forty indicators because their scope is too specialized. Nevertheless, they played a key role in particular labor market outcomes.

INSTITUTIONS REINFORCING EACH OTHER. The redistribution of income is, as indicated previously, an integral feature of the economic system. Although such an outcome can be traced to governmental actions, three other critical institutions can also influence the results:[21] (i) Labor unions have generally acted to narrow wage differences, and changes in labor-union membership affect the degree of equalization in many (but not all) groups of the labor

---

[19] The data for the earlier period were drawn from Maddison (2003). Nevertheless, with the possible exception of the AS+ nations, the differences between one system and another in the 1950s and 1960s were not statistically significant when we hold constant such control variables as per capita GDP in the initial year.

[20] I draw especially on the work of Blanchard (1997); Blanchard and Wolfers (2000); Bertola, Blau, and Kahn (2001); and Lazear (1990) for the discussion in this paragraph.

[21] Discussion in this paragraph draws on the empirical and theoretical work of Blau and Kahn (1994) and Card (1998).

force. (ii) Strong legal support for collective bargaining reinforces the equalizing effect of union activity. (iii) Income equality is further strengthened by wage bargaining at the industry or national level rather than at the enterprise level. Thus, in the United States, which experienced a decline in both union membership and collective bargaining in the latter part of the twentieth century, and where wages tended to be negotiated at the enterprise level, we would expect (and, in fact, find) growing inequality of wages, a trend reinforced in the late twentieth century by the impact of greater imports from low-wage nations.

INSTITUTIONS COUNTERACTING EACH OTHER'S EFFECTS. Peter Lindert (2004a, 2004b) asks an interesting question: Why did the Nordic nations, which tax heavily and spend lavishly on social welfare, show growth rates little different from other nations? Certainly, conventional belief, as well as sophisticated statistical studies (e.g., De Avila and Strauch, 2003), suggests that such taxes should discourage investment and growth. Among other things, Lindert points out that the mix of taxes in some of these Nordic nations was more pro-growth than in many OECD countries with lower tax rates; that these Nordic nations adopted several measures to minimize young adults' incentive to avoid work and training; that their government subsidies to early retirement took the least productive employees out of work, thereby raising labor productivity; and that much of social spending, especially on education, raised productivity. Blau and Kahn (1994) also point out that although compressed wage differentials discourage a person from investing in more training, Sweden circumvents this disincentive by subsidizing advanced training, thus making it less of a financial burden to the recipient. Slemrod (1995) notes that a high degree of interpersonal trust and governmental honesty (both are discussed in the next section) also aided Nordic economic growth.[22]

From this array of considerations, two main conclusions can be quickly drawn. First, in linking the economic system to economic performance, it is

---

[22] In many cases, it is difficult to determine whether the reinforcement effects of economic institutions or their counteracting effects are stronger. For instance, Nickell and Layard (1999) show that in the 1983–94 period, unemployment in twenty OECD nations was significantly and positively related to union density, union contract coverage, the ratio of unemployment payments to wages, the length of unemployment benefits, and the tax wedge between wages and income, and was negatively related to coordination of wage bargaining above the level of the enterprise and to active labor-market policies. These various institutions and policies do not, however, occur in a single package but rather in varying degrees in different countries, so that assessing their overall impact in a particular country requires a comparative analysis of many countries.

essential to take into account variables representing the changing economic environment. Second, in many cases, the economic system variable is too broad to link directly to economic performance, and we must look instead at the individual components of the system and the ways they reinforce or counteract each other.

C. Possible Causes Underlying the Adoption of an Economic System

Why do certain industrialized market economies have one type of economic system rather than another? In this section, I look at three sets of possible causes: historical/geographical, political/ideological, and social/cultural.

1. Long-term Historical/Geographical Determinants[23]

A VERY LONG VIEW. An historical detour to look at economic conditions around the turn of the first millennium yields some relevant insights. In outlining various ideal types of political authority in agricultural societies, Max Weber (1947: 341–58) distinguished systems with highly centralized political authority (e.g., sultanism) from systems in which political authority and economic power were more dispersed. Among the latter, he argued that the most decentralized was feudalism, where local political leaders inherited authority and were only nominally bound to the center by a formal promise of fealty.[24] In between these extremes was a type of "decentralized patrimonialism," where the ruler tried to forestall the growth of an independent landed aristocracy by awarding benefices only to an office, not a person or family; such a system was characterized by a pyramid of patron–client relations, with the top administrators exercising considerable power. The peasants at the lowest level of the feudal structure were serfs, who had very little freedom of movement. In a patrimonial system, however, peasants had a variety of statuses, depending on the situation; they might have been serfs, landless laborers, or independent peasant farmers.

For many centuries after the turn of the first millennium, according to many political historians, patrimonialism distinguished the political systems in Southern Europe (and later in Latin America) from those in the rest of

---

[23] The analysis in the first two paragraphs is heavily indebted to a conversation with James Kurth.
[24] Such an approach defines "centralization" by looking down from the top of the political pyramid.

the European continent.[25] Europe north of the Alps was distinguished by different forms of feudalism, all of which varied considerably from that found in the Western European core countries, which generally serve as our model for feudalism. For instance, this form of social organization was much less embedded in English society than in Western Europe and featured more individualism, greater personal mobility, a free yeomanry, and more extensive rights of private property (for both men and women), including the free disposal of land and a certain degree of commercial activity (Macfarlane, 1979).[26] In the Nordic countries, feudalism also took a much lighter form, if we can speak of feudalism at all,[27] and historians have explained this in several ways. For instance, Heckscher (1963) notes the important role of internal colonization within several of these Nordic countries, a process that emphasized equality among people rather than dependency. Moreover, in all of these countries (as in England), the long coastal strips in relation to the remaining land mass allowed traders and travelers to avoid road tolls, an easy income source for landlords elsewhere. This placed a brake on feudal expansion. Individual land ownership also seemed to play a more important role than in Western Europe. For instance, at the threshold of modern times, peasant private land holdings accounted for 96 percent of all agricultural land in Finland and slightly more than 50 percent in Sweden (Heckscher, 1963: 31); in Denmark, however, the percentage was apparently much smaller. Although serfs, villains, and rules binding certain people to the land were found in parts of Scandinavia, their significance was less than in Western Europe. To this list I might add that in these Nordic nations, the social impact of tribes and the extended family units lasted far longer than in Western Europe, another aspect of social structure that discouraged feudal tendencies.

Thus, the four economic systems of the industrialized OECD nations of Europe today roughly correspond in their geographical distribution to the four forms of social organization that prevailed in the same regions in Europe a millennium ago: north of the Alps, three quite distinct forms

---

[25] This argument is summarized by Kurth (1993), who cites many past and contemporary authorities. For instance, he notes that, according to Talleyrand, "Europe stops at the Pyrenees" and Italy was only "a promontory that links Europe to Africa." Metternich added that Greece lay "beyond the pale of civilization." To these statesmen, the politics of the countries of Southern Europe were considerably different from that of the countries in Western Europe.

[26] The consequences of these differences were noted by many continental travelers in England. For instance, in 1729 Montesquieu wrote, "I am here in a country [England] which hardly resembles the rest of Europe" (cited by Macfarlane, 1979: 168).

[27] Heckscher (1963: 36) entitles one section of his history of Sweden as "The Absence of Feudalism."

of feudalism (i.e., Anglo-Saxon, Nordic, and Western European); in the south, patrimonialism. It is certainly tempting to posit a causal link between current economic systems and these earlier political/economic/social systems. Such an explanation, however, is too neat. It means that the systemic differences between these four groups of nations have lasted for many centuries and, as we shall see in Chapter 7, the evidence to support this intriguing argument is a bit shaky.

HISTORICAL/GEOGRAPHICAL CONNECTIONS. It is also worth noting that the OECD nations sharing the same type of economic system in 1990 had stronger historical connections with each other than with other nations. With the exception of Japan and Switzerland, the AS+ nations consisted exclusively of England and its former colonies or conquered lands; the former colonies drew most of their early European population from the British Isles, founded their legal systems on English principles, and continue to speak English to this day. Most of the nations of Western Europe were politically united at various times: for instance, during much of the Carolingian years and under Napoleon. These nations are geographically contiguous and they have had close political and economic contacts for a millennium. The Nordic nations fought each other, occupied each other's lands, and for brief periods formed political unions for particular purposes. For instance, all four entered into the Kalmar Union in the late fourteenth century; and at various times, Sweden and Norway were united, as were Sweden and Finland. The legal systems of the four Nordic countries had similar origins, all have been predominantly Protestant for many centuries, and (except Finland) they have spoken related languages. The Southern European nations have also had close commercial relations, relying for many centuries on the Mediterranean Sea as their primary transportation linkage. Their current legal systems had the same origin in French civil law; except for Greece, they have been predominantly Roman Catholic; and, again except Greece, their languages are similar.

Such historical/geographic factors, which favored diffusion of ideas and institutions, might also provide some explanation of why France, a nation with both strong Western and Southern European contacts, appears close to the boundary between Western and Southern European economic systems. This type of argument also helps to explain the Japanese case, a country that moved away from a type of feudalism only in the second half of the nineteenth century and, to catch up economically, heavily borrowed ideas from many different nations. This factor, combined with Japan's unique culture, explains why this country is so hard to classify and appears close to the boundary between the Anglo-Saxon-plus nations and Western Europe.

RELATIVE LEVELS OF ECONOMIC DEVELOPMENT. These historical/geographical factors were reinforced by one important economic factor: namely, the disparities in levels of economic development among the four groups of nations in the last two or three centuries.[28] More specifically, the average per capita GDP of Southern European nations was considerably lower than that of the other three groups of nations by 1700 and has remained so ever since. Because they industrialized later than the AS+ and Western European nations, the average Nordic nations also had a somewhat lower per capita GDP, at least until 1970.

INTERNAL POLITICAL FACTORS. Several broad-scale political factors deserve brief mention. Certain political scientists, such as Kurth (1993), have argued that the relatively late industrialization in Scandinavia brought about conditions favorable to a distinctive political coalition between agricultural and industrial workers, one that had a considerable impact on the development of their welfare states. Among the Southern European nations, three – Italy, Portugal, and Spain – went through long periods in which the government pursued policies of centralized corporatism, which heavily influenced certain economic institutions in later years, at least up to the end of the twentieth century.[29] Acemoglu, Johnson, and Robinson (2004) tie the existence of particular property institutions to the form of government, the *de facto* political power held by certain important groups in the economy, and the political dynamic between these groups.

EXTERNAL POLITICAL FACTORS – A CASE STUDY OF ITALY AND JAPAN. Although it is satisfying to find some deep-rooted historical and geographical causal factors underlying the four types of economic systems in the OECD nations in 1990, I must add the precautionary note that random external

---

[28] I base the generalizations in this paragraph on estimates by Maddison (2003) of per capita GDP of the OECD nations for 1500, 1700, 1820, and every half century thereafter. For estimates of the average per capita GDP for the AS+ nations for 1500 and 1700, I omitted Australia, Canada, New Zealand, and the United States because they were being colonized in this period; and for 1820, I also omitted New Zealand for the same reason. For 1870, however, I used the full sample of all groups (excluding France and Switzerland because of the ambiguous designation of their economic systems).

[29] Other interesting comparisons of the economic history of two of these Southern European nations can be found in Prados and Zamagni (1992).

factors, particularly of a political nature, had in some cases an important influence as well. This can be seen by a brief comparative examination of how the economic systems of Italy and Japan evolved.

Although both nations had quite different histories, both were poor when they started to industrialize in the last decades of the nineteenth century.[30] Both nations began with the same model for the administration of enterprises: namely, a pyramidal system of holding companies whereby a small group – often a family – would control a vast number of enterprises, with little interference from other stockholders at lower levels of the pyramid.[31] Both nations also had an extraordinarily large number of small and medium-size enterprises and both had relatively underdeveloped banking systems.

Nevertheless, subsequent events caused their economic systems to diverge greatly. In Italy, many of the companies suffered financial difficulties in the 1930s and were nationalized, thus creating several very large government holding companies that lasted for many decades. In Japan, the American occupation led to the destruction of the large conglomerates (*zaibatsu*), whose successors only palely reflected their previous economic power. Italy never developed an extensive banking system, so the government served as a key lender to private enterprises, whereas in Japan, by contrast, the *zaibatsu* created banks to serve their own financial needs, and these large banks survived and prospered for many decades. Although the governments of both nations attempted to implement various types of industrial policies, Japan's strategy was more consistently and skillfully carried out and, as a result, large enterprises benefitted much more from these government incentives than in Italy. The Japanese government's economic policies also had a particularly strong impact on the structure of exports. After World War II, Japan's exports shifted from steel and ships in the 1950s to cars and low-tech electronics in the next two decades, and to more knowledge-intensive goods thereafter, all produced primarily by large firms. In Italy, the commodity composition of exports has not changed so greatly and continues to be dominated by more traditional manufactured goods produced by small and middle-size enterprises.

Many other differences between Italy and Japan could be mentioned. The main point is that the economies of these two latecomers to industrialization diverged considerably from each other in the last century, primarily because

---

[30] According to the calculations of Maddison (2003), Japan and Italy had per capita GDPs (in 1990 Geary-Khamis dollars) of $863 and $1,581, respectively, in 1880.

[31] For this paragraph and the following discussion, I draw heavily on various essays in Boltho, Vercelli, and Yoshikawa (2001).

of a series of incremental changes, influenced in large measure by strong forces, particularly of a political nature, from outside the economic system.

2. Political/Ideological Determinants

The rich literature on the origins and development of particular economic institutions offers a variety of conjectures based on political/ideological variables. But how can we tell if the variable under examination was a cause or an effect of the economic system? What do such variables today tell us about conditions many decades (or centuries) ago, when these economic systems were being formed? In the following brief discussion, I present various correlations between political/ideological phenomena and then interpret these results to show their relevance to the formation of economic systems. Appendix 6-5 presents a fuller analysis, as well as the data sources.

More specifically, I look at three sets of political/ideological variables. The first focuses on *attitudes and beliefs:* the degree of leftism, interest in politics, and confidence in the political system. The first might underlie certain welfare-state measures; the other two might affect other aspects of the government's role in the economy. The second set of variables focuses on *political processes:* the extent of party competition, legislative effectiveness, and degree of democracy. These could influence governmental initiatives to create certain types of economic institutions. The third group focuses on *political disorders,* which could make private property rights less secure, discourage investment, and force more governmental regulation of economic activities in order to prevent chaos. I mention statistically significant results only when the per capita income is held constant; Appendix 6-6 provides a more complete discussion of all my results, along with more exact definitions of the indicators underlying the generalizations discussed herein.

The Southern European nations reveal the most distinctive political/ideological pattern of the four economic systems. When we hold the level of economic development constant, these nations differed from the others by having had a higher share of the population claiming to hold a leftist ideology, a smaller share of the population declaring a personal interest in politics, and less public confidence in the political system. However, when we look at more impersonal indicators of ideology, such as seats in the legislature, we see that this self-declared leftism did not translate into direct political influence. Data for the second group of indicators reveal that the Southern European countries had less competition between political parties, less democracy, and less effective legislatures. One consequence, revealed by the third set of indicators, is that they also had significantly greater political turmoil, reflected in various types of civil disturbances and disorders, more political instability, and higher turnover in the leadership of the government.[32]

In a country with a left-leaning population, even a conservative government has to follow certain leftist policies if it wants to retain power. For example, it was Otto von Bismarck, a conservative German imperial chancellor, who introduced the world's first social security system, in order to take the political wind out of the sails of the Socialists. Although the Southern European nations have not had notably leftist governments, the greater political turmoil in these nations, lower governmental legitimacy, greater self-declared leftism among their populations, and possibly greater insecurity of tenure of officeholders have provided a challenge to their rightist or centrist governments.[33] As a result, these governments have tried to maintain power by structuring the economy so that it accords with some of the perceived interests of the population (i.e., the Bismarck phenomenon). For instance, the Southern European governments tend to give stronger protection to the employment rights of labor (Table 6-1), perhaps to make up for the fact that although collective bargains extend over a large part of the labor force, the actual share of union members in the labor force is lower than in the other economic systems (Traxler, et al., 2001: 82). The greater political turmoil may also explain some of the other features of their economic system, such as greater national governmental intervention in the economy, greater regulation of industry, and higher barriers to new enterprises. Of course, the political turmoil and lower confidence in the government may also have been a consequence of a bureaucratic style of government, which, among other things, has led to a less effective court system for market activities (Table 6-1).

The Nordic nations also have had a distinctive pattern of political/ideological indicators. Although the share of their population describing itself as leftist was no larger in the Nordic nations than elsewhere, their governments had more representatives of the left in their legislatures. Moreover, these governments enjoyed greater confidence by the citizenry. These

---

[32] Di Tella and MacCulloch (2004) add an important additional interpretation, based on a careful statistical analysis using data from the World Value Study. When the population of a poor country perceives the government to be corrupt, they either vote for leftist parties or for politicians of the right who are willing to impose more regulation on the private sector to eliminate such corruption. (Unfortunately, additional regulation of private activities gives rise to more potential avenues of corruption and seems self-defeating.) The basic premise underlying this voting pattern is that corruption is due exclusively to unrestrained activity by the private sector, not to underpaid governmental bureaucrats.

[33] Lindert (2004b: 57) shows that the extent of regime insecurity (represented by turnover of the political leadership) is one of the factors explaining high welfare expenditures.

characteristics tended to create an economic system more favorable to the rights of labor and also a more highly developed welfare state, in which the government directly provided certain services, rather than merely distributing cash grants. We also see greater competition between political parties in these nations and, at the same time, fewer strikes and other small-scale civil disturbances.

For nations with the two other economic systems, the results are much less dramatic. The AS+ nations are distinctive only in having fewer left-leaning politicians in the lower house of the legislature and fewer citizens describing themselves as leftist. Such a political orientation may account for their weaker protection of employment and their more *laissez-faire* economic system (Table 6-1).

For the nineteen indicators for attitudes and beliefs, political processes, and political disorders, the Western European nations had no scores significantly different from those of the other types of economic systems. As a result, we cannot tell how these political/ideological indicators influenced their economic system.

I experimented with a number of other political variables that did not prove very fruitful. These included indicators related to postwar difficulties arising from damage and deaths occurring in World War II.[34] I also explored the argument that it is the type of legal system that explains the origins of the different types of economic systems but, for reasons discussed in Appendix 6-7, I do not find this conjecture compelling. It is possible that closer attention to participation in elections and, in the past, the sequencing of the extension of the voting franchise, might be useful in explaining why certain nations have one economic system rather than another. This type of analysis, used skillfully by Lindert (2004a, 2004b) to explain different levels of governmental social expenditures, might be difficult to apply to certain economic institutions but is certainly worth trying.

3. Social/Cultural Determinants

Many scholars argue that a variety of social/cultural variables have also influenced the formation of economic systems. As in the case of the political/

---

[34] Of the combatant nations, the population of the Southern and Western European nations suffered roughly the same percentage of war deaths and injuries, which was also about four times the percentage in either the AS+ or the Nordic nations (Ellis, 1993: 253–54). This, of course, affected the population structure and, in later years, social security payments. Moreover, because the incidence of such casualties fell unequally on various income groups, it fostered support for many governmental welfare programs and institutions in these nations. Unfortunately, statistical experiments along these lines did not yield many notable insights.

ideological factors, we face causality and data problems. Again, I present correlations and then interpret them in the light of other evidence in order to show their relevance to the formation and functioning of economic systems.

In the following discussion, I briefly examine four sets of indicators: *population heterogeneity, social capital, social breakdown*, and *values*. In this discussion, I also mention only significant correlations that emerge after controlling for per capita income. I also experimented with a variety of other indicators, which, unfortunately, did not provide much insight into the formation of economic systems.[35] Appendix 6-6 presents a much more thorough analysis of the twenty-one indicators on which this discussion is based.

Again, the Southern European nations reveal a distinctive pattern when per capita income is held constant. The average adult had fewer years of formal education, behavior was governed by more "traditional" practices (as reflected in lower suicide rates, greater marriage stability, fewer single-parent families), and less trust was expressed in others. The lack of trust, which not only increased market risks and the costs of carrying out business, undoubtedly reinforced their distrust in government (discussed previously).

The Nordic nations had a significantly stronger work ethic, more trust in others, and a more pronounced tendency toward competitive individualism; at the same time, they exhibited significantly less religious diversity and, in previous decades, probably less ethnic heterogeneity as well. All of this was consistent with their confidence in the political system and their fewer

---

[35] The role of religion may be important, but I didn't know how to interpret the data. Following the well-known argument of Max Weber, some see a crucial link between religion (particularly the split between Protestants and Catholics) and economic life in the West. Among the OECD nations, there is some correlation between religion and the economic system. More specifically, around 1990 in the adult population (excluding the two "wandering nations," France and Switzerland; and, because of its high Buddhist population, Japan), the following percentages of the adult population classified as either Protestant or Catholic (Roman or Greek Orthodox) were Southern European economic system, less than 1 and 93 percent; AS+, 37 and 46 percent; Nordic economic system, 88 percent and less than 1 percent; and Western European economic system, 18 and 61 percent.

In the Southern European, Western European, and Nordic nations, one of these religions has predominated, but the data do not indicate the degree of actual belief in, or adherence to, the religion. Nevertheless, I find it difficult to link these statistics with important institutions of the economic systems.

For each type of economic system, I used unweighted averages of the individual nations. The underlying data came from the *Encyclopedia Britannica* (1993: particularly pp. 783–85). Given the degree to which these numbers change from year to year, they can represent only approximations.

civil disturbances. These unique characteristics (excepting the competitive individualism) provide support for the particular type of welfare state found in the Nordic nations, with its very high rate of government consumption, especially for health, education, and welfare.

As in the case of the political/ideological variables, the AS+ and the Western European nations show few distinctive characteristics. A significantly higher percentage of adults in an average AS+ nation showed less tolerance for governmental corruption practices; and, in the average Western European nations, a significantly lower percentage. The latter also had a weaker work ethic. The other differences of these two economic systems with the rest of the sample were few and reveal no general social/cultural pattern that might have had a noticeable influence on the economic system.

4. An Overview of Possible Determinants of Industrial Economic Systems

This section surveys several broad sets of possible factors that might explain why individual OECD nations have developed and/or maintained one type of economic system rather than another. The results suggest certain linkages of historical/geographical/political/social-cultural factors with the particular economic systems.

Many hundreds of years ago, four quite distinct political/economic/social systems existed in Europe and they prevailed in the same geographic regions that now define the four types of economic systems. In the past, the countries in these four areas also had more contact with each other than with other areas, thus facilitating the diffusion of institutions. Using the examples of Italy and Japan, I show that in some cases, external political events have played a critical role in systemic changes as well.

The sets of nineteen political/ideological and twenty-one social/cultural indicators show very distinctive patterns for the Southern European and Nordic nations and many fewer distinguishing characteristics among the AS+ and Western European nations. In particular, the Southern European societies appeared to be more "traditional" and their members expressed lower levels of interpersonal trust, of interest in politics, and of confidence in the government. These nations have also been less democratic and have experienced political turmoil in the last century. Among other things, these conditions appear consistent with more governmental regulation of the economy. By contrast, the citizens of the Nordic nations expressed greater interpersonal trust and confidence in government and greater actual (in contrast to verbal) leftism. These nations also showed greater party competition and fewer political disorders. Certain aspects of governmental intervention – particularly their greater reliance on direct provision of health, education, and welfare services by the government, rather than transfer payments – were consistent with these social characteristics.

The citizens in AS+ nations expressed less leftism than other OECD nations, which was consistent with their relatively smaller governmental intervention. Otherwise, neither the AS+ nor the Western European nations appeared to have significant differences in their political/ideological or social/cultural characteristics that would have left a distinctive impact on their economic system.

Two caveats must be added to this analysis. First, this is only an initial foray into the reasons why a particular nation has one economic system rather than another. A more extensive analysis would undoubtedly unearth more subtle and important causal factors – political, social, cultural, or economic – than I have examined. Second, it is often difficult to distinguish the causes of an economic system from its effects and, therefore, in a more extensive analysis, this problem needs to be directly addressed. Only after making a more exhaustive analysis of this type will we begin to understand the key forces underlying the logic of institutions, which determine the clusters characterizing the individual economic systems.

D. A Brief Summary

The cluster analysis reveals four different types of economic systems among the industrialized OECD nations at the end of the twentieth century: namely, the AS+, the Nordic, the Western European, and the Southern European systems. The countries sharing a particular economic system usually had considerable historical connections and geographical proximity.

Holding the level of economic development constant, the cluster analysis shows that AS+ countries had the most liberal market economy with a relatively weak position of labor and a smaller government measured in terms of transfers or employment. The Nordic countries had a more organized economy, with greater participation of labor in firm decision-making, wages bargained at industry and national levels, a stronger role of labor unions and employer organizations, and a larger public sector, as measured by government consumption expenditures and coverage of the social security system. In many respects, countries with the Western European economic system were somewhat between those of the AS+ and Nordic nations; however, they had significantly greater unionization, fewer stockholder rights, and a larger government, as measured by government transfer payments. Finally, the nations with a Southern European economic system, which generally had lower levels of economic development than the other OECD nations, also had a poorer legal environment for markets, more regulated product markets, higher entry barriers of new enterprises, high unionization, and stronger protection of the rights of labor.

These various aspects of the four types of economic system are in accord with common perceptions. Moreover, the designation of economic system provides a framework within which to analyze a variety of economic activities and to distinguish those characteristics common to all advanced industrial economies and those traits common to those nations with the same economic system from those institutions unique to the particular economy.

For certain economic performance variables, such as the distribution of income, the direct impact of the economic system can be easily seen. For many other indicators of performance, such as the rate of economic growth, the impact of the economic system cannot be directly determined and we must turn toward the impact of particular institutions or governmental policies for an explanation of differences between nations.

Although correlation of the economic system with various political, ideological, social, and cultural variables reveals some interesting patterns, only in the Southern European and Nordic nations did they seem to have a discernable impact on it.

The analysis of systemic change in advanced market economic systems is the focus of the following chapter. At this point, however, several broader conclusions can be drawn. The four industrial market economic systems I have isolated allow us to summarize in a simple and brief manner a great many differences in the institutional configuration of a large number of economies. The four designated systems allow us to account for somewhat more than 40 percent of the institutional variation of these economies – considerably more than the agricultural systems and roughly the same as the foraging systems. As in the case of the other types of economies, distinguishing these economic systems allows us to determine more easily complementarities between particular economic institutions (the logic of institutions) and also between the economic system and important aspects of the political and social system. Unlike the other types of economies, these systems provide us with sufficient data to explore some of the linkages between economic system and economic performance. Such an exercise draws our attention to the question of whether it is the entire configuration or only certain institutions composing it that determine particular aspects of the economic performance.

Although many of the results obtained in this analysis should come as no surprise to those familiar with the OECD economies, they validate the approach also used for the foraging and agricultural economies, with which we are less familiar. In the next chapter, I investigate how these economic systems in the OECD nations have changed in the past and will be transformed in the future.

SEVEN

Systemic Changes in Advanced Market Economies

In this chapter, I explore certain dynamic properties of the economic systems of industrial/service market economies. For foraging and agricultural economic systems, we could only gain general insights into the processes of systemic change, primarily with regard to the change in the focus of production. In contrast, for industrial/service economic systems, we can begin to explore other aspects of their evolution over time. The first half of this chapter focuses on these systemic change in the past and the second half, on systemic change in the future.

Changes in both the economies and the economic systems of the OECD nations have accelerated. In the two centuries between 1500 and 1700, the average per capita GDP of the nations composing my OECD sample grew 30 percent; in the two decades between 1980 and 2000, 51 percent.[1] Many have commented on this increase in economic growth; many fewer have noted a similar acceleration of change in the economic institutions and systems of the same nations. This neglect of systemic change arises both from our lack of theory about such matters and from the lack of detailed empirical studies on the impact of technology and other exogenous factors on the formation and development of institutions.

The rapid institutional and systemic changes in recent years allow us to explore some critical aspect of the process. In particular, we can look for four different types of systemic change.

FIXED VERSUS FLUID PATTERNING. Fixed patterning means that the overall configurations of institutions defining particular economic systems are

---

[1] The data are drawn from Maddison (2003).

relatively fixed over time, whereas fluid patterning means that this patterning of institutions changes over the course of economic development. Given the vastly different development elasticities of the various institutions shown in previous chapters, fluid patterning seems much more likely.

PARALLEL VERSUS POLYVALENT CHANGE. Parallel change indicates that over the course of time, the nations with the same economic system change in the same manner so that they remain grouped together. The hypothesis discussed in the previous chapter that the grouping of nations by particular aspects of their political/economic institutions a millennium ago was roughly the same as their grouping according to the forty institutional variables discussed in the previous chapter is a dramatic example of parallel change. If, by contrast, systems change in a polyvalent fashion, nations that are grouped together at one point in time may be in quite different groups at other points in time. In polyvalent change, the logic of institutions is much weaker than in the parallel change.

CONTRACTING VERSUS EXPANDING CLUSTERS. Contracting change indicates that the multidimensional distance *among* nations with the same economic systems becomes smaller. This means that the clustering of nations with a given economic system has become tighter; that is, the technological/environmental constraints influencing variations within a given economic system have become stronger. Expanding change is the reverse. Of course, it is also possible that the tightness of the clustering remains unchanged.

CONVERGENT VERSUS DIVERGENT CHANGE. Convergent change indicates that the multidimensional distance *between* economic systems becomes smaller. This means that the clusters of nations have become closer and reveals in another way that the technological/environmental constraints limiting systemic variation have become stronger. Divergent change is the reverse. Of course, it is also possible that the inter-cluster distance remains the same.

The latter three characterizations of systemic change represent different dynamic characteristics of the logic of institutions. In all cases, the logic of institution may be strong at a single point in time, but this strength can vary over time, depending on technological and other exogenous changes in the economic environment.

With this framework of four characteristics of systemic change in mind, my discussion focuses on two topics. First, I briefly summarize the results of a cross-section analysis of the economic system of nations outside the OECD that had relatively low levels of economic development in 1990. This provides direct evidence on three of the four characteristics of systemic change. Then, I examine the economic systems of OECD nations at various points in time in the second half of the twentieth century, an exercise which, although limited by the lack of sufficient data to allow a refined empirical analysis, does provide some important insights.

Unfortunately, we encounter a sufficient number of unresolved issues in the analysis of past changes in the economic system that we cannot easily predict the future. For this reason, the discussion of future systemic change is less elaborate and focuses primarily on the most important factors that will influence changes in both the economy and the economic system in the coming decades. Such factors include aging of the population, increasing globalization, and changing relationships between capital and labor.

A. Some Clues about Systemic Change from the Economic Systems of Developing Nations

Comparisons of the economic systems of developing nations and of the OECD in 1990 provides some important insights about general systemic changes. Before plunging into the discussion, however, we must consider two hazards of using evidence from a single point in time in other parts of the world to generalize about events occurring over several centuries. First, poor and rich countries respond differently to certain important economic forces. For instance, the development elasticities of certain institutional variables, such as the share of public consumption in the GDP, are much different. Second, some causal forces operate quite differently over a period of time than at a single point in time. For instance, from 1879 to the present, the ratio of government expenditures to the GDP in the OECD nations was highly correlated with per capita income; but, at a single point in time, I could find no such relation.[2] These two methodological pitfalls mean that we must proceed cautiously.

---

[2] Total government expenditures include consumption, transfers, subsidies, and capital consumption. In the OECD nations, the ratio of these expenditures to the GDP increased from an average of 9.2 percent in 1870 to 45.9 percent in 1990, and the relationship between this ratio and per capita GDP was strongly significant. By contrast, I could find no significant relationship between per capita GDP and this government expenditure ratio among the OECD nations at single points in time, taking cross sections for 1870, 1910, 1950, and 1990. New technologies, new ideas and values, and new political or economic opportunities can influence changes in the economic system over time; at a single point in time, however, they are roughly the same for all nations.

Rather than exploring these developing nations in detail, I summarize the major results of a cluster analysis of these countries (Appendix 6–8), which employs most of the same institutional variables used for the OECD nations in the previous chapter.[3] This allows us to focus on the results most relevant to the problem of systemic change, of which the following seem particularly important.

FLUID PATTERNING OF THE ECONOMIC SYSTEM. The institutions and organizations that served to distinguish the economic systems in the OECD from each other were quite different from those defining the economic system of developing nations. For instance, regulation of product markets, which differentiated OECD economic systems, did not emerge as important distinguishing characteristics between the economic systems of developing nations. This suggests that the institutional configurations defining economic systems of OECD nations could have been quite different thirty or fifty years ago, a topic taken up at greater length in the next section. To investigate this matter further, I combined the samples of OECD and developing economies and carried out a supervised cluster analysis, which means that I forced the program to classify the economic system of each developing nation into one of the four economic systems of the OECD nations. Almost all of them fell within the Southern European cluster, which constituted that group of OECD nations with the lowest levels of per capita GDP. This exercise provides yet another example of the interrelations between the economic system and the level of economic development, so it is not surprising that the economic systems of developing nations would be defined by quite different characteristics than those of the industrialized market economies of the OECD.

CONTRACTING CLUSTERS DURING MODERNIZATION. The statistical analysis yields tighter clusters for OECD nations than for developing countries, whose clusters appear to have roughly the same tightness as preindustrial

The ratios of total government expenditures to GDP come from Cusack and Fuchs (2003). I have made rough estimates of the OECD countries not included in the earlier years. The per capita GDP data come from Maddison (1995, 2001). This topic receives greater attention in the following discussion.

[3] The developing-country sample consists of forty-one countries in 1990, all with a per capita GDP of less than $10,000, and thirty-one indicators of institutions and organizations. The OECD sample consists of twenty-one countries in 1990, all with a per capita GDP of more than $10,000, and forty indicators. For the comparisons with the developing nations, however, I have used roughly the same indicators as those in the analysis of developing nations.

agricultural societies.[4] This is schematically shown in Chart 7-1, in which (similar to Chart 1-1) the axes represent the institutions defining the economic system (only two axes are drawn because it is difficult to draw graphs in thirty-one dimensions), and the ellipses represent the spaces within which all nations belonging to the same economic system are found.

Although systemic change appears contracting, such a conclusion must be drawn cautiously for several reasons. The developing nations had a greater percentage variation in per capita GDP than the OECD nations and, because many institutions are related to the level of economic development, these developing nations would reveal greater differences in particular institutions. Moreover, the developing nations were spread over the entire world (except Europe and Oceania) and, as a result, the forces of diffusion (i.e., borrowing of institutions) between them were weaker. Finally, a successfully functioning agricultural economy is less complex and, therefore, requires fewer restriction on its constituent elements.

DIVERGING CHANGE. The distances between the individual clusters among the developing nations were shorter than among the OECD nations, a characteristic also shown in the chart.[5] Thus, at the same time that the OECD nations with the same economic system were more similar than developing countries with the same economic system, the individual economic systems of the OECD nations were more different. In other words, over the course of economic development, the patterning of the individual economic systems becomes more distinct, even as the possibilities of variation between particular systems increase. A rough analogy might be a collection of bonsai trees which, in their early months, show few overall differences and which also cannot be easily distinguished into distinct groups; years later, however, the same collection reveals great differences and can also be easily separated into groups with distinct styles of induced growth.

IMPACT ON ECONOMIC PERFORMANCE. Unlike the OECD countries, the economic systems of developing economies have important consequences for such macroeconomic indicators as the growth of per capita GDP and inflation. This provides additional support for the conjecture discussed in

---

[4] For these comparisons, I used roughly the same institutional indicators for OECD and developing countries. The cluster analysis reduces the variance of the sample of OECD countries 44 percent; the sample of developing countries, 31 percent; and the sample of preindustrial agricultural societies (using different institutional indicators), 30 percent.

[5] In this comparison, I used the same samples as in footnote 4 and measured the multidimensional distance of the center of each cluster with every other cluster. The comparisons noted in the text refer to the sum of the distances of each economic system with every other economic system.

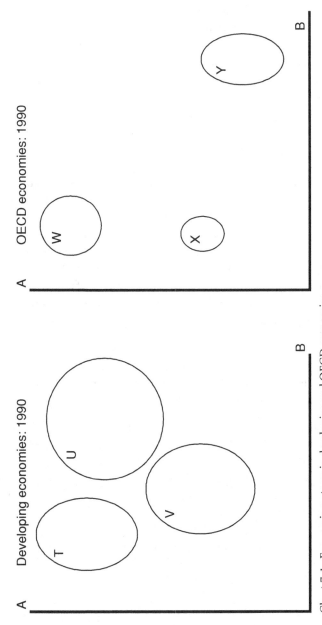

Chart 7-1. Economic systems in developing and OECD economies.
Note: A and B are the institutions defining the economic systems. T, U, and V and W, X, and Y are the economic systems.

Chapter 5 that the early industrialization of many OECD nations can be attributed to certain characteristics of their economic systems that set them apart from other countries that were not industrializing. Moreover, those European nations that industrialized relatively late were more able to borrow and modify institutions from their more successful neighbors, unlike the nations in Asia, Africa, or Latin America, which either had a colonial status or had less opportunity to communicate with the pioneering nations of the industrial revolution.[6]

In brief, this glance at a cross-section of developing economies yields some interesting clues about the long-term evolution of the economic systems of the OECD nations. The characteristics differentiating the economic systems of developing countries are not the same as those that differentiate the four economic systems of the OECD nations. The functional requirements of industrialization (and postindustrialization) appear to tighten the complementarities between particular institutions, even while allowing greater variation of the institutional patterns as a whole. Finally, the economic system previously in place had an important impact on the speed of industrialization, as shown by the higher average growth rates of those developing nations with a particular economic system. The impact of the economic system on growth rates attenuates, however, at higher levels of economic development, and this, in turn, reduces the political impetus for a convergence of systems.

B. Recent Evolution of the OECD Economic Systems: Clues from a Small Sample

In this section, I explore changes in the economic systems of OECD nations over the second half of the twentieth century. In the theoretical literature,

---

[6] Some argue that political factors have a much stronger influence on the economic system and its performance in the developing countries than in OECD nations (a proposition rigorously investigated by Przeworski et al., 2000a). For instance, various studies find more corruption and more autocratic governments among these developing nations. Other than the obvious impact such characteristics might have on the security of private property rights, generalizations are difficult to make. This indeterminacy arises from the very nature of autocracy: Each ruler had his own notions about a desirable economic system, often quite unrelated to the actual economic conditions of the country, and the results might as easily have encouraged as discouraged economic growth (Glaeser et al., 2004).

I might add that the literature on politics and the economic system is confusing. Some argue that dictatorship and a market economy are incompatible, but a half-century ago, many argued the reverse – that a market economy and democracy are contradictory. For my purposes, neither line of argument seems promising. Moreover, statistical experiments using my sample of developing nations shows that the economic system was a more important determinant of various measures of economic performance than various political indicators.

which I briefly review in the first section, major differences of opinion arise about the characteristics of systemic change. I then turn to the scanty available data to investigate these issues for the second half of the twentieth century, especially with regard to whether such changes were parallel or polyvalent.

1. Different Views on How Economic Institutions and Systems Change

In dynamic economies, institutions composing the economic system are mutating for a variety of reasons. Some institutional changes arise from shifts in the economic environment – for instance, a higher per capita GDP, particular economic crises, a shifting demand for various goods and services, new technologies, new values,[7] or new developments in the domestic and international economic environment. Some institutional changes arise from endogenous causes – for instance, certain institutions are not performing well (due to poor management). Other changes occur because policy dilemmas can be solved in quite different ways in nations with the same economic system, depending on the particular balance of political forces or on changes in opinion of certain key institutional players, such as the Roman Catholic church in particular European countries.[8] Finally, economic institutions and systems change for direct political reasons – for instance, the East European nations changing from market economies to planned economies in the late 1940s and then back again in the 1990s. As a result, many assertions about institutional change rest more on intuition than on rigorous theorizing or empirical study.

The variety of causes underlying institutional and systemic change mean that prediction about parallel or polyvalent change is difficult. It is usually assumed that groups of nations with the same economic systems will continue to have similar economic systems in the future, even while the nature of these systems are changing, but such an implicit assumption is questionable. Of course, particular institutions may have strong complementarities,

---

[7] An interesting example is provided by the system of income taxation in the United States. According to a survey commissioned by the U.S. Internal Revenue Service (cited by Anon., "Tax Points," 2004), the percentage of people who "completely agree" with the statement that it is the duty of all Americans to pay their fair share of taxes decreased from 81 to 68 percent between 1999 and 2003. Further, those who said it is acceptable to cheat "a little" rose from 8 to 12 percent; and those who said taxpayers should cheat "as much as possible" rose from 3 to 5 percent. If such a shift in values continues, the current income tax system in the United States would become unsustainable. Perhaps it already is.

[8] For instance, Lindert (2004b: 79) points out that Catholicism had a positive impact on social transfers after World War II, but not before.

which make it seem likely that the composition of the groups of nations with the same economic systems will not change. For instance, unions will always play a stronger economic and political role in those nations with the so-called Ghent system of unemployment insurance, whereby the national system is administered by unions, not the government. Moreover, insofar as natural resource endowments influence the economic system (e.g., in the oil-rich nations in the Mideast), a changing composition of nations with the same economic system will be inhibited. Nevertheless, such complementarities may weaken as the institutions themselves change in response to external factors. Moreover, as Dani Rodrik (2003) has forcefully pointed out, different institutions can serve the same function, so that the tasks sloughed off by a changing institution can be picked up by others. Perhaps the strongest reason for (erroneously?) believing in parallel rather than polyvalent change is that our mental maps of the economies of different countries mutate more slowly than the actual economic systems of these nations.

Assertions about contracting clusters and convergent change rest on the notion that the functional requirements for an advanced industrial or postindustrial economy are increasingly restrictive in all dimensions and, moreover, globalization is bringing about a homogenization of certain economic institutions throughout the industrialized world.

But, some contrary arguments are also strong. For instance, in recent years, several groups of economists (see Kitschelt et al., 1999b; Hall and Soskice, 2001) have pointed out that by working within a given economic system, the work force of a nation develops core competencies that are advantageous in the international marketplace. As a result, strong economic interests would oppose both contracting and convergent change. Moreover, the citizens of different nations have quite different institutional preferences, which would also work against international homogenization of economic institutions.

Obviously, these different views of systemic change should be assessed empirically by studying the economic institutions of OECD nations at earlier points in time, using a cluster analysis to divide them again into distinctive types of systems. Although this prescription is easy to write, it is hard to fill because, unfortunately, quantitative indicators for economic institutions at different points in time are difficult to find. More specifically, of the forty indicators used in the previous chapter to define the economic systems of OECD nations in 1990, time-series data are readily available for only eleven. Moreover, for several institutions, less satisfactory indicators than those employed for the 1990 sample must be used and, moreover, the various data series also have more blanks. In some cases, therefore, I use alternative statistical procedures.

2. Parallel versus Polyvalent Systemic Change

An indirect method of determining whether the same nations remain grouped together over the postwar period focuses on the relative ranking of each economic system for each institutional indicator. If systemic change is parallel, then the rank orders of these various institutional variables for the different groups of nations should remain the same over time.

Because the OECD nations had largely recovered from the effects of World War II by 1960, I start the analysis with data for four benchmark years thereafter: namely, 1960, 1970, 1980, and 1990. Then, I determine the rank orderings of the average values of the four economic systems for each of the eleven indicators in each benchmark year. Finally, I investigate whether these rank orderings for the eleven indicators were related in the four years by calculating a Kendall concordance coefficient. This coefficient ranges between zero (where there is no relationship in the rank orderings for a particular indicator in the four benchmark years) and one (where the rank orderings are the same for all four years). The resulting coefficient can then be tested for statistical significance.[9]

The test results are clean. For ten out of the eleven institutional indicators, the relative rank orderings of the four economic systems are similar over the period under investigation – that is, the concordance coefficient is statistically significant for all four years under investigation. The only exception is the indicator showing the government's share in total investment. Such results suggest that regardless of whether the particular characteristics of the economic systems in the OECD changed from 1960 through 1990, the four groups of countries maintained their distinct differences with each other – in brief, they revealed parallel institutional change and the groups of nations with a similar economic system did not greatly change.

More insight can be gained by looking at indicators whose rank orderings changed somewhat over the years, even though the degree of concordance remained significant. For instance, the ratio of public consumption to total (public plus private) consumption in the Nordic nations was roughly the same as the OECD average in 1952 (not included in the test results), but it had moved ahead of all other OECD systems by 1960 and, in the following years, this gap widened. Thus, this distinctive characteristic of the current Nordic economic system in the 1990s began to emerge only in the mid-1950s,

---

[9] I follow the procedure for calculating concordance coefficients described by Sheskin (1997: 641–51). In the text, I describe the results only from 1960 through 1990, but roughly similar results are obtained when 1952 is included in the calculation. The data are presented in Appendix 7-2.

even though the ideological seeds may have been planted decades earlier. An alternative method of redistributing income is to provide cash transfer and, in this regard, Western European nations led the rest of the OECD economic systems throughout the second half of the twentieth century. In the immediate post-World War II years, this was undoubtedly a response to assist quickly those suffering from war injuries or property damage, a daunting administrative task most easily solved by giving funds directly to needy individuals, who could then purchase the necessary services themselves. The Nordic system of providing the needed welfare services directly was administratively too complicated for Western European governments in these early postwar years, but their system of transfer payments persisted thereafter.[10]

One immediate objection to this analysis must be raised. These comparisons of rank orderings cover only thirty years. Would such relationships hold over a longer period? For instance, data on public expenditures extending back to 1870 show sharp breaks in the rank ordering before and after World War II.[11] Similarly, with regard to the openness of foreign trade, as measured by average tariff rates, the rank orderings of the four groups of nations greatly changed over the last 120 years, showing sharp breaks after both world wars.[12] In addition, certain institutional features, such as the relative importance of cartels or direct governmental measures to direct production

---

[10] Other factors also played roles in these different approaches to the welfare state. For instance, the relatively homogeneous populations in the Nordic countries, combined with the greater trust of citizens in each other and their greater degree of leftism (Appendix Table A6-2), played a key role. Equally important, as some have argued, the relatively late (but not as late as in Southern Europe) industrialization in the Nordic nations encouraged a political alliance between industrial workers and farmers, which gave greater power to social democratic parties and their program of direct supply of welfare services.

[11] The underlying data come from Cusack and Fuchs (2003). However, I have had to make a number of estimates to extend some of the series back to 1870. Another series of public expenditures for social purposes by Lindert (2004a, 2004b) goes back to the eighteenth century, but these appeared too late to be used in this study. He shows that many of the changes in the rank orderings among nations can be traced to changes in the extent of the voting franchise and the degree of democracy.

[12] The long-term pattern of trade openness is complex. Tariff rates in a worldwide sample of thirty-five nations slowly rose from the 1870s to the first decade of the twentieth century, then rose dramatically from the 1920s to the late 1930s so that at their peak, they were roughly twice as high as the late-nineteenth-century average, and then slowly declined from the late 1940s to the 1990s (Blattman, Clements, and Williamson, 2003). During these three periods, the relative position of countries changed considerably. For instance, the United States was a high-tariff nation in the late nineteenth century, but in the interwar period (up to the enactment of the Smoot–Hawley tariff bill in the early 1930s) had relatively low tariff rates, in comparison both to its previous rates and rates in other countries. Obviously, certain changes in the external international economic environment, such as the influence of GATT and the European common market after World War II, greatly influenced these tariff differences among nations.

were not very important in the latter part of the twentieth century in most OECD nations, but played an important role in the economic systems of certain of my sample nations during the period between the world wars. In these ways as well, the economic systems did not appear to change in a parallel fashion over the century.

An economic system, however, is not just a set of economic institutions randomly assembled; rather, it comprises institutions that have a distinctive relationship to each other, and we must look at the overall pattern of these institutional variables as well. Therefore, the eleven indicators might be used to derive economic systems just as the forty indicators were used in the previous chapter for the OECD nations in 1990.

Unlike the forty indicators used in the previous chapter, the eleven indicators available for the historical analysis are not necessarily representative of the entire economic system. Thus, the two data sets might not necessarily yield the same results for 1990, the overlapping year. Such a calculation put this fear to rest and showed that for 1990, slightly more than three-fourths of the countries in the eleven-indicator sample were in the same clusters derived from the cluster analysis for the same year using forty indicators.[13] It is noteworthy that distinct Nordic and AS+ groups emerged in the eleven-indicator sample as in the more extensive analysis. This finding gives us a certain confidence to proceed, especially because comparability problems are not as serious when we use the same eleven indicators for each of the benchmark years. To avoid any confusion with actual economic systems, however, I labeled the results of the eleven-indicator cluster analysis as "pseudosystems."

The results of this exercise suggest a certain degree of polyvalent change. More specifically, the similarity of composition of the pseudosystems seems also to decline as we move back in time. For instance, in 1980, 48 percent of the nations remained in the same cluster that the forty-indicator analysis had assigned them; for 1970, 57 percent; and, for 1960, 38 percent (all shown in Appendix Chart A7-1). Moreover, because most of the eleven indicators do not necessarily capture the key systemic elements, the derived pseudosystems should also be more volatile over time than systems derived from an analysis using more indicators. As expected, only slightly more than one third of the nations remained in the same pseudosystem from one decade to the next.

---

[13] The MDL analysis of the eleven-indicator samples suggests that a grouping of five different economic systems is the most appropriate in 1990, 1980, and 1960, but not 1970. To achieve comparability, I use a five-cluster analysis for all years and also for the comparisons with the forty-indicator sample in 1990. The percentage of variance explained by the cluster analysis was roughly 60 percent for all four benchmark years.

The results from the cluster analysis are also supported by other evidence. For instance, the calculations in Chapter 6 show that the economic system of France appears close to the border separating the Western and Southern European systems, and that the economic system of Switzerland is similarly situated close to the border of the Western European and the AS+ nations, which suggests that in later years they might be grouped by the statistical analysis in different clusters than their present location. As I discuss in the next section, the United Kingdom appeared to move from one economic system to another over the last half of the twentieth century, which provides additional evidence about polyvalence.

Thus, the results of the rank-order concordance and the cluster-analysis tests provide rather different answers to the question about parallel versus polyvalent change. Although the latter test appears to me to be more appropriate, I do not believe that a definite conclusion can be drawn at this time.

3. Contracting and Convergent Systemic Changes

Looking at the results of the cluster analysis for the four benchmark years, no long-term trends in the degree of clustering can be detected from 1960 through 1990.[14] In sum, *within* the various clusters, no apparent trend toward contracting nor expanding systemic change was apparent over the thirty years.

This cluster analysis for the four benchmark years also showed no trend in the multidimensional distances *between* the various clusters.[15] In this respect, therefore, the systems experienced no convergence or divergence, at least between 1960 and 1990 before the nations in the European Union began to accelerate their economic integration. Such a result confirms the conjectures of Herbert Kitschelt, Peter Hall, and David Soskice discussed briefly herein.

Because of the nature of the data, these two results are by no means conclusive. Nevertheless, as a working hypothesis, they suggest that in the

---

[14] The amount of sample variance explained by a five-group cluster analysis for 1990, 1980, 1970, and 1960 are, respectively, 59, 53, 53, and 53 percent. Although the difference between the sample variance for 1990 and 1980 is statistically significant, more years would be needed to determine if 1990 represents a new trend.

[15] More specifically, for each of the benchmark years, the cluster program calculated the multidimensional distance of the mean values of each dimension in the different economic systems to each other to determine the average distances between the various systems. I then added up each of these average distances and found no statistically significant difference in the four benchmark years. The sums of the multidimensional distances in the four benchmark years were, respectively, 20, 17, 18, and 19.

middle-run, systemic change among the OECD nations showed no significant trends toward contracting or convergent change.

4. A Brief Word about the Logic of Institutions

The cluster results presented in the previous chapters show that, at a single point in time, the logic of institutions is unchallengeable because we can explain a considerable share of the difference between the configuration of economic institutions in various countries by grouping them into distinct economic systems. Because institutions and systems change over time, however, a strong version of the logic of institutions explains nothing. A weaker version, however, would suggest that systemic change would be parallel, not polyvalent and that systemic change would not be either contracting or expanding, nor would it be either convergent or divergent. At least the latter two predictions receive some support.

C. Forces for Change in the OECD Economic Systems in the Next Half-Century

In this discussion, I look first at some general features of the rapidity and direction of change of institutions because they underlie the transformation of the economic system. Then, I turn to three specific forces that will have, I believe, a critical impact on the changes of the economic systems of the OECD nations in the future.

1. Rapidity and Direction of Institutional Changes

Sometimes institutions change suddenly in response to a crisis. Examples include the introduction of the social security system in the United States several years after the onset of the economic depression in the 1930s and the rapid nationalization of banks and factories in many Western European nations after the end of World War II. In many cases, these rapid institutional innovations were the result of a new constellation of political forces emerging from a considerable realignment of political forces and/or a dramatic change in the economic environment.

In other cases, institutions seem frozen in time.[16] For instance, in the OECD, the measures of central-bank independence varied little from the 1950s to the 1990s. The most noticeable development was the increasing

---

[16] Unless otherwise indicated, the generalizations in this and the following paragraphs are drawn from data on the eleven OECD historical indicators reported in Appendix Table A7-3.

independence of the Southern European central banks, rising from well below the OECD average in 1951 to about average in 1990. Of course, the independence of national central banks may greatly change in the future as the European Central Bank gains more and more power.[17] In the labor market, the level of the economy at which wages were bargained also did not appear to change greatly in most of the post–World War II period.

For other institutions, the direction of change was steady and in one direction. A notable case was the rapid rise in all economic systems of the ratio of current government expenditures, both consumption and transfers. The average ratio of these combined expenditures to the GDP in the OECD nations rose from 26.3 to 44.5 percent between 1952 and 1990. Such growth in public expenditures represents the most visible institutional change in OECD economic systems in the post–World War II period – the expenditures increased in terms of percentage points one and a half times more in the four decades following 1950 than in the eighty years from 1870 to 1950 (Cusack and Fuchs, 2003). In like manner, indicators of other institutions, such as worker protection against job loss and openness of trade in goods, services, and capital (measured in terms of barriers against such flows), also showed a steady increase over time.[18]

Finally, some institutions rose and fell in relatively short periods. For instance, in the four decades following the postwar wave of nationalizations in Europe, public ownership of the means of production declined in many of the same nations (Toninelli, 2000). Some argue that corporatist institutions revealed a similar rise and fall in the same period, but this would depend on what we mean by corporatism. Although some trappings of corporatism disappeared in some countries after the mid-1970s, following the oil shock and economic difficulties, I find no evidence that the tide of corporatism was ebbing in the OECD as a whole, even though such a pattern is found in some countries.[19]

From such snapshots of institutional change, it is difficult to gain an overall view of the entire economic system. For the United Kingdom, however, a sufficient number of economic institutions changed between 1960 and 1990

---

[17] The measures of central-bank independence do not capture the loss of independence arising from greater cooperation with foreign central banks. In Europe, intensive cooperation began in 1964 and was reinforced by the establishment of the European Monetary System in 1979 and its transformation into the European Monetary Union two decades later, the founding of the European Central Bank in 1998, and the introduction of a common currency in 2001. As a result, the role of the national central banks in many European nations has diminished; my measure of independence is becoming an anachronism.

[18] Data on these indicators are presented in Appendix Table A7-1.

[19] I discuss certain aspects of corporatism in greater detail in Appendix 7-4; see also Pryor (1988).

to allow us to observe the relationship between institutional and systemic transformations.

The changing role of government regulation in the United Kingdom provides a useful starting point for the discussion. Myron Ross (1965) surveyed a small group of specialists in economic systems, and a majority rated Great Britain in the early 1960s as having more national planning and governmental direction of the economy than other OECD nations. My own analysis of pseudosystems in 1960 placed the United Kingdom among the other Western European nations rather than in the AS+ group, which had more laissez-faire economic systems. For the late 1990s, a much more systematic study using both legal and observer surveys (Nicoletti and Pryor, forthcoming), put the United Kingdom among those OECD nations with the least governmental participation in the economy. Correspondingly, my own analysis of pseudosystems in 1990 positioned the United Kingdom among those with an AS+ economic system.

The high degree of government intervention in the United Kingdom in the 1950s and early 1960s can be attributed to the self-reinforcing process of a slow wartime recovery and inertia in removing inappropriate wartime controls of the economy. But, as a result of disappointing economic performance in the first three decades following World War II, both ideology and the balance of political forces shifted. Most public attention has focused on the 1979 election of Margaret Thatcher, whose government sold off state enterprises, cut back its other governmental roles in the economy, and reduced the influence of labor unions in national economic policymaking. By her last year in office, the United Kingdom's economic system had become like those of other nations in the AS+ group. But, if we look at the eleven historical indicators discussed previously, this process appears to have begun in the mid-1970s. Thatcher's policies simply reflected the culmination of a previous trend. Without a full-scale cluster analysis with many indicators for a series of years, however, we cannot easily tell when a series of small institutional changes resulted in a significant transformation of the entire economic system.

Much more can be said about processes of institutional change, a topic on which the *régulation* school in France has focused much effort (e.g., Boyer and Saillard, 2002).[20] We can, however, analyze more directly the future transformation of the economic systems of OECD nations by looking at three critical forces acting on these economies: namely, the aging of the population, globalization, and shifts in the relative power of labor, management, and capital.

---

[20] In Appendix 7-5, I also have a brief discussion on certain other aspects of institutional change.

2. Critical Forces Influencing Future Systemic Changes: Aging of the Population

According to United Nations estimates (2003), the median age in the twenty-one OECD nations in my sample will rise from 37.8 in 2000 to 46.9 in the following half-century.[21] The nations with the Southern European economic system will experience the highest increase (12.6 years), while the Nordic nations, the lowest (7.1 years). For our purposes, the key demographic implication of this change is the fall in the ratio of those in the traditional working ages (20 through 64) to those 65 and above, a tendency reinforced by the lengthening of life expectancy. These data, reported in the first two columns of Table 7-1, show that in 2040, there will be roughly half as many people in the working ages for every person over 65 than there were in 2000. In 2040, this ratio will be highest in the AS+ nations and lowest among the Southern European nations, where low birth rates will exacerbate the problem. These different ratios argue against any convergence of OECD economic systems because they will influence all economic systems in two major ways.

INCREASING GOVERNMENT EXPENDITURES. Obviously, the aging of the population will place enormous strains on the pension payments of the social security system. According to the estimates in Table 7-1, such payments as a percent of GDP for the OECD as a whole will rise about 6 percentage points between 2000 and 2040 if current laws remain in force.[22]

If the ratio of workers to retirees is falling, the governments face three choices: raise taxes on the working population, cut non–social security public expenditures, or reduce social security payments per recipient. The first two options will, of course, meet fierce resistance on the part of those in the labor force.

Governmental health payments to the aged will also rise, not just because of population aging but also because health care is becoming increasingly more expensive as costly new medical techniques are developed and more extensively used (it is difficult for any elected government to ration life-saving health care). According to the estimates in Table 7-1, governmental health expenditures for the aged as a percent of GDP for the OECD as

---

[21] These are unweighted averages of the twenty-one countries from the "medium variant," which includes medium fertility estimates and normal projections of mortality and international migration. If the median ages are weighted by the population of the nation, the rise in the median age will be 6.3 rather than 9.1 years. The unweighted averages that I report give a better picture of the problems facing each country. Unless otherwise indicated, all other data cited in this section were estimated from projections for individual countries from the United Nations (2003).

[22] An alternative set of estimates by Kraemer (2004) places this rise in public expenditures somewhat lower.

Table 7-1. *Estimates of population structure and future governmental expenditures on the aged if present laws remain in force*

| | Ratio of Workers to Retirees | | Ratio of Public Expenditures on the Aged to GDP | | | | | | |
| | | | Total | | For Pensions | | For Health | | |
	2000	2040	2000	2040	2000	2040	2000	2040	
AS+									
Australia	4.89	2.30	0.090	0.166	0.042	0.061	0.027	0.070	
Canada	4.90	2.12	0.089	0.229	0.049	0.117	0.033	0.098	
Ireland	5.15	2.40	0.058	0.167	0.034	0.080	0.026	0.078	Est
Japan	3.59	1.26	0.118	0.270	0.069	0.145	0.038	0.109	
New Zealand	4.96	2.35	0.088	0.201	0.057	0.114	0.027	0.065	Est
UK	3.71	2.37	0.121	0.176	0.065	0.065	0.028	0.066	
USA	4.79	2.76	0.094	0.203	0.052	0.091	0.037	0.105	
Average	4.57	2.22	0.094	0.202	0.053	0.096	0.031	0.084	
Nordic									
Denmark	4.07	2.11	0.108	0.217	0.074	0.119	0.025	0.080	Est
Finland	4.07	2.01	0.104	0.219	0.077	0.131	0.028	0.078	Est
Norway	3.82	2.01	0.095	0.204	0.058	0.102	0.033	0.091	Est
Sweden	3.37	1.93	0.133	0.230	0.073	0.113	0.039	0.080	
Average	3.83	2.01	0.110	0.218	0.071	0.116	0.031	0.082	
Western European									
Austria	4.00	1.69	0.140	0.273	0.104	0.171	0.036	0.092	Est
Belgium	3.51	1.93	0.127	0.245	0.088	0.150	0.030	0.078	
Germany: all	2.39	1.34	0.151	0.255	0.103	0.154	0.038	0.084	
Netherlands	4.57	2.14	0.117	0.256	0.065	0.138	0.030	0.078	
Average	3.62	1.77	0.134	0.257	0.090	0.153	0.034	0.083	
Southern European									
Greece	3.46	1.57	0.109	0.249	0.085	0.167	0.019	0.057	Est
Italy	2.32	1.04	0.173	0.320	0.121	0.200	0.030	0.090	
Portugal	3.88	1.82	0.085	0.213	0.059	0.129	0.023	0.062	Est
Spain	3.65	1.47	0.126	0.331	0.077	0.203	0.027	0.093	
Average	3.32	1.47	0.123	0.278	0.086	0.175	0.025	0.076	
France	3.67	1.99	0.158	0.293	0.113	0.182	0.033	0.092	
Switzerland	3.88	1.62	0.128	0.263	0.067	0.133	0.061	0.123	Est
Sample avg.	3.93	1.92	0.115	0.237	0.073	0.132	0.032	0.084	

Note: The expenditure data assume current laws. The data for health and pensions do not add up to total governmental expenditures because a category of miscellaneous public expenditures for the aged, which is quite small, is omitted. The ratio of workers to retirees is, more exactly, the ratio of those 65 and older to those 20 to 65; these estimates come from the United Nations (2003). The expenditure data for twelve nations come from Jackson and Howe (2003: Table 2). For the expenditures of the remaining nine nations, I have made rough estimates that are described in Appendix 7-6; these are designated with "Est."

a whole will rise about 5 percentage points.[23] The same type of clashing intergenerational interests will undoubtedly occur for governmental health expenditures to the aged as for social security.

Table 7-1 shows that, under current laws, total governmental expenditures for the aged will rise on the average about 12 percentage points of the GDP for the various OECD nations between 2000 and 2040. The increase will be least in the AS+ and Nordic nations and greatest in the Southern European countries. Although any such estimates are subject to a considerable margin of error, they point to one unavoidable fact: unless fundamental changes are made in current programs (e.g., raising the retirement age or limiting payments for certain expensive medical procedures to those under a given age), governmental payments to the aged will lead to a significant rise in total governmental expenditures.[24] Cutting benefits, of course, requires considerable political courage: witness the strikes and other labor disorders in France (and electoral defeats in 2004) when the government of Jacques Chirac attempted to change the retirement age in 2003.

Using data on the adjustment of social-security expenditures to an aging of the population in the late twentieth century, Lindert (2004a: 193–209) provides evidence that the major brunt of the adjustment will probably be on the recipients, despite the fact that in terms of the number of voters, they will become stronger. If true, this means that public expenditures will not rise as rapidly as portrayed in Table 7-1 and, at the same time, a larger share of the elderly will be living in poverty. The looming intergenerational battle about governmental taxes and expenditures will be prolonged and painful. Nevertheless, if tax revenues do not increase as fast as expenditures for the aged and if other public expenditures are not cut, the national debt of the country will soar, interest rates on government debt will rise, and governmental interest payments will sharply rise.

---

[23] I must add that estimates of future governmental health expenditures for the aged under current law in OECD nations vary considerably. For the United States alone, this also holds true. For instance, Kraemer (2004) has much lower estimates than in Table 7-1; the Board of Trustees of Medicare (2004) estimates a rise in these governmental health expenditures between 2000 and 2040 at 6.2 percentage points (and about 11.5 percentage points between 2000 and 2080); whereas the estimates of Kotlikoff and Burns (2004), who draw on careful generational accounting studies, are roughly similar to those in the table in 2050, but are very much higher in 2075.

[24] Kraemer (2004) estimates an increase in total "age-related" governmental expenditures of about 6 percentage points. However, he foresees a total increase in governmental expenditures for all purposes of 10 percentage points. Another recent study of age-related expenditures by Heller (2003) points to similarly large increases in governmental expenditures.

LOWER SAVING AND ECONOMIC GROWTH. If we assume that people save during their working years (either directly or indirectly through some type of social security system) and spend down their wealth during their retirement years, then overall savings should decline as the number of workers per retirees declines. A number of empirical studies are available that have estimated the impact of a 1 percent rise in the elderly dependency ratio (i.e., the ratio of those in retirement ages to those in the working ages) on the net savings rate (the ratio to the GDP of saving by workers to dissaving of retirees), a statistic I will call the population-saving elasticity (PSE). Taking the PSE to be 0.30, which is at the low end of the range of available empirical estimates, this would indicate that net savings rate in the OECD will be slightly more than half the 2000 level by 2040.[25] If this fall in saving is spread over forty years, the average growth of per capita GDP over the period would be roughly 16 percent less than it would have been if the elderly dependency rate had remained the same and, at the end of the period, saving would not cover all of depreciation. As a result, all growth of the GDP would be due only to technical change.[26] If the PSE were 0.6 (which is still lower than the average of the empirical estimates), the average growth over the period would be roughly 39 percent less than it would have been without any change in the population structure.

Another more theoretical approach to the problem is to assume a very simple economy in which people save so as to even out consumption over their lifetime.[27] By looking at the number of people in working and retirement ages, we can then determine net saving. For the United States, such an approach using a simulation model yields a decline in the net savings rate and in GDP growth of roughly the same magnitude as that when the PSE is 0.30. The simulation model, however, also allows us to easily explore what happens when life expectancy or the retirement age rises. Looking just at the ratio of work years to retirement years when life expectancy increases, we

---

[25] The elderly retirement ratio (the inverse of the ratio in the first two columns of Table 7-1) will rise on average about 29 percentage points among the OECD nations between 2000 and 2040. The results of various empirical studies of the impact of a rise in the elderly dependency ratio on savings are summarized by England (2002: 84), who draws from published and unpublished work by Guy Meredith.

[26] These estimates on the impact of a fall in the savings rate on GDP growth was derived by a simulation model. I assumed a 1 percent increase in disembodied technical change, a Cobb–Douglas production function, a depreciation rate of 5 percent, an initial savings rate of 20 percent, and an initial capital/output ratio of three.

[27] By a "simple economy," I mean one with no interest rate, no economic growth (so that earnings are the same every year), and perfect foresight by workers and retirees. A simulation model using this approach can be found in Pryor (2002a).

obtain the counterintuitive result that net saving falls when the retirement age increases the same number of years as life expectancy, and rises if the retirement age remains the same. By itself, this suggests that the strategy adopted by most governments of staving off bankruptcy of their social security systems in the face of rising life expectancy by raising the retirement age may lower the overall net savings rate and, as a result, economic growth.[28]

The population data in Table 7-1 combined with the results from either the empirical or theoretical model allow us to determine that the decline in net saving will be greatest in the nations of Southern Europe, in large part because their populations are aging faster, and least in the AS+ and Nordic nations. This means that the level of economic development in the Southern European nations will fall further behind that of the other OECD nations unless domestic saving is supplemented by capital inflows.

These considerations also suggest that for the domestic savings rate to be maintained in the future, governments will have to either resort to forced saving (where tax revenues are greater than expenditures) or take politically costly steps to reduce expenditures. One certainty must be emphasized – in the coming decades, it will be less likely that a nation can "grow out" of particular economic and social problems. This points toward greater social unrest and institutional change in the future.

A CONJECTURE. The rising governmental expenditures for pensions and health costs, combined with decreased saving and economic growth, can be handled in a variety of ways, many of which will have an important impact on the institutions of the nation. The variety of possible responses to these problems suggests that countries with the same economic system might opt for different solutions. If so, this means that polyvalent systemic change may prevail in the future.

3. Critical Forces Influencing Future Systemic Changes: Economic Globalization

Globalization has many meanings – political, legal, cultural, economic – and it can also refer to the international transmission of such diverse phenomena

---

[28] Governments might also have to borrow to finance state pension schemes that currently are primarily financed on a pay-as-you-go basis. This raises problems because their borrowing has been rising for other reasons as well. A Standard and Poors estimate says that nine of the EU's fifteen member states will have an accumulated government debt of 150 to 300 percent of GDP by 2050 (Kraemer, 2004), and this could be exacerbated by disability or special unemployment schemes for older workers that essentially provide early-retirement benefits.

as diseases or economic crises.[29] For purposes of this discussion of world market integration, three macroeconomic indicators deserve our attention: the flows of trade, people, and capital.

TRADE FLOWS. Over the second half of the twentieth century, trade became an increasingly important part of national economies. The ratio of foreign trade (the average of exports and imports) to the GDP is a useful measure of international market integration. For all of the OECD nations, this indicator rose from 21.3 percent in 1952 to 38.0 percent in 2000,[30] with the greatest acceleration in the 1970s and 1990s. Within the OECD, these ratios grew fastest for the Southern European nations and slowest for the Nordic nations. Another indicator of market integration is international price convergence. Although the evidence is mixed, it appears that a certain amount of price convergence also occurred among the OECD nations.[31]

IMMIGRATION. Immigration into the OECD nations increased considerably in the second half of the twentieth century, although this is difficult to document for the early years of the period. One measure of integration of the world labor market is the ratio of annual immigrants to total population. For the twenty-one OECD nations, this ratio rose steeply toward the end of the twentieth century, from 0.2 percent in 1984 to 0.8 percent by 2000. Another measure is the ratio of the foreign-born to the total population, which, in the same seventeen-year period for the same group of nations, rose from 4.7 to 6.5 percent.[32] If illegal immigrants are included, the increase would be

---

[29] The former is exemplified by international transmission of AIDS or SARS; the latter, by the wave of financial crises among developing nations. Although we might conjecture that globalization is also leading to the synchronization of business cycles, the evidence is mixed.

[30] These estimates are unweighted average five-year ratios of [(exports + imports)/2]/GDP, using the definitions of the 1968 system of national accounts. The data come from OECD (Annual-b for years 1980, 1998, and 2003). Findlay and O'Rourke (2003: 41) present a longer series, reaching back to 1820, which shows the steady rise (except from 1929 to 1950) of the export/GDP ratio.

[31] Using World Bank data, Findlay and O'Rourke (2003) could find no discernible trend toward commodity price convergence in the last four decades of the twentieth century. By contrast, Nicoletti et al. (2001: 158) examined more than two hundred goods and services and did find price convergence between 1985 and 1996, both among the EU countries and among seven other OECD nations (although to a lesser degree). Measuring integration in this manner is tricky. For instance, in a study using detailed price statistics underlying the U.S. consumer price index, I found (1995) no movement toward integration in U.S. retail markets in the latter half of the twentieth century.

[32] The immigration data come from World Bank (2004) and include only those countries for which relatively long series are available. If my estimates for the other countries are to be believed, the results are practically the same. The percentage of foreign-born come from the same source and, again, include only those countries with long series and, according to my estimates for the other

undoubtedly higher. Data on net immigration for the entire second half of the twentieth century point to the same picture.[33] For perspective, however, it is worth noting that annual immigration as a share of the population in the early part of the twentieth century before World War I appears to have been higher than it was at the end of the same century (McBride, 2000).

CAPITAL. International capital flows have increased enormously and point toward considerable integration of world capital markets. In the quarter-century between 1972 and 1997, estimated world capital flows, both direct and portfolio investment measured in constant prices, increased at an average annual rate of 8.3 percent,[34] more than twice as fast as the world GDP. In my sample of OECD nations, direct foreign investment as a share of GDP increased from 0.7 percent between 1971 and 1980 to 2.6 percent between 1991 and 2000; for foreign direct investment in the home country, the corresponding ratios are 0.2 and 1.0 percent.[35] This increase in foreign direct investment can also be seen in the rising ratio of foreign-owned assets as a percentage of the world GDP, from 6 percent in 1960 to 62 percent in 1995 (Obstfeld and Taylor, 2003: 141). Another measure of the integration of the world capital market is the convergence of the rates of return on various types of assets. This turns out to be a highly technical measurement problem, but at least in some capital markets, Obstfeld and Taylor (2003) find such convergence.

countries, the increase was from 5.5 to 8.0 percent. Unfortunately, both series only extend from 1984 to the end of the century.

[33] Net immigration (immigration minus emigration) increased from 0.02 percent of the population in 1952, when a majority of my sample of OECD nations had a net outflow of population, to 0.28 percent of the population in 1997. In the latter year, all of the OECD nations were net receivers of immigrants. These percentages are calculated from the difference between estimated population growth and the births minus deaths in the various countries for five-year intervals. The underlying data come from the United Nations (2003).

[34] For this estimate of capital flows, I adjusted "old IMF data" for 1970–84 (from Lipsey, 1999: 327) so that it was roughly comparable with "new IMF data" for 1980–92 using data for the overlap year as the adjustment factor. The new IMF data have an inconsistent treatment of Hong Kong and Taiwan, which I could not take into account. The combined results are deflated by the GDP price index of the United States. The overall growth of GDP for roughly the same period comes from Maddison (2003).

[35] These ratios for capital outflows were calculated from data from the OECD (2001). To convert these data into 1990 dollars, I deflated the current price data using the implicit price deflator of gross investment in the United States. The data for capital inflows were estimated from data from the OECD (Annual -c, 1999, 2001) and are more uncertain. The GDP data come from Maddison (2003).

These three facets of globalization have varied effects, but convergent systemic changes seem more likely. Several of the most important arguments deserve attention.

HOMOGENIZATION OF GOVERNMENT POLICIES. As nations become more deeply enmeshed in the world market, governmental policy tools to steer the economy become less and less effective, just as the integration of the American economy has left state governments with very little power to influence the aggregate economy under their jurisdiction. Federal governmental expenditures to stimulate domestic demand will have a smaller impact when these disbursements serve more than formerly to increase the imports of foreign goods (more technically, when the marginal propensity to import rises). Governmental monetary power to stimulate investment by lowering interest rates will becomes less effective if lenders can easily send their funds abroad to receive a higher return.[36] This reduction in the effectiveness of governmental intervention in the economy makes such policymaking in all nations more similar.

EXTERNAL PRESSURES. Increasing economic integration encourages an international convergence of institutions in certain narrow arenas of activity. For instance, the Bank for International Settlements in Basel has been trying to standardize certain banking practices worldwide, and such groups as the World Intellectual Property Organization and the European Patent Convention are trying to create some uniformity in patent procedures, in large measure to avoid bitter international disputes about intellectual property. Many other international organizations, such as the World Trade Organization, could also be mentioned in this regard. Clive Crook (2003) also argues that because of increasing international oversight, existing income support and other forms of subsidies – for instance, those to farmers – will become more explicit and, therefore, harder to sustain. The measures taken to standardize laws and regulations among nations belonging to the European Union are an extreme example of such convergence.

---

[36] On a microeconomic level, the policy options of governments are also narrowed because they are limited by international agreements. For instance, President George W. Bush's attempt in March 2002 to bolster his nation's steel industry (and gain more political support among steel workers) by increasing tariffs on imported steel was censured by the World Trade Organization, which forced the United States to rescind such tariffs or face special tariffs against a variety of U.S. goods produced in politically sensitive states.

INCREASING IMPACT OF LARGE MULTINATIONAL ENTERPRISES. For many decades, we have heard that greater globalization leads to a greater importance of multinational firms and this, in turn, will lead to a standardization of corporate practices in various nations. The first part of this assertion is undoubtedly true, and some changes, such as the coming standardization of accounting practices throughout the world, point toward a standardization of corporate structures and activities. Nevertheless, I have found no evidence that a general homogenization of corporation structures and procedures has actually taken place or will occur in future decades: The management traditions of the various countries act strongly to offset such tendencies, especially because most multinational firms are firmly embedded in the business culture of their home country, even though they operate in other countries as well.

CONVERGING LEVELS OF ECONOMIC DEVELOPMENT. International trade has winners and losers, and many have argued that globalization points toward widening disparities of world income, which might, in turn, influence different institutional changes.[37] Although income inequalities between and within nations appear to have increased in the latter half of the twentieth century, this may not have been the result of globalization. Lindert and Williamson (2003) present evidence that those nations "strongly open to trade" have, other factors held constant, grown faster than other nations and that these nations show a certain convergence in their levels of economic development with those of high-income nations. Within the OECD where all nations have been open to trade, differences in per capita GDPs have narrowed considerably between the early 1950s and 2000.[38] According to standard arguments, this tendency – if it lasts – should encourage convergent change.

HIGHER SOCIAL TRANSFERS. Various econometric comparisons of nations have shown that more open economies have had high social transfers, other causal factors held constant. It is hypothesized that this has come about

---

[37] This paragraph draws heavily on a broad survey of these issues by Lindert and Williamson (2003).

[38] The data come from Maddison (2003). Two tests can be used for income convergence: a fall in the coefficient of variation (the standard deviation divided by the mean) and an inverse relation between the initial level of per capita GDP and the growth rates of these levels of development. The OECD nations pass both tests.

because of greater vulnerability to external economic shocks accompanying greater openness (Lindert, 2004b: 71-2).

All of these arguments are based on the notion that globalization will continue at the same rapid pace as in the latter part of the twentieth century. This is by no means certain. Moreover, in many situations, the effects of globalization can lead to considerable disruption of the domestic economy – for instance, the turmoil in Asia in 1997–98. Such economic difficulties, in turn, invite a retreat from open markets and greater national regulation of the economy.

If rapid globalization does continue, a certain homogenization of particular economic institutions outside the government may also take place, in part as the result of the greater impact of the same external economic environment on these nations. As noted before, it seems unlikely that a general systemic convergence will occur in the short and middle run, in part because of differences in values and national traditions that will be difficult to submerge. This is despite their membership in broader political entities, such as the European Union. Whether larger nations will be more able to resist systemic homogenization than smaller nations is another open question.

4. Critical Forces Influencing Future Systemic Changes: Relative Power of Capital, Labor, and Management

To explore these issues, it seems useful to separate the particular forces affecting the institutions defining the relative economic power of capital and labor.

Trends in the ownership and management of enterprises do not point toward dramatic systemic changes. In the popular press, we frequently encounter the argument that the size and concentration of enterprises are increasing. If true, this could have an important impact on the functioning of markets, various types of property rights, the manner in which the government makes its decisions, and, of course, wage bargaining.

Three quite different indicators can be used to examine these issues: monopolization, as measured by the share of a narrowly defined industry's shipments accounted for by the top four or eight firms; agglomeration, as measured by the share of total employment or industrial assets accounted for by the largest one hundred or one thousand firms; and the average size of enterprises, as measured by labor force or assets. Despite the growing number of mergers between enterprises, particularly in the 1990s, trends in these indicators in the latter part of the twentieth century give no cause for alarm and provide little evidence of dramatic changes in the coming decades.[39]

One other argument is often raised: In the latter part of the twentieth century, corporate tax rates declined. If globalization proceeds, competition among nations for new foreign investment (to offset a decline in domestic saving) may become more severe and encourage the continuation of this trend.

Nevertheless, future systemic changes of OECD nations will more likely come from forces arising from labor, rather than product markets, and from management, rather than ownership. Several interrelated trends are apparent.

DECLINE IN WORKING-CLASS SOLIDARITY. As the labor force becomes more and more heterogeneous in terms of skills, ethnicity, and life style, working-class solidarity appears to be declining in many countries. In a number of OECD countries, union density (i.e., the share of unionized workers in the labor force) has declined, and only in the four Nordic nations has it risen (ILO, 1997; Golden, Wallerstein, and Lange, 1999). In three of these Nordic nations and in Belgium (where union density has remained roughly stable), the unions have administered the unemployment insurance fund so that union membership has certain clear advantages. Moreover, in most countries, labor unions have been losing many of their initial functions, as the state has begun to enforce labor protection laws. As noted herein, globalization has placed less-skilled workers in a more precarious position in the OECD, and unionization has not solved the problem of foreign competition.

GREATER WAGE INEQUALITY. The weakening of labor unions has some important implications for the economic system. Several economists, such as Blau and Kahn (1994) and Card (1998), provide evidence that unionization is one of the key institutional factors influencing the dispersion of wages.[40] Other considerations held constant, wage inequalities should widen

---

[39] Evidence supporting these generalizations come from Franko (2003), Ghemawat and Ghadar (2000), Nicoletti et al. (2001), Pryor (2002a), and White (2002, 2003). A possible exception to my optimistic conclusion is the growing share of production covered by inter-firm alliances (Friedheim, 1998), which may portend the growth of cartel-like activities in certain industries in the future.

[40] Other institutional factors of importance include the level at which wages are negotiated (plant, enterprise, industrial, or national level) and various foreign trade and immigration institutions.

as unionization declines,[41] a trend reinforced by an increasing willingness by employers in many countries to use wage differentials as part of incentive packages to workers. Burgeoning international trade also has an adverse influence on wage equalization, at least in all but the poorest OECD nations. More specifically, because most of the OECD nations have a comparative advantage in the production of goods requiring highly skilled and/or educated workers, the rising imports of goods from the developing nations that embody unskilled labor will put a downward pressure on the wages of their own less skilled or educated labor force; and growing immigration of low-skilled workers will exacerbate this problem.

MORE JOB INSECURITY. Trade openness may also lead to greater job insecurity, not only because each country is more vulnerable to shocks from the others but also because fewer domestic industries are safe from foreign competition. Moreover, because more and more firms have branches in many countries, a firm experiencing labor difficulties in one nation can more easily shift production to another.

DECLINING INSTITUTIONAL SUPPORT FOR WELFARE EXPENDITURES. Union density is also correlated with the size of the government sector in general and government welfare expenditures in particular. It is possible that as unions weaken, visible public support for these programs, which is important for legislators, will decline as well.

Although the previous discussion points to a shift in the relative power of labor and capital toward the latter, the impact of these tendencies should not be exaggerated. Stephen McBride (2000) argues that nation-states are not powerless in the face of globalization, particularly with regard to labor policies, and that in many cases neoliberalism is not a structural necessity in a globalizing world but an ideological victory. Multinational companies are still nationally embedded and can be regulated; immigration can, to a certain extent, be controlled; and labor market policies in various countries have shown little tendencies to converge. Webb (2000) also notes that even in the

---

[41] Some orthodox Marxists also argue that the ratio of labor to property income will fall as the economic power of unions declines, a proposition disputed by neoclassical economists, who argue that wages are determined solely by the marginal productivity of labor, so that this ratio is indeterminate. Turning to the empirical evidence, it appears, although we cannot be certain, that the share of wages in the national income in all of the twenty-one industrialized OECD nations rose in the third quarter of the twentieth century and either stayed roughly constant or rose in the remaining quarter-century as well. I hesitate, however, to pronounce on this issue because of the statistical difficulties in making long-term comparisons of the relative shares of capital and labor income for many countries.

area of corporate tax policy, there is as yet no race to the bottom, corporate tax rates vary considerably between countries, and such differentials are likely to persist. And, governmental welfare expenditures have broader support than just labor-union members.

The very close tie between labor and management relations to other aspects of the economic system suggests that the systemic changes of these institutions will be path-dependent. If so – and we cannot be sure – then it is quite possible that the degree of clustering and the distance between clusters may not also change.

SHIFTING STRENGTH OF MANAGEMENT OVER CAPITAL. The separation of ownership and control, which accompanied the rise of large corporations in past decades, appears a *fait accompli,* a phenomenon that has run its course in many OECD nations. In the United States, however, one facet of this managerial revolution continues and is manifested in the accelerating labor income of the very rich. Piketty and Saez (2003) show that since the 1960s not only have the incomes of those in the top 10 percent of the income distribution increased markedly faster than those of others, but also their share of labor income has increased more rapidly. For instance, the share of total wage income of the top 1 percent rose from 5.1 percent of all wage income in 1965 to 10.9 percent in 1998. An important part of this seems due to the explosive increase in executive compensation compared to ordinary wages, a phenomenon that does *not* seem due to more superior executive performance or to the larger size of enterprises but rather to the ability of top managers to appropriate for themselves a higher share of the profits that would have ordinarily gone to stockholders.

This trend is not yet apparent in most OECD nations, although business executives in these other nations have not given up the battle. For instance, in 2004 during the criminal trial in Germany of executives from Mannesman, who distributed 57 million Euros of bonuses to themselves shortly before Vodafone took over their firm, one defendant declared his innocence to the press: It was unfair that German business leaders are paid under their true international market value, as determined by U.S. norms, so they were only trying to recover their true worth from the firm that had been exploiting them!

The struggle between management and ownership is constrained by various institutions, not only legal but economic as well. For us, the real questions are why restraining influences on management have withered in the last quarter of the twentieth century and whether other countries will follow the same path. Such interesting issues await detailed study, although I suspect that such changes, if they will occur at all in other OECD countries, will be found primarily in the AS+ nations.

5. Final Observations

Many exogenous factors that will undoubtedly have an important impact on the future economy come readily to mind. These include the introduction and spread of new technologies (especially in biomedicine and information services), the changing international environment as the developing countries try to roll back some of the neoliberal policies currently pursued by international organizations, and the rising costs of extreme weather events caused by gradual global warming (Heller, 2003: 23 ff.). Certain evidence, such as the decreasing saltiness of the North Atlantic resulting from melting glaciers in the polar regions, point toward abrupt climate change as the flow of the Gulf Stream is diverted. According to a scenario submitted to the Pentagon, which allowed it to be published on the Internet (Schwartz and Randall, 2004), such an event could bring about decreased global agricultural production, decreased supplies of fresh water in key regions, more frequent floods and droughts, and increased warfare to obtain needed resources. Finally, in coming decades, certain raw materials – especially those connected with energy production – may become scarcer and rise in price, circumstances that I have shown elsewhere (2002a) will lead to greater consumption inequalities because consumption expenditures by low-income families are much more material-intensive than those by higher income households.

A number of endogenous factors will also have an important influence on the economy. These include the ever-rising demand for more highly educated workers, the growing distrust of government, and the increasing economic instabilities arising from growing national debt burdens (according to Heller, 2003: 70, all but a few of the twenty-one OECD nations had unsustainable fiscal policies at the turn of the millennium).

These lists can, of course, be considerably extended and for each item, the various impacts could be specified more precisely – although, in some cases, there is a large margin of error. Once we turn from the influence of such factors on the economy to their influence on the economic system, the analysis becomes even more problematic. This is both because of the greater number of factors to take into account and because of our lack of knowledge about the causal forces underlying institutional and systemic change.

What should be clear from this discussion of three major influences on the future economic system is that a strong element of uncertainty clouds our view. The aging factor may lead to expanding divergent change; the globalization factor, to contracting and convergent change; the shift in the relative power of capital and labor (and perhaps the shift in power between management and ownership), to neither. Because we do not understand exactly what happened in the past, predictions of the future are even more difficult to make.

D. A Brief Overview

The economic system of an industrial market economy is strongly influenced by its level of economic development; at different levels of per capita GDP, different sets of institutions distinguish one economic system from another. This is a critical factor to bear in mind when analyzing changes in such systems. Moreover, the impact that the economic system can have on various performance indicators can vary from one level of economic development to another. For instance, among contemporary developing economies, the type of economic system had a considerable impact on the rate of economic growth, whereas among the twenty-one current OECD nations it did not. As discussed in Chapter 5, the developing countries with the economic system showing the fastest growth also shared certain of the same institutional characteristics as the OECD nations.

My analysis of the characteristics of systemic change in the past yields several results. Comparisons between a group of developing nations and the OECD show that in the long-term course of economic development, the clusters defining the various economic systems become tighter but, at the same time, the differences between the different economic systems become greater. Focusing just on middle-term (i.e., 1960–1990) changes within the OECD and using a much smaller sample of institutions, the results are not as conclusive. No trends in either the degree of clustering or the distances between the clusters are apparent. In testing for parallel versus polyvalent change – that is, whether or not the nations with the same economic systems remained grouped over time – I use two tests. One test suggests that such groups maintained roughly the same composition and a second test showed that, to a certain degree, they did not. In this case, we cannot draw any conclusions. When we look at specific cases of institutional change, we see a multiplicity of factors at work; not all of them may be present at any given point in time in the countries that share the same economic system. Moreover, a brief look at the United Kingdom suggests that a country can peacefully change its economic system – that is, move from one cluster of nations to another in a span of three decades – which provides further evidence of a weak logic of institutions.

Finally, I look at three factors that should markedly influence changes in the economic systems of the OECD nations in the future. These include the aging of the population, globalization, and shifts in the relative power of ownership, management, and labor. This analysis provides further evidence of the complexity of systemic change and the difficulties of prediction.

EIGHT

Marxist Economic Systems

In this chapter, I speak of Marxist regimes rather than socialist or communist governments because the Marxist ideal may have pointed toward socialism, but many of these regimes fell far short of such a goal. Indeed, as I note herein, some so-called capitalist nations achieved certain Marxist goals to a greater extent than some so-called socialist nations.

Marxist economic systems were created and sustained by authoritarian governments that, on the basis of a particular ideology, formed in many countries economic institutions quite different from those found in market economies. As I argue, even though these Marxist economic systems rose and fell primarily for political, not economic, reasons, it is useful to survey them, both to determine how much an ideology can influence a system and how their divergence from a market economic system affected their economic performance. The results also provide some indication of the viability of economic systems different from those examined in the previous two chapters.

My analysis is based on the assumption that the impact of the ideology, rather than the authoritarianism *per se*, was more important for determining the way these economies functioned. Of course, Marxism in its Leninist garb has few uses for democracy. Indeed, most leaders in Marxist regimes argued that some type of autocracy or dictatorship is necessary to carry out the radical institutional changes they had in mind, even though they knew that some changes had severely adverse economic consequences, at least in the short and middle run.[1] Thus, it should come as no surprise

---

[1] For instance, Amílcar Cabral, a university-trained agronomist and one of the most important Marxist theorists in Africa (and also the leader of the liberation struggle in Cape Verde and Guinea-Bissau) wrote that agricultural land must be collectivized, even though this major

that, in comparing market and Marxist economies in the mid-1980s, the average degree of democracy was higher in the former than in the latter nations. Although comparisons between the OECD and Eastern Europe show these differences to be statistically significant, the results in the developing countries are more ambiguous. Two different ratings give rather different answers as to whether the differences in the degree of democracy in developing Marxist and market economies were statistically significant.[2] For my purposes, the findings of Adam Przeworski and his colleagues (2000b) in a detailed quantitative analysis of developing nations are critical: They show that for developing nations, the degree of democracy or dictatorship makes little difference in economic performance. Thus, any economic differences I might find between market and Marxist economies seem due more to the impact of the ideology than the degree of democracy *per se*.

Two immediate problems in carrying out a survey of Marxist economic systems must be faced. First, because of a paucity of readily available quantitative information on their institutions and how they actually function (in contrast to how they were supposed to function), it did not prove feasible to carry out a cluster analysis of the type used in previous chapters. Nevertheless, it is possible to carry out a more informal examination so as to gain an understanding of some of their key institutional characteristics and their economic performance in comparison with that of market economies at similar levels of economic development. Second, it proved difficult to define a Marxist regime. Of course, no country achieved communism in the classical Marxist sense – from each according to his ability, to each according to his need. So it is necessary to arrive at a less strict definition.

In the first section of this chapter, I lay out several criteria to define a "Marxist regime" in order to select thirty-three nations for further analysis.

---

institutional change would have the effect of lowering agricultural production ("people do not love the land in the same way as farmers who own the land themselves"), because he associated collectivization with "real" socialism. The citation is from Rudebeck (1974: 88).

[2] Marshall and Jaggers (2003) have a combined democracy–autocracy scale (Polity 2) running from +10 to −10. For the sample of nations used in Table 8-3 covering both market and Marxist economies in Europe (for Western Europe, I use all of the industrialized OECD nations), Asia, the Caribbean Basin, and Africa, the average scores (with the market economies' scores first and then the Marxist economies) are, respectively: +9.8 and −7.1; −1.4 and −7.3; +3.3 and −5.0; and −4.6 and −6.3. In all but the African case, the market economies have significantly higher scores (0.05 level of confidence). Another coding is by Przeworski et al. (2000a, 2000b), who have a two-point scale, with 0 = dictatorship and 1 = democracy. The average scores of these four world regions are, respectively, 1.00 and 0.00; 0.21 and 0.00; 0.67 and 0.50 (they had only two Marxist countries in their sample of Caribbean Basin nations and rated Nicaragua in 1985 as a democracy); and 0.03 and 0.00. In their ratings, the average scores for the market economies were significantly higher only in Europe.

Thereafter, I explore four issues: What were the circumstances underlying the establishment of these regimes? What were some of the most important and novel institutional features of their economies? What particular impacts did the regimes have on the functioning of their economies, particularly with regard to their long-term viability? And why did most of these regimes drop their Marxist program/policies at the beginning of the 1990s? Many other topics about Marxist economic systems would be interesting to analyze – in particular, the transition of the various planned economies to market economies, a process that is still underway. The questions I do focus upon, however, are most relevant to the broad themes of this book.

A. The Universe of Marxist Regimes

We can classify "Marxist regimes" by various criteria, of which three seem particularly important: the self-identification of the party in power as Marxist (or Marxist–Leninist); a firm goal of establishing a de facto one-party rule; and a serious intention to achieve direct control over the key sectors and enterprises of the economy for the purpose of facilitating highly detailed economic planning. These three criteria are difficult to apply. Some Marxist–Leninist parties took considerable pains to disguise the nature of their true beliefs. The one-party criterion does not exclude the existence of many nominal parties, if the ruling Marxist party manipulated these other parties and/or the outcomes of elections; unfortunately, such maneuvers are often difficult for outsiders to detect. Specification of the key sectors and enterprises raises additional analytical problems and, moreover, the serious-ness of the published plan that was really meant to be implemented cannot often be determined.[3] And, finally, "firm goals" and "serious intentions" are difficult to pin down.

Given such uncertainties, I do not apply these criteria too rigidly and include in Table 8-1 those governments in the second half of the twentieth century that apparently had these Marxist intentions or goals, even though they did not immediately carry them out. I also include only those that lasted long enough to attempt to implement their program, which excludes certain left-wing governments that proved unable to carry out their intended

---

[3] A telling case is the Madagascar long-term plan for 1986–90, which was never widely diffused to the population and was accessible only in the official law journal. Most government officials ignored it and knowledgeable Malagasy not working for the government speculated that its primary purpose was to convince the World Bank to extend the nation more credit (Pryor, 1990b: 236), rather than providing a statement of the government's true economic intentions.

Table 8-1. *Classification of Marxist regimes in the mid-1980s*

| | Date | Percent Adults in Marxist Party | U.N. Vote Index 1979–1987 | Percent of Economically Active in Each Branch by Sector | | | | | | |
| | | | | | State Sector | | | Cooperative Sector | | |
				Date	AFF	Other Branches	Total Economy	AFF	Other Branches	Total Economy
Africa										
Angola	1985	0.9	+1.00	1984	2.2%	30–50%	9–14%	—	—	—
Bénin	1986	<0.1	+0.10	1980	0.4	11.7	3.5	—	—	—
Cape Verde	1986	5.5	−0.05	1985	—	—	51.2	—	—	—
Rep. of Congo	1985	1.1	+0.38	1982	—	—	14.7	—	—	—
Ethiopia	1985	0.3	+1.00	—	—	—	—	—	—	—
Guinea-Bissau	—	—	−0.14	1984	—	—	13.4	—	—	—
Madagascar	—	—	+0.38	1980	0.8	41.3	5.3	—	—	—
Mozambique	1983	1.9	+0.52	1980	2.9	70.4	12.9	0.6%	0.4%	0.5%
São Tomé	1985	6.2	−0.05	1981	86.0	60.0	74.5	—	—	—
Seychelles	—	—	+0.24	1985	57.5	58.3	58.2	—	—	—
Somalia	1977	0.8	−1.00	1981	0.6	47.8	4.8	1.7	8.4	2.2
Zimbabwe	—	—	−0.43	1983	4.0	28.4	25.5	—	—	—
Americas										
Cuba	1986	8.2	+1.00	1981	75.6	98.5	93.3	3.8	0.0	0.9
Grenada	1982	0.2	+0.80	1981	15.7	38.1	31.9	—	—	—
Guyana	—	—	−0.33	1981	42.3	23.4	25.6	—	—	—
Nicaragua	1985	0.3	+0.52	1983	11.0	33.0	22.8	2.2	0.0	1.0
Asia										
Afghanistan	1987	0.5	+1.00	1981	0.6	26.1	10.6	8.7	0.0	5.3
Cambodia	1985	0.2	no vote	—	—	—	—	—	—	—

(continued)

Table 8-1 (continued)

| | Date | Percent Adults in Marxist Party | U.N. Vote Index 1979–1987 | Date | Percent of Economically Active in Each Branch by Sector | | | | | |
| | | | | | State Sector | | | Cooperative Sector | | |
					AFF	Other Branches	Total Economy	AFF	Other Branches	Total Economy
China	1987	7.9	−1.00	1986	3.3	64.4	27.1	0.1	16.9	6.7
Korea, North	1985	24.8	no vote	1965	8.0	100.0	43.2	92.0	0.0	56.8
Laos	1985	5.0	+1.00	—	—	—	—	—	—	—
Mongolia	1985	8.4	+1.00	1979	—	—	63.1	—	—	—
Viet Nam	1985	5.8	+1.00	1984	10.9	21.1	13.8	70.0	—	50.3
Yemen, South	1985	2.7	+1.00	1982	10.7	47.5	42.8	30.7	5.3	5.5
Europe										
Albania	1981	6.7	−0.33	1979	—	—	49.8	—	—	—
Bulgaria	1985	14.1	+1.00	1965	16.3	90.1	57.3	82.7	8.4	41.3
Czechoslovakia	1985	15.5	+1.00	1985	99.1	98.8	98.9	(included in state sector)		
Germany, East	1985	17.9	+1.00	1987	19.8	87.6	80.2	78.7	7.0	14.8
Hungary	1985	11.4	+1.00	1985/6	22.0	82.7	70.5	70.1	6.4	19.2
Poland	1985	8.4	+1.00	1978	14.1	96.4	71.6	6.8	—	2.0
Romania	1985	23.1	+0.14	1977	11.9	92.5	62.8	72.2	5.9	30.3
U.S.S.R.	1984	10.1	+1.00	1970	39.4	99.2	84.1	59.5	0.9	15.5
Yugoslavia	1985	14.0	−0.86	1981	11.6	94.0	68.5	0.4	—	—

Notes: Adults include all the population over 19 years old. AFF = agriculture, forestry, and fishing. — = not available. The U.N. vote index is calculated from U.N. data taken from twenty-one votes on the Afghanistan and Cambodian questions that came up in the U.N. between 1979 and 1987: +1.00 = complete similarity with Soviet votes; −1.00 = complete dissimilarity. All data come from Pryor (1992: 19, 363) with corrections for Hungary.

reforms. As a result, the list presented in Table 8-1 contains a number of borderline cases – for instance, Benin, Somalia, and Zimbabwe. Some analysts who have carried out a similar exercise[4] place more weight on whether the Marxist party in power was Leninist or whether a highly centralized political group controlled the government, rather than on their declarations of intention. The Soviets also had several baroque classification systems that seemed, in part, to be based on "friendship" with the U.S.S.R. In general, the various lists differ the most in their treatment of particular developing nations in Africa. A brief look at some of the specific indicators provides a greater understanding of additional classification problems, especially in nonindustrialized nations.

MASS PARTY. Defining a "mass party" as one whose membership comprises more than 6 percent of the adult population, the table shows that outside of Europe, only five nations had such a Marxist party. In most African nations, party membership was quite low and surpassed the 6 percent limit only in São Tomé (and almost in Cape Verde). In the Americas, only Cuba could boast a mass party. In Asia, the share of adults having party membership was noticeably high in China, Mongolia, and North Korea, and low in Afghanistan, Cambodia, and South Yemen (with Laos and Viet Nam falling in between).

U.N. VOTING. The U.N. vote index shows the extent to which the country voted the same as the Soviet Union on particular issues. It also varied considerably among the Marxist regimes, especially because China and the Soviet Union were often on opposite sides of the issues of those that I took into account in calculating the index.

PUBLIC OWNERSHIP. The degree of nationalization (or, in the case of agriculture, cooperativization) varied enormously from country to country. The data in Table 8-1 show that, outside of Europe, roughly half of the Marxist regimes had nationalized to the extent that at least a quarter of the labor

---

[4] In the rest of this paragraph, I refer to studies by Rubinstein (1988), Szajkowski (1982), and, about the Soviet classifications, Spaulding (1982, 1983) and Starr (1987). My list contains all the countries named by Rubinstein, but I also include Cape Verde, Guinea-Bissau, Guyana, Seychelles, Somalia, and Zimbabwe, which he does not. Szajkowski's list contains all of the same countries as mine except Somalia; however, he also includes Burkina Faso, Ghana, and Surinam, which I do not. The Soviets included as "socialist" all of the countries on my list except Somalia, but they also counted Algeria, Burkina Faso, Burma, Burundi, Ghana, Guinea, Libya, Mali, Sierra Leone, Syria, Tanzania, Uganda, and Zambia as socialist, which I do not.

force was working either directly in governmental agencies or in state and cooperative enterprises. Given that the share of the labor force employed directly in traditional governmental activities (e.g., defense, police, education) was relatively low, the bulk of this employment must have been in state-owned enterprises or farms. These numbers can be placed in perspective by comparing them to similar figures for other nations. At the end of the 1990s among the industrial OECD nations, for instance, the percentage of the labor force employed in government (central or local) enterprises was relatively small – ranging from 3 to 7 percent (Pryor, 2002a: 314) – but the share of the civilians in the labor force employed in governmental agencies (e.g., administration, education, health) was much higher, running from 7 percent (Japan) to 15 percent (U.S.) to 23 percent (Sweden).[5] Thus, the total share of the labor force in the public sector ranged from 10 to 30 percent in these "capitalist" nations, which was higher than the corresponding percent in about half of the Marxist regimes outside of Europe, at least in their early years.

In countries such as Afghanistan, Bénin, Madagascar, and Somalia, the socialist sectors (state enterprises and cooperatives) were noticeably low. In most of the developing nations, in contrast to Eastern Europe, the transfer to state ownership of previously privately owned enterprises was often not painful to the citizens of the country because it frequently involved nationalization of foreign-owned enterprises and farms and was, thus, an aspect of the national liberation movement. A particularly dramatic case occurred in São Tomé, where the Portuguese plantation owners fled within days of independence, so that without bloodshed or major difficulties, the government quickly ended up owning more than three quarters of the agricultural land.

PUBLIC EXPENDITURES. Although it might seem obvious to some that public expenditures as a share of the GDP would be much higher in Marxist than non-Marxist nations, this turns out *not* to be the case. In 1985, for instance, general governmental expenditures as a share of GDP in Marxist regimes were not statistically different from those of non-Marxist countries in Eastern Asia, Africa, and the small nations bordering the Caribbean (national account data from the World Bank, 2002). In Europe, certain problems arise

---

[5] These data come from the Japan Statistical Bureau (2003); U.S. Bureau of the Census (2002); and the website of the CEEP (European Center of Enterprises with Public Participation and of Enterprises of General Interest) <www.ceep.org/>. Other data (not cited) on public employment in the OECD nations come from Eurostat.

because for Marxist and non-Marxist nations, the readily available data are not easily comparable. My own attempts to adjust them for comparability show that for the seven "standard" functions of government expenditure (i.e., administration, national defense, police, health, education, welfare, and research and development), no significant differences between Marxist and non-Marxist nations can be found during the 1950s (Pryor, 1968); and during the 1960s and early 1970s, these public expenditures as a share of GDP were possibly higher in the West (Pryor, 1984). In sum, the share of general public expenditures (i.e., those not destined for commercial activities or investment) as a share of the GDP did not distinguish Marxist and non-Marxist regimes. As shown in the following discussion, the major differences lay in the way the economy functioned.

B. The Rise of Marxist Regimes

It would be useful to have a general theory of why some regimes become Marxist and others do not. But, the variety of ways by which nations developed Marxist regimes has been sufficiently diverse that any general theory is not likely to be very helpful for empirical research. Table 8-2 summarizes the major ways in which Marxist regimes came to power, and from this starting point we can search for patterns.

Marx argued that, as their per capita income increases, capitalist economies become increasingly dysfunctional: their business cycles are more severe, unemployment rises; social classes become more polarized as incomes become more unequal; profit rates fall; and the means of production become concentrated into ever fewer owners. To Marx (1950 [1867]: Chapter 32), the consequences were obvious:

The monopoly of capital becomes a fetter upon the mode of production, which has sprung up and flourished alone with, and under it. Centralization of the means of production and socialization of labor at last reaches a point where they become incompatible with their capitalist integument. This integument is burst asunder. The knell of private property sounds. The expropriators are expropriated.

The rhetoric is thrilling, but Table 8-2 shows that this has not actually happened, at least not up to now. For a better answer, it is helpful to start by charting the geographical/temporal pattern. In the period up to 1949, all of the new Marxist regimes were contiguous to the Soviet Union (except Albania, Bulgaria, and Yugoslavia); and, except Mongolia and North Korea, all were in Europe. From 1949 to 1959, two more Asian countries (China and Viet Nam) joined the group. In these first two stages, the spread

Table 8-2. *How Marxist regimes came to power*

	Independence	Political Power Achieved	Per Capita GDP	Circumstances of the Takeover
Europe				
Albania	1944*	1944–45	10%	Marxist partisans liberated nation, formed the new government.
Bulgaria	—	1944–47	17	Marxists gradually took over coalition government with Soviet help, later won manipulated elections.
Czechoslovakia	1945*	1948	37	Marxists won plurality in 1946; outmaneuvered others in cabinet shuffle in 1948.
Germany, East	—	1945–49	29	Soviets installed pro-Soviet government after WWII; formal Marxist government in 1949.
Hungary	1945*	1949	26	With Soviet aid, minority Marxist party fused with socialists; single list in election.
Poland	1945*	1945–47	26	Soviets installed pro-Soviet government; then Marxists won 1947 manipulated election.
Romania	—	1944–46	12	Soviet-installed governments became progressively more Marxist.
U.S.S.R.	—	1917	30	Marxists staged coup during disorders resulting from WWI, consolidated regime after civil war.
Yugoslavia	1945*	1945	17	Marxist partisans with Soviet army liberated nation; took over government.
Africa				
Angola	1975	1975	11	Marxists seized power in a civil war with other liberation parties.
Bénin	1958	1972–74	11	Military staged a coup, appointed Marxist leader.
Cape Verde	1975	1975	5	Marxist party won election.
Rep. of Congo	1960	1968–69	13	Military staged a coup, appointed Marxist leader.
Ethiopia	—	1974	3	Military coup, appointed Marxist leader.
Guinea-Bissau	1974	1974	3	After insurrection in one area, party moved into vacuum after independence.
Madagascar	1960	1975	10	President was assassinated; military directorate named Marxist president.

Country	Independence	Political power	Per capita GDP (1950, % of U.S.)	Path to power
Mozambique	1975	1975	12	After insurrection, Marxists dominated interim government and gained full power at independence.
São Tomé	1975	1975	5	Party dominated interim government; achieved full power at independence.
Seychelles	1976	1977	20	Domestic and foreign guerillas staged a coup.
Somalia	1960	1969	11	Military staged a coup.
Zimbabwe	1965	1980–82	7	After guerilla action and British-brokered peace, party won majority in subsequent election.
Americas				
Cuba	—	1959	36	Marxist party staged a revolution.
Grenada	1973	1979	10	Marxist party staged a coup.
Guyana	1966	1966	11	Previously elected Marxist-dominated transition government achieved power.
Nicaragua	—	1979	11	Insurrection/revolution.
Asia				
Afghanistan	—	1978	7	Military with crucial Marxist influence staged a coup.
Cambodia	1954	1975	5	Party staged a civil war/revolution.
China	1945*	1949	5	Party staged a revolution.
Korea, North	1945*	1945–48	8	Marxist dominated transition government with Soviet help; formal state in 1948.
Laos	1954	1975	6	Marxists took over coalition government by military actions and electoral successes.
Mongolia	1921	1921–24	5	Party led insurrection.
Viet Nam	1945	1954	7	Marxist party led independence war; in 1975, won war to gain control of south.
Yemen, South	1967	1969	10	Through semi-coup, party gained control of government apparatus.

Notes: Independence = year when the nation achieved independence or effective self-government; or, if previously occupied by an enemy power (designated with an *), years that occupation ended. Political power achieved = year when Marxist party achieved effective power. Per capita GDP for 1950 as percent of U.S. per capita GDP in the same year.

GDP data come from Maddison (2001). The estimates for East Germany were based on data from Maddison (personal communication); São Tomé was estimated from World Bank (2002) data; Viet Nam and Yemen estimates cover the entire country, rather than just the Marxist region. Information on dates and path to power drawn from a variety of historical sources for each country.

of communism represented a special type of political diffusion. Thereafter, however, most that became Marxist regimes were in Africa and far removed from the mother country.

As shown in the third column of Table 8-2, Marxist regimes usually did *not* come to power in economically advanced capitalist nations but rather in nations with relatively low levels of per capita GDP. The advent of Marxist regimes in the few industrialized nations (Czechoslovakia and East Germany) did not follow the classical revolutionary route but was the result of a coup or military occupation. From calculations of the GDP where similar goods and services in all countries are valued in the same prices, we find that in 1950, the per capita GDP in the thirty-three nations that had – or were to have – a Marxist regime averaged about 13 percent that of the United States in the same year. If we compare these 1950 levels of production of Marxist regimes to that of the United States in 1870, only a few years after Marx was tolling the knell of capitalism, the ratio would be 53 percent.[6] In 1913, a few years before the Marxist takeover, Russia had a per capita GDP of 63 percent of the United States in 1870, so it also had a relatively low level of economic development, no matter what standard is employed.

Five major routes to power can be quickly distinguished: In six of the thirty-three nations (18 percent), the Marxist regime took power via the "classical route": namely, a revolution or civil war (Cambodia, China, Cuba, Laos, Nicaragua, and the U.S.S.R.). In seven (21 percent), the Marxist regime was the direct outcome of a national liberation struggle against colonialism in which Marxist parties played a critical role.[7] In eight (24 percent), the regime took power as a result of a coup d'etát or installation by the country's military.[8] In another nine (27 percent), the regime came into power within five years of a military defeat or the removal of an enemy occupier (German or Japanese).[9] Finally, in three (9 percent), the regime was the result of an

---

[6] The U.S. per capita GDP in 1870 and the Russian per capita GDP in 1913 come from Maddison (2001). It is also noteworthy that in 1950, the average European nation in the future OECD had a per capita GDP roughly 55 percent that of the United States in the same year.

[7] These included Angola, Cape Verde, Guinea-Bissau, Mongolia, Mozambique, São Tomé, and Zimbabwe. It is interesting to note that in Sub-Saharan Africa, all of Portugal's former colonies, which were given independence relatively late, became Marxist regimes; whereas in both the former British and French colonies, Marxist parties come to power after independence in only about one sixth of the countries. Thus, in certain cases, the colonial government played a causal role in the type of national liberation struggle in which Marxist groups serve as leaders.

[8] These included Afghanistan, Benin, Republic of the Congo, Ethiopia, Grenada, Madagascar, Seychelles, and Somalia.

[9] These included Albania, Bulgaria, Czechoslovakia, East Germany, Hungary, North Korea, Poland, Romania, and Yugoslavia.

election or political maneuvering of the domestic Marxist party without extensive assistance from other Marxist nations.[10]

Stepping back from this detailed information, it is noteworthy that in all but four (12 percent) of the thirty-three countries, the formation of the Marxist regime occurred within a decade of national liberation, a major war, or a previous civil war.[11] The radical break from the past, which was accompanied by a considerable change in elites, was felt to be necessary to prevent a restoration of the old order that had brought misery to a significant portion of the population. Although other ways of categorizing these paths to power have been offered, most are of limited usefulness.[12]

From this discussion, five critical generalizations can be quickly drawn: (1) Almost all countries with a Marxist regime either started at a relatively low level of economic development or had such a regime foisted on them by the U.S.S.R. (2) In relatively few countries did the regime come to power as the result of a class-based revolution. (3) In most developing countries, the regime came to power either as a direct result of the national liberation struggle or as the result of a coup by a relatively small number of people. (4) Although many lives were lost in the national liberation struggle, the final transfer of power to a Marxist party in these countries or in the other nations was, in most cases, relatively bloodless. (5) As far as I can tell, economic factors stemming from the economic system played a relatively unimportant role in the installation of most Marxist regimes.

C. Major Institutional Features of a Marxist Economic System

Given the variety of economic systems found among Marxist regimes or within the same regime over time, I use the Soviet economy in the late 1950s as the canonical case with which to compare all others because its

[10] These included Czechoslovakia, Guyana, and South Yemen. With regard to political maneuvering, the Czechoslovak case is particularly instructive (Korbel, 1959: Chapters 11 and 12). After the first postwar election, the communist party gained a plurality (but not a majority) and its leader, Klement Gottwald, became Prime Minister. His cabinet, however, was dominated by noncommunists and in February 1948, a political crisis developed. To bring down the government and force a new and free election, the noncommunist cabinet members resigned. Gottwald, however, was able to intrigue with certain leaders of the Social Democratic Party so that the government would not fall and, with no opposition in the cabinet, they structured the subsequent election so that the communists won almost total control for the next forty-two years.

[11] These four were Afghanistan, Cuba, Ethiopia, and Nicaragua.

[12] Szajkowski (1982: Chapter 3) presents various typologies of this sort and then disparages their usefulness.

institutions were firmly established and functioning for a long time. This decision is not arbitrary, however, because in a triple sense the Soviet system served as the model for other Marxist regimes. The Soviet Union forced its version of Marxist–Leninist institutions onto some countries where its troops were stationed or where the country was heavily dependent on Soviet aid. Moreover, because the domestic Marxist parties had few experienced technicians, economic advisors from the U.S.S.R. or other Marxist nations helped to set up the economy and they often seemed to favor the establishment of institutions that they had in their own country.[13] Finally, the U.S.S.R. served as an inspiration, the embodiment of socialism for many (but not all) Marxist leaders, at least in the early years of the newly founded Marxist regimes.[14] In major part, this was because at that time there were no other models of Marxist economic systems, with the possible exception of Yugoslavia. Unfortunately, for many countries, we do not now know which of these factors was the most important in the establishment of their economic systems.

Although many institutional and organizational aspects of the economic systems of Marxist regimes differed from those of the market economies in Western industrial nations, it is most useful to focus attention primarily on those allocation mechanisms that underlay the property system and the distribution of goods and services, rather than discussing institutions that were unique to certain sectors of the economy – for instance, collective and state farms. In the following summary of three major institutional characteristics of a Marxist economic system, I first discuss the canonical case and then the variations that could be found in the "core" Marxist regimes. These include those in Europe plus Cuba, China, North Viet Nam, and North Korea, which had high levels of state or cooperative ownership and had sufficient political power and administrative abilities to launch some type of planned economy. I do not discuss in any detail the economic systems of the remaining Marxist regimes, most of which featured a hodgepodge of market elements, government regulation, and governmental intervention at both the central and local levels.

---

[13] Advisors from Czechoslovakia, for instance, assisted the Cuban government in setting up a planning system similar to that in the Soviet Union or their own nation. In Grenada, by way of contrast, the Soviet advisors felt that the island did not have the prerequisites for such a planning system and tried to slow down that nation's attempt to adopt "socialist institutions" (Pryor, 1986b).

[14] The role of the Soviet Union as an inspirational model was also readily apparent in Cuba, China, Czechoslovakia, and Viet Nam, though no Soviet soldiers were stationed in these nations. Footnote 1 provides an example of this inspirational role in Guinea-Bissau.

1. Nonmarket Allocation of Goods and Services

a. The Canonical Case

Marx had a considerable distrust of markets, and so it was highly likely that nations with Marxist leaders would attempt to find a substitute. By the end of the 1920s, the Soviets began to employ physical allocation systems to determine how many goods and services should be produced. The chief planning tool became the material-balance, which was simply a sheet of paper with the various sources of supply (domestic production, imports, and inventory drawdowns) and demand (from consumers, producers, the government, exports, and inventory buildups). If more production of a particular good was desired, this would require more production of its inputs, and this additional production would, in turn, require more production of other inputs, and so on down the line. The chief task of the planning office was to keep in balance all of the material-balances in a manner consistent with the production capacities of all branches of industry.

These material-balances had several important properties:

- They could be maintained either in physical or monetary units and, moreover, at any level of aggregation.
- They could cover many goods or just a few and could be administered at various levels of the hierarchy. The Soviet Central Planning Office maintained from 800 to 1,600 material-balances, and the various ministries maintained another 5,000. Planning units farther down the line maintained still more.
- Supply and demand could be equated for each of the material-balances in the system through a systematic iterative process, so that sophisticated computer methods were not necessary.[15]

For the material-balance system to function efficiently, the production enterprises had to be held to strict production goals. A preliminary plan would be sent down to producers, who would send up to the planners their estimates (usually exaggerated) of needed inputs. The planners would then use this information and readjust production quotas so that the supply and demand of all goods and services were equalized. These plans, specifying

---

[15] These are discussed, with a number of illustrations, by Montias (1959 and 1962, Chapter 1). See also Manove (1971).

production, labor force, finance, and other goals, were then aggregated into the final yearly plan. To widen production bottlenecks and to raise productivity through additions to the capital stock, long-term investment plans were also promulgated.

Supplementing the allocation of resources through the material-balance system was an extensive system of government controls, so that Soviet leaders could have as complete an overview and power over as many economic activities as possible. This meant a concerted effort to eliminate all private economic activities and to erect elaborate hierarchies of overlapping controls by governmental and party agencies. Such centralization allowed little autonomous decision-making roles to be played either by enterprise managers or by workers and their labor unions.

In the finance sector, the drive toward direct administrative control meant that all transactions had to be carried out through branches of a single state bank. In agriculture, private farms were rare and farmers were herded onto the state and collective farms that took over the land once privately owned. However, private garden plots were allotted to those working on the state and collective farms; in the Soviet Union in the 1950s, these accounted for roughly one third of the total produced food (Pryor, 1992: 176).

The foreign-trade sector was also brought under central control. Shortly after the Russian Revolution, Lenin declared that all foreign trade was to be carried out by state enterprises and all foreign financial transactions through state banks. Such controls were instituted for several reasons: to prevent a capital flight or the accumulation of assets abroad; to prevent exports and imports from creating production difficulties; to prevent foreigners from gaining sensitive information about the state of the economy; and to regulate contacts with foreigners, who might have hostile intentions toward the U.S.S.R.

b. Variants Among the Core Nations

Most but not all of the Eastern European nations maintained a material-balance planning system from the 1950s up to the end of the central planning system. Around 1950, Yugoslavia appeared to drop its material-balance system when its labor-managed enterprise system began to flower. In Hungary after 1968, the planning system was drastically changed and the material-balances no longer served their former planning/administrative function. In China, with the devolution of control over production to local private and township/village enterprises after the mid-1980s, the material-balance system appeared to have been retained only for a limited number of products produced in the state sector.[16]

Some countries, such as East Germany, Hungary, and Yugoslavia, also tried to decentralize decision-making in industry. East Germany's "New Economic System," which started in the 1960s but gradually reverted in the 1970s, was primarily a reorganization of industry and the newly created industrial units still received an output plan although, perhaps, less detailed than before. Hungary's "New Economic Mechanism" was more ambitious, for it eliminated the output plan targets and tried to devolve real decision-making authority to firm directors.

In some of these cases, the move away from the material-balance system as a tool for allocation meant that more emphasis was placed on indirect governmental controls, which were intended to make room for a utilization of local talents and knowledge on particular problems. Toward the end of the Marxist era, for instance, the foreign-trade monopoly in a number of Eastern European countries was relaxed by allowing state firms to participate directly in export and import trade rather than funneling such trade through special foreign-trade enterprises. In the rural sector, Yugoslavia, Poland (after the mid-1950s), Viet Nam (in the 1970s), and China (after 1979), decollectivized agriculture so that farming was essentially private, even though the farmers may not have had formal ownership of the land.

Nevertheless, direct administrative controls and central commands continued to be issued. Keren (1992) argues that in countries attempting decentralization, enterprise directors did not, as hoped, maximize profits but rather paid greater attention to directives (and informal targets) from higher administrative organs. This was manifested, at least in Hungary, by the continuation of "storming" (i.e., a dramatic increase of production at the end of the plan period in order to meet plan goals). Kornai (1983: 233–34) also points to the continued lack of budgetary discipline (a "hard-budget constraint") in Hungary that would have forced unprofitable firms into bankruptcy. The most radical decentralization of industry was in Yugoslavia but, even there, enterprise decision-making was considerably constrained by the interventions of higher government agencies. The lack of a well-functioning market system was shown by the absence of a hard-budget constraint and the minuscule fraction of production units that were subject to bankruptcy (Keren, 1992).

---

[16] Township/village enterprises did exist in a different form before the mid-1980s, but as commune/brigade enterprises subordinate to the agricultural communes rather than as independent decision-making units.

In brief, East Germany, Hungary, and Yugoslavia certainly did not have market systems but rather hybrid systems, with only indirect influences of the forces of supply and demand. If we were able to carry out a cluster analysis of the Marxist nations, they would undoubtedly lie in a different cluster than the U.S.S.R. and other core Marxist countries.

Although the Eastern European nations made a relatively quick (and painful) jump to some form of a market economy in the 1990s, some of the Asian Marxist nations opted for a slower transition. It seems unlikely, however, that such a process will suddenly stop at mid-point, in major part because their mixed economic systems have given rise to some difficult microeconomic problems. In China, for instance, competition from the relatively free industrial sector has forced a number of state-controlled enterprises into bankruptcy.

2. Wage and Price Controls

a. The Canonical Case

In the Soviet Union, the prices of all major producer and consumer goods were, with the exceptions noted herein, set by a price office of the central government, whereas most other prices were set by other administrative units of the central and local governments. In theory, all goods were available to all consumers at the same price. Such prices, however, did not necessarily equate demand with supply, which meant that shortages were endemic, as were long queues of consumers waiting for scarce goods in particular stores.[17] Moreover, the feedback between the existence of scarcities and the producers of the goods was indirect and highly imperfect, so that scarcities could persist for long time periods. In brief, there was no consumer sovereignty and, insofar as shortages were allowed to persist, no consumer choice either.[18] Money also played a relatively passive economic role in the process of buying and selling – that is, it facilitated transactions but did not have the wide-ranging impacts on decision-making and activities that it has in a market economy.

Industrial workers were free to move around where they wished, except during World War II and a brief period thereafter, and were constrained only

---

[17] Data on shopping time in various Eastern and Western European nations are presented and analyzed by Pryor (1977d).

[18] Shleifer and Vishny (1998) argue that the endemic shortages were not merely a structural fault in the planning system but rather a deliberate policy by the government employees to enrich themselves and the managers by creating a ready climate for bribery.

by difficulties in finding housing. For most of the period, workers on collective farms, by way of contrast, needed permission from farm authorities to leave for the city.

Wages were centrally set and were outside the direct concerns of the labor unions. Some material incentives supplemented fixed wage payments, including certain types of piecework payments, as well as special bonuses for working in unpleasant conditions (e.g., in mines or in the far north) or for exceeding work norms. High bonuses were awarded to managers for exceeding plan goals. To a limited extent, Russia also employed certain moral incentives through systems of special recognition and medals for exemplary workers, such as awards for Stakhanovites for exceeding plan norms; sometimes these were accompanied by monetary bonuses as well.

b. Variants Among the Core Nations

In the last quarter of the twentieth century, a number of European Marxist regimes began loosening the fixed-price system, setting certain prices centrally, while allowing some to be set by the sellers and to fluctuate between fixed limits, and other prices to be set by enterprises so as to respond freely to the changing forces of supply and demand. Several countries with considerable reliance on foreign trade also began to adjust certain fixed domestic prices to reflect changes in international market prices, thereby avoiding the necessity of subsidizing those goods that sold for less at home than they did abroad. Nevertheless, in the East German and Yugoslav reforms, the most important prices continued to be centrally set. In Hungary, most centrally fixed prices were removed after 1968, but firms usually had to follow strict rules when setting prices and to take account of administrative injunctions and laws against unfair profits (Kornai, 1986).

Most core Marxist regimes followed the Soviet system of wage controls for most jobs, but there were certain marked exceptions. A left-deviation from the canonical case could be found in Cambodia, China, Cuba, and, to a certain extent, North Korea, where material incentives were downgraded and moral incentives played a much more important role. In these nations, jobs were assigned, a worker's employment and mobility were severely restricted, and unpaid "volunteer" work was also required. The right-deviation from the canonical case was found in Yugoslavia, where strikes were permitted and wages were flexible, at least upward (Keren, 1992). In Hungary, firms had a certain control over the wages that they paid as well.

3. Supplementary Markets: Open and Hidden

a. The Canonical Case[19]

Despite Soviet attempts to stamp out private markets, several types of markets persisted where prices fluctuated according to the forces of supply and demand. Some of these were legal ("white markets"), some were disliked but tolerated ("gray markets"), and some were illegal ("black markets").

The most important legal and officially recognized markets were the so-called collective-farm markets, designated places in almost all towns and cities where collective and state farmers could bring the surplus food from their private plots to be sold at any price they could obtain. Shops selling secondhand goods on commission and flea markets were also part of the white market.

Among the gray markets were the various "informal" ways of renting apartments, tutoring, giving medical service, making auto or house repairs, tailoring, and offering other specialized services. In some cases, such as medical services, the service was sold at the official price but the customer was expected to give a tip to ensure prompt service in the future. An important exchange of goods needed for production was also carried out between enterprise managers. Although such exchange was on a strict barter basis, the rate of exchange between the goods was, of course, an implicit price. This barter activity often resulted in long chains of exchanged goods and was facilitated by special go-betweens, shadowy characters whose contacts with a large number of managers allowed them to know where surplus goods for barter were available.

Finally, several kinds of black markets played important roles in the allocation of goods. Consumers often made special payments to sales clerks for goods held under the counter, or they bought goods obtained either legally or illegally by their vendors that were forbidden by law to be sold. Similar arrangements were also made between producers.

Although various economists have estimated the relative importance of the gray and black markets in the Soviet Union, it is difficult to gauge their accuracy. Several estimates for the 1970s and late 1980s run from 10 to 25 percent of the GDP (Feldbrugge, 1989; Schneider and Enste, 2002). In the successor states after the fall of communism, the size of the gray and black economy increased. World Bank estimates (cited by Feige, 1997) set the ratio as 37 percent in 1992, whereas Schneider and Enste (2000) cite estimates

---

[19] This discussion draws heavily from Katsenelinboigen (1977).

from 8 percent (Uzbekistan) to 63 percent (Georgia) in the mid-1990s, after the central planning systems had disintegrated.[20]

b. Variants Among the Core Nations

As shown in Table 8-1, some of the Eastern European Marxist regimes had larger private sectors than the Soviet Union. For the same reasons as in the Soviet Union, their physical allocation system was supplemented by a variety of white, gray, and black markets. It is noteworthy that some of the Marxist nations that had more legal free markets than the U.S.S.R., such as Yugoslavia, also appeared to have had larger shadow economies, mainly because it was easier to evade governmental restrictions and regulations on production.[21] In certain core countries such as China, markets were also permitted for small consumer goods, which meant that their stores featured a greater variety of goods and that queuing for them was less frequent.

4. A Note on the Economic System of Marxist Regimes Outside the Core

In most of the third-world Marxist regimes outside the core, a number of critical factors lowered the probability of a significant change in the economic system. These nations were primarily agricultural, and they were much more heavily reliant on foreign trade than the relatively autarkic Soviet Union. They also did not have the prerequisites for a totally planned economy, such as a system to provide accurate and timely economic statistics or a large cadre of trained economists and administrators.[22] Even more

---

[20] For perspective, according to Schneider and Enste (2002), the shadow economy in the early 1990s for twenty-one industrial OECD nations averaged roughly 14 percent, running from 8 percent (Switzerland) to 26 percent (Greece). But, the accuracy of any estimates of a shadow economy may be challenged. For instance, Frey and Pommerehne (1989) point out that for the United States in the 1970s, estimates ran from 3.4 to 33 percent of the GDP. Moreover, the Schneider–Enste estimates for the OECD nations apparently do not include the costs of crime (which represent the impact of illegal activities) which, in the U.S., amounted to more than 7 percent of the GDP in the mid-1990s (according to D. Anderson, 1999).

[21] At the end of the 1980s and early 1990s, production in the shadow economy amounted to 20 to 40 percent of the reported GDP in Croatia, Macedonia, and Slovenia (Schneider and Enste, 2000: 101). This magnitude might also be inferred from the trends in the 1970s and 1980s for Yugoslavia as a whole, as reported by Bićanić (1990).

[22] Such conditions did not mean that the introduction of a planned economy was impossible: China, Cuba, North Korea, and North Viet Nam, for instance, were able to adopt most of the key aspects of the Soviet economic system. But, these four countries had extraordinarily capable leaders, who had enormous political authority and did not feel constrained in using their power to create a Soviet-style economic system.

important, most also lacked leaders with sufficient political muscle to impose dramatic changes on the economy. As a result, their economic systems combined production for one's own consumption (in agriculture), private enterprises operating under various types of government regulation, and government enterprises that responded partly to pressures from the export market, partly to directives from the government. Because of this mixture of institutional features, which differed somewhat from country to country, it is difficult to characterize the economic systems of these third-world Marxist regimes.

5. A Requiem for the "New Socialist Man"

Although the physical planning, price and wage controls, and peripheral markets constitute the most important differences between these Marxist regimes and Western market economies, the list of other differences worth noting would be much longer. I must, unfortunately, leave this task for others. I would, however, like to emphasize one aspect in which the economies of the core Marxist regimes did *not* appear to differ from market economies: namely, the economic values of the individuals who participated in them.[23]

Party spokespersons in these Marxist regimes emphasized the development of the "New Socialist Man," who worked for the good of society rather than his own material interests. From infancy on, teachers and government officials were instructed to inculcate children with such values. But, judging from the World Value Study for the years 1990–93 (Inglehart et al., 2001), the results of these efforts did not seem to have been successful. This study reports survey results from forty-one nations of a series of standardized questions about their values from a random sample of the population. Focusing just on economic values, my analysis (forthcoming-c) of these data found no significant differences between Eastern and Western Europe. Certain anecdotal information supports this conclusion as well.[24] Perhaps the

---

[23] More interesting than economic values are those that deal with interpersonal relations and, in this respect, certain differences between nations in Eastern and Western Europe are readily apparent. In Germany, for instance, public opinion pollsters found greater interpersonal trust and greater value placed on friendship in East than in West Germany.

[24] For instance, shortly after the first free election in the former East Germany in 1990, I interviewed a very high-level official in the communist party (Sozialistische Einheitspartei Deutschlands) about the social/political changes during the Marxist period and the recent election results. According to my notes, he replied: "We had forty years to change the mentality of our people – and we failed."

New Socialist Man existed or still lives in North Korea or Cuba, which were not included in the survey. He certainly could not be found in China or East Germany, whose economic values were not statistically different from those found, respectively, in Taiwan or in West Germany.

D. Some Macroeconomic Consequences

Many argue that Marxist regimes fell because of poor economic performance. To show this widespread belief to be mistaken, it is necessary to review certain indicators of their economic achievements. I focus particularly on the growth of per capita GDP because Marxist officials seemed to consider this as their most important measure of success; moreover, the data needed for meaningful comparisons are readily available. Such an analysis shows that, except for the OECD–Eastern Europe comparison, Marxist and market economic systems did not have greatly different growth rates. I also touch more briefly on several other criteria of economic performance.

1. Economic Growth

Table 8-3 presents estimates of the average annual growth rates, calculated by fitting exponential curves (using a standard regression technique) to the data on per capita GDP for the years when the country had a Marxist regime. For the European Marxist regimes, which lasted longer than most countries in other areas, I also calculated a second regression that allows determination of the deceleration of growth over the period.[25] Finally, for perspective, I also report data for market economies in the same region (or, in the case of Europe, the industrialized OECD nations) during roughly the same years in which the Marxist regimes were in existence. Because each continent raises particular problems of analysis, it is useful to consider them separately.

For Sub-Saharan Africa, the per capita GDP growth rates of the Marxist regimes were not significantly different from zero. Although they were somewhat higher than those of the non-Marxist nations in the region, the differences were not statistically significant, even when we control for the per capita GDP in the initial year of the growth calculation, which allows us to

---

[25] More specifically, the regression formula is: $\ln YCap = a + bT + cT^2$, where $\ln YCap$ is the logarithm of per capita GDP and T is time. Differentiating this formula we derive: $AAYCap = b_1 + 2cT$, where $AAYCap$ is the average annual percentage growth of per capita GDP, $b_1 = $ "controlled growth rate" and $c = $ "change coefficient."

Table 8-3. *Average annual growth of per capita GDP of Marxist and non-Marxist nations*

Sub-Saharan African Nations during Period of Marxist Regime	Growth Rate	European Marxist Regimes: 1950–89	Growth Rate	Average Annual Change in Growth
Angola	−1.8*%	Albania	—	—
Benin	+1.4*	Bulgaria	+3.6*%	−0.048*%
Cape Verde	+5.3*	Czechoslovakia	+2.5*	−0.024*
Rep. of Congo	+1.6*	Hungary	+2.7*	−0.027*
Ethiopia	−0.7*	Poland	+2.5*	−0.029*
Guinea-Bissau	+0.1	Romania	+3.5*	−0.040*
Madagascar	−2.7*	U.S.S.R.	+2.5*	−0.027*
Mozambique	−2.7*	Yugoslavia	+4.2*	−0.028*
São Tomé	+0.5			
Seychelles	+2.1*	Average of 7 Marxist regimes	+3.1% (0.2%)	−0.033% (0.003%)
Somalia	+1.7*	Average of 21 OECD nations, 1950 through 1989	+3.3 (0.2)	−0.021 (0.003)
Zimbabwe	+1.8			
Average of 12 Marxist regimes	+0.6% (0.7%)			
Average of 30 non-Marxist regimes, 1975–90	−0.7 (0.4)			

Small Caribbean Nations during Period of Marxist Regime		Eastern Asian Nations during Period of Marxist Regime	
Cuba	−0.8%*	Afghanistan	+0.5%
Grenada	—	China	+3.8*
Guyana	−0.2	Cambodia	+2.5*
Nicaragua	−3.6*	Laos	+1.4*
Average of 3 Marxist regimes	−1.6% (1.3%)	North Korea	—
		Mongolia	+3.0*
		Viet Nam	—
		South Yemen	—
Average of 10 non-Marxist regimes, 1966–90	+1.1 (0.35)	Average of 5 Marxist regimes	+2.2% (0.5%)
		Average of 15 non-Marxist regimes, 1975–90	+3.3 (0.5)

Note: The non-Marxist nations are those on the same continent that never had a Marxist government. All growth rates are for per capita GDP and are calculated by fitting exponential curves to the data. An asterisk designates a growth rate significantly different from zero. The dates of the Marxist periods are found in Tables 8-2 and 8-4. The data in parentheses are standard deviations, corrected for degrees of freedom. Appendix 8-1 discusses the sources of the underlying data.

factor out the effect that low-income nations often grow faster than high-income nations.[26] Because most of these nations did not move very far toward installing the canonical Marxist system, such results are not surprising.

By contrast, the Eastern Asian Marxist regimes experienced growth rates significantly higher than zero. Although the non-Marxist regimes in Asia had higher average growth rates of per capita GDP between 1975 and 1990, the differences between the two groups of nations were not statistically significant, even when we control for the level of per capita GDP in the initial year.[27] Looking at the long-run average annual growth, which allows us to use only China and Mongolia in the comparisons, we obtain the same results: no significant difference between the systems.

For the Caribbean area, the growth rates of per capita income were either zero or negative for the three Marxist regimes in the table. For Grenada, during the four years that this island had a Marxist regime, the situation is unclear because some estimates show an increasing GDP, while others show the opposite.[28] In the period from 1966 through 1990 (the years when Guyana had a Marxist regime), the average growth of per capita GDP for other countries bordering the Caribbean (excluding the micro states and the three large nations) was positive and significantly higher than those achieved under the Marxist regimes, but only when per capita income was held constant.

In the period 1950 through 1989 for Europe (before the various Marxist regimes collapsed), the results are more interesting. By Western calculations, both parts of Europe showed impressive growth rates. Simple comparisons of means show that twenty-one comparable non-Marxist regimes had roughly the same average growth rates and, in the same period, a lower rate of growth deceleration. Holding per capita income constant, however, the Marxist regimes performed less impressively on both criteria, but only

---

[26] The OLS regression is:

$$\text{AAYCap} = -0.0025 - 2.81 \times 10^{-6}\,\text{Ycap} + 0.0117\,\text{System} \qquad R^2 = 0.1012$$
$$\phantom{\text{AAYCap} = }(0.0057) \quad (2.25 \times 10^{-6}) \qquad\quad (0.0078) \qquad\qquad\quad n = 42$$

where AAYcap = average annual growth of per capita GDP (Marxist period for Marxist regimes, 1975–90 for non-Marxist regimes); Ycap = per capita GDP in 1975; System = 1 if Marxist regime, 0 if not; R^2 = coefficient of determination (uncorrected for degrees of freedom); n = size of sample.

[27] Using the same notation as in the previous footnote (with an asterisk designating statistical significance at the 0.05 level), the OLS regression is:

$$\text{AAYCap} = +0.024 + 2.90 \times 10^{-6}\,\text{Ycap} - 0.0044\,\text{System} \qquad R^2 = 0.2212$$
$$\phantom{\text{AAYCap} = }(0.007) \quad (1.56 \times 10^{-6}) \qquad\quad (0.0099) \qquad\qquad\quad n = 20$$

[28] I (1986b: 333–36) present these various results, including my own two estimates.

the higher growth rate difference in the West was statistically significant.[29] Many observers argue that the deceleration of growth would have become more severe in Eastern Europe had the Marxist systems persisted there because of their slowness in adapting to the information revolution and advances in other new technologies. That is, most of the core Marxist regimes continued to stress traditional smokestack industries far longer than many industrialized countries in the West. Unless we assume a long-term rigidity of their economies that is unsupported by the available evidence, this situation seems unlikely to have lasted if these nations had remained Marxist regimes.

It might be added that since 1990, the transition of these Eastern European nations to a market economy has proven difficult and the growth picture has been disastrous. By 2000, for instance, the per capita GDP in 1988 was exceeded only in Hungary and Poland.

One related aspect to economic growth also deserves note. Volatility of the growth path, as measured by fluctuations of per capita GDP from the trend, was also no different in the East than in the West.[30]

2. Economic Efficiency

The dynamic efficiency of the growth process – the amount of growth achieved by an additional unit of input – can only be discussed for Eastern Europe and the industrialized OECD nations. Because the Marxist regimes of Eastern Europe had a somewhat higher investment rate than the non-Marxist OECD nations, but experienced lower economic growth, it seems likely that they probably had lower dynamic efficiency, although we cannot

---

[29] Using the same abbreviations as in the previous footnotes (but with Ycap = per capita GDP in 1950 and AAChge = average annual change in the growth rate of per capita GDP), the OLS regressions are:

$$\text{AAYcap} = +0.051^* - 3.71^* \times 10^{-6} \, \text{Ycap} - 0.0115^* \, \text{System} \quad R^2 = 0.7909$$
$$\phantom{\text{AAYcap} = } (0.002) \quad (0.47 \times 10^{-6}) \quad\quad (0.0018) \quad\quad\quad n = 24$$
$$\text{AAChge} = -0.00036^* + 2.42 \times 10^{-8} \, \text{Ycap} - 0.000043 \, \text{System} \quad R^2 = 0.3230$$
$$\phantom{\text{AAChge} = } (0.00007) \quad (1.36 \times 10^{-8}) \quad\quad (0.000059) \quad\quad\quad n = 24$$

[30] For measuring volatility, I used a statistic similar to the coefficient of variation (the standard deviation divided by the mean). More specifically, for each year, I calculated the squared ratio of the difference between the actual and predicted values of per capita GDP to the predicted value, where the predicted value was estimated from the following regression equation for the entire 40 years: $\ln \text{Ycap} = a + bT + cT^2$. I then took the square root of the average of these values for the entire time span. Such volatility was significantly and inversely related to per capita GDP (in 1950). Although the Eastern European nations had a somewhat lower volatility than Western European countries when controlling for per capita income, such differences were not statistically significant. The same conclusion was reached without controlling for income and also with other measures of volatility.

be completely sure until we take account of the growth of labor inputs. This was particularly evident in agriculture, where the share of overall investment going to agriculture was very much higher than in Western Europe, even though the growth rate of agriculture was considerably lower (Pryor, 1992).

With regard to static efficiency, the Marxist regimes adopting the canonical Soviet model appear to have performed generally worse than comparable market economies. The system of physical planning and price controls made it difficult for planners to calculate the true costs of production; and, as thousands of economists have argued, this leads to economic inefficiencies. The central planners also had trouble in arranging an incentive structure to encourage hard work and careful use of resources. Unfortunately, empirically demonstrating the lower static efficiency of the canonical model proves difficult because the available data usually do not allow a clean distinction between differences in efficiency (either allocative or technical)[31] and differences in productivity.

Most of the empirical studies of allocative efficiency for the economy as a whole or for the industrial sector have revealed lower efficiency in centrally planned economies when compared to market economies. In most studies, however, the estimated amount was relatively small, usually running from 2 to 12 percent (e.g., Desai and Martin, 1987; Kemme, 1990; or Barreto and Whitesell, 1992).[32] Moreover, as Bergson (1992) has underlined, despite the sophisticated statistical techniques employed, the underlying data leave much to be desired and the results of such aggregate studies should be taken with caution.

During the communist period, it was difficult for Western economists to carry out studies of technical efficiency. Although several extensive joint Soviet–U.S. studies were made for the particular Soviet industries (i.e., cotton refining, textile production, and candy manufacturing) and many showed relatively high technical efficiency, considerable controversy has arisen about the proper analysis and meaning of the results.[33] Perhaps more

---

[31] Allocative inefficiency reflects the additional production that could be gained by a reallocation of productive resources over the economy; technical inefficiency reflects the additional production that could be gained by reorganizing single production units.

[32] Some studies have used a time-series approach with the calculation of dynamic frontier production functions. One such study (Whitesell, 1990) showed substantially greater allocative inefficiency in Hungary than in West Germany, whereas another study employing the same methodology (Whitesell, 1994) shows less inefficiency in the Soviet Union than in the United States.

[33] The original study by Danilov et al. (1985) showed that roughly half of the firms produced within 7 percent of the production possibility frontier. Some reanalysis of these data, however, suggest that technical efficiency was much lower (Nowakowski, 1994). Other studies on the same theme are found in a volume edited by Rosefielde (1998).

revealing are eighteen different comparisons of enterprise performance in Russia and Eastern Europe after privatization (summarized by Megginson and Netter, 2001). Most of these studies show a considerable improvement in productivity or other measures in comparison either with previous performance or with enterprises not yet privatized.[34] For the agricultural sector, relevant data on efficiency are more plentiful, and analysts have carried out three quite different kinds of comparisons (summarized by Pryor, 1992: 238–57). Some analysts compared productivity before and after decollectivization and marketization, particularly in China, where they found a dramatic increase in productivity (studies summarized by Rozelle and Swinnen, 2004). Others compared productivity on private and collective farms in the same country, and generally found greater efficiency in the former; whereas still others have examined farming areas in a sample of non-Marxist and Marxist nations (or in comparable farming areas in these countries) and, again, generally showed greater static efficiency in the market economies.

3. Distribution

On one performance criterion – namely, equality in the distribution of income – the Marxist regimes appear to have performed better than market economies. The existing data reveal, at least in Eastern Europe, that the Marxist regimes generally exhibited less inequality of money income than in Western Europe (Atkinson and Micklewright, 1992; Pryor, 1973b: 67–90). Such studies, of course, do not take into account nonmonetary income in the form of privileges and perks, although my subjective impression is that this would not alter the general conclusion because such nonmonetary income is significant in market economies as well.

4. A Brief Summary

The major results of this brief survey can be quickly summarized. The growth experience of the Marxist regimes was not noticeably different from market economies in most parts of the world except Europe, where the canonical economic system yielded lower growth than in the industrialized OECD nations. Nevertheless, the growth performance of Eastern Europe was still quite respectable. The only exception to my argument that growth

---

[34] Serious problems also arise in making such comparisons. For instance, part of the change in productivity might be due to more diligence of the workers or greater access to credit, rather than any reallocation of resources or changing of production arrangements.

performance was not important in the fall of the Marxist regime was Nicaragua, where the per capita GDP fell almost by a half between 1978 and 1989 in the reign of the Sandinistas.

The canonical Marxist economic systems appeared, however, to have lower allocative efficiency and lower dynamic efficiency, but these are issues of secondary political importance. Nevertheless, these problems had important qualitative effects that were felt in the everyday life of most citizens, at least in Eastern Europe. Such impacts included, for instance, the low quality and meager selection of consumer goods, the endemic shortages and the long queues to obtain them, and the governmental allocation of certain scarce goods and services according to political criteria.[35]

But, it seems to me that such daily difficulties hardly ignite the forceful overturn of a regime, nor does it seem likely that any candidate could win an election by promising to eliminate shortages. The evidence presented herein belies the common assertions that Marxist regimes collapsed primarily because of the alleged "miserable" economic performance resulting from their economic system. We must, therefore, turn to broader considerations to explore the real causes.

E. The Downward Path of Marxist Regimes

1. The Key Events

Charting the decline of Marxist regimes raises analytic problems because it is often difficult to determine when a given government or party deviated sufficiently from the Marxist path to no longer warrant the label and should be considered as another authoritarian regime. In some of the third-world nations, the end dates reported in Table 8-4 must be considered as approximations.

The most striking aspect of the table is that between 1989 and 1994, twenty-five of the thirty-three nations had ceased to be Marxist regimes, joining the three others (Somalia, Guinea-Bissau, and Grenada) that had left the camp somewhat earlier. After the early 1990s, only four or five Marxist regimes remained[36]: namely, China, Viet Nam, Cuba, North Korea,

---

[35] These qualitative failings were not necessarily an essential feature of the system. For instance, in the Chinese variant of the canonical Marxist model, the variety of goods available to consumers appeared much greater than in Eastern Europe and the quality problems seemed less severe, especially after the death of Mao.

[36] Laos is particularly difficult to classify; but since the government appeared to have abandoned more of the traditional Marxist economic policies and institutions than either China or Viet Nam, I have not considered it as a Marxist regime after 1989.

Table 8-4. *Changes in the status of Marxist regimes up to 2002*

	Key dates	Circumstances
Europe		
Albania	1991–92	Demonstrations forced multiparty election. Non-Marxists won and privatization/liberalization began.
Bulgaria	1990–93	Ideology attenuated; after multiparty election, Marxist became minority party and liberalization began.
Czechoslovakia	1989–90	Government resigned; non-Marxists won multiparty election; and privatization/liberalization began.
Germany, East	1989–90	Berlin Wall fell; Marxist party lost multiparty election; and nation united with West Germany.
Hungary	1989–91	Marxist party changed ideological direction; lost a multiparty election; privatization/liberalization began.
Poland	1989–90	Marxist party defeated in multiparty election; rapid liberalization and some privatization began.
Romania	1989–91	Army coup overthrew political leaders; after multiparty election, slow economic liberalization began.
U.S.S.R.	1991–92	After failed army coup, non-Marxists won multiparty election; privatization/liberalization began.
Yugoslavia	1990–91	Nation broke up. In multiparty election, Marxists won in several republics, lost in others; and economic program attenuated.
Africa		
Angola	1990–91	Party publicly abandoned M–L ideology; multiparty elections and slow liberalization began.
Benin	1989–91	Marxist group renounced M–L; multiparty election took place and Marxist leader defeated.
Cape Verde	1991	Marxist party lost multiparty election; new constitutions 1994.
Rep. of Congo	1990–92	Marxist party dropped M–L; non-Marxists won parliament after multiparty election.
Ethiopia	1990–91	Marxist party dropped M–L; lost civil war to non-Marxist group; began decollectiving and liberalizing.
Guinea-Bissau	1980–84	After army coup, privatization and structural-adjustment program began.
Madagascar	1989–93	Party abandoned economic program and began privatization; later defeated in multiparty election.
Mozambique	1989–94	Party abandoned M–L rhetoric and planning; after multiparty election, started gradual liberalization.

(continued)

253

Table 8-4 *(continued)*

	Key dates	Circumstances
São Tomé	1990–91	Marxists lost in multiparty election.
Seychelles	1993	Although Marxists won multiparty election, attenuated Marxist economic program.
Somalia	1977–78	After nation lost Ogaden war, party attenuated M–L program; switched from U.S.S.R. to U.S. patronage.
Zimbabwe	1990–91	Mugabe lost attempt to institute one-party state. Party abandoned Marxist economic program and rhetoric; nation undertook structural adjustment program.
Americas		
Cuba	—	Marxist regime is still in full power.
Grenada	1983	Party split. After brief civil war, U.S. invaded and installed new government; M–L party later lost in multiparty election.
Guyana	1989–91	Party abandoned M–L program, started structural-adjustment program and privatization of state farms.
Nicaragua	1990	Marxist party defeated in multiparty election and dismantling of Marxist economy began.
Asia		
Afghanistan	1988–91	Soviets began withdrawing army and financial aid; civil war intensified; Taliban dominated by 1996.
Cambodia	1991–93	Party abandoned economic program; multiparty election took place.
China	—	Marxist party is still in full power, but undertaking slow transition to market economy since 1979 with semi-decollectivization.
Korea, North	—	Marxist party is still in full power.
Laos	1987–89	Party started decollectivizing, liberalizing; a great deal of privatization in 1990s; but Party retains political control; much more privatization in 1990s.
Mongolia	1990–92	Party abandoned M–L ideology, began liberalizing/privatizing but reformed Marxist party won multiparty election.
Viet Nam	—	Marxist party in full power, but economy has been in transition to market from mid-1980s.
Yemen, South	1989–90	Party voted to merge with non-Marxist North Yemen; dropped M–L program and began liberalization.

Note: M–L = Marxist–Leninist. Semi-decollectivization means that the land was not privatized but private farmers were given long-term leases on the land.

and perhaps Laos. Of these, the first two and Laos were in transition to a market economy in the 1990s and soon might not be considered Marxist regimes, at least by the criterion used in the definition at the beginning of this chapter. Why these four or five nations have remained Marxist regimes raises a host of issues that must be left for others to discuss. Nevertheless, it is noteworthy that all these nations had, at one time, engaged in some type of military action against the United States or its direct proxies, and that all but North Korea achieved power through a revolution, a civil war, or a national liberation struggle. These circumstances may have given these governments a higher probability for durability, even though it did not prove sufficient to prevent the collapse of certain other Marxist regimes.[37]

In six of the nations (Afghanistan, Angola, Cambodia, Ethiopia, Mozambique, and Nicaragua), the movement away from a Marxist regime was accelerated by civil war, which forced both economic and political changes.[38] In Somalia, the process was hastened by an unsuccessful border dispute with Ethiopia. By way of contrast, a long-term war that resulted in the unification of the country undoubtedly strengthened the authority of the Viet Namese government. In about three quarters of the countries that turned away from Marxism, the transition was accompanied by relatively little loss of life. In 1989 in Czechoslovakia, the government simply resigned and peacefully handed over power to the leaders of a large crowd of antigovernment protesters.

The transition from a Marxist regime also did not mean that the Marxist party was exiled to the political wilderness. In some countries, such as Benin, Congo, Mongolia, Mozambique, Seychelles, or Zimbabwe, the party (or its renamed successor) retained power for some time, although it had changed its economic and political direction. In other countries, such as Albania, Cambodia, Cape Verde, Laos, Hungary, Poland, São Tomé, or Somalia, the Marxist party (or its renamed successor) later regained political power through an election. In Madagascar, the previous party leader was

---

[37] Although China's direct military conflict with the United States during the Korean War and Cuba's conflict with U.S. proxies in the Bay of Pigs invasion were relatively short, the resulting political tensions remained high for many years. Direct conflict with the United States or its proxies, however, did not always guarantee regime stability – Nicaragua is a particular case in point. And, of course, any such added legitimacy given to the government of the Soviet Union for its leading role in the cold war against the United States was not strong enough to counter successfully other forces pushing toward regime change.

[38] Contributing to the fall of the Marxist regime in Nicaragua was the supreme confidence of the Sandinista leaders that they would handily win the 1990 election against the National Union of the Opposition (UNO). This optimism was bolstered by pre-election poll results; of course, political polling results in an authoritarian nation raise certain problems of interpretation.

reelected president several years after his ouster. In yet other countries, the Marxist party has remained an influential political player.

2. A Brief Case Study of Decline: The U.S.S.R.

Most explanations of the collapse of the Soviet regime (or, for that matter, Eastern Europe) focus primarily on political factors – for instance, the reduction of terror and the resulting opening of expanded political possibilities (Bunce, 1998). Turning to more economic or political/economic factors, especially those related to the economic system, it is useful to treat separately the U.S.S.R., the other nations in Eastern Europe, and the developing nations because the critical causes of the collapse were, I believe, rather different in these three cases and formulating a general theory of collapse of Marxist regimes seems a dubious activity. I start first with the U.S.S.R., both because it serves as the canonical model and because events in the Soviet Union had a major impact in most other Marxist regimes.[39]

The economic system of the Soviet Union faced four critical long-term problems of viability, even though these were not directly related to the downfall of the regime.

COMPLEXITY AND CONTROL PROBLEMS. The economy was growing more complex and this, in turn, increased information costs to the central planners. Greater problems also arose both in setting effective economic incentives for managers and in maintaining effective central control. This was paralleled by a rising importance of the shadow economy, increasing official corruption, and the growth of informal horizontal relations between producers at the expense of their vertical relations – all of which subverted the planned economy (Grossman, 1998). The use of terror as an inducement for greater managerial effort had been discarded after Stalin's death, but the economic stimuli for producers and the officially sanctioned profit incentives had little impact on raising growth, efficiency, or productivity in an environment where prices were fixed.[40] The increasingly serious problems in managing the canonical Marxist economic system, which arose from the growing complexity associated with higher levels of per capita GDP,

---

[39] A fuller discussion of these problems can be found in Pryor (1994) and on my web page (www.swarthmore.edu/SocSci/Economics/fpryor1/) in the file labeled "External Appendices to 'The Future of U.S. Capitalism,'" Appendix 1.3.

[40] Using Cuba as his case in point, Rutgaizer (1992) argues that the second economy can flourish, even in the face of terror. See also Michalowski and Zatz (1990).

occurred in all industrialized Marxist economies and, undoubtedly, were a key factor underlying the deceleration of growth in these nations shown in Table 8-3. Bunce (1999) also argues that the growing complexity of the economy and society had important political consequences by giving rise to different interests of various segments of the elite. Such divisions among the elite weakened the unitary state and, moreover, allowed islands of political autonomy to arise.

LOSS OF INDUSTRIAL DISCIPLINE. With the decline in the use of force to ensure compliance with the economic plans, Soviet authorities had not devised a suitable set of substitute incentives to encourage higher productivity and plan fulfillment.

INVESTMENT DIFFICULTIES. Easy investment opportunities (i.e., investments with a high payoff per unit of invested capital) were gradually exhausted and the demand for more capital-intensive investments, particularly in housing, was increasing.

MILITARIZATION OF THE ECONOMY. To match the military strength of the United States, a much richer country, the U.S.S.R. was forced to spend a much larger share of its GDP on its military, a problem exacerbated after President Reagan's strategic defense initiative increased the perceived U.S. military threat. For the mid-1970s to the mid-1980s, Western estimates of the share of Soviet defense expenditures in the GDP range from 6 to 30 percent; but the middle to higher part of this range appears more probable.[41] What is more important is that military claims on goods and services had higher priority than civilian claims, which meant that the consumption needs of the population were neglected.

On top of these long-run factors, the U.S.S.R. faced some serious short-term economic problems as well. These were primarily caused by policy failures, which, although not directly related to the economic system, did play a critical role in the downfall of the regime.

RISING GOVERNMENT DEFICITS AND THE RESULTING INFLATION. This situation was, in part, due to the relative decline of four major government

---

[41] CIA estimates of Soviet defense expenditures were, in the mid-1980s, roughly 15 percent of the GDP (Firth and Noren, 1998: 129–30). Rosefielde (1998) severely criticizes these estimates and, for some years, his estimates are twice as high. The highest estimates are presented (without justification) by Marshall (1987). For other estimates, see U.S. Congress (1987).

revenues: tax on liquor sales (because of Gorbachev's anti-alcohol campaign), profits from oil exports (because of the fall in international oil prices), profit taxes from enterprises (because of new policies encouraging firms to reduce profits by raising wages), and revenues withheld by governments of the various constituent republics. Three major expenditures also began to rise: industrial investment outlays, subsidies on food, and social benefits (especially pensions). The rising deficits were covered by the printing of money, which led to inflation.

CONSTANT INSTITUTIONAL FLUX AND THE RESULTING UNCERTAINTIES. Gorbachev lurched from one attempt at institutional reform to another in order to improve economic performance: Between 1986 and 1991, his economic program (*perestroika*) had three distinct phases with quite different and conflicting regulations and policies. As a result, the rules of the economic game became increasingly unclear, and the power of the central bureaucratic apparatus was weakened.

DECLINE OF PARTY AND GOVERNMENTAL AUTHORITY. The government lost considerable authority by earnestly attempting to increase freedom of open expression (*glasnost'*) in order to tap the ideas and expertise of the population for restructuring the economy. Such measures included curtailing the propagandizing of Marxism–Leninism to reduce the power of party conservatives, permitting greater criticism of the government in the Soviet media, and enhancing the relative power of industrial managers vis-á-vis party officials. The net result was a weakening of the party's authority and a dissolution of the ideological glue holding the system together, accompanied by a rise in social turmoil (strikes and protests) as more political players entered the game.

NATIONALISM. A rise in open nationalism accompanied *glasnost'*, manifested by popular demand for less political dominance by Moscow and greater local and republic political autonomy. The unresolved grievances of the peoples of the various Soviet republics, which had been suppressed during the seventy years of Soviet power by Gorbachev's predecessors, sprang into open public discussion and were fed by a series of clumsy policy errors. For instance, the central government's mishandling of the Chernobyl incident in the Ukraine in 1986 was a key factor in the growth of nationalistic fervor in that republic. One repercussion of the rise of nationalism was, as noted previously, a withholding of certain tax revenues that the constituent republics were supposed to remit to the central government.

RISING MISTRUST AND DISCONTENT. The gap between the glowing promises by governmental and party officials and actual performance became increasingly apparent in the period from 1988 to 1991, when per capita GDP decreased about 10 percent (Maddison, 2001). The real collapse of the Soviet economy, it must be added, came after the downfall of the Marxist regime.

THE GORBACHEV FACTOR. From one perspective, the collapse of the Soviet Union appears to be the consequence of a bizarre series of random events. Leonid Brezhnev died in 1982 and, were it not for the failures of Yuri Andropov's kidneys and Konstantin Chernenko's lungs, Mikhail Gorbachev would never have become the Soviet leader less than two and a half years later. Gorbachev was an intelligent, well-meaning, energetic, and impetuous leader, with little desire to rule with an iron fist. But, he was also a leader with little understanding of the adverse implications of his various (and changing) policy initiatives. The final collapse of the Soviet regime in 1991–92 was also not inevitable but rather the result of a botched coup d'état by a small group of left-oriented military and party officials and of the quick seizure of power by Boris Yeltsin, the president of the Russian Republic. This led to the dissolution of the union into its constituent republics and the flawed transition to a market economy, which represented Yeltsin's attempt to break sharply with the past.

These various short-run economic problems strengthened two critical political trends: the growing political weakness of the Soviet government and the rising demands of the population for change. I strongly suspect that if a Soviet leader of the old ruthless mold had taken over after the death of Chernenko, the regime could have persisted, at least for several decades, despite the problems of long-term viability discussed herein. Moreover, a case can be made that under the proper political leadership and carefully designed systemic changes, a modified planned economy might have had long-term political and economic viability.

This did not happen, of course. Moreover, many of the changes instituted by Gorbachev – particularly his loosening of Soviet control over Eastern Europe – might not have been reversible. The peaceful economic changes in China, which occurred without a political upheaval, suggest that it was Gorbachev's incompetent political and economic policies that were primarily responsible for the fall of the Marxist government in the U.S.S.R. in the early 1990s, not impersonal economic forces originating from the economic system or poor long-term economic performance.

3. Special Factors in the Decline of Marxist Regimes in Eastern Europe

Some of the political causes weakening the Soviet government and encouraging political activity for change at lower levels could be found in various Eastern European nations. Moreover, many of the long-term economic factors adversely influencing the economic system of the Marxist regime in the U.S.S.R. also held for Eastern Europe. But, two special causal factors deserve emphasis.

A VIABLE ALTERNATIVE MODEL. Western Europe, with its growing prosperity and extensive political freedoms, provided an increasingly attractive model for Eastern Europeans to follow. The increasingly stark and growing contrasts between the two parts of Europe also provided dramatic evidence of the gap between regime promises and actual performance in the East, especially to those who could travel or who lived in countries that could receive Western TV broadcasts.

A CHANGE IN SOVIET POLICY. The most important political element in the decline of Marxist regimes in Eastern Europe was the U.S.S.R.'s change in political policies toward that region. By 1988, according to Fowkes (1993: 171), Gorbachev had reached the conclusion that the "governments of Eastern Europe should be left to govern as they wished, without outside interference: in other words, the Brezhnev doctrine of limited sovereignty was finally thrown overboard." This was reflected in theses prepared for the nineteenth Party Congress in May 1988 and represented an *ex post facto* repudiation of the Soviet military actions undertaken in East Germany (1953), Hungary (1956), and Czechoslovakia (1968) to maintain the Marxist party in power in the face of popular resistance and civil unrest. This made political action by dissatisfied citizens in Eastern Europe both safer and more likely to succeed.

4. Special Factors in the Decline of Marxist Regimes Among Developing Nations

Marxist regimes in the developing world faced three special problems.

SHORT-TERM PROBLEMS. Many Marxist regimes, particularly in Africa, ran into severe short-term economic difficulties and requested aid from the IMF and the World Bank. These international institutions began to require certain "structural adjustments," a procedure followed with non-Marxist governments as well. But, such adjustments forced both the abandonment of many of the Marxist policies of these regimes and also critical changes in some of their new economic institutions.

PROBLEMS OF ADOPTING THE CANONICAL MODEL. It became readily apparent that the traditional economic policies and institutions of the Soviet Union were not easily applicable to the developing nations. The countries did not have the requisite infrastructure and the autocratic governments were not sufficiently strong to force certain crucial changes. Moreover, while facing seemingly insoluble economic problems, the leaders of many Marxist regimes in the developing countries became increasingly oriented toward private political goals: namely, retention of power. Of course, a similar evolution also took place in a number of non-Marxist states in the third world, where the formerly idealistic leaders of the anticolonial struggle, who achieved political leadership, could not solve the economic problems facing their nations and turned instead to private enrichment. As long as these Marxist regimes received foreign aid from the East or the West (or both), they could maintain their political position without imposing great hardship on the population, but as the competition in foreign aid between East and West waned during the late 1980s, these Marxist leaders had less to deliver to their populations (or to their own bank accounts), their political rule became increasingly harsh, and political discontent rose.

DIFFERENCES BETWEEN PROMISES AND PERFORMANCE. A gap widened between the glorious economic promises of the various Marxist regimes and the reality on the ground. Of course, most of the non-Marxist economies in these areas also did not exhibit impressive economic performance, but expectations in these countries were often lower because the governments made fewer promises. The gap between promises of the Marxist regimes and their performances was unsustainable in the long run and, not unexpectedly, political discontent – as manifested by various demonstrations, rebellions, and civil unrest – grew stronger. Usually, popular demands for genuine multiparty elections also grew louder and in countries torn by civil war, such as Angola, Mozambique, and Nicaragua, multiparty elections were often a key demand of the antigovernment forces as well.

The decline of Marxist regimes in many of these developing nations was much less dramatic than in Eastern Europe. This was, in major part, due to the lack of great differences in their economic and political systems with other authoritarian third-world nations.

F. Conclusions and a Note on Systemic Convergence

Most Marxist regimes were not long-lived. Combining the data from Tables 8-2 and 8-4 and excluding those nations that were still under Marxist regimes by the end of the twentieth century, such governments lasted on average twenty-six years. Excluding the European Marxist nations from this sample, where system change was prevented by the activities (actual or threatened, at least up to the late 1980s) of the Soviet army, this average falls to seventeen years.[42]

For the developing nations, Marxist regimes appeared primarily as a political reaction to the previous colonial regime and, in a number of cases, Marxism served merely as the ideological fig leaf behind which a particular group obtained and maintained political power (and/or enriched itself). Orthodox Marxists were quite justified in arguing that such an attempt to remold the economy was premature and that these countries did not have the prerequisites for a genuine socialist revolution. I might add, however, that their very inability to imitate the canonical Soviet model made their transition back to a market economy less painful. The fall of these Marxist regimes, often aided by civil unrest, primarily resulted from political disenchantment: In essence, much of the population felt that the political costs of the regime overshadowed the promised economic benefits, which did not materialize.

For the economically developed Marxist regimes in Eastern Europe, the economic systems were, in most cases, installed and held together by political force, both domestic and external. The political and economic costs of such systems became increasingly apparent as the populations of these nations became more aware of the quality of life in Western Europe and as these costs were associated with the major role of the Soviet Union in their domestic affairs. Thus, the fall of the Marxist regimes in Eastern Europe represents a type of decolonialization rather than a decisive vote against a particular economic system.

From this analysis, it is useful to return to the strange debate in the West, noted in Chapter 1, that raged in the 1950s and 1960s about whether Marxist and market economic systems would converge to a system somewhere between these extremes that would combine the strong features of each.[43] Those arguing for convergence, including Nobel laureate Jan Tinbergen,

---

[42] I have not seen any comparable data on the life span of non-Marxist nations, so it is difficult to place the results of this calculation in perspective.

[43] The various arguments are spelled out in detail in Pryor (1973b: 356–71) and in various essays in Dallago, Brezinski, and Andreff (1992).

used one or more of three basic arguments: (a) an optimal performing economic system lies somewhere between the market economies and the canonical Soviet model; (b) economic determinism is so overpowering that it produces a strong similarity between societies at a given level of economic development, with the Western showing signs of creeping socialism and the authoritarian regimes of the East beginning to liberalize their economies; and (c) increasing globalization would accelerate this uniformity among economic systems as the impacts of particular institutions became more apparent.

Those arguing against convergence also made three crucial points: (a) convergence of economic systems implies similar social, political, and economic goals, which is highly doubtful; (b) vested interests would prevent the adjustments necessary for convergence; and (c) most tellingly, a basic incompatibility between the physical and market allocation of goods and services in the same country could not be bridged in the long term.[44] Or, in the vocabulary used in Chapter 7, the logic of institutions suggests that in the long term, it is impossible to combine within a single economy a market allocation of goods and services and its attendant incentives with physical planning, fixed prices and wages, and suppression of market forces.

Since the 1970s, the Western European nations have not moved toward a greater economic role of the state and the introduction of physical planning but rather in the opposite direction. They sold off state enterprises, tried to curtail public expenditures, reduced their efforts at national economic planning, and attempted to substitute indirect controls for direct administrative measures. Since their collapse, most Marxist regimes have moved passed the alleged "optimum system" toward a market economy, not stopping at any point in between. The final test of the convergence hypothesis will be the experience of China and Viet Nam, two nations that have attempted a slow transition toward a market economy. The key question is whether they can stop the process in midstream or, more theoretically phrased, whether a stable economic system can exist between a centrally planned economy and a market economy with relatively little direct government interference in production and distribution.

---

[44] For instance, China had the same goods produced by both state and privately owned factories, with the former operating according to a government plan and selling their goods at government-set prices. Because the prices of the same goods sold in the private sector were different, this gave rise to all sorts of arbitrage possibilities that, although very profitable, caused numerous difficulties and adversely affected economic development. When the gap between government-set and private prices was narrowed, the state enterprises found it difficult to compete against the private enterprises.

PART FIVE

FINAL WORDS

NINE

Conclusions and an Agenda for Future Research

This study applies a uniform method of analyzing economic systems at various stages of development, ranging from foraging to advanced industrial/ service economies. Although such an approach does not result in a generalized "theory of economic systems," whatever that may mean, it does permit us to discover for economies with any given focus of production an important order arising out of the chaos of case studies, statistics, anecdotes, and factoids that govern most discussions. As a result, theorizing can begin about their institutional orders from a solid empirical base.

The most important empirical results can be quickly summarized: Economies at every stage of development feature a small number of distinct economic systems, defined in terms of particular groups of institutions that cluster together. From the statistical analysis presented in previous chapters, many of these economic systems do not seem to be generally determined by the social structure, political organization, or physical environment of the societies but rather appear as independent entities, worthy of study in their own right.

These economic systems provide an analytical framework within which a variety of economic activities can be placed in context and examined. Designation of the economic system also allows us to distinguish those characteristics typical of all societies with the same focus of production from those that are shared only by those societies with the same system and those that are unique to a given society. Moreover, in certain cases, these economic systems have an important impact on the performance of the economy.

In the transition from foraging to agriculture, the particular economic systems did not appear to have influenced which societies made this transformation. Instead, other factors such as the stress on the land played more important roles. Unfortunately, we currently do not have enough evidence to determine in what manner the system influenced this transformation. By contrast, the characteristics of the economic system appeared to play an important role in the transition from agriculture to manufacturing, as evidenced by data on eighteenth- and nineteenth-century industrialization and also on developing economies at the end of the twentieth century.

The preceding chapters have, of necessity, focused on details; the general conclusions summarized herein would not have stood on a firm foundation without a careful analysis of the available statistical data. Now, at the end of this study, it is time to reexamine my results from a broader perspective and to ask how they can be extended and deepened.

A. The Existence and Delineation of Economic Systems

1. A Brief Review

In the previous chapters, I use a cluster analysis to show that, at each stage of economic development, only a small number of different economic systems can meaningfully be isolated. This approach takes into account the major institutions and organizations in these economies that define property relations and structure the distribution of goods and services. The results of such an analysis for the industrial/service economies, which accord with our expectations about such systems, give us confidence in the results of economies at lower levels of economic development.

The type and number of institutions taken into account depend on the complexity of the economy. For my sample of forty-four foraging societies, I use ten key institutional and organizational variables to determine the clusters (which are, in turn, used to examine another twelve foraging societies that had begun the transition to agriculture). For my sample of forty-one agricultural societies, I select twenty-two such key institutions and organizations for this statistical analysis. For the analysis of the transition from agriculture to industry, I use two samples. The first is a sample of more than twenty national economies in the eighteenth and nineteen centuries, although the available data do not lend themselves to a cluster analysis. The second is a sample of forty-two developing nations where such an analysis could be carried out using thirty-one indicators (Appendix 6-8). For the exploration of industrial/service market economies at high levels of economic development and complexity, I examine forty indicators of institutions and organizations for twenty-one OECD nations. Finally, I investigate particular characteristics of thirty-three Marxist economies and compare their impact on economic performance with various market economies. In brief, in this analysis I take account of more than two hundred different economies, ranging along the entire development spectrum from extremely simple gathering economies to the most complex industrial/service economies.

If the proposition about the limited number of economic systems were wrong, the empirical analysis would reveal either a large number of clusters defining the economic systems at each level of economic development or relatively little reduction in the multidimensional variance of the institutional variance. But this does not happen.

The level of economic development plays a critical role in this analysis because it is correlated not just with many of the particular systemic characteristics, but also, in many cases, with the type of economic system. Such correlations, of course, do not tell us which caused which; unfortunately, the nature of the available data does not easily allow refined statistical tests to separate the direction of causality. For our purposes, however, it is sufficient to realize that the level of economic development is a crucial key to understanding these systems and their characteristics.

The importance of the level of economic development becomes particularly apparent when we compare the economic systems of high- and low-income market economies at the end of the twentieth century. The economic systems of the two groups of countries had quite different characteristics and clusters of institutions. Indeed, over a span of thirty years in the latter part of the twentieth century, the defining characteristics of the different economic systems of the OECD nations changed as the level of per capita GDP rose.

2. Some Implications of the Results

METHOD AND THEORY. The research presented in the previous chapters shows that all types of economies – foraging, agricultural, or industrial/ service – can be successfully analyzed using the same approach and with the same statistical methods. This does not, however, imply that we can develop a grand typology of economic systems over all time and space or that some overarching theory can explain how they all function. These different types of economic systems at various levels of development seem to me to be too diverse to allow many useful generalizations.[1]

---

[1] Nevertheless, in special cases, meaningful comparisons can be made. For instance, although I have not placed great emphasis on nomadism in the chapters on preindustrial societies, in comparison with other societies with the same focus of production, both nomadic foragers and

Despite my skepticism that a single theory can be developed that will embrace all economic systems, some parallelisms between the economic systems of foraging, agricultural, and industrial/service economies can be found. For instance, within each of these major groups, we find some economic system in which political forces were significantly more centralized: the politically oriented system among the foragers, the individualistic societies among the agriculturalists, and the Nordic and West European systems among the advanced market economies (as well as the East European Marxist systems, if we wish to include all industrialized economies). Nevertheless, this political emphasis is tied to quite different social and economic characteristics so that these parallelisms lie primarily on the surface. For instance, in the politically oriented foraging societies, the leaders collected taxes or tributes but were limited in what they could extract because of the relative ease with which a family could leave the band and join another. At higher levels of development, however, the leaders of the more politically centralized societies faced no such constraints. Other parallelisms along social or cultural dimensions are even more difficult to find.

THE LOGIC OF INSTITUTIONS. My delineation of different economic systems implies that the logic of institutions – that is, complementarities and coherence in the configuration of economic institutions of a society – has analytical usefulness. The tightness of this logic, however, is a key issue. For instance, societies at the same level of development and with the same type of system can have somewhat different economic institutions. That is, not all of the economies with a given type of system necessarily feature all of the same economic institutions and organizations that are typical of the system. For a given nation, such differences with the average characteristics of the system can be slight, so that we can consider it to lie close to the center of the cluster; whereas other nations might have greater differences and lie closer to the border separating one economic system from another. For instance, in Chapter 7, I show that France appeared close to the border separating the West and South European systems and that Switzerland was

---

nomadic agriculturalists (herders) are more likely to exhibit group possession of a territory than the private ownership of land. All types of nomads, however, have some other kinds of private ownership: the foragers own their tools and, perhaps, certain trees; and the herders own their flocks. Greater inequalities of wealth (at least before redistribution of income occurs) might also be more likely to arise among nomads than settled foraging or agricultural communities. For instance, a nomadic hunter, gatherer, or fisher might have a run of bad luck for a considerable period of time; or a nomad herder's animals could be wiped out in a short time because of disease, attacks by wild animals, or theft.

close to the border between the AS+ and the West European systems. Thus, the logic of institutions has some flexibility and represents a general tendency rather than a binding constraint. Of course, if this logic were completely inflexible, economic systems would have difficulty adapting to the functional necessities of a higher level of economic development, and economic progress might be considerably hampered.

In considering why certain economies perform better than others, many have focused their attention on "key institutions." If the logic of institution holds, however, such institutions are related to others so that the question is whether it is the impact of the "key institution" alone or together with related institutions that provides the crucial explanation. For instance, is it primarily the strength of property institutions alone, as some have argued, or in conjunction with institutions facilitating trade, labor mobility, and the flow of capital that caused such differences in growth between West Europe and the rest of the world in the nineteenth century?

The logic of institutions also raises some important issues about how institutions change. When nations sharing the same type of economic system change, do these institutions mutate in the same way or in different ways? When we examine the transition from foraging to agriculture, or from agriculture to industry, are the functional necessities more or less constraining, so that the types of economic systems in all nations with a given economic system become ever more similar (contracting clusters) or different (expanding clusters)? The cluster analysis suggests that the functional necessities that shape economic systems are less restrictive for agricultural societies than for either foraging or industrial/service economies, even though we cannot assess at this time whether these functional necessities in industrial/service economies are becoming ever more restrictive as the level of economic development rises.

EVOLUTION. This investigation of the economic systems of preindustrial societies has an important implication for a long-standing debate among anthropologists about the meaningfulness of the concept of "societal evolution." Robert Carneiro (1970; 2003) provides a useful cumulative scale of societal complexity in which the societies at a lower level do not have certain key characteristics of societies at a higher level (e.g., the extraction of metal from ore), whereas those at a higher level have all of the key characteristics of those at a lower level (e.g., the making of pottery). His scale gives a very concrete meaning to societal evolution, and I use it as a measure of economic development. Although his scale employs several hundred cultural characteristics, it does not focus on economic institutions and organizations, which define the economic system.

My results are relevant to this debate on evolution in two respects: First, I show that certain economic systems occur only in specific ranges of the development scale, which supports Carneiro's schema of unidirectional evolution. Then, I also demonstrate that at particular levels of economic development, several different economic systems may be found. This means that alternative configurations of institutions can exist at any given level of societal complexity and, hence, we must consider societal evolution as a multilayered process. Such an approach takes into account a different array of traits than Carneiro's scale, thereby deepening our understanding on how these preindustrial societies develop.

ECONOMIC FUNCTIONS AND INSTITUTIONS. The institutions through which certain activities are carried out are also greatly different among those in foraging, agricultural, and industrial/service economies. For instance, one type of distribution mechanism – namely, the sharing of food – appeared more prevalent among the foragers than the agriculturalists.[2] In part, this was because random elements played a more important role in hunting, gathering, and fishing than in plant or animal production; in part, because the foraging communities were generally smaller and, one can conjecture, socially more cohesive. In industrialized economies, however, the sharing of food has been carried out primarily through transfer expenditures by the government, a type of transaction that, in most preindustrial societies, was a relatively minor method of food redistribution.

3. Possible Extensions of the Analysis

The type of cluster analysis I use to delineate economic systems can be extended in a number of directions.

TYPES OF ECONOMIES. In my investigation of preindustrial societies, I focus on those that are predominantly foraging or agricultural. But, a large number of societies lie somewhere in between, relying partly on foraging and partly on agriculture for their food. They deserve investigation. In my sample, I also have relatively few instances of societies where a strong state played an

---

[2] Because I could not develop a consistent code for food sharing in agricultural societies, this proposition could not be proven; it is based on impressions gained from ethnographical observations of agricultural societies when the ethnographers focused interest on such matters.

important economic role, and even in the few that I have, I focus primarily on the economy at the village level. Certainly, the economic role of ancient states deserves greater attention. For lack of readily obtainable information, I also do not carry out a cluster analysis on Marxist economic systems; this would also be a very important investigation.

TYPES OF INDICATORS. For the preindustrial societies, I coded only those indicators of the major economic institutions and organizations that could be most easily gleaned from the more than seven hundred ethnographies I consulted. This coding task, though wearisome, should be extended to cover a broader range of indicators. For the advanced market economies, I also rely primarily on the most readily available indicators of institutions and organizations, most of which were calculated by others. This same tedious research needs to be expanded for yet more indicators because not all important economic institutions have been covered. Furthermore, for the advanced market economies, we need such indicators not just for the current period, but also for years in the past. For instance, in the period between the world wars, cartels and certain state administrations of industry were very important in certain countries (e.g., Germany and Japan), and these institutional elements are not well captured in my list of indicators. The task of devising such indicators for the past raises some difficult estimation problems, especially because some of the indicators for 1990 are based on surveys that were not carried out in the past.

REFINEMENTS OF THE ANALYSIS. In carrying out the various cluster analyses, I employ some indicators of economic institutions and organizations that do not serve to differentiate one economic system from another. And, as mentioned, some economic indicators, which might possibly be important, do not come readily to hand and, therefore, are not included – for instance, the security of property rights in preindustrial societies. Although I am sure that the economic systems derived from my analysis broadly delineate those which exist, much closer attention needs to be given to determining the most effective types and numbers of indicators so that the boundaries of the various economic systems can be drawn with greater confidence.

A TESTABLE THEORY OF THE LOGIC OF INSTITUTIONS. My method of analysis has been primarily inductive. It shows which institutions cluster together in various economic systems but does not explain why such clusters are found. More specifically, do institutions cluster together because, as a group, they can operate more efficiently or effectively? Or do they cluster together because they emanate from the same political or social forces? (Such issues are investigated briefly in Chapter 6 for advanced market economies and shown to be crucial for the Marxist economies in Chapter 8.) Or do they cluster together because they stem from the same set of external causes?

Given the mathematical tools available to economists, it would certainly be easy to generate such a theory, even though it could never be empirically tested. Although such intellectual games may be useful for young scholars to obtain their doctorates or to gain promotion to a higher academic rank, such an approach is useless for the long-run advancement of the study of economic systems. In the words of Bertram Russell, it has all the advantages of theft over honest toil. Instead, such general theories of economic systems must be testable, preferably by the scholar proposing them, so that their usefulness can be demonstrated.

B. Causal Independence of the Economic System

Heavily influenced by Karl Polanyi and his epigone, most social scientists seem to believe that preindustrial economic systems are embedded in a social–political–environmental matrix, which ultimately determines the major shape of the system. They also seem to argue that this is not the case with modern industrial economies. In previous chapters, I address this matter in a very simple way: by lining up a series of indicators for important social, political, and environmental variables and testing whether the particular values for these indicators vary significantly from one economic system to another while holding the level of development constant. If any significant correlation emerges, I then try to determine if the relationship is real or spurious and in which direction the arrow of causality points.

For preindustrial societies, this investigation is very straightforward because I find very few such statistical relationships. Thus, their economic systems appear quite independent of these social–political–environmental forces that have received such loving attention and such determined protection by anthropologists. Moreover, cultural diffusion also seems to have played a relatively minor role in determining the type of economic system a preindustrial developed because most – but not all – of the various types of preindustrial economic systems were found in widely separated locales.

By contrast, the four types of economic systems of the OECD nations were correlated with some political, ideological, social, and cultural variables. This suggests that such noneconomic factors might well have played a certain role in the development of these systems. For instance, the countries with a Nordic economic system have had more left-leaning populations;

and almost all of the countries with Marxist economic systems were dictatorships, which held their economic systems together.[3] The OECD nations with the same economic system also appear geographically and historically linked; thus, diffusion also appears to have had a causal role in their formation. In brief, my results appear to turn the conventional wisdom about the role of noneconomic factors in preindustrial and industrial economic systems upside down.

Again, my analysis can also be extended in different directions. In particular, more subtle types of social–political–environmental variables and their relation to the economic systems need to be explored. As noted in Chapter 6, the form of government, the de facto political power held by certain important groups, and the dynamic between these groups have an important impact on the security of property rights, which is a very important institutional variable influencing economic groups. The relationships between the various types of economic systems and a variety of these noneconomic variables need to be modeled in a more sophisticated fashion, as demonstrated in recent studies by Lindert (2004a, 2004b) and Acemoglu, Johnson, and Robinson (2004).

Such research efforts are vitally important for focusing attention on a key theoretical question left unanswered in this study: namely, the causal factors underlying institutional complementarities. In brief, the logic underlying the logic of institutions is far from clear and needs to be explained before we can fully understand either the structure or the functioning of economic systems.

C. Impact of the Economic System on Economic Performance

Unfortunately for this study, preindustrial societies did not have central statistical offices and most visiting anthropologists evinced little interest in filling this void. Because of a lack of comparable data on such outcome as growth, fluctuations, inflations, and other macroeconomic measures of economic success, I could not determine the impact of the economic system on economic performance.

Even without such comparative macroeconomic performance tests, however, we can still test hypotheses about the relationships between different

---

[3] Of course, a number of market economies are (or were) dictatorships as well, so that it was the combination of a Marxist ideology and a monopoly on political power that gave the relatively economically advanced Marxist nations their distinctive economic systems.

types of economic systems and their microeconomic performance. More specifically, existing ethnographic case studies of societies with different economic systems can certainly provide considerable insight into a number of such questions. For instance, which of two or three societies with different economic systems was best able to handle a famine, drought, or some other external shock with the least loss of life? Which was best able to handle the consequences of contact with the West – for instance, forced sedentarism, restriction of territory, or elimination of entrenched local practices such as the slave trade? Which was best able to handle the economic demands of a war or a welcoming feast thrown for a neighboring community or some other situation requiring a large mobilization of resources? Which had the economy most troubled by social tensions or internal warfare over food or other vital resources? Which was the most likely to feature individual economic behavior that damaged the smooth functioning of the economy?[4]

Such comparisons, of course, require an enormous amount of digging into the ethnographic literature. Moreover, this research must be carried out with the realization that such comparisons of two or three societies with different economic systems cannot provide conclusive evidence for the proposition under investigation, even while they can permit the systematic accumulation of evidence from which generalizations can later be drawn. Such work also provides some useful guides for future ethnographic field-work of aboriginal societies – assuming, of course, that any such societies remain uncontaminated by contact with the West.

For the industrial/service economies, several different extensions of the analysis of economic performance in this study can also be envisioned. Given limitations of space, I deal with only the most obvious macroeconomic indicators of performance. Investigation of the impact of the economic system on more subtle macroeconomic phenomena is vitally important for policy-makers. For instance, what is the differential impact of various monetary and fiscal policies on the performance of nations with different economic systems? What is the impact on economic performance if a nation with a given economic system is lacking one or more institutions that the other nations with the same economic system have? Or, what are the types of special economic difficulties that arise in nations whose institutional configurations lie close to the border of another economic system? A considerable number of other questions about microeconomic performance can be added to this list.

---

[4] Given the emphasis of Marxism on the struggle between different economic groups in the formation and growth of industrial/service economies, it is surprising that Marxist anthropologists have not paid more attention to such struggles in preindustrial societies.

An equally difficult and fundamental task is separating the influence on economic performance of specific economic institutions from the influence of the economic system as a whole. As noted in Chapter 1, adherents of the "new institutional economics" have set themselves the task of investigating the impact of individual institutions on performance. But, certain institutions reinforce (or negate) the impact of others, so that it is not enough to correlate performance with one institution; rather, a whole cluster of institutions must be taken into account. For instance, as mentioned in Chapter 6, Timur Kuran analyzes the economic underdevelopment of nations in the Middle East in terms of the interaction of three economic institutions. Of course, once we begin to talk about clusters of institutions, we are focusing on whole economic systems or at least on sizable segments (subsystems) of them. The analysis of economic performance thus becomes more difficult because we are not just exploring which institutions influence the economic outcome and then assessing the relative importance of each. We must also determine which combination of these institutions plays the leading causal role.

D. Change of Economic Systems

Systemic change can occur within or without a change in the focus of production, and it is useful to discuss these two processes separately because external forces might operate quite differently in the two cases.

1. Systemic Change Accompanying a Change in the Focus of Production

The change of economic systems occasioned by a shift either from foraging to agriculture or from agriculture to industry can be approached by looking at either the beginning or the end of the process. In this study, I focus most attention on the beginning. Concerning the transition from foraging to agriculture, I draw two major conclusions.

FUNCTIONAL NECESSITIES. Many argue that this transition cannot proceed without certain functional necessities being met, especially the development of a sense of private property, so that the harvest of a particular plot is understood to belong to the person who prepared its soil, planted the seeds, and weeded it. Most of the foraging societies in my sample were, in this respect, quite prepared for the transition, and I believe this issue to be overdrawn.[5] Even when the concept of private property in land is lacking, it can readily evolve under suitable conditions. In the past, this may have taken hundreds of years, but sometimes it can take hold in just a few decades – for instance, among the !Kung San of the Kalahari desert (Yellen, 1998) or the Sirionó of Bolivia (Stearman, 1987).

THE ROLE OF THE EXISTING ECONOMIC SYSTEM AND OTHER VARIABLES. In Chapter 3, I find little relationship between a foraging society's economic system and its transition to agriculture, although the sample for this analysis is small. I also determine that the transition did not seem consistently related to most social-structural or many environmental variables because their possible causal roles differed considerably at different times and places. More promising explanatory variables were sedentarism and increasing population density, accompanied by diminishing returns in foraging. If, because of the growth of population in adjoining areas, small groups within the society were no longer free to move elsewhere to forage when foraging returns declined, then agriculture became an increasingly important option for obtaining sufficient food for survival. Nevertheless, neither sedentarism nor higher population density, taken in isolation, appeared to be sufficient causes for the transition. Moreover, some societies returned from agriculture to foraging, when the technology of foraging improved (e.g., the introduction of the horse), and the introduction of agriculture could be delayed by various artificial means for limiting population growth.

The passage from an agricultural to a manufacturing/service economy appeared to be a different type of transformation. The evidence from the industrial revolution in Europe in the eighteenth and nineteenth centuries suggests that a number of important institutional factors were involved, many of which appeared to be related to the economic system. These included high literacy, high agricultural productivity, increasing commercialization, and farms with stable tenure arrangements, where influences of the community or the landlord on farming decisions were minimal. Using a sample of developing countries at the end of the twentieth century, I find further support for the linkage between economic system and economic development. Nevertheless, as I argue in Chapter 5, although a commercialized agricultural economic system seems *most likely* to make the transition into

---

[5] As noted in footnote 19, Chapter 3, even our nonhuman primate cousins have certain notions of private property in regard to both territories and nonfood items. See also Pryor (2003b) and Boehm (2004).

manufacturing, it is neither a necessary nor a sufficient condition for such a transition. For instance, the Netherlands was the most commercialized nation in Europe in the eighteenth century and it shared the other features aiding industrialization but was one of the laggards in industrialization. Many developing nations today have highly developed commercial sectors and some of the other reinforcing characteristics as well but have relatively little manufacturing except, perhaps, for that financed and managed by Western entrepreneurs.

From these studies of the quite different transitions from foraging to agriculture and from agriculture to industry, I must conclude that the search for a single all-embracing theory (in Marxist terminology, for the "laws of motion") is probably fruitless. Nevertheless, the separate investigation of each of these transitions yields useful insights into the impact of economic systems.

2. Systemic Change Without a Change in the Focus of Production

With the exception of a few words about the U.K. economy in the second half of the twentieth century, I say little in this book about how a society might shift from one economic system to another while maintaining the same focus of production. Such an analysis would involve investigation of the behavior of economic systems of various societies over a long period of time; for the most part, I rely on snapshots of societies at particular moments in time. At least for foraging societies, moreover, such historical studies are very rare indeed because most of these groups lived their lives "outside of history." Of course, the lack of much factual information has not prevented theorists from speculating: some have explained such systemic changes in terms of gains in efficiency or productivity, for example; others, in terms of population movements involving the conquest of groups with one economic system by those with another system. Such armchair theorizing is a pleasant way to pass the time, especially while leaving the hard work of empirical validation to others. Given the incentive system in academic economics, this may not ever happen.

For agricultural societies, the historical record is more complete, especially for Europe. For instance, for Europe we have a large number of studies on particular institutions, such as the rise and fall of serfdom or various land-rental arrangements, or the emergence of such other institutions as banks, guilds, and various types of industrial endeavors. The search for the underlying causes of these changes, and their impacts on the economic system as a whole, has revealed a variety of endogenous factors ranging from the purely economic, such as changes in population density or inflation, to more political/economic factors, such as the structuring of economic and power relationships between tenant farmers and landlords. The role of exogenous factors was also substantial, like warfare or increased economic contact with other nations. In a large number of these historical studies, however, the focus has been on exploring the path of the society toward industrialization or capitalism, rather than on its shift from one agricultural economic system to another.

Relating such historical materials to the typologies I have developed from cross-section evidence requires more than a shift of viewpoint to determine how economic systems change while maintaining the same focus of production. As noted previously, the research in this book on preindustrial societies deals mostly with communities, whereas many of the historical studies deal more with states and empires. As shown in Chapter 5, however, it is possible to bridge these different levels of analysis. Moreover, as far as I have been able to determine, we have few comparative studies of systemic change in agricultural societies outside of Europe from which to derive hypotheses that could be linked to the cross-section evidence. In brief, a comparative study of how societies change from one agricultural economic system to another would be a very useful full-length book – but it has yet to be written.

Problems also arise in studying how advanced industrial/service market economies move from one economic system to another, in part because of the lack of comparable data (as shown in Chapter 7), in part because the defining characteristics of economic systems have been mutating as the international economic environment has constantly changed, the level of technology has increased, and the general level of economic development has risen. For instance, a defining characteristic of nations with the Nordic economic system in 1990 – namely, an especially high ratio of public consumption to total public and private consumption – began to emerge in these nations only in the late 1950s.

Other critical and unsolved theoretical problems about the patterns of systemic change are raised in this study. For instance, are systemic changes parallel or polyvalent? Do the clusters contract or expand with systemic change? How do the distances between the clusters also change? The evidence on these such patterns is mixed. In Chapter 3, analysis of the change from foraging to agriculture suggests polyvalent change because some causal forces, such as increasing population density, are external to the societies and societies with the same economic system might experience quite different changes in population density. As noted herein, the clusters also appear to expand as agriculture is adopted. In Chapter 5 and Appendix 6-8, analysis of the change from agriculture to manufacturing suggests parallel change because one type of economic system seems most likely to reach the threshold of industrialization; and, moreover, the clusters appear to contract with industrialization. Finally, the brief discussion in Chapter 7 on systemic changes in OECD nations in both the short and middle run yields mixed results. Nevertheless, I hope to have framed the problem of the characteristics of systemic change so that it can be answered in the future.

E. Coda

Although I hope that this study contributes to our understanding of economic systems, its persistent and much more important message is that we have much more to learn – about their constituent elements, their impact on economic performance, and the ways in which they change. As I repeatedly emphasize, at the present time we have no overall theory of economic systems and, consequently, we cannot explain why, for instance, certain institutions and organizations cluster together or are found in one society but not in another. Although such general theories will probably emerge in the future, they must be constrained by the stylized facts bringing order out of the chaos of existing information. Premature theorizing without such a factual basis – for instance, in the many studies of the role of property rights in the transition to agriculture – will only divert attention from the real economic (and intellectual) problems.

In brief, this study presents a new perspective for defining and analyzing the economic system of any type of economy and it can later serve as the basis for theorizing. This new viewpoint will, I believe, help us understand more clearly the link between complementary institutions and various types of economic performance indicators. The particular economic systems that I have isolated will provide an overall view of the multitude of institutions structuring economic activities as a whole, so that we can step beyond reference to specific economic customs or behaviors and focus more on those with crucial causal implications. It will also provide the framework of analysis for a variety of specific questions about these economies. Most important, I hope to have provided the key empirical results needed by future analysts to build on firm foundation theories about the logic of institutions and about economic systems.

Bibliography

Acemoglu, Daron, Simon Johnson, and James A. Robinson. 2000. "The Colonial Origins of Comparative Development: An Empirical Investigation." NBER Working Paper 7771. Cambridge, MA: National Bureau of Economic Research.

———. 2002. "The Rise of Europe: Atlantic Trade, Institutional Change and Economic Growth." Sloan School of Management, MIT, Working Paper 4269-02, <http://ssrn.com/abstract_id=355990>.

———. 2004. "Institutions as the Fundamental Cause of Long-Run Growth," NBER Working Paper 10481. Cambridge, MA: National Bureau of Economic Research.

Adelman, Irma, and Cynthia Taft Morris. 1978. "Patterns of Market Expansion in the Nineteenth Century: A Quantitative Study." Pp. 231–324 in George Dalton, ed., *Research in Economic Anthropology*, vol. 1. Greenwich, CT: JAI Press.

———. 1980. "Patterns of Industrialization in the Nineteenth and Early Twentieth Centuries: A Cross-Sectional Quantitative Study." Pp. 1–85 in Paul Uselding, ed., *Research In Economic History*, vol. 5. Greenwich, CT: JAI Press.

Afonso, António, Ludger Schuknecht, and Vito Tanzi. 2003. "Public Sector Efficiency: An International Comparison." European Central Bank, Working Paper 242. Frankfurt.

Alesina, Alberto, Arnaud Devleeschauwer, William Easterly, Sergio Kurlat, and Romain Wacziarg. 2003. "Fractionalization." *Journal of Economic Growth* 8, no. 1: 155–94.

Allen, Robert C. 1999. "Tracking the Agricultural Revolution in England." *Economic History Review* 52, no. 2: 209–35.

———. 2003. "Progress and Poverty in Early Modern Europe," *Economic History Review* 56, no. 3: 403–44.

Anderson, David A. 1999. "The Aggregative Burden of Crime," *Journal of Law and Economics* 42, no. 2 (October): 611–43.

Anderson, Patricia C. 1991. "Harvesting of Wild Cereals During the Natufian as Seen from Experimental Cultivation and Harvest of Wild Einkorn Wheat and Microwear Analysis of Stone Tools." Pp. 527–56 in Bar-Yosef and Valla, eds., 1991.

1999a. "Introduction." Pp. 1–6 in Anderson, ed., 1999b.

ed. 1999b. *Prehistory of Agriculture: New Experimental and Ethnographic Approaches.* Los Angeles: Institute of Archaeology.

Andreski, Stanislav. 1964. *Elements of Comparative Sociology.* London: Weidenfeld and Nicolson.

Anon. 2002. "A Survey of Pensions." *The Economist,* February 16.

2004. "Tax Points," *Tax Line* 24, no. 1 (January): 1.

Aston, T. H., and C. H. E. Philpin, eds. 1985. *The Brenner Debate: Agrarian Class Structure and Economic Development in Pre-Industrial Europe.* New York: Cambridge University Press.

Atkinson, Anthony B., and John Micklewright. 1992. *Economic Transformation in Eastern Europe and the Distribution of Income.* New York: Cambridge University Press.

Atkinson, Anthony B., Lee Rainwater, and Timothy M. Smeeding. 1995. *Income Distribution in OECD Countries: Evidence from the Luxembourg Income Study.* Paris: OECD.

Australian Bureau of Statistics. 1991. *Enterprise Statistics, Australia, 1986/87.* ABS Publication 8103.0. Canberra.

Austria, Statistik Austria. 2002. *Statistisches Jahrbuch Österreiches.* Vienna: Verlag Österreich.

Bailey, H. 1960. "A Method of Determining Warmth and Temperateness of Climate." *Geografiska Annaler* 45: 1–16.

Bairoch, Paul. 1982. "International Industrialization Levels from 1750 to 1980." *Journal of European Economic History* 11, no. 2 (Fall): 269–325.

1993. *Economics and World History: Myths and Paradoxes.* Chicago: University of Chicago Press.

Bairoch, Paul, Jean Batou, and Pierre Chèvre. 1988. *The Population of European Cities: Data Bank and Short Summary of Results.* Geneva: Librarie Droz.

Banks, Arthur R. 2003. "Cross-National Time-Series Data Archive." A proprietary database distributed by Databanks International. <http://www.databanks.sitehosting.net/>.

Barreto, Humberto, and Robert S. Whitesell. 1992. "Estimation of Output Loss from Allocative Inefficiency: A Comparison of the Soviet Union and the USA." *Economics of Planning* 25, no. 3: 219–36.

Barro, Robert J., and Jong-Wha Lee. 1994. "Data Set for a Panel of 138 Countries." <www.nber.org/pub/barro.lee>.

Barry, Herbert III, and Alice Schlegel, eds. 1980. *Cross-Cultural Samples and Codes.* Pittsburgh: University of Pittsburgh Press.

1982. "Cross-Cultural Codes on Contributions by Women to Subsistence." *Ethnology* 21: 165–88.

Barry, Herbert III, Lili Josephson, Edith Lauer, and Catherina Marshall. 1976. "Traits Inculcated in Childhood: Cross-Cultural Codes." *Ethnology* 15, no. 1 (January): 83–114.

Barth, James R., Gerard Caprio, Jr., and Ross Levine. 2001. "Banking Systems Around the Globe: Do Regulation and Ownership Affect Performance and Stability?" Pp. 31–88 in Frederic S. Mishkin, ed., *Prudential Supervision: What Works and What Doesn't.* Chicago: University of Chicago Press.

Bar-Yosef, Ofer, and Richard H. Meadow. 1995. "The Origins of Agriculture in the Near East." Pp. 39–94 in Price and Gebauer, eds., 1995.

Bar-Yosef, Ofer, and François K. Valla, eds. 1991. *The Natufian Culture in the Levant.* International Monographs in Prehistory. Ann Arbor, MI: University of Michigan.

Baslé, Maurice. 2002. "Acknowledged and Unacknowledged Institutional Antecedents of Regulation Theory." Pp. 21–27 in Boyer and Saillard, eds., 2002.

Beck, Thorsten, Asli Demirgűç-Kunt, and Ross Levine. 2003. "Law and Finance: Why Does Legal Origin Matter?" *Journal of Comparative Economics* 31, no. 3 (December): 620–53.

Bender, Barbara. 1975. *Farming in Prehistory: From Hunter-Gatherer to Food-Producer.* New York: St. Martin's Press.

———. 1978. "Gatherer-Hunter to Farmer: A Social Perspective." *World Archaeology* 10, no. 2: 204–22.

Bergson, Abram. 1992. "The Communist Efficiency Gap: Alternative Measures." *Comparative Economic Studies* 36, no. 1 (Spring): 1–13.

Bertola, Giuseppe, Francine D. Blau, and Lawrence M. Kahn. 2001. "Comparative Analysis of Labor Market Outcomes: Lessons for the U.S. from International Long-Run Evidence." NBER Working Paper 8526. Cambridge, MA: National Bureau of Economic Research.

Bićanić, Ivo. 1990. "Unofficial Economic Activities in Yugoslavia." Pp. 85–100 in Maria Łoś, ed., *The Second Economy in Marxist States.* New York: St. Martin's Press.

Binford, Lewis R. 1968. "Post-Pleistocene Adaptions." Pp. 313–41 in Sally R. Binford and Lewis R. Binford, eds., *New Perspectives in Archaeology.* Chicago: Aldine.

———. 1980. "Yellow Smoke and Dogs' Tails: Hunter-Gatherer Settlement Systems and Archaeological Site Formation." *American Antiquity* 45: 4–21.

———. 2001. *Construction Frames of Reference: An Analytical Method for Archaeological Theory Building Using Hunter-Gatherer and Environmental Data Sets.* Berkeley, CA: University of California Press.

Blanchard, Olivier. 1997. "The Medium Run." *Brookings Papers on Economic Activity,* no. 2: 89–158.

Blanchard, Olivier, and Justin Wolfers. 2000. "The Role of Shocks and Institutions in the Rise of European Unemployment: The Aggregate Evidence." *Economic Journal* 110, no. 1 (March): C1–C33.

Blattman, Christopher, Michael A. Clemens, and Jeffrey G. Williamson. 2003. "Who Protected and Why? Tariffs the World Around, 1870–1938." Harvard Institute of Economic Research Discussion Paper 2010. Cambridge, MA.

Blau, Francine D., and Lawrence M. Kahn. 1994. "International Differences in Male Wage Inequality: Institutions versus Market Forces." NBER Working Paper 4678. Cambridge, MA: National Bureau of Economic Research.

Blomme, Jan, and Herman Van der Wee. 1994. "The Belgium Economy in a Long-Term Historical Perspective: Economic Development in Flanders and Brabant, 1500–1812." In Angus Maddison and Herman Van der Wee, eds. *Economic Growth and Structural Change: Comparative Approaches over the Long Run.* Bocconi, Italy: Università Bocconi.

Board of Governors, Federal Reserve System. 2002. *Flow of Funds Accounts of the United States,* 5 vols. Washington, D.C.

Board of Trustees, Federal Hospital Insurance and Federal Supplementary Medical Insurance Trust Funds. 2004. *2004 Annual Report.* Washington, D.C.: GPO.

Boehm, Christopher. 2004. "What Makes Humans Economically Distinctive?" *Journal of Bioeconomics* 6, no. 2.

Boltho, Andrea, Alessandro Vercelli, and Hiroshi Yoshikawa, eds. 2001. *Comparing Economic Systems: Italy and Japan.* New York: Palgrave.

Bordo, Michael D., Alan Taylor, and Jeffrey G. Williamson, eds. 2003. *Globalization in Historical Perspective.* Chicago: University of Chicago Press.

Bordo, Michael D., and Thomas Helbling. 2003. "Have National Business Cycles Become More Synchronized?" NBER Working Paper 10130. Cambridge, MA: National Bureau of Economic Research.

Botero, Juan, Simeon Djankov, Rafael La Porta, Florencio Lopez-de-Silanes, and Andrei Shleifer. 2003. "The Regulation of Labor." NBER Working Paper 9756. Cambridge, MA: National Bureau of Economic Research.

Bowles, Paul, Osvaldo Croci, and Brian MacLean. 2000. "Creating the Institutions of the Global Economy? Central Bank Independence in Japan and Italy." Pp. 55–67 in McBridge and Wiseman, eds., 2000.

Bowles, Samuel, and Jung-Kyoo Choi. 2003. "The First Property Rights Revolution." Paper delivered at the Workshop on the Co-evolution of Behaviors and Institutions, Santa Fe Institute. Santa Fe, NM.

Bowman, Mary Jean, and C. Arnold Anderson. 1963. "Concerning the Role of Education in Development." Pp. 247–79 in Clifford Geertz, ed., *Old Societies and New States.* Glencoe, IL: Free Press.

Boyer, Robert, and Yves Saillard, eds. 2002. *Régulation Theory: The State of the Art,* trans. by Carolyn Shread. New York: Routledge.

Brenner, Robert. 1985. "The Agrarian Roots of European Capitalism." Pp. 213–327 in Aston and Philpin, eds., 1985.

Bunce, Valerie. 1998. "Subversive Institutions: The End of the Soviet State in Comparative Perspective." *Post-Soviet Affairs* 14, no. 1 (January): 323–54.

  1999. *Subversive Institutions: The Design and the Destruction of Socialism and the State.* New York: Cambridge University Press.

Butlin, N. G. 1962. *Australian Domestic Product, Investment and Foreign Borrowing, 1861–1938/39.* Cambridge, U.K.: Cambridge University Press.

Buyst, Erik. 2002. "Estimates of Economic Growth in the Southern Low Countries/Belgium, 1770–1846." Unpublished paper.

Card, David. 1998. "Falling Union Membership and Rising Wage Inequality: What's the Connection?" NBER Working Paper 6520. Cambridge, MA: National Bureau of Economic Research.

Carneiro, Robert L. 1969. "The Transition from Hunting to Horticulture in the Amazon Basin." Pp. 244–48 in *8th International Congress of Anthropological and Ethnological Sciences: Proceedings,* vol. 3. Tokyo: Science Council of Japan.

  1970. "Scale Analysis, Evolutionary Sequences, and the Rating of Cultures." Pp. 834–72 in Naroll and Cohen, eds., 1970.

  2003. *Evolution in Cultural Anthropology: A Critical History.* Boulder, CO: Westview.

Carter, George F. 1977. "A Hypothesis Suggesting a Single Origin of Agriculture." Pp. 89–135 in Reed, ed., 1977.

Cauvin, Jacques. 2000. *The Birth of the Gods and the Origins of Agriculture*, trans. by Tevor Watkins. New York: Cambridge University Press.

Chao, Kang. 1982. "Textile Production in Traditional China." In Deyon, ed., 1982, vol. 1.

Cipolla, Carlo M. 1969. *Literacy and Development in the West*. Hammondsworth, U.K.: Penguin.

Clague, Christopher, Philip Keefer, Stephen Knack, and Mancur Olson. 1999. "Contract-Intensive Money: Contract Enforcement, Property Rights, and Economic Performance." *Journal of Economic Growth* 4, no. 2 (June): 185–211.

Coates, David. 2002. *Models of Capitalism: Debating Strengths and Weaknesses*. Northampton, MA: Elgar.

Cohen, Marc Nathan. 1977a. *The Food Crisis in Prehistory: Overpopulation and the Origins of Agriculture*. New Haven, CT: Yale University Press.

———. 1977b. "Population Pressure and the Origins of Agriculture." Pp. 135–77 in Reed, ed., 1977.

———. 1985. "Prehistoric Hunter-Gatherers: The Meaning of Social Complexity." Pp. 99–119 in Price and Brown, eds., 1985.

Cooper, John M. 1946. "Patagonia and Pampean Hunters." Pp. 127–60 in Julian H. Steward, ed., *Handbook of South American Indians*, vol. 1, *The Marginal Tribes*. Smithsonian Institution, Bureau of American Ethnology, Bulletin 143. Washington, D.C.: GPO.

Cooper, J. P. 1985. "In Search of Agrarian Capitalism." Pp. 138–91 in Aston and Philpin, editors, 1985.

Crafts, N. F. R. 1983. "British Economic Growth, 1700–1831: A Review of the Evidence." *Economic History Review*, 2nd ser., 36, no. 2 (May): 177–99.

———. 1985. *British Economic Growth During the Industrial Revolution*. Oxford: Clarendon Press.

Crocker, William H. 1990. "The Canela (Eastern Timbira) I: An Ethnographic Introduction." *Smithsonian Contributions to Anthropology* 33. Washington, D.C.: Smithsonian Institution Press.

Crook, Clive. 2003. "Globalization in Interdisciplinary Perspective." Pp. 549–52 in Bordo, Taylor, and Williamson, eds., 2003.

Cukierman, Alex. 1992. *Central Bank Strategy: Credibility and Independence, Theory and Evidence*. Cambridge, MA: MIT Press.

Cusack, Thomas R. 2003. "Public Expenditure Statistics." <http://www.wz-berlin.de/mp/ism/staff/cusack.en.htm>.

Cusack, Thomas R., and Susanne Fuchs. 2003. "Parteien, Institutionen und Staatsausgaben." Pp. 321–54 in Herbert Obinger, Uwe Wagshal, and Berhard Kittel, eds. *Politische Ökonomie: Politik und wirtschaftliche Leistungsprofile in OECD Demokratien*. Opladen, Germany: Leske und Büdrich.

Cutler, David M., and Ellen Meara. 1999. "The Concentration of Medical Spending: An Update." NBER Working Paper 7279. Cambridge, MA: National Bureau of Economic Research.

Dallago, Bruno, Horst Brezinski, and Wladimir Andreff, eds. 1992. *Convergence and System Change: The Convergence Hypothesis in the Light of Transition in Eastern Europe*. Brookfield, VT: Dartmouth.

Danilov, V. I., Ivan S. Materov, Steven Rosefielde, and C. A. Knox Lovell. 1985. "Measuring Enterprise Efficiency in the Soviet Union: A Stochastic Frontier Analysis." *Economica* 52: 225–33.

Dare, Ron. 1974. "The Ecology and Evolution of Food Sharing." *California Anthropologist* 2: 13–25.

de Ávila, Romero, and Rolf Strauch. 2003. "Public Finances and Long-Term Growth in Europe: Evidence from a Panel Data Analysis." Working Paper 246, European Central Bank. Frankfurt am Main, Germany.

Deane, Phyllis, and W. A. Cole. 1969. *British Economic Growth, 1688–1959: Trends and Structure.* London: Cambridge University Press.

Deininger, Klaus, and Lyn Squire. 1988. "New Ways of Looking at Old Issues: Inequality and Growth." *Journal of Development Economics* 57, no. 2 (December): 259–87.

Demirgüç-Kunt, Asli, and Ross Levine, eds. 2001. *Financial Structure and Economic Growth: A Cross-Country Comparison of Banks, Markets, and Development.* Cambridge, MA: MIT Press.

Desai, Padma, and Ricardo Martin. 1987. "Efficiency Loss from Resource Misallocation in Soviet Industry." Pp. 117–33 in Desai, ed. *The Soviet Economy: Problems and Prospects.* Oxford: Blackwell.

D'Evreux, Yves. 1864. *Voyage dans le nord du Brésil fait durant les années 1613 et 1614,* ed. by Ferdinand Denis. Human Relations Area File SO-09. New Haven, CT: Yale University.

Deyon, Pierre, ed. 1982. VIIIe Congres international d'histoire économique, Section A2: *La protoindustrialisation: Théorie et réalité.* Lille, France: Université des Arts, Lettres, et Science Humaines de Lille.

Di Tella, Rafael, and Robert MacCulloch. 2004. "Why Doesn't Capitalism Flow to Poor Countries?" <http://papers.ssrn.com/sol3/papers.cfm?abstract_id= 511986>.

Diamond, Jared. 1999. *Guns, Germs, and Steel: The Fates of Human Societies.* New York: Norton.

Dirks, Robert. 1993. "Starvation and Famine: Cross-Cultural Codes and Some Hypotheses Tests." *Cross-Cultural Research* 27: 28–69.

Divale, Willliam, and J. Patrick Gray. 2001. "Coded Variables for the Standard Cross-Cultural Sample." *World Cultures,* Spring edition, CD-ROM. Jamaica, NY.

Djankov, Simeon, Edward L. Glaeser, Rafael La Porta, Florencio Lopez-de-Silanes, and Andrei Shleifer. 2003. "The New Comparative Economics." NBER Working Paper 9608. Cambridge, MA: National Bureau of Economic Research.

Domar, Evsey. 1970. "The Causes of Slavery or Serfdom: A Hypothesis." *Journal of Economic History* 30 (March): 18–31.

Duplessis, Robert S. 1997. *Transitions to Capitalism in Early Modern Europe.* New York: Cambridge University Press.

Eisner, Robert. 1989. *The Total Income Systems of Accounts.* Chicago: University of Chicago Press.

Ellis, John. 1993. *World War II: A Statistical Survey.* New York: Facts on File.

Ember, Carol R. 1975. "Residential Variation Among Hunter-Gatherers." *Behavior Science Research* 10, no. 3: 199–229.

Ember, Carol R., and Melvin Ember. 1992. "Codebook for 'Warfare, Aggression, and Resource Problems: Cross-Cultural Codes." *Behavior Science Research* 26: 169–85.

Ember, Marvin. 1975. "On the Origin and Extension of the Incest Taboo." *Behavior Science Research* 10, no. 4: 249–83.

Encyclopedia Britannica. 2001. "World Data," *2001 Britannica Book of the Year.* Chicago.

Encyclopedia Britannica. 1993. Chicago.

Engerman, Stanley, and Kenneth L. Sokoloff. 2003. "Institutional and Non-Institutional Explanations of Economic Differences." NBER Working Paper 9989. Cambridge, MA: National Bureau of Economic Research.

England, Robert Stowe. 2002. *The Macroeconomic Impact of Global Aging.* Washington, D.C.: Center for Strategic and International Studies.

Ercolani, Paolo. 1969. "Documentazione statistica di base." Pp. 380–463 in Giorgio Fua, ed., *Lo sviluppo economico in Italia,* vol. 3. Milan: Franco Angeli.

Estevez-Abe, Margarita, Torben Iversen, and David Soskice. 2001. "Social Protection and the Formation of Skills: A Reinterpretation of the Welfare State." Pp. 145–83 in Peter A. Hall and David Soskice, eds., *Varieties of Capitalism.* New York: Oxford University Press.

European Commission, Eurostat. 1994. *Enterprises in Europe:* Third Report. Brussels.

Feige, Edgar L. 1997. "Underground Activity and Institutional Change." Pp. 21–33 in Joan Nelson, Charles Tilly, and Lee Walker, eds., *Transforming Post-Communist Political Economies.* Washington, D.C.: National Academy Press.

Feld, Lars P., and Stefan Voigt. 2003. "Economic Growth and Judiciary Independence: Cross-Country Evidence Using a New Set of Indicators." CESifo Working Paper 906. <www.CESifo.de>.

Feldbrugge, F. J. M. 1989. "The Soviet Second Economy in a Political and Legal Perspective." Pp. 297–338 in Edgar L. Feige, ed., *The Underground Economies.* New York: Cambridge University Press.

Findlay, Ronald, and Keven H. O'Rourke. 2003. "Commodity Market Integration, 1500–2000." Pp. 13–65 in Bordo, Taylor, and Williamson, eds., 2003.

Firestone, O. J. 1958. *Canada's Economic Development, 1867–1953.* London: Bowes & Bowes.

Firth, Noel E., and James H. Noren. 1998. *Soviet Defense Spending: A History of CIA Estimates, 1950–1990.* College Station, TX: Texas A&M University Press.

Flannery, Kent V. 1968. "Origin and Ecological Effect of Early Domestication in Iran and the Near East." Pp. 73–100 in Peter J. Ucko and G. W. Dimbleby, eds., *The Domestication and Exploitation of Plants and Animals.* London: Duckworth.

Food and Agricultural Organization/UNESCO. 1971–78. *Soil Maps of the World.* Paris: UNESCO.

Fowkes, Ben. 1993. *The Rise and Fall of Communism in Eastern Europe.* New York: St. Martin's Press.

Franko, Lawrence G. 2003. "Corporate Concentration and Turnover in Global Industries, 1960–2000." *Competition and Change* 7, nos. 2–3: 163–84.

Frey, Bruno S., and Werner W. Pommerehne. 1989. "Measuring the Hidden Economy." Pp. 3–27 in Vito Tanzi, ed., *The Underground Economy in the United States and Abroad.* Lexington, MA: Lexington Books.

Friedheim, Cyrus. 1998. *The Trillion Dollar Enterprise: How the Alliance Revolution Will Transform Global Business*. Reading, MA: Perseus Books.

Fuller, Jill E., and Burke D. Grandjean. 2001. "Economy and Religion in the Neolithic Revolution: Material Structure and the Proto-Religious Ethnic." *Cross-Cultural Research* 35, no. 4: 370–99.

Galor, Oded. 2003. "Why Are a Third of People Indian and Chinese? Trade, Industrialization, and Demographic Transition." Paper delivered at the American Economic Association Convention, Washington, D.C.

Galor, Oded, Omer Moav, and Dietrich Vollrath. 2003. "Land Inequality and the Origin of Divergence and Overtaking in the Growth Process: Theory and Evidence." <http://papers.ssm.com/paper.taf?abstract_id378161>.

Gamble, Andrew. 1993. "The Decline of Corporatism." Pp. 41–68 in Derek Crabtree and A. P. Thirlwall, eds., *Keynes and the Role of the State: 10th Keynes Seminar*. New York: St. Martin's Press.

Gebauer, Anne Birgitte, and T. Douglas Price. 1992. "Foragers to Farmers: An Introduction," in Gebauer and Price, eds., *Transitions to Agriculture in Prehistory*. Madison, WI: Prehistory Press.

Germany, Statistisches Bundesamt. 1995. *Statistisches Jahrbuch für die Bundesrepublic Deutschland*. Wiesbaden.

Gerschenkron, Alexander. 1966. *Economic Backwardness in Historical Perspective: A Book of Essays*. Cambridge, MA: Belknap Press of Harvard University Press.

Ghemawat, Pankaj, and Fariborz Ghadar. 2000. "The Dubious Logic of Global Megamergers." *Harvard Business Review* 78, no. 4 (July–August): 64–75.

Gill, Frank B. 1995. *Ornithology*. New York: Freeman.

Ginarte, Juan C., and Walter G. Park. 1997. "Determinants of Patent Rights: A Cross-National Study," *Research Policy* 26, no. 3: 283–301.

Glaeser, Edward L., Rafael La Porta, Florencio Lopez-de-Silanes, and Andrei Shleifer. 2004. "Do Institutions Cause Growth?" NBER Working Paper. Cambridge, MA: National Bureau of Economic Research.

Goland, Carol. 1991. "The Ecological Context of Hunter-Gatherer Storage: Environmental Predictability and Environmental Risk." Pp. 107–25 in Preston T. Miracle et al., eds., *Foragers in Context: Long-Term, Regional and Historical Perspectives in Hunter-Gatherer Studies*. Michigan Discussions in Anthropology 10. Ann Arbor: University of Michigan, Department of Anthropology.

Golden, Miriam, and Michael Wallerstein. 2002. "Union Centralization Among Advanced Industrial Societies: Update to 1995." <www.shelley.polisci.ucla.edu/data>.

Golden, Miriam A., Michael Wallerstein, and Peter Lange. 1999. "Postwar Trade-Union Organization and Industrial Relations in Twelve Countries." Pp. 194–230 in Kitschelt, Lange, Marks, and Stephens, eds., 1999a.

Goldin, Claudia Dale. 1976. *Urban Slavery in the American South, 1820–1860*. Chicago: University of Chicago Press.

Goldsmith, Raymond. 1961. "The Economic Growth of Tsarist Russia, 1860–1913." *Economic Development and Cultural Change* 9, no. 3 (April): 441–75.

Goossens, Martine. 1993. *The Economic Development of Belgian Agriculture: A Regional Perspective, 1812–1846*. Leuven, Belgium: Leuven University Press.

Gottschalk, Peter, and Timothy M. Smeeding. 1997. "Cross-National Comparisons of Earnings and Income Inequality." *Journal of Economic Literature* 35, no. 2 (June): 633–87.

Gowdy, John M., ed. 1998. *Limited Wants, Unlimited Means: A Reader on Hunter-Gatherer Economics and the Environment*. Washington, D.C.: Island Press.

Grannato, Jim, Ronald Inglehart, and David Leblang. 1996. "The Effect of Cultural Values on Economic Development: Theory, Hypotheses, and Some Empirical Tests. "*American Journal of Political Science* 40, no. 3 (August 1996): 607–31.

Grantham, George, and Carol S. Leonard, eds. 1989. *Agrarian Organization in the Century of Industrialization: Europe, Russia, and North America*, Supplement 5, Part A, Research in Economic History. Greenwich, CT: JAI Press.

Grassby, Richard. 1999. *The Idea of Capitalism before the Industrial Revolution*. Lanham, MD: Rowman & Littlefield.

Gray, J. Patrick. 1996. "Is the Standard Cross-Cultural Sample Biased? A Simulation Study." *Cross-Cultural Research* 30, no. 4 (November): 301–15.

2001. See Divale and Gray (2001).

Greenfeld, Liah. 2001. *The Spirit of Capitalism: Nationalism and Economic Growth*. Cambridge, MA: Harvard University Press.

Gregory, Paul R. 1982. *Russian National Income, 1885–1913*. New York: Cambridge University Press.

1997. "Searching for Consistency in Historical Data: Alternative Estimates of Russia's Industrial Production, 1887–1913." *Journal of Economic History* 57, no. 1 (March): 196–203.

Grilli, Vittori, Donato Masciandaro, and Guido Tabellini. 1991. "Political and Monetary Institutions and Public Financial Policies in the Industrial Countries." *Economic Policy* 13: 342–92.

Groningen Growth and Development Centre. 2003. Website: <www.eco.rug.nl/ggdc/index.html>.

Grossman, Gregory. 1998. "Subverted Sovereignty: Historic Role of the Soviet Underground." Pp. 24–50 in Stephen S. Cohen et al., eds., *The Tunnel at the End of the Light*. Berkeley, CA: University of California Press.

Gwartney, James D., and Robert A. Lawson. 1997. *Economic Freedom of the World: 1997 Annual Report*. Vancouver: Fraser Institute.

Hall, Peter A., and David Soskice. 2001. "An Introduction to Varieties of Capitalism." Pp. 1–71 in Hall and Soskice, eds., *Varieties of Capitalism: The Institutional Foundation of Comparative Advantage*. New York: Cambridge University Press.

Hann, Christopher. M., ed. 1998. *Property Relations: Renewing the Anthropological Tradition*. New York: Cambridge University Press.

Hansen, Svend Aage. 1974. *Økonomisk vækst Danmark*, vol. 2. Copenhagen: Akademisk Forlag.

Harlan, Jack R. 1988. "Plant Domestication: Diffuse Origins and Diffusion." Pp. 21–35 in C. Barigozzi, ed., *The Origin and Domestication of Cultivated Plants*. Amsterdam: Elsevier.

1999. "Harvesting of Wild-Grass Seed and Implications for Domestication." Pp. 1–6 in Anderson, ed., 1999b.

Harris, David R. 1977. "Settling Down: An Evolutionary Model for the Transformation of Mobile Bands into Sedentary Communities." Pp. 401–17 in J. Friedman and M. J. Rowlands, eds., *The Evolution of Social Systems*. London. Institute of Archaeology, University of London.

Hayden, Brian. 1990. "Nimrods, Piscators, Pluckers, and Planters: The Emergence of Food Production." *Journal of Anthropological Archaeology* 9, no. 1: 31–69.

1993. *Archaeology: The Science of Once and Future Things*. New York: Freeman.

1995a. "A New Overview of Domestication." Pp. 273–97 in Price and Gebauer, eds., 1995.

1995b. "Pathways to Power: Principles for Creating Socioeconomic Inequalities." Pp. 15–86 in Price and Feinman, eds., 1995.

Heckscher, Eli F. 1963. *An Economic History of Sweden*. Trans. by Gören Ohlin. Cambridge, MA: Harvard University Press.

Heller, Peter S. 2003. *Who Will Pay? Coping with Aging Societies, Climate Change, and Other Long-Term Fiscal Challenges*. Washington, D.C.: International Monetary Fund.

Henley, Andrew, and Euclid Tsakalotos. 1993. *Corporatism and Economic Performance: A Comparative Analysis of Market Economies*. Brookfield, VT: Elgar.

Hjerppe, Riitta. 1989. *The Finnish Economy, 1860–1985*. Helsinki: Bank of Finland Government Printing Center.

Ho, S. P. S. 1982. "The Simple Analytics of Proto-industrialization and Deindustrialization." In Deyon, ed., 1982, vol. 1.

Hoffmann, Walther G. 1965. *Das Wachstum der deutschen Wirtschaft seit der Mitte des 10. Jahrhunderts*. Berlin: Springer Verlag.

Hölldobler, Bert, and Edward O. Wilson. 1990. *The Ants*. Cambridge, MA: Harvard University Press.

Holmberg, Alan R. 1950. *Nomads of the Long Bow: The Sirionó of Eastern Bolivia*. New York: Natural History Press.

Hoselitz, Bert F. 1960. "Theories of Stages of Economic Growth." Pp. 193–239 in Bert F. Hoselitz et al., eds., *Theories of Economic Growth*. Glencoe, IL: Free Press.

Huber, Evelyne, Charles Ragin, and John D. Stephens. 1997. "Comparative Welfare States Data Set." <www.lisproject.org/publications/welfaredata/welfareaccess. htm>.

Hwa, Erh-Cheng. 1988. "The Contribution of Agriculture to Economic Growth: Some Empirical Evidence." *World Development* 16, no. 11: 1329–39.

Inglehart, Ronald et al. 2000. *World Value Surveys and European Values Surveys, 1981–1984, 1990–1992, and 1995–1997*. Inter-university Consortium for Political and Social Research (ICPSR) Study No. 2790. <www.icpsr.umich.edu>.

Inglehart, Ronald, Miguel BasaZez, and Alejandro Moreno. 2001. *Human Values and Beliefs: A Cross-Cultural Sourcebook*. Ann Arbor, MI: University of Michigan Press.

Institute for Management Development (IMD). 1999. *The World Competitive Yearbook*. Lausanne.

2001. *World Competitiveness Yearbook*. Lausanne.

International Labour Office (ILO). 1996. *Yearbook of Labour Statistics 1996*. Geneva.

1997. *World Labour Report 1997–1998*. Geneva.

1997–98. *World Labour Report 9*. Geneva.

International Monetary Fund. Monthly. *International Financial Statistics*. Washington, D.C.

International Financial Statistics, Database and Browser, CD-ROM. Washington, D.C.

Internet Center for Corruption Research 2002. Website. <www.gwdg.de/~uwvw/icr.htm>.

Jackson, Richard, and Neil Howe. 2003. *The 2003 Aging Vulnerability Index*. Washington, D.C.: Center for Strategic and International Studies.

Japan, Statistical Bureau, Ministry of Public Management, Home Affairs, Post and Telecommunication. 2003. *Japan Statistical Yearbook*. Tokyo.

Jefferson, Philip N. 1998. "Seigniorage Payments for Use of the Dollar: 1977–1995." *Economic Letters* 58: 225–30.

Jones, Eric L. 1981. *The European Miracle: Environments, Economies, and Geopolitics in the History of Europe and Asia*. New York: Cambridge University Press.

Jones, Eric L., and Stuart J. Woolf. 1969. "The Historical Role of Agrarian Change in Economic Development." Pp. 10–23 in Jones and Woolf, eds., *Agrarian Change and Economic Development*. London: Methuen & Co.

Kappeler, Peter. 1999. "Convergence and Divergence in Primate Social Systems." Pp. 158–79 in John G. Fleagle et al., eds., *Primate Communities*. New York: Cambridge University Press.

Katsenelinboigen, Aron. 1977. "Coloured Markets in the Soviet Union," *Soviet Studies* 29, no. 1 (January): 62–86.

Kaufmann, Daniel, Aart Kraay, and M. Mastruzzi. 2003. "Governance Indicators for 1996–2002." <www.worldbank.org/wbi/governance/pubs/govmatters3.html>.

Kausel, Anton. 1979. "Oesterreichs Volkseinkommen 1830 bis 1913." Pp. 689–720 in Oesterreichische Statistischen Zentralamt, *Geschichte und Ergebnisse der zentralen amtlichen Statistik in Oesterreich 1829–1979*. Vienna.

Keefer, Philip. 2002. "DPI2000: Database of Political Institutions: Changes and Variable Definitions," <www.worldbank.org>.

Keeley, Lawrence H. 1995. "Proto-agricultural Practices Among Hunter-Gatherers." Pp. 243–73 in Price and Gebauer, eds., 1995.

1999. "Use of Plant Foods among Hunter-Gatherers: A Cross-Cultural Survey." Pp. 6–23 in Anderson, ed., 1999b.

Keller, Gerald, and Brian Warrack. 2003. *Statistics for Management and Economics*. Pacific Grove, CA: Thompson, Brooks/Cole.

Kelly, Robert L. 1983. "Hunter-Gatherer Mobility Strategies." *Journal of Anthropological Research* 39, no. 3: 277–306.

1995. *The Foraging Spectrum: Diversity in Hunter-Gatherer Lifeways*. Washington, D.C.: Smithsonian Institution Press.

Kemme, David. 1990. "Losses in Polish Industry Due to Resource Misallocation." *Jahrbuch der Wirtschaft Osteuropas*, 14, no. 2: 139–58.

Kent, Susan. 1989. *Farmers as Hunters: The Implications of Sedentism*. New York: Cambridge University Press.

Keren, Michael. 1992. "The New Economic System, the New Economic Mechanism, and the Yugoslav Labor-Managed Firms: Bureaucratic Limits to Reform." *Economic Systems* 16, no. 1 (April): 89–111.

Khamis, Salem H. 1984. "On Aggregation Methods for International Comparisons." *Review of Income and Wealth* 30, no. 2 (June): 185–207.

Kitschelt, Herbert, Peter Lange, Gary Marks, and John D. Stephens, eds. 1999a. *Continuity and Change in Contemporary Capitalism.* New York: Cambridge University Press.

1999b. "Convergence and Divergence in Advanced Capitalist Democracies." Pp. 427–60 in Kitschelt et al., eds., 1999a.

Knack, Stephen, and Philip Keefer. 1997. "Does Social Capital Have an Economic Payoff? A Cross-Country Investigation." *Quarterly Journal of Economics* 112, no. 4 (November): 1251–88.

Kondo, Edson Kenji. 1994. *Patent Laws and Foreign Direct Investment: An Empirical Investigation.* Ph.D. dissertation, Harvard University, Cambridge, MA.

Korbel, Josef. 1959. *The Communist Subversion of Czechoslovakia, 1938–1948.* Princeton, NJ: Princeton University Press.

Kornai, János. 1983. "Comments on the Present State and the Prospects of the Hungarian Economic Reform." *Journal of Comparative Economics* 7, no. 3 (September): 225–53.

1986. "The Hungarian Reform Process: Visions, Hopes, and Reality," *Journal of Economic Literature* 24, no. 4 (December): 1687–1737.

Kotlikoff, Lawrence, and Scott Burns. 2004. *The Coming Generational Storm.* Cambridge, MA: MIT Press.

Knack, Stephen, and Philip Keefer. 1997. "Does Social Capital Have an Economic Payoff? A Cross-Country Investigation." *Quarterly Journal of Economics* 112, no. 4 (November): 1251–88.

Kraemer, Moritz. 2004. "The Western World Past Its Prime – Sovereign Rating Perspectives in the Context of Aging Populations," *Standard & Poors Credit Ratings,* <www2.standardandpoors.com/NASApp/cs/ContentServer?pagename=sp/page/HomePg>

Krantz, Olle, and Carl-Axel Nilsson. 1975. *Swedish National Product 1861–1970.* Stockholm: CWK Gleerup.

Kraus, Stephen J. 1995. "Attitudes and the Prediction of Behavior: A Meta-Analysis of the Empirical Literature." *Personality and Social Psychology,* Bulletin 21, no. 1: 58–75.

Kriedte, Peter, Hans Medick, Jürgen Schlumbohm. 1981. *Industrialization Before Industrialization.* New York: Cambridge University Press.

Kuran, Timur. 2003. "Why the Middle East Is Economically Underdeveloped: Historical Mechanisms of Institutional Stagnation." *Journal of Economic Perspective* 18, no. 3 (Summer): 71–90.

Kuran, Timur. 2004. "Why the Middle East Is Economically Underdeveloped: Historical Mechanisms of Institutional Stagnation," *Journal of Economic Perspectives* 18, no. 3 (Summer): 71–90.

Kurth, James. 1993. "A Tale of Four Countries: Parallel Politics in Southern Europe, 1815–1990." Pp. 27–66 in James Kurth and James Petras, eds., *Mediterranean Paradoxes: Politics and Social Structure in Southern Europe.* Providence, RI: Berg.

Lains, Pedro. 1995. *A Economia Portuguesa no Século XIX.* Lisbon: Impresa Nacional Casa da Moeda.

Lambsdorff, Johann. 2003. "Historical Statistics of Corruption." University of Passau, Internet Center for Corruption Research. <wwwuser.gwdg.de/~uwvw/corruption.cpi_olderindices.html>.

La Porta, Rafael, Florencio Lopez-de-Silanes, and Andrei Shleifer. 1998. "Corporate Ownership around the World." NBER Working Paper 6625. Cambridge, MA: National Bureau of Economic Research.

La Porta, Rafael, Florencio Lopez-de-Silanes, Andrei Shleifer, and Robert W. Vishny. 1996. "Law and Finance." NBER Working Paper 5661. Cambridge, MA: National Bureau of Economic Research.

— 1997. "Legal Determinants of External Finance." NBER Working Paper 5879. Cambridge, MA: National Bureau of Economic Research.

Lazear, Edward P. 1990. "Job Security Provisions and Employment." *Quarterly Journal of Economics* 105, no. 3: 699–726.

Léon, Jorge. 1977. "Origin, Evolution, and Early Dispersal of Root and Tuber Crops." Pp. 20–36 in James Cock, Reginald MacIntyre, and Michael Graham, eds., *Proceedings of the Fourth Symposium of the International Society for Tropical Root Crops.* Ottawa: International Development Research Center.

Levine, Ross, and David Renelt. 1992. "A Sensitivity Analysis of Cross-Country Growth Regressions," *American Economic Review* 82, no. 4 (September): 942–64.

Lieth, Helmut. 1975. "Modeling the Primary Productivity of the World." Pp. 237–63 in Lieth and Whittaker, eds., 1975.

Lieth, Helmut, and Robert H. Whittaker, eds. 1975. *Primary Productivity of the Biosphere.* New York: Springer-Verlag.

Lindert, Peter H. 2004a. *Growing Public: Social Spending and Economic Growth Since the Eighteenth Century,* vol. 1. New York: Cambridge University Press.

— 2004b. *Growing Public: Social Spending and Economic Growth Since the Eighteenth Century,* vol. 2. New York: Cambridge University Press.

Lindert, Peter, and Jeffrey Williamson. 2003. "Does Globalization Make the World More Unequal?" Pp. 227–77 in Bordo, Taylor, and Williamson, eds., 2003.

Lipsey, Robert. 1999. "The Role of Foreign Direct Investment in International Capital Flows." Pp. 307–30 in Martin Feldstein, ed., *International Capital Flows.* Chicago: University of Chicago Press.

MacFarlane, Alan. 1979. *The Origins of English Individualism.* New York: Cambridge University Press.

MacNeish, Richard S. 1991. *The Origins of Agriculture and Settled Life.* Norman, OK: University of Oklahoma Press.

MacQueen, J. 1965. "On Convergence of k-Means and Partitions with Minimum Average Variance." *Annals of Mathematical Statistics* 36: 1084 ff.

Maddison, Angus. 1983. "A Comparison of Levels of GDP Per Capita in Developed and Developing Countries, 1700–1980." *Journal of Economic History* 43, no. 1 (March): 27-43.

— 1985. *Two Crises: Latin America and Asia, 1929–38 and 1973–83.* Paris: OECD.

— 1991. *Dynamic Forces in Capitalist Development.* New York: Oxford University Press.

— 1995. *Monitoring the World Economy, 1820–1992.* Paris: OECD.

— 2001. *The World Economy: A Millennial Perspective.* Paris: OECD.

— 2003. *The World Economy: Historical Statistics.* Paris: OECD.

Manove, Michael. 1971. "A Model of Soviet-Type Economic Planning," *American Economic Review* 61, no. 3 (June): 390–407.

Marcano, Gabriel. 1998. "Measuring Central Bank Independence: A Tale of Subjectivity and Its Consequences," *Oxford Economic Papers* 50 (July): 468–92.

Marshall, Andrew W. 1987. "Commentary." Pp. 481–85 in U.S. Congress, Joint Economic Committee (1987).

Marshall, Monty G., and Keith Jaggers. 2003. "Polity IV Project: Regime Characteristics and Transitions, 1800–2001." <www/cidcm.umd/edu/inscr/polity/>.

Marx, Karl. 1950 [1867]. *Capital*, vol. 1. New York: Modern Library.

——— 1953. *Grundrisse der Kritik der politischen Ökonomie (Rohentwurf) 1857–1858.* Berlin: Dietz.

Mathias, Peter, and P. O'Brien. 1976. "Taxation in Britain and France, 1715–1819." *Journal of European Economic History* 5, no. 3 (Winter): 601–51.

Maxwell, Bruce A., and Robert W. Buddenmeier. 2002. "Coastal Typology Development with Heterogeneous Data Sets." *Journal of Regional and Evolutionary Change* 3 (December): 77–87.

Maxwell, Bruce A., Frederic L. Pryor, and Casey Smith. 2002. "Cluster Analysis in Cross-Cultural Research." *World Cultures* 13, no. 1 (Spring): 22–39.

McBride, Stephen. 2000. "The Politics of Globalization and Labour Strategy." Pp. 24–37 in McBride and Weisman, eds., 2000.

McBride, Stephen, and John Wiseman, eds. 2000. *Globalization and Its Discontents.* New York: St. Martin's Press.

McGrew, William C. 1992. *Chimpanzee Material Culture: Implications for Human Evolution.* New York: Cambridge University Press.

Megginson, William L., and Jeffery M. Netter. 2001. "From State to Market: A Survey of Empirical Studies on Privatization." *Journal of Economic Literature* 39, no. 2 (June): 321–89.

Mendels, Franklin F. 1972. "Proto-industrialization: The First Phase of the Industrialization Process." *Journal of Economic History* 32, no. 1: 241–62.

Michalowski, Raymond J., and Marjorie S. Zatz. 1990. "The Cuban Second Economy in Perspective." Pp. 101–22 in Maria Łoś, ed., *The Second Economy in Marxist States.* New York: St. Martin's Press.

Miers, Suzanne, and Igor Kopytoff. 1977. "African 'Slavery' as an Institution of Marginality." Pp. 3–84 in Miers and Kopytoff, eds., *Slavery in Africa.* Madison, WI: University of Wisconsin Press.

Mitchell, Brian R. 1998. *International Historical Statistics: Europe, 1759–1993.* 4th edition. New York: Stockten Press.

Mocan, Naci. 2004. "What Determines Corruption? International Evidence from Micro Data." NBER Working Paper 10460. Cambridge, MA: National Bureau of Economic Research.

Mokyr, Joel, ed. 1985a. *The Economics of the Industrial Revolution.* Totowa, NJ: Rowman and Allanheld.

——— 1985b. "The Industrial Revolution and the New Economic History." Pp. 1–53 in Mokyr, ed., 1985a.

——— 2002. *The Gifts of Athena: Historical Origins of the Knowledge Economy.* Princeton, NJ: Princeton University Press.

Montias, John Michael. 1959. "Planning with Material Balances." *American Economic Review* 49, no. 5 (December): 963–85.

——— 1962. *Central Planning in Poland.* New Haven, CT: Yale University Press.

Morris, Cynthia Taft, and Irma Adelman. 1988. *Comparative Patterns of Economic Development, 1859–1914.* Baltimore: Johns Hopkins University Press.

Mulvaney, Darek John, and Johan Kamminga. 1999. *Prehistory of Australia.* Washington, D.C.: Smithsonian Institution Press.

Murdock, George P., and Caterina Provost. 1973. "Measurement of Cultural Complexity." *Ethnology* 12: 379–92.

Murdock, George P., and Douglas R. White. 1969. "The Standard Cross-Cultural Sample and Its Codes." *Ethnology* 8: 329–69; also pp. 3–45 in Barry and Schlegel, eds., 1980.

Murdock, George P., and Suzanne F. Wilson. 1972. "Settlement Patterns and Community Organizations: Cross-Cultural Codes 3." *Ethnology* 11: 254–95.

Myška, Milan. 1996. "Proto-industrialization in Bohemia, Moravia, and Silesia." Pp. 188–208 in Ogilvie and Cerman, eds., 1996a.

Naroll, Raoul. 1956. "A Preliminary Index of Social Development." *American Anthropologist* 56, no. 4 (August): 687–715.

Naroll, Raoul, and Ronald Cohen, eds. 1970. *A Handbook of Method in Cultural Anthropology.* Garden City, NY: Natural History Press.

Neale, R. S. 1975. "The Bourgeoisie, Historically, Has Played a Most Revolutionary Part." Pp. 84–104 in Eugene Kamenka and R. S. Neale, eds., *Feudalism, Capitalism, and Beyond.* Canberra: Australian National University Press.

Netting, Robert McC. 1977. *Cultural Ecology.* Menlo Park, CA: Cummings Publishing Company.

———. 1990. "Population, Permanent Agriculturae, and Polities: Unpacking the Evolutionary Portmanteau." Pp. 21–61 in Upham, ed., 1990b.

Nickell, Stephen, and Richard Layard. 1999. "Labor Market Institutions and Economic Performance." Pp. 3029–84 in Orley Ashenfelter and David Card, eds., *Handbook of Labor Economics,* vol. 3c. New York: Elsevier.

Nicoletti, Giuseppe, and Frederic L. Pryor. Forthcoming. "Subjective and Objective Measures of Governmental Regulation in OECD Nations." *Journal of Economic Behavior and Organization.*

Nicoletti, Giuseppe, Robert C. G. Haffner, Stephen Nickell, Stefano Scarpetta, and Gylfi Zoega. 2001. "European Integration, Liberalization, and Labor Market Performance." Pp. 147–235 in Giuseppe Bertola, Tito Boeri, and Giuseppe Nicoletti, eds., *Welfare and Employment in a United Europe.* Cambridge, MA: MIT Press.

Nicoletti, Giuseppe, Stefano Scarpetta, and Olivier Boylaud. 2000. "Summary Indicators of Product Market Regulation with an Extension to Employment Protection Legislation." OECD Working Paper 226. Paris.

Nieboer, Herman J. 1971 [1910]. *Slavery as an Industrial System: Ethnological Researches.* 2nd revised edition. The Hague: M. Nijhoff.

North, Douglass C. 1998. "Economic Performance through Time." Pp. 78–90 in Carl K. Eicher and John M. Staatz, eds., *International Agricultural Development.* 3rd edition. Baltimore: Johns Hopkins University Press.

North, Douglass C., and Robert Paul Thomas. 1977. "The First Economic Revolution." *The Economic History Review,* Second Series 30, no. 2: 229–241.

Norway, Statistisk Sentralbyrå. 1965. *Nasjonalregnskap 1865–1960.* Oslo.

Nowakowski, Joseph M. 1994. "Efficiency at Different Stages of Production in the Soviet Union," *Comparative Economic Studies* 36, no. 4 (Winter): 79–99.

Obstfeld, Maurice, and Alan M. Taylor. 2003. "Globalization and Capital Markets." Pp. 121–91 in Bordo, Taylor, and Williamson, eds., 2003.

O'Dea, Kerin. 1992. "Traditional Diet and Food Preferences of Australian Aboriginal Hunter-Gatherers." Pp. 73–80 in Whiten and Widdowson, eds., 1992.

OECD. Annual-a. *Labour Force Statistics* (alternative title, *Manpower Statistics*). Paris.

Annual-b. *National Accounts of OECD Countries* (title varies slightly from year to year). Paris.

Annual-c. *International Direct Investment Statistics Yearbook*: 1989–2000. Paris.

1980. *National Accounts of OECD Countries, 1950–1978*. Paris.

1994. *Employment Outlook 1994*. Paris.

1997a. *Employment Outlook 1997*. Paris.

1997b. *Family, Market and Community: Equity and Efficiency in Social Policy*. Paris.

1997c. *Indicators of Tariff and Non-tariff Trade Barriers*. Paris.

1997d. *Measuring Public Employment in OECD Countries: Sources, Methods, and Results*. Paris.

1999. *A Caring World: The New Social Policy Agenda*. Paris.

2000a. *OECD Health Data*. CD-ROM. Paris.

2000b. *Labour Force Statistics, 1978–1998*. Paris.

2000c. *OECD Health Data 2000*. CD-ROM. Paris.

2001. *OECD Science, Technology and Industry Scoreboard*. Paris.

OECD and Statistics Canada. 2000. *Literacy in the Information Age: Final Report of the International Adult Literacy Survey*. Paris: OECD.

Ogilvie, Sheilagh C., and Markus Cerman. 1996a. "Proto-industrialization, Economic Development and Social Change in Early Modern Europe." Pp. 227–40 in Ogilvie and Cerman, eds., 1996c.

1996b. "The Theories of Proto-industrialization." Pp. 1–15 in Ogilvie and Cerman, eds., 1996c.

eds. 1996c. *European Proto-Industrialization*. New York: Cambridge University Press.

Ohkawa, Kazushi, and Miyohei Shinohara. 1979. "Appendix Tables." In Kazushi Ohkawa and Miyohei Shinohara, eds., *Patterns of Japanese Economic Development*. New Haven, CT: Yale University Press.

Olsson, Ola. 2003. "The Rise of Neolithic Agriculture." Göteborg University Working Paper in Economics 57, Göteborg, Sweden.

Olsson, Ola, and Douglas A. Hibbs, Jr. Forthcoming. "Biogeography and Long-Run Economic Development."

Papadakis, Juan. 1966. *Climates of the World and Their Agricultural Potential*. Buenos Aires: Papadakis.

1970. *Agricultural Potentialities of World Climates*. Buenos Aires: Papadakis.

Patterson, Orlando. 1982. *Slavery and Social Death: A Comparative Study*. Cambridge, MA: Harvard University Press.

Piketty, Thomas, and Emmanuel Saez. 2003. "Income Inequality in the United States, 1913–1998," *Quarterly Journal of Economics* 118, no. 1 (February): 1–41.

Pomeranz, Kenneth. 2000. *The Great Divergence: China, Europe, and the Making of the Modern World Economy*. Princeton, NJ: Princeton University Press.

Postan, M. M., and John Hatcher. 1985. "Population and Class Relations in Feudal Society." Pp. 64–78 in Aston and Philpin, eds., 1985.

Prados de la Escosura, Leandro. 2003. *El progreso económico de EspaZa, 1850–2000.* Madrid: Fundación BBVA.

Prados de la Escosura, Leandro, and Vera Zamagni, eds. 1992. *El desarrolo económico en la Europa del Sur.* Madrid: Alianza Editorial.

Price, T. Douglas. 1995. "Social Inequality at the Origins of Agriculture." Pp. 129–51 in Price and Feinman, eds., 1995.

Price, T. Douglas, and James A. Brown, eds., 1985. *Prehistoric Hunter-Gatherers: The Emergence of Cultural Complexity.* Orlando, FL: Academic Press.

Price, T. Douglas, and Gary M. Feinman, eds. 1995. *Foundations of Social Inequality.* New York: Plenum Press.

Price, T. Douglas, and Anne Birgitte Gebauer, eds. 1995. *Last Hunters, First Farmers.* Santa Fe, NM: School of American Research Press.

Price, T. Douglas, Anne Birgitte Gebauer, and Lawrence H. Keeley. 1995. "The Spread of Farming into Europe North of the Alps." Pp. 95–126 in Price and Gebauer, eds., 1995.

Pryor, Frederic L. 1968. *Public Expenditures in Communist and Capitalist Nations.* Homewood, IL: Irwin.

1973a. The Diffusion Possibility Method: A More General and Simpler Solution to Galton's Problem. *American Ethnologist* 3: 731–49.

1973b. *Property and Industrial Organization in Communist and Capitalist Nations.* Bloomington: Indiana University Press.

1977a. "A Comparative Study of Slavery." *Journal of Comparative Economics* 1, no. 1 (March): 81–102.

1977b. "The Origins of Money." *Journal of Money, Credit, and Banking* 9, no. 3 (August): 391–409.

1977c. *The Origins of the Economy: A Comparative Study of Distribution in Primitive and Peasant Economies.* New York: Academic Press.

1977d. "Some Costs of Markets: An Empirical Study." *Quarterly Journal of Economics* 91, no. 1 (February): 81–102.

1980a. "The Asian Mode of Production as an Economic System: A Review Essay." *Journal of Comparative Economics* 4, no. 4 (December): 420–42.

1980b. "Feudalism as an Economic System: A Review Essay." *Journal of Comparative Economics* 4, no. 1 (March): 56–77.

1982a. "The Classification and Analysis of Precapitalist Economic Systems by Marx and Engels." *History of Political Economy* 14, no. 4 (Winter): 521–43.

1982b. "Plantation Economies as Economic Systems: A Review Essay." *Journal of Comparative Economics* 6, no. 3 (September): 288–317.

1983. "Causal Theories About the Origins of Agriculture." *Research in Economic History* 8: 93–124.

1984. "Interpretation of Public Expenditure Trends in East and West." Pp. 362–89 in Gustav Ranis et al., eds., *Comparative Development Perspectives: Essays in Honor of Lloyd Reynolds.* Boulder, CO: Westview Press.

1985a. "Climatic Fluctuations as a Cause of Differential Economic Growth of the Orient and Occident: A Comment." *Journal of Economic History* 45, no. 3: 667–75.

1985b. "The Invention of the Plow." *Comparative Studies in Society and History* 27, no. 4 (October): 727–43. 1985c. "The Islamic Economic System: A Review Article." *Journal of Comparative Economics* 9, no. 2 (June): 197–224.

1986a. "The Adoption of Agriculture: Some Theoretical and Empirical Evidence." *American Anthropologist* 88, no. 4 (December): 879–97.

1986b. *Revolutionary Grenada: A Study in Political Economy*. New York: Praeger.

1988. "Corporatism as an Economic System." *Journal of Comparative Economics* 12, no. 3 (September): 317–44.

1990a. "A Buddhist Economic System – In Principle." *American Journal of Economics and Sociology* 49, no. 3 (July): 339–51.

1990b. *The Political Economy of Poverty, Equity, and Growth: Malawi and Madagascar*. New York: Oxford University Press.

1991. "A Buddhist Economic System – In Practice." *American Journal of Economics and Sociology* 50, no. 1 (January): 17–33.

1992. *The Red and the Green: The Rise and Fall of Collectivized Agriculture in Marxist Regimes*. Princeton, NJ: Princeton University Press.

1993. "The Roman Catholic Church and the Economic System: A Review Essay." *Journal of Comparative Economics* 17, no. 1 (March): 129–51.

1994. "Growth Deceleration and Transaction Costs." *Journal of Economic Behavior and Organization* 25, no 3: 121–33.

1995. "Behavior of Retail Prices: A Note on Market Integration in the U.S.," *Eastern Economic Journal* 21, no. 1 (Winter): 83–97.

2001. "Will Most of Us Be Working for Giant Enterprises by 2028?" *Journal of Economic Behavior and Organization* 44, no. 4 (April): 363–82.

2002a. *The Future of U.S. Capitalism*. New York: Cambridge University Press.

2002b. "Quantitative Notes on the Extent of Government Regulation in Various OECD Nations." *International Journal of Industrial Organization* 20, no. 5 (May): 693–715.

2003a. "Demographic Effects on Personal Saving in the Future." *Southern Economic Journal* 69, no. 3 (January): 541–60.

2003b. "What Does It Mean to Be Human? A Comparison of Primate Economies." *Journal of Bioeconomics* 5, no. 2: 97–146.

2003c. "Economic Systems of Foragers," *Cross-Cultural Research* 37, no. 4 (November): 393–427.

2004. "Reply to Boehm." *Journal of Bioeconomics* 6, no. 2.

Forthcoming-a. "Economic Systems of Developing Market Economies." *Comparative Economic Studies*.

Forthcoming-b. "The Rise and Fall of Communist Economies." *ORBIS*.

Forthcoming-c. "Economic Values and Economic Growth," *American Journal of Economics and Sociology*.

Webpage.<http://www.swarthmore.edu/SocSci/Economics/fpryor1>.

Pryor, Frederic L., and Eleanor F. Beach. 1995. "What Did Adam and Eve Do for a Living?" *BR: Bible Review* 11, No. 2 (April): 38–42.

Pryor, Frederic L., and Nelson Graburn. 1980. "The Myth of Reciprocity." Pp. 215–39 in Kenneth J. Gergen, et al., eds. *Social Exchange: Advances in Theory and Research*. New York: Plenum Press: 215–39.

Przeworski, Adam, Michael E. Alvarez, José Antonio Cheibub, and Fernando

Limongi. 2000a. *Democracy and Development*. New York: Cambridge University Press.

2000b. "Database."<http://pantheon.yale.edu~jac236/Research.htm>.

Putnam, Robert D. 2000. *Bowling Alone: The Collapse and Revival of American Community*. New York : Simon & Schuster.

Quinn, Dennis, and Maria Toyoda. 2003. Unpublished monograph.

Reed, Charles A. ed. 1977. *Origins of Agriculture*. The Hague: Mouton Publisher.

Republic of China. 2003. *Statistical Abstract of National Income in Taiwan Area, Republic of China*. <http://61.60.106.83/nis/enisd.htm>

Reynolds, Lloyd G. 1985. *Economic Growth in the Third World, 1850–1980*. New Haven: Yale University Press.

Richardson, Peter J., Robert Boyd, and Robert L. Bettinger. 2001. "Was Agriculture Impossible During the Pleistocene But Mandatory During the Holocene? A Climate Change Hypothesis, *American Antiquity* 66, no. 2 (July): 387–413.

Rindos, David. 1984. *The Origins of Agriculture: An Evolutionary Perspective*. Orlando, FL: Harcourt, Brace, Jovanovich.

Rissanen, Jorma. 1989. *Stochastic Complexity in Statistical Inquiry*. Singapore: World Scientific Publishing Co.

2001. "Information, Complexity and the MDL Principle." Pp. 339–51 in Lionello F. Punzo, ed., *Cycles, Growth and Structural Change: Theories and Empirical Evidence*. New York: Routledge.

Rodrik, Dani. 2003. "Growth Strategies." NBER Working Paper 10050. Cambridge, MA: National Bureau of Economic Research.

Rodrik, Dani, Arvind Subramanian, and Francesco Trebbi. 2002. "Institutions Rule: The Primacy of Institutions over Geography and Integration in Economic Development." Centre for Economic Policy Research Paper 3643. London.

Roosevelt, Anna Curtenius. 1984. "Population, Health, and the Evolution of Subsistence: Conclusions from the Conference." Pp. 559–81 in Mark Nathan Cohen and George J. Armelagos, eds., *Paleopathology at the Origins of Agriculture*. Orlando, FL: Academic Press.

Rosefielde, Steven, ed. 1998. *Efficiency and the Economic Recovery Potential to the Year 2000 and Beyond*. Brookfield, VT: Ashgate.

Rosenberg, Michael. 1990. "The Mother of Invention: Evolutionary Theory, Territoriality, and the Origins of Agriculture." *American Anthropologist* 92, no. 2: 399–415.

Rosenzweig, Michael L. 1968. "Net Primary Productivity of Terrestrial Communities: Predictions from Climatology." *The American Naturalist* 102, no. 923: 67–74.

Ross, Marc H. 1981. "Political Decision Making and Conflict: Additional Cross-Cultural Codes and Scales." *Ethnology* 22, no. 2: 169–92.

Ross, Myron H. 1965. "Fluctuations in Economic Activity." *American Economic Review* 55, no. 1 (March): 158–61.

Rosser, J. Barkley, Jr., and Marina V. Rosser. 2004. *Comparative Economics in a Transforming World Economy*, 2nd edition. Cambridge, MA: MIT Press.

Rostow, W. W. 1960. *The Stages of Economic Growth: A Non-Communist Manifesto*. Cambridge, UK: Cambridge University Press.

Rozelle, Scott, and Johan F. M. Swinnen. 2004. "Success and Failure of Reform: Insights from the Transition of Agriculture." *Journal of Economic Literature,* 42 (June 2004): 404–56.

Rubinstein, Alvin Z. 1988. *Moscow's Third World Strategy.* Princeton, NJ: Princeton University Press.

Rudebeck, Lars. 1974. *Guinea-Bissau: A Study of Political Mobilization.* New York: Africana Publishing Company.

Rudolph, Richard L. 1982. "Agricultural Structure and Proto-Industrialization in Russia: Economic Development with Unfree Labor," in Deyon, ed., 1982, vol. 2.

Rutgaizer, Valeriy M. 1992. "Sizing Up the Shadow Economy." Pp. 39–77 in Rutgaizer, *The Shadow Economy in the USSR.* Berkeley–Duke Occasional Papers on the Second Economy in the USSR. Bala-Cynwyd, PA: WEFA Group.

Sachs, Jeffrey D., and Andrew Warner. 1995. "Economic Reform and the Process of Global Integration." *Brookings Papers on Economic Activity,* no. 1: 1–119.

Sahlins, Marshall D. 1972. *Stone Age Economics.* Chicago, Aldine-Atherton.

Samuelsson, Kurt. 1964. *Religion and Economic Action: A Critique of Max Weber.* New York: Harper & Row.

Sanday, Peggy Reeves. 1981. *Female Power and Male Dominance: On the Origins of Sexual Inequality.* New York: Cambridge University Press.

Sanderson, M. 1972. "Literacy and Social Mobility in the Industrial Revolution in England." *Past and Present* 56 (August): 75–104.

Sauer, Carl O. 1969. *Seeds, Spades, Hearths, and Herds: The Domestication of Animals and Foodstuffs,* 2nd edition. Cambridge, MA: MIT Press.

Schneider, Friedrich, and Dominik H. Enste. 2000. "Shadow Economies: Size, Causes, and Consequences," *Journal of Economic Literature* 38, no. 1 (March): 77–114. 2002. *The Shadow Economy: An International Survey.* New York: Cambridge University Press.

Schwartz, Peter, and Doug Randall. 2004. *Imagining the Unthinkable: An Abrupt Climate Change Scenario,* <www.ems.org/climate/pentagon_climatechange.pdf>

Sharpe, D. 1975. "Methods of Assessing the Primary Productivity of Regions." Pp. 147–60 in Lieth and Whittaker, eds., 1975.

Sheskin, David. 1997. *Handbook of Parametric and Nonparametric Statistical Procedures.* Boca Raton, FL: CRC Press.

Shleifer, Andrei, and Robert Vishny. 1998. *The Grabbing Hand: Government Pathologies and Their Cures.* Cambridge, MA: Harvard University Press.

Shonfield, Andrew. 1965. *Modern Capitalism: The Changing Balance of Public and Private Power.* New York: Oxford University Press.

Siaroff, Alan. 1999. "Corporatism in 24 Industrial Democracies: Meaning and Measurement." *European Journal of Political Research* 36, no. 2 (October): 175–205.

Sleifer, Jaap. 2003. *Falling Behind: The East German Economy in Comparison with West Germany from 1936 to 2002.* Monograph Series, no. 6: Groningen, Netherlands: Groningen Growth and Development Centre.

Slemrod, Joel. 1995. "What Do Cross-Country Studies Teach About Government Involvement, Prosperity, and Economic Growth?" *Brookings Papers on Economic Activity,* no. 2: 373–415.

Smeeding, Timothy. 2000. "Changing Income Inequality in OECD Countries: Updated Results from the Luxembourg Income Study." LIS Working Paper 252. Luxembourg: Luxembourg Income Study.

Smith, Bruce. 1995. *The Emergence of Agriculture*. New York: Scientific American Library.

Smith, Eric Alden, and Bruce Winterhalder, eds. 1992. *Evolutionary Ecology and Human Behavior*. New York: Aldine de Gruyter.

Smith, Philip E. L. 1973. *The Consequences of Food Production, Module in Anthropology* 31. Reading, MA: Addison-Wesley.

Smits, Jan-Pieter, Edwin Horlings, and Jan Luiten van Zanden. 2000. *Dutch GNP and Its Components, 1800–1913*, GGDC Monograph Series, no. 5. Groningen: Groningen Growth and Development Centre.

Sokoloff, Kenneth L., and Stanley L. Engerman. 2000. "History Lessons: Institutions, Factor Endowments, and Paths of Development in the New World." *Journal of Economic Perspectives* 14, no. 3 (Summer): 217–30.

Sombart, Werner. 1902. *Der Moderne Kapitalismus*. Leipzig: Duncker & Humblot.

Soskice, David. 1999. "Divergent Production Regimes: Coordinated and Uncoordinated Market Economies in the 1980s and 1990s." Pp. 101–34 in Kitschelt et al., eds., 1999.

Spaulding, Wallice H. 1982. "Checklist of the 'National Liberation Movements.'" *Problems of Communism* 31, no. 2 (March/April): 77–83.

———. 1983. "The Communist Movement and Its Allies," Pp. 25–60 in Ralph M. Goldman, ed., *Transnational Parties: Organizing the World's Precincts*. Lanham, MD: University Press of America.

Starr, Richard. 1987. *Foreign Policy After Détente*, Revised edition. Stanford, CA: Hoover Institution Press.

Stearman, Allyn MacLean. 1987. *No Longer Nomads: The Sirionó Revisited*. Lanham, MD: Hamilton Press.

Steinfeld, Robert J. 1991. *The Invention of Free Labor: The Employment Relation in English and American Law and Culture*. Chapel Hill, NC: University of North Carolina Press.

Stodder, James P. 1995a. "The Evolution of Complexity in Primitive Economies: Theory," *Journal of Comparative Economics* 20, no. 1 (February): 1–31.

———. 1995b. "The Evolution of Complexity in Primitive Economies: Empirical Tests," *Journal of Comparative Economics* 20, no. 2 (May): 190–210.

Sweden, Statistiska Centralbyrån. 1969. *Historisk statistik for Sverige*, vol. 1. Stockholm: KL Beckmans Tryckerier AB.

Szajkowski, Bogdan. 1982. *The Establishment of Marxist Regimes*. London: Butterworths.

Temin, Peter. 2001. "The Labour Supply in the Early Roman Empire." Massachusetts Institute of Technology, Department of Economics Working Paper 01/45.

Testart, Alain. 1982. "The Significance of Food Storage Among Hunter-Gatherers: Residence Patterns, Population Densities, and Social Inequalities." *Current Anthropology* 23: 523–37.

Thornthwaite, C. W., and Associates, Laboratory of Climatology. 1962–65. *Average Climatic Water Balance Data of the Continents*. Parts 1–8. Centerton, NJ: Thornthwaite and Associates.

Tilly, Charles. 1982. "Flows of Capital and Forms of Industry in Europe, 1500–1900." Pin Deyon, ed., 1982, vol. 2.

Tökai, Ferenc. 1979 (1965). *Essays in the Asiatic Mode of Production*. Budapest: Akadémiai Kiadó.

Toninelli, Pier Angelo. 2000. *The Rise and Fall of State-Owned Enterprise in the Western World*. New York: Cambridge University Press.

Toutain, Jean-Claude. 1987. *Le produit intérieur brut de la France de 1789 à 1982*. Cahiers de l' I.S.M.E.A., Série: *Histoire quantitative de l'Économie française*, no. 15. Grenoble, France: Presses Universitaires de Grenoble.

Traxler, Franz, Sabine Blaschke, and Berhard Kittel. 2001. *National Labour Relations in Internationalized Markets*. New York: Oxford University Press.

Tuden, Arthur, and Catherine Marshall. 1972. "Political Organization: Cross-Cultural Codes 4." *Ethnology* 11, no. 4: 436–64.

Tudge, Colin. 1998. *Neanderthals, Bandits and Farmers: How Agriculture Really Began*. New Haven, CT: Yale University Press.

Turnbull, Colin M. 1972. *The Mountain People*. New York: Simon & Schuster.

United Kingdom, Statistical Office. 2000. *Regional Trends*, no. 35. London: Stationery Office.

United Nations. Annual-a. *Yearbook of International Trade Statistics*. New York.

Annual-b. *Yearbook of the United Nations*. New York.

Annual-c. *Demographic Yearbook*. New York.

2000. *National Account Statistics: Main Aggregates and Detailed Tables, 1996–1997*. New York.

2003. *World Population Prospects: The 2002 Revision*, vol. 1. New York.

U.S. Bureau of the Census. Annual. *Statistical Abstract of the United States*. Washington, D.C.: GPO.

1975. *Historical Statistics of the United States: Colonial Times to 1700*. Washington, D.C.: GPO.

1997. *1992 Enterprise Statistics: Company Summary*. Washington, D.C.: GPO.

U.S. Congress, Joint Economic Committee. *Gorbachev's Economic Plans*. Washington, D.C.: GPO.

U.S. Department of State. Annual. *Report to Congress on Voting Practices in the United Nations*. Washington, D.C.: GPO.

U.S. Patent and Trademark Office (USPTO). 2002. "TAF Special Report, All Patents, All Types, January 1977–December 2001. "<www.uspto.gov/web/offices/ac/ido/oeip/taf/apat.pdf>.

Upham, Steadman. 1990a. "Analog or Digital? Toward a Generic Framework for Explaining the Development of Emergent Political Systems." Pp. 87–115 in Upham, ed., 1990b.

ed. 1990b. *The Evolution of Political Systems: Sociopolitics in Small-Scale Sedentary Societies*. New York: Cambridge University Press.

Visser, Jelle. 2001. "Industrial Relations and Social Dialogue." Pp. 184–242 in Peter Auer, ed., *Changing Labour Markets in Europe: The Role of Institutions and Policies*. Geneva: International Labour Office.

Vries, Jan de, and Ad van der Woude. 1997. *The First Modern Economy*. New York: Cambridge University Press.

Watson, Patty Jo. 1995. "Explaining the Transition to Agriculture." Pp. 21–37 in Price and Gebauer, ed., 1995.

Webb, Michael. 2000. "Global Markets and State Power: Explaining the Limited

Impact of International Tax Competition." Pp. 113–27 in McBride and Wiseman, eds., 2000.

Weber, Max. 1947. *The Theory of Social and Economic Organization*, trans. by A. M. Henderson and Talcott Parsons. New York, Oxford University Press.

1958 [1904]. *The Protestant Ethic and the Spirit of Capitalism.* New York: Scribner.

1961 [1923]. *General Economic History*, trans. by Frank H. Knight. New York: Collier Books.

Weisdorf, Jacob L. 2003a. "Explaining the Neolithic Revolution: A Guided Tour for Growth Economists." Unpublished paper, Institute of Economics, University of Copenhagen.

2003b. "Stone Age Economics: The Origins of Agriculture and the Emergence of Non-Food Specialists." Unpublished paper, Institute of Economics, University of Copenhagen.

Weiss, Thomas. 1994. "Economic Growth Before 1860: Revised Conjectures." Pp. 11–28 in Thomas Weiss and Donald Schaefer, eds., *American Economic Development in Historical Perspective.* Stanford, CA: Stanford University Press.

West, Edwin G. 1985. "Literacy and the Industrial Revolution." Pp. 227–40 in Mokyr, ed., 1985.

Wheeler, Valeri (Nammour). 1974. *Drums and Guns: A Cross-Cultural Study of the Nature of War.* Ph.D. dissertation, University of Oregon.

White, Lawrence J. 2002. "Trends in Aggregate Concentration in the United States," *Journal of Economic Perspectives* 16, no. 4 (Fall): 137–60.

2003. "Aggregate Concentration in the Global Economy," unpublished paper.

Whiten, A., and E. M. Widdowson, eds. 1992. *Foraging Strategies and the Natural Diet of Monkeys, Apes, and Humans.* Oxford: Clarendon Press.

Whitesell, Robert S. 1990. "Estimates of the Output Loss from Allocative Inefficiency: A Comparison of Hungary and West Germany." Pp. 95–126 in Josef Brada and Istvan Dabozi, eds., *Money, Incentives and Efficiency in the Hungarian Reforms.* Armonk, NY: M.E. Sharpe.

Whyte, Martin E. 1978. "Cross-Cultural Codes Dealing with the Relative Status of Women." *Ethnology* 17: 211–37.

Will, Pierre-Étienne, and R. Bin Wong, eds. 1991. *Nourish the People: The State Civilian Granary System in China, 1650–1850.* Ann Arbor, MI: Center for Chinese Studies, University of Michigan.

Woodburn, James. 1982. "Egalitarian Societies." *Man* 17: 431–51.

1998. "'Sharing Is Not a Form of Exchange': An Analysis of Property-Sharing in Immediate Return Hunter-Gatherer Societies." Pp. 48–63 in Hann, ed., 1998.

World Bank. 1995. *Bureaucrats in Business: The Economics and Politics of Government Ownership.* New York: Oxford University Press.

2002. *World Development Indicators, 2002.* CD-ROM version. Washington, D.C.

2004. *World Development Indicators, 2004.* <www.worldbank.org>.

World Cultures: CD-ROM. See Divale and Gray (2001).

World Economic Forum. 1991. *World Competitiveness Report 1991.* Lausanne and Geneva.

World Economic Forum and Center for International Development, Harvard University. 2000. *The Global Competitiveness Report 2000.* New York: Oxford University Press.

World Intellectual Property Organization. 2003. "25 Years of Industrial Property Statistics." <www.wipo.int.ipstat/en>

Wright, Gavin. 1986. *Old South, New South: Revolutions in the Southern Economies of the Civil War.* New York: Basic Books.

Wrigley, E. A. 1987. *People, Cities, and Wealth: The Transformation of Traditional Society.* New York: Blackwell.

Wrigley, E. A., and R. S. Schofield. 1981. *The Population History of England, 1541–1871.* Cambridge, MA: Harvard University Press.

Yellen, John T. 1998 (1990). "The Transformation of the Kalahari !Kung." Pp. 223–35 in Gowdy, ed., 1998.

Index

Printed in the United States
by Baker & Taylor Publisher Services